Berkeley University of California, Berkeley. Junior Class. cn
University of California

The blue and gold

Berkeley University of California, Berkeley. Junior Class. cn University of California

The blue and gold

ISBN/EAN: 9783742883063

Manufactured in Europe, USA, Canada, Australia, Japa

Cover: Foto ©Andreas Hilbeck / pixelio.de

Manufactured and distributed by brebook publishing software (www.brebook.com)

Berkeley University of California, Berkeley. Junior Class. cn
University of California

The blue and gold

When we are old and worn with years, we'll read
    This record of our youth, the day, the place;
And we will suit our memory to our need,
    And long-forgotten name to faded face.

Sadness will come to us who fail to trace
    The dreams we dreamed so certain to succeed.
Time's later generations will erase
    The dreamer and the doer and the deed.

Then let us see these tranquil hills again,
    Fog-laden trees, the lighted homeward street,
Let us not seek our former years in vain,
    Let us find youth unspoiled, and living sweet.
For us once more the splendor and the pain
    Dreaming the old world trembles at our feet.

                                    Genevieve Taggard '18

FOREWORD

IN THIS, the 1918 Volume of the BLUE AND GOLD, it has been our utmost aim to consolidate into as few pages as possible a record of the past college year—a record, that we, who are Juniors now, may keep and cherish more and more as the years go by, which may be referred to in after life as a true reminder of the fading reminiscences of our college days. That it is not a complete record we have no doubt. True it is, that there are many incidents, personalities, indeed names which do not even appear on these pages. On the other hand, it may be that too much lead or copper has been expended upon some happening—some individual or his or her name. If anyone has been offended by either the former or the latter, we beg forgiveness.

In gathering together the material which has gone to make up this volume we have realized that there is no end to the matter, both printed and half-toned which might be forced in between these covers. We have further realized that a book of this kind may be easily and unknowingly overdone, and supersaturated with uninteresting and irrelevant material, thus evading the primary purpose for which it was intended—that is, a record of the college year. Consequently, we have endeavored to be as concise as possible, eliminating those things which have appeared as extraneous.

If we have but assembled a partial mass of material which has been gleaned from the happenings of the past college year and have presented them in an interesting and coherent manner, then our efforts have not been in vain. We sincerely hope that our successes may serve as an aid and our mistakes as a warning to the editors who will have in their hands the fates of the Blue and Golds which are to follow in the future.

TO
HIRAM WARREN JOHNSON
OF THE CLASS OF 1888

UNITED STATES SENATOR FROM CALIFORNIA

GOVERNOR OF THE STATE AND REGENT OF
THE UNIVERSITY 1911-1917

AT A CRITICAL TIME IN THE HISTORY OF OUR
PUBLIC AFFAIRS, HE LED THE PEOPLE OF
CALIFORNIA IN SECURING EFFECTIVE GOVERN
MENT IN A REINVIGORATED DEMOCRACY.
NOW IN A PERIOD OF UNMEASURED TRIAL
WE FOLLOW HIS LEADERSHIP IN THE GREATER
SERVICE OF THE NATION

CONTENTS

THE UNIVERSITY
   The Campus — — — — — — — — — 15
   Regents — — — — — — — — — 32
   In Memoriam — — — — — — — — 36

THE COLLEGE YEAR
   Illustrated College Year — — — — — — — 41
   Rallies — — — — — — — — — 67
   Dances — — — — — — — — — 75

ACTIVITIES
   Military — — — — — — — — — 83
   Publications — — — — — — — — 93
   Debates — — — — — — — — — 107

DRAMATICS
   Extravaganzas and Partes — — — — — — 113
   Campus Productions — — — — — — — 115
   Authors and Co-Authors — — — — — — 134

ORGANIZATIONS
   Student Body Organizations — — — — — — 137
   Athletic Organizations — — — — — — — 143
   Alumni Organizations — — — — — — — 144
   Religious Organizations — — — — — — — 146
   Debating Societies — — — — — — — 150
   Departmental Societies — — — — — — — 152
   Music — — — — — — — — — 159

HONOR SOCIETIES — — — — — — — 173

ATHLETICS
   Football — — — — — — — — — 203
   Basketball — — — — — — — — 239
   Baseball — — — — — — — — — 247
   Track — — — — — — — — — 259
   Crew — — — — — — — — — 269
   Tennis — — — — — — — — — 277
   Minor Sports — — — — — — — — 283
   Women's Athletics — — — — — — — 291

CLASSES
   Seniors — — — — — — — — — 305
   Juniors — — — — — — — — — 351
   Sophomores — — — — — — — — 364
   Freshmen — — — — — — — — 383

FRATERNAL ORGANIZATIONS
   Fraternity Statistics — — — — — — — 387
   Fraternities — — — — — — — — 389
   Sororities — — — — — — — — 489
   Men's House Clubs — — — — — — — 525
   Women's House Clubs — — — — — — 547

JOSHES — — — — — — — — — 561

ADVERTISEMENTS — — — — — — — 568

INDEX — — — — — — — — — 628

EDITOR
John L. Reith

ASSISTANT EDITORS
Fuller Clarkson Margaret Wilson Honeywell
Chester Leroy Isaacson

MANAGER
Wilson Meyer

ASSOCIATE MANAGERS
Vera Lillian Christie John Ritchie McKee
William Griffiths Pillsbury

THE UNIVERSITY
Olin Wellborn III, Editor
Leo Roy Moody, Assistant Editor

THE COLLEGE YEAR
George Magee Cunningham, Editor
John O'Melveny Ruth Benjamin Walker
Heber Spencer Steen Catherine Helene Woolsey

ATHLETICS
Arthur Reihl Wilson, Editor
Charles Franklin Harper Carroll Hutchinson Smith
Preston Edward Snook

MINOR ATHLETICS
Paul Wilbur Masters, Editor
Orville Robert Caldwell Blanche G. Coulter

DRAMATICS
Anthony Laurence Mitchell, Editor
Florence Isaacs Genevieve Taggard

MILITARY
Max Weston Thornburg, Editor
John Bradburn McKinlay, Assistant Editor

DEBATES
Martin Stern Rosenblatt, Editor

THE CLASSES
Albert Brodie Smith, Editor

PUBLICATIONS
Victor Lavenson Furth, Editor
Amy Dinkelspiel, Assistant Editor

ORGANIZATIONS
John Louis Cooley, Editor

Marian Brown
Walter Budd Champlin

Carl King
Camille Avila Purdy

HONOR SOCIETIES
William Hill Thomas, Editor

Leslie Scott Nelson

Irene Ray

FRATERNAL ORGANIZATIONS
Max Weston Thornburg, Editor
Edwin French Steen, Assistant Editor

Russell White Bell
Margaret Eddy House

Edith Louise Monroe
Amy Daphne Noell

Jean Wright

RECORDS
Charles William Suits, Editor
Leonard Roland Dykes, Assistant Editor

JOSHES
Chester Leroy Isaacson, Editor

Leslie Brown
Donald Cline Bull
Wymond Bradbury Garthwaite

Edward Moss Jaffa
Donald Linn Kieffer
Cloyd Jonathan Sweigert

SENIOR RECORDS
William Ross McKay, Editor

ASSISTANT MANAGERS

Donald Cline Bull
Everett Johnson Gray

Harvey Maher Kilburn
Dohrmann Kaspar Pischel

MANAGERIAL STAFF

Howard Maurice Baldwin
Harold Edgar Bradley
Muriel Margaret Cameron
Vivian Everett Carlson
Valance Scott Cowan
Walter John Escherich
Pauline Finnell
Charles Lawrence Frost
Victor William Galvin

Margaret Eddy House
Mary Edith Lipman
Edward Ramsay Moran
Madeline Ann Muldoon
Clyffice Bernadine Nevin
Edwin Sprague Pillsbury
Frank Combs Ransom
Dorothy Jean Waterhouse
Thomas Carroll Winstead

THE UNIVERSITY

SATHER GATE AND THE CAMPANILE

THE UNIVERSITY

Student Life and Its Campaigns

SENIOR MEN'S HALL

THE FOOTBALL STATUE

BRIDGE ACROSS STRAWBERRY CREEK

HARMON GYMNASIUM

ALONG STRAWBERRY CREEK

THE MINING BUILDING

THROUGH THE IVY BEDS

BOALT HALL OF LAW

ONE OF THE NORTH FORK'S MANY PICTURESQUE CROSSINGS

AGRICULTURAL HALL

TRAVERSING FACULTY GLADE

THE CAMPANILE

THE GREEK THEATRE.

NORTH ENTRANCE TO THE CAMPUS

UNIVERSITY LIBRARY ACROSS THE BOTANICAL GARDENS

STRAWBERRY CREEK NEAR FACULTY GLADE

MECHANICS BUILDING

ON THE PATH TO THE BIG "C"

NORTH HALL

THE GREATER UNIVERSITY

THE PRESIDENT'S HOUSE

ADMINISTRATION BUILDING—CALIFORNIA HALL

LEADING TO THE GREEK THEATRE

STEPS APPROACHING THE PRESIDENT'S HOUSE

OLD SENIOR BENCH

APPROACH TO UNIVERSITY LIBRARY

THE FACULTY CLUB

SENIOR WOMEN'S HALL

REGENTS

REGENTS EX OFFICIO

His Excellency William Dennison Stephens, Governor and President of the Regents.
Clement C. Young, B. L., Speaker of the Assembly
Edward Hyatt, State Superintendent of Public Instruction
John M. Perry, President of the State Agricultural Society
Livingston Jenks, A. B., LL. B., President of the Mechanics Institute
Benjamin Ide Wheeler, Ph. D. LL. D., Litt. D., L. H. D., President of the University

APPOINTED REGENTS

Philip Ernest Bowles, Ph. B.
John Alexander Britton, Esq.
William Henry Crocker, Ph. B.
Edward Augustus Dickson, B. L.
Guy Chaffee Earl, A. B.
Arthur William Foster, Esq.
Mrs. Phoebe Apperson Hearst
Isaias William Hellman, Esq.
Garrett William McEnerney, Esq.
James Wilfred McKinley, B. S.
James Mills, Esq.
James Kennedy Moffitt, B. S.
Charles Adolph Ramm, B. S., M. A., S. T. B.
Chester H. Rowell, Ph. B.
Rudolph Julius Taussig, Esq.
Charles Stetson Wheeler, B. L.

OFFICERS OF THE REGENTS

President, His Excellency William Dennison Stephens
Secretary, Victor Hendricks Henderson
Treasurer, Mortimer Fleishhacker
Comptroller, Ralph Palmer Merritt
Attorney, Warren Olney, Jr.

Wheeler Hall
By John Galen Howard

BENJAMIN IDE WHEELER HALL was designed primarily to house the humanities — roughly speaking, that group of university subjects which make up the regular course of instruction in the old-time American college. The building has been given therefore the character of early American or Colonial architecture.

The dominating feature of the main (south) front is an Ionic colonnade running through the height of the second and third stories and crowning an arched and rusticated first story. The rhythm of the colonnade is accented above the entablature by carved urn-shaped lamps, which, with their flames, symbolize the light of learning. The lamps are decorated with heads of rams, symbolizing procreant power, and garlands, symbolizing the flowers of wisdom. The key-block of each arch is enriched with the head of Apollo, wreathed with bay and garlanded with oak.

The arcade on the south side of the ground story opens into a spacious vaulted vestibule, paved with cork tile, from which opens an auditorium with one thousand seats. This is the largest apartment and occupies the center of the building, being lighted from above by means of an open court.

Most of the rest of the building is occupied by class rooms of a great variety of sizes and shapes, each adapted to special class purposes. The entire fourth story is divided into department offices and studies.

The building, in addition to corridors, stairs, etc., contains 126 rooms.

BENJAMIN IDE WHEELER HALL

The University

REMARKABLE GROWTH in all departments of the university during the past year has adequately preserved the continuous and progressive development that has placed and maintained California in the foreground of American collegiate institutions. Owing to the ever-increasing demands of the people of the state, the university is experiencing an era of growth and expansion never before paralleled in its history.

Within the last seven years the Student Body has practically doubled, and during the last year a net total of 6,601 students was reached at a single semester's enrollment at the university proper in Berkeley. To these figures should be added 5,928 to include the enrollment in professional schools in San Francisco, students in the farm school at Davis, students registered in the summer session, and other outlying departments.

Turning back now from the university in its wider influence to the university at Berkeley as based on fixed graduations and prerequisites and adjusted to the highest recognized standards, we find that the growth has been well distributed among its various colleges. The College of Chemistry during the past three years has increased sixty per cent. in size, the Graduate Division fifty-six per cent., Dentistry fifty-four per cent., Letters and Science forty-two per cent., Commerce, Medicine, and Agriculture nineteen per cent.

This pressure of population has led to an enormous building construction during the present year. From the initiative by the people of the state, providing a total of $1,800,000, five new buildings are in present erection. All of these are well along towards completion and will be finished within one year. Benjamin Ide Wheeler Hall, the new class-room building costing more than $700,000, stands imposingly just inside of the Sather Gate. This splendid architectural masterpiece, designed by Professor John Galen Howard, contains an auditorium adequate for the larger lecture courses, together with sixty-two class rooms seating a total of 4,899 persons, and forty-seven professors' offices. In its combined beauty and adaptation to use it ranks with any academic building in the land. Wheeler Hall replaces old North Hall which is to be demolished in May, 1917, along with its traditions of half a century.

The new wing of the Library will cost over $547,000 and represents about seventy-one per cent. of increase in working floor space, with book space for over a million volumes, twenty new seminar rooms, and additional professors' offices. There is further the Agriculture Building costing $375,000 and the Chemistry Building, $220,000, both of re-enforced concrete. These latter two buildings will be ready for occupancy August 15, 1917. With the necessity for more heat and light a new unit has been added to the power plant.

But these great additions seem to afford only partial and temporary relief. There is the greatest and most definite need of a Student Union. Such a building in a larger measure must take the place of the old North Hall basement, and be wholly devoted to student life and student interests. There is need too of an auditorium adjusted to the size of the university. Aside from the Greek Theatre we must meet in Harmon Gymnasium where there are seats for barely half the population. There is essential to the life of the university a place in which it can assemble itself and become conscious of its own existence. A unit of the Reserve Officers' Training Corps will almost certainly be established at the university in the near future and then there will be a great need of additional armory space, preferably a new and proper building in keeping with the newer and larger system.

Provision for the social life and shelter of the students has ever been a pressing problem, suggesting the building of dormitories. However, the thirty-six men's fraternities, eleven men's house clubs, seventeen women's fraternities, and six women's house clubs have helped to remedy this need. These organizations have responded to their responsibilities and have strengthened and bettered themselves in many ways. They have consented to the publication of the relative scholastic standing of the various organizations with an effort to further improvement, even though the organization average is now above the general student average. This general improvement has given the fraternities and clubs a proper and justifiable place in student life and has removed much of the adverse criticism that has been directed against them in past years by people opposed to fraternities.

Government of the Student Body by the students has been maintained with very little friction and difficulty, and student self-government has become a complete working part of the university.

So, as the year draws to a harmonious and successful close, with each body doing its own work in the interest of the whole, every indication points to the continued prosperity of one of the state's greatest assets, the University of California.

BACON HALL

In Memoriam

Horace Davis
July 12, 1916, San Francisco, California
President of the University from 1888 to 1890

Lambert Henry Werson
September 4, 1916, San Francisco, California
Instructor at the Wilmerding School of Industrial Arts

Josiah Royce, Ph. D., LL. D., Litt. D.
September 14, 1916, Cambridge, Massachusetts
Instructor in English Literature and Logic from 1878 to 1882

Everett Gillis Morgan
November 9, 1916, Berkeley, California
A Junior in the College of Letters and Science

George Leslie Albright '14
December 15, 1916, Seville, Spain
Native Sons' Traveling Fellow in History

Albert Bonnheim
December 23, 1916, San Francisco, California
A Friend and Benefactor of the University

George Holmes Howison, LL. D.
December 31, 1917, Berkeley, California
Professor of Philosophy Emeritus

Elizabeth Josselyn Boalt
February 10, 1917, Santa Barbara, California
Giver of Boalt Hall and Founder of Boalt Professorships

Arnold Valentine Stubenrauch '99
February 12, 1917, Berkeley, California
Professor of Pomology in the University

Irene Marguerite O'Brien
March 5, 1917, Berkeley, California
A Freshman in the College of Letters and Science

Verne Frye Graves
March 26, 1917, Berkeley, California
A Freshman in the College of Mechanics

THE COLLEGE YEAR

THE PAJAMARINO RALLY

THE COLLEGE YEARS

The Paramino Press

Programme for Senior Week, May, 1916

FRIDAY, MAY 12

6:30 P. M.   Senior Men's Banquet   Leslie Hollis Brigham, Toastmaster
                          SENIOR HALL

7:00 P. M.   Senior Women's Banquet   Agnes Marie Flinn, Toastmistress
                          HOTEL SHATTUCK

SATURDAY, MAY 13

8:30 P. M.   Senior Extravaganza, "Absent on Leave,"
                                           by Hazel Havermale and Roger Goss
                          GREEK THEATRE

SUNDAY, MAY 14

4:00 P. M.   Baccalaureate Sermon   Rt. Rev. William H. Moreland
                          GREEK THEATRE

MONDAY, MAY 15

9:00 A. M.   Senior Pilgrimage   CAMPUS
9:00 P. M.   Senior Ball   HOTEL OAKLAND

TUESDAY, MAY 16

4:00 P. M.   Phi Beta Kappa Address   Prof. J. S. P. Tatlock
                          101 CALIFORNIA HALL

WEDNESDAY, MAY 17

9:45 A. M.   Commencement Exercises   GREEK THEATRE
              Invocation: Rev. Francis Greenwood Peabody

        Speakers: Philip Conley, Lena Meta Schafer, Hugh Samuel Johnson, and
                          Paul Longstreth Fussell

              University Medal awarded to Kathleen Harnett

COMMENCEMENT WEEK

Commencement Day

COMMENCEMENT DAY was celebrated by the Class of 1917 on May 17. The Greek Theatre was the place of gathering for the Seniors for the last official get-together of their undergraduate career. Following the invocation by Reverend Francis Greenwood Peabody, Philip Conley spoke on "Discipline and National Efficiency." Miss Lena Meta Schafer was the second one of the graduates to deliver an address. Her subject was "True Democracy." Paul Longstreth Fussell, as the next speaker, discussed "The New Internationalism." After talks by Governor Johnson, President Wheeler and Hugh Samuel Johnson the university medal was awarded to Miss Kathleen Harnett, a student of history.

Senior Pilgrimage

MEMBERS OF THE CLASS OF 1917 bade farewell to the university campus in the annual Pilgrimage on the morning of Monday, May 15. The women met, attired in white dresses and carrying white parasols, at Senior Women's Hall where they were greeted by Helen Lawton, president of the

PASSING THE MECHANICS BUILDING

WOMEN'S PILGRIMAGE

Senior women. The men met at Senior Men's Hall where Lloyd Hamilton spoke of the place of Senior Hall in the control of the undergraduate affairs of the university. In this connection he told of the development of the honor spirit in examinations and the growth of the institution of Senior control.

At Hearst Hall the men and women met. Here Marjorie Hyland reviewed the part which Hearst Hall had played in the undergraduate life of the women students. Lead by the University Cadet Band the

MEN'S PILGRIMAGE

Pilgrimage then proceeded to the Chemistry Building. At this building Charles Cron, after demonstrating the use of liquid air and color reagents, spoke of the development of the Chemistry Department which would follow the completion of the new building.

Frances Marion Hook was honored by being the first speaker at the Sather Campanile. Harlowe Stafford told of the peculiarities of the civil engineering curriculum which precluded the members of that college from participating in college activities. Leon Gazarian was the speaker at the Hearst Memorial Mining Building. Roy Heffner spoke at the Mechanics Building.

The Pilgrimage then proceeded to the Architecture Building and was addressed by Henry Howard. At the North Hall steps, Les Brigham, yell leader, told of the place of North Hall in the life of the undergraduate student and mourned the day when the bench and its surroundings should be destroyed by removal of North Hall.

Vira Georgeson, president of the Associated Women Students, spoke from the steps of the University Library Building. Knowles Ryerson was the speaker at the Agriculture Building. Charles Street, president of the Associated Students, spoke at California Hall. Howard Judy told of the development of the Law School under the direction of Professor William Carey Jones. After hearing Osgood Murdock at Wheeler Hall and Theodore Preble at Harmon Gymnasium, the Pilgrimage proceeded to Senior Oak. Here Matthew Hazeltine, president of the class, spoke of the achievements of the class during its four years in the university. After the singing of "All Hail," the Pilgrimage dispersed.

PRESIDENT HAZELTINE SPEAKS FAREWELL WORDS AT SENIOR OAK

1916 Senior Extravaganza
"Absent on Leave"

"AN EXTRAVAGANZA WORTHY OF A COPYRIGHT," was the comment of one newspaper critic. And that was the impression the audience got that saw "Absent on Leave" produced in the Greek Theatre on the evening of May 13. The 1916 Extravaganza, written by Hazel Halma Havermale and Roger Fulton Goss, reached a new height in this type of class fantasy, for the authors evaded the element of the personal and centered the merit for the production in the dialogue and lyrics.

SENIOR EXTRAVAGANZA
ROMERT LIGHT AND ELSIE LEE

"Absent on Leave" was more than a bevy of whimsy choruses, elaborate costumes and grotesque situations. There was a point to the central action. At the same time the spectacular f e a t u r e s, characteristic of former extravaganzas, were not left out, but were the result of clever thinking on the part of the authors rather than plain barbaric bigness.

The 1916 Extravaganza was a queer mixture of the modern and the medieval, the sensational and the intangible for the plot combined the spirit of present day college life with that of three centuries ago at the University of Paris.

The spectacular was interspersed throughout the production. In the opening number a steam curtain played about Satan and his flaming-red costumed chorus. "The Warder's Song" was sung by L. H. Brigham from the very top of the grey walls, and in the finale Satan sitting there with steam and lights centered on him provided a scene no less impressive. Large groups of choruses took full advantage of the depth of the stage and the massive opportunities which the Greek Theatre makes possible. The towering walls backed numerous settings of splendid and brilliant coloring.

Elsie Lee and W. S. Rainey carried the leads. The demands upon them were arduous for they were called upon to sing, dance and carry out the main action of the plot. R. M. Light played the other important role.

From the standpoint of artisticness and plot development "Absent On Leave" set a higher mark for future authors to reach. It proved a fitting vehicle for the closing of college dramatic careers and was not hampered on the night of production by the wet, drizzling weather of the year before.

CAST OF CHARACTERS

Bill, *the unintellectual outcast, formerly a gay student* ..... W. S. RAINEY
Jonothan Wise, *the intellectual Phi Bet* .... R. M. LIGHT
Satan, *who accomplishes the metamorphosis* .... H. P. SCARBOROUGH
The Jongleur, *a wanderer* .... R. G. DUDLEY
Peter, *who keeps the "Students' " Inn* .... J. E. KRUEGER
Prexy, *the High Priest of Intellectualism* .... L. H. BRIGHAM
Flossy, *a coed, the cause of it all* .... ELSIE LEE
Abbess, *the Jongleur's Fleur de Lys* .... LOUISE SHEPPA
Lizette, *the tavern maid* .... CLAIRE TUCKER

MORALITY PLAY

Maidenhood, *very sweet and very good* .... FLOSSIE
Worldly Wisdom, *the tempter* .... GERTRUDE WOODWARD
Piety .... RUTH TULLY
Passion .... GRACE PARKER
True Love .. .. ELINORE EARL

SENIOR EXTRAVAGANZA—"THE JONGLEUR"

1916 Senior Ball Committee

PATRONS AND PATRONESSES

President and Mrs. Benjamin Ide Wheeler
Professor and Mrs. William Brodbeck Herms
Professor and Mrs. Joel Henry Hildebrand
Professor and Mrs. Ruliff Stephen Holway
Professor and Mrs. Carleton Hubbell Parker
Doctor Romilda Paroni
Professor Henry Morse Stephens
Mr. and Mrs. Ralph Palmer Merritt
Professor and Mrs. Walter Morris Hart
Professor and Mrs. Matthew Christopher Lynch
Mr. and Mrs. F. C. Torrey

Class President, Matthew Emery Hazeltine
General Chairman Senior Week, Jean Carter Witter
General Chairman Senior Ball, John Lendell Browning
Floor Manager, Kenneth Auran Hays

ARRANGEMENTS COMMITTEE
Chairman, Kenneth Charles Watson

Dorothy Daniels	Loui Charles Beauman
Mabel Harrison Longley	Donald Lorenzo Campbell
Belle Tuttle Radcliff	Morse Erskine
Ruth Almede Smith	Robert Edward Graf
Mirabel Minnie Stewart	Reginald Heber Linforth
Hazel Adette Thompson	Thomas Andrew Reid

RECEPTION COMMITTEE
Chairman, John Douglas Short

Evelyn Dierrsen	Katherine Helen Westbrook
Elinore Hayes Earl	Archie Munroe Edwards
Frances Agnes Peterson	Jarvis Lewis Gabel
Virinda Lynn Pratt	Edmund Earl Hazelrigg
Lena Meta Schafer	Harlowe McVicker Stafford
Dorothea Torrey	John Boardman Whitton

HOGABOOM AND RYAN LOOK OVER THE FROSH

1930'S FIRST YELL

SOPHOMORE-FRESHMEN CONTESTS — THE JOUST MATCH

SOPHOMORE-FRESHMAN CONTESTS—THE TIE UP

SOPHOMORE-FRESHMAN CONTESTS—SOPHS BEING DRENCHED WITH WATER IN TUG OF WAR

"ENGINEERING" SUMMER CAMP

STUDENTS IN THE ENGINEERING COLLEGES of the university were in attendance at the camp maintained for practice surveying at Swanton in the Santa Cruz Mountains during the summer of 1916. The work was divided into two sections. The first of these was composed of Juniors in the College of Civil Engineering together with about twenty Freshmen. This party left Berkeley immediately after the close of Senior Week. The second party, composed of students from all the engineering colleges occupied the camp a month later.

For the Junior Civil Engineers, the work consisted of railroad location problems carried on to duplicate as nearly as possible the practice in actual construction work. For them the camp is a dismal drudge. There is nothing at Swanton that they had not already seen during the Freshman year. They had already climbed all the peaks, carried transits over all the trails and endured all the varieties of poison oak that thrive in the vicinity of the camp.

AROUND THE FIRE AT NIGHT

But for the Freshmen, new vistas appear with every day. They are treated, many of them for the first time with the trials of camp life; with bedclothes that won't stay put, straw mattresses that develop great holes and mounds with each night's sleep, lunches that defy the most ravishing of appetites, and hills that grow steeper and higher even as one climbs them. But these, the new men soon became used to.

The work of the Freshmen and of the men of the second party consists of the practice of surveying methods as carried on in field work. The men are divided into parties of three, the position of the men changing in the party each day. Each party is required to complete all the allotted problems before leaving the camp.

While the camp life is new to many, it is nevertheless enjoyed by all. There are occasional long walks through the woods, fishing expeditions, all night penny-ante games, and baseball contests. One feature of the camp life is the morning newspaper, issued by each party in camp in turn, generally under a new name each morning. This paper contains all of the scandal of the camp gossip. During the latter part of the session the paper generally is forced to combat with the activities of Mike Dillon, camp janitor and news censor.

Camp breaking is a festivity that every one remembers. Half the members of the camp are busy finishing maps and completing note-books. The other half see to it that the camp is closed with due ceremony. Then every one boards the train for Santa Cruz, with "Oski's" ringing in the air.

READY FOR HOME — WAITING FOR THE TRAIN

CHARTER DAY

CALIFORNIA CELEBRATED the forty-ninth anniversary of the founding of the university in the annual Charter Day ceremonies in the Greek Theatre, March 23. Professor George Herbert Palmer of Harvard University, speaker of the day, found a subject of common interest to himself and his audience in the life of George Berkeley, patron saint of the city.

Professor Palmer told of the three enthusiasms that characterized the life of Bishop Berkeley: "An enthusiasm for the non-existence of the material world, for the founding of a college in America, and for the drinking of tar-water."

In turn the speaker dealt with the activities of Berkeley's life, and demonstrated that, although his enthusiasms were not those which ordinarily stir the blood of mankind, they, nevertheless, resulted from orderly and accurate thought. In regard to the first enthusiasm, Professor Palmer

DR. PALMER SPEAKING AT GREEK THEATRE

told of the advance made by Berkeley over his friend and teacher, Locke, in the development of idealistic philosophy. Professor Palmer related the incidents which lead to Berkeley's attempt to found a college in America for the training of ministers, which was his second great enthusiasm. Berkeley's faith in the curative properties of tar-water founded upon experiences in America was cited as the third of Berkeley's beliefs.

Previous to the principal speech of the day President Wheeler announced gifts of more than half a million dollars from friends of the university which had been received in the past year.

Members of the Class of 1896 celebrated the twenty-first anniversary of their graduation by the dedication of a marble chair in the Greek Theatre to the memory of Martin Kellogg, former president of the university. Mr. Sidney M. Ehrman, as spokesman, told of the devotion of the members of his class to Martin Kellogg, and pledged their support to the university. "Unified and collective service should be given by every graduating class to its Alma Mater. The gift of the Class of 1896 typifies its devotion to the university and its hopes to do further service. The next twenty-one years must be dedicated to united effort to accomplish the ideals that formed the life of Martin Kellogg."

During the afternoon, the guardianship of the Big "C" was transferred to the Freshman Class by the Sophomores. Members of both classes assembled on Charter Hill where the new and retiring chairmen of the Big "C" committees spoke in behalf of the classes which they represented.

FACULTY-SKULL AND KEY BASEBALL GAME—MOBBING THE UMPIRE

SKULL AND KEY RUNNING

...

FOR THE FIRST TIME in the history of the organization, the Skull and Key Society held its annual initiation running without the attendance of the women of the university. A taboo placed upon the society by the Pan-Hellenic organization was the cause.

Throughout the morning, the neophytes played knight errant on the paths leading to the campus. At eleven o'clock, the time honored limericks were recited on California Field. No women were present.

The second radical departure from custom occurred when the new members of the society, being denied the privilege of serving lunch at the sororities, placed a cordon of pickets in front of the boycotting houses.

The afternoon's festivities consisted of a chemically pure series of travesties on campus situations given in pantomime on California Field. The following men were initiated:

Honorary—Stanley Barton Freeborn, James Townsend Barstow, Hollis Mansfield Black, Fred Thomas Brooks, Edward Porter Bruck, Charles Stanley Dixon, Edwin Madison Elam, Waldemor A. Falck, Theodore Randolph Finley, Jr.

SKULL AND KEY RUNNING—ENTERTAINING THE CROWD

SKULL AND KEY RUNNING—NEOPHYTES FURNISH NO END OF SERVICE

Benjamin Blackwood Foster, Fred Gray Gibbons, Charles Franklin Harper, William Knox Holt, Walter John Hulting, Grant James Hunt, Harry Bluett Liveright, Russell Haveus Macyonaki, Mervin Louis McCabe, Bradford Morse Melvin, Kenneth Monteagle, John O'Melveny, J. R. Murray, Jr., John L. Reith, Ray Rohmer, Henry Augusto Ruffo, Harry Hall Scheeline, Albert Carnahan Simonds, Elmer Ellsworth Stone, Chester Benson Tonkin, John Stewart Weeks, Harry Kirk White, Pierre Works and George Washington Young.

FARM COLLEGE YEAR

By Don L. Kieffer

THE THREE HUNDRED AND EIGHTY STUDENTS enrolled at the University Farm may be divided into two academic groups. First are the regular Farm students and secondly are those students from Berkeley who must spend at least one semester at Davis as a requisite for the College of Agriculture.

The Davis school has a student body organization called the Associated Students of the University Farm. Students from Berkeley for the spring semester affiliate with the A. S. U. F. for the time being, with full privileges and powers and a place on the executive committee for one member.

Picnic Day is the "Big Event" of the Farm and the one held this year on April 28 far surpassed any previous one. Visitors, numbering to the thousands, flocked to Davis as the guests of the "farm boys."

AT WORK IN THE GARDENS

Those in charge of this year's picnic were Colby Slater, general chairman; Howard Burson, athletics; Jack Hunsaker, parade; Randolph Sevier, reception; Elmer Struve, refreshments; Harry Drobish, publicity; Arthur Folger, stock judging; Fred Janney, entertainment and Grant Hunt, dances.

Life among the U. C. Students at the Farm tends toward the ideal existence, for the wily woman is conspicuous by her absence. Consequently, having enjoyed the pleasures and contentments of college without the co-ed, every student of the farm is an anti-co-education booster for good. Women are necessary evils at dances but we rarely dance— here at the Farm. We even tolerate stenographers for necessity's sake. Faculty and students alike enrobe in the oldest of togs and many a youth tries his first crop of down on the Farm.

Life at Davis is made up of work only in the day time with evenings all to oneself. These evenings, as a rule, are spent in the neighboring towns of Sacramento, Woodland or Davis, according to the inclination of the individual.

The work of the Farm curriculum consists chiefly of practical experiments in farming.

JUDGING STOCK   FARM SCHOOL SCENES   A CATTLE CORRAL

WOMEN'S COLLEGE YEAR

Sports and Pastimes Jinx

THE FIRST NOTABLE EVENT of the women's college year was the annual Sports and Pastimes Jinx, held in the form of an Italian carnival or street fair. La Festa, as it was called, took place on November 11th, in Hearst Hall. The main floor was arranged with numerous booths, decorated with chili, garlic, and onions, in which artists and fortune-tellers were busily engaged. Italian peasant girls in bandanas, bright-colored aprons and skirts, sold balloons, flowers, and candy. Organ grinders, singers, tarantula and dagger dancers afforded entertainment, and in the gaily decorated annex there was dancing. Down-stairs, peasant girls sold fruit, spaghetti, raviolas, and tamales. The proceeds of this very successful evening were given to women's athletics.

CAPTAIN BRUD MONTGOMERY SPEAKS AT WOMEN'S RALLY

THE PRYTANEAN FETE

Women's Football Rally

On November 15th, in Hearst Hall, the women held a football rally in anticipation of the Big Game. It was in the nature of a basket supper, followed by speeches. The girls were divided according to their classes, and during supper, contests were held between the classes in singing bleacher songs and giving yells, each class having its own leader. After supper speeches were made by President Wheeler, Dean Stebbins, Graduate Manager Stroud, Eddie Mahan, who explained the important rules and plays of the American game, Captain Brud Montgomery '17, and Leila Berry '17. The Women's Big "C" Society stunt was a burlesque of various football plays. The rally was well attended and very enthusiastic.

The Prytanean Fete

The annual Prytanean Fete was held on March 3, in Harmon Gym. This year it was a Kubist Karnival, original and startling in every feature. The gym was a riot of color, the ceiling was covered in great cubes, and the walls and booths all carried out the effect. "Down the Bloc" were numerous attractions. One whole corner was devoted to fortune-telling, where seven different methods of making known the future were employed. A Futuristic Theatre furnished amusement with Kubist dancers and Vogue tableaux; in another section remarkable Kubist silhouettes were cut. One of the main attractions was the Bohemian cafe, arranged on the stage, where refreshments were served.

ART SCHOOL COLLEGE ·· YEAR ··

California School of Fine Arts

DURING THE PAST YEAR the name California School of Design was changed to the California School of Fine Arts. Originally founded in 1874 it is now completing its forty-third year. In 1893 it was affiliated with the University of California, thereby becoming privileged to confer a University Certificate of Proficiency in the Graphic Arts.

The building in which the school is now conducted under the direction of the San Francisco Art Association, is built upon the foundation of the former Mark Hopkins Institute of Art and is considered temporary.

The school has a total enrollment of about 230 students. Night classes and a Saturday class are conducted in addition to the regular courses held during the day. The subjects are taught by a faculty staff composed of ten regular instructors and several special teachers. The curriculum is composed of drawing and painting from antique, still life, life and costumed

THE ART SCHOOL JINX

A CLASS AT WORK

models, modeling, illustration, composition, decorative and commercial design, etching, handicrafts and a normal course.

In the last National competition conducted by the Art Students' League of New York in which all art students compete, the students of the California School of Fine Arts received distinguished honors, winning eight of the total seventeen awards granted. This has placed the school in the foremost ranks of art institutions in America, causing much favorable comment in Eastern art circles.

With these successes behind the school, a bright future is ahead and plans are already being laid to provide increased facilities for the expected stimulus in attendance.

STUDENTS RECEIVING PRACTICAL INSTRUCTION

The College of Dentistry at San Francisco

THIS YEAR MARKS the completion of certain building activities at the College of Dentistry calculated to meet the demand for larger and better clinical facilities to provide instruction for the increasing number of students enrolled.

A new building has been erected in which the most modern type of equipment has been installed with the view to individualizing the student's activities. Each section is planned and arranged to represent a dental office in so far as it is possible in a large clinic room. Each student is taught both by precept and practice, the generally accepted and approved methods of practicing dentistry both as to his professional work and his relations with his clientele.

On Thursday, October 5, 1916, the Faculty and students observed "Labor Day" to install the new equipment. The greater portion of the work was completed in the morning, after which the toilers sat down to a feed provided by the Faculty and served by the members of the Freshman class. By evening the work was practically finished. The following two days were spent in getting settled in the new quarters.

With the beginning of the next regular session in August, 1917, the four-

JUNIORS AT COLLEGE OF DENTISTRY

DENTAL CO-EDS LEND A HAND

year course of study will be inaugurated in all dental schools in this country. This is the first step taken in placing dentistry ultimately as a specialty in the broad field of general medicine, toward which it has been gravitating for several years.

At present all courses of instruction will be given in the dental school. When the departments of Physiology, Pathology and Anatomy are moved to San Francisco it is planned to have instruction in these basic medical sciences given by the respective departments.

Although the course prescribed occupies the greater portion of the students' time, students' affairs and matters of general importance are considered by the Student Body as a whole. Meetings are held on the last Thursday of each month. Students' affairs are transacted, generally followed by talks by outside men of standing on subjects of interest and benefit to the members. The Student Body has a membership of 175, the largest in the history of the college. With the extension of the course in dentistry and the transferring of the entire medical course to this side of the Bay the students of dentistry look forward to an organization composed of students of medicine, pharmacy and dentistry.

In all the universities where both medicine and dentistry are being taught, this general plan is being adopted, a striking reversion of the ideas which caused the separation of the schools and the profession, and which brought American dentistry into such prominence throughout the world in the past seventy-five years. Dentistry is more and more becoming to be recognized as one of the vital professions and as a result, the professional men are giving it more of a place.

AGRICULTURAL TRIPS

During the summer of 1916 summer travelling courses in agriculture were conducted by five divisions of the College of Agriculture. These courses, or equivalent work during the summer, are required at the end of the Sophomore year.

The trips, extending for six weeks, were taken by students in the divisions of agronomy, pomology, citriculture, soils and landscape gardening. The first three groups named travelled in automobiles during the entire trip which allowed them to stop at their convenience.

The value to be derived from these interdivision courses lies in the student being able to become acquainted with agricultural conditions throughout the state, not only in his particular field but in other branches as well. Students come in contact with men engaged in the actual work of farming and can learn much from such men's experiences. In addition the summer work gives students a better preparation for the work to be taken up in the upper division of the college.

RESTING AFTER A HARD DAY OF EXPERIMENTING

SOPHOMORE LABOR DAY

For the purpose of repairing the Big "C" and the Charter Hill path, the members of the 1919 Class participated in the first Sophomore labor day on November 11. The men met under the leadership of the Sophomore Big "C" committee at the North Hall steps at nine o'clock. Tools for the work of the day were provided by loans from construction companies of the Bay region.

During the morning the concrete emblem was painted and a new system of wiring was installed for the illumination of the Big "C" on the eve of University anniversaries. Along the path, new gravel was placed. The drain ditch above the path was repaired to prevent the erosion of the path by the winter rains.

At noon the workers assembled at Hearst Hall where the women of the class had prepared lunch of the "Labor Day" variety. Beans, coffee, and "dogs" were served in large quantities.

After lunch, members of the class provided music for dancing in Hearst Hall which lasted until the crowd broke up to attend the St. Mary's-Varsity football game.

This was the first annual labor day held by Sophomores.

ODD MOMENTS DURING SOPHOMORE LABOR DAY

Programme for Senior Week, May, 1917

THURSDAY, MAY 10

7:00 P. M. Senior Men's Banquet   Charles Josef Carey, Toastmaster
              HOTEL WHITCOMB, SAN FRANCISCO

8:00 P. M. Senior Women's Banquet   Frances Leslie Brown, Toastmistress
              KEY ROUTE INN, OAKLAND

SATURDAY, MAY 12

12:00 M.   Faculty Club Garden Party   FACULTY GLADE
8:00 P. M. Senior Extravaganza, "Youth Comes Up"
              by Edwin Marshall Mashn and John Robert Bruce
              GREEK THEATRE

SUNDAY, MAY 13

4:00 P. M. Baccalaureate Sermon,
              Most Reverend E. J. Hanna, D. D., Archbishop of San Francisco
              GREEK THEATRE

MONDAY, MAY 14

9:00 A. M. Senior Pilgrimage
4:00 to 6:00 P. M. President's Reception to Graduating Class
              PRESIDENT'S HOUSE
9:00 P. M. Senior Ball   HOTEL OAKLAND, OAKLAND

TUESDAY, MAY 15

4:00 P. M. Phi Beta Kappa Address
              Frederick James Eugene Woodbridge of Columbia University

WEDNESDAY, MAY 16

9:45 A. M. Commencement Exercises   GREEK THEATRE
12:45 P. M. Alumni Luncheon   STRAWBERRY CANYON
2:00 P. M. Farewell Ceremonies, North Hall
2:30 P. M. Dedication of Benjamin Ide Wheeler Hall.

1917 Senior Week

WHILE THE COLLEGE YEAR of 1916-1917 draws to a close preparations are complete for commencement week of the Class of 1917. Under the direction of the Senior Week committees, plans have been formulated for the ceremonies and festivities incident to the graduation of the class from the university.

Preceding Senior Week, the final University Meeting was held in Harmon Gymnasium on Friday, April 13, at which chosen speakers gave the advice of the Senior Class based upon undergraduate experiences.

Senior Week is scheduled to open with the banquets of the men and women on the evening of Thursday, May 10. The men of the class are to gather at Hotel Whitcomb in San Francisco, while the women meet at the Key Route Inn. The toastmaster of the evening is Charles Josef Carey. Graduates, members of the Faculty and members of the graduating class who have been chosen to speak at the banquet of the men are Benjamin Ide Wheeler, Matthew Christopher Lynch, Charles Frank Stern, Jay Dwiggins, Milton Swartz and Harry Boyd Seymour.

The speakers chosen for the women's banquet are Frances Leslie Brown, toastmistress; Dr. Romilda Paroni, Leila Berry, Margaret Marchant, Anna Barrows, Carol Eberts and Mary Kleinecke.

The evening of Saturday, May 12, has been set aside for the 1917 Extravaganza "Youth Comes Up", by John Robert Bruce and Edwin Marshall Muslin. The play has been coached by Reginald Travers and Fred Carlyle. Alice Bunnell Elliot and James Somers Candee have the leads in the production.

The Most Reverend E. J. Hanna '99, D. D., has been selected to deliver the Baccalaureate Sermon on Sunday, May 13. Members of the class are to attend the services in a body.

Class Day, the climax of the festivities of Senior Week, has been set for Monday, May 14. On this day the members of the graduating class, headed by the Cadet Band, march in turn to the different buildings of the campus where they bid farewell to the scenes of undergraduate activity. From four to six o'clock of the afternoon of Class Day, President Wheeler is to hold a reception for the members of the class at his mansion. Following the step of the 1916 Class, the Senior Ball is to be held off the campus, at Hotel Oakland, on the evening of Class Day.

After the commencement exercises, which are to be held on Wednesday, May 16, the alumni will banquet in Strawberry Canyon.

Other plans included in the programme for this last day are the formal dedication of the new Benjamin Ide Wheeler Hall and farewell ceremonies to Old North Hall.

RALLIES

Freshman Rally

When Professor Henry Morse Stephens faced his audience from the stage of the Greek Theatre at the annual Freshman Rally, according to his own statement he found for the first time in his fourteen years experience at welcoming the newcomers, no extraneous material. And that one fact—unimportant as it may seem—makes the official entrance of 1920 into the university community one to be reckoned apart from those of previous classes.

As the "Father of Freshman Classes" looked out over the fitfully leaping flames which lit up the faces of the thousands of spectators he saw but one thing—California Spirit. For on that night the walls of the Greek Theatre enclosed Californians alone. In welcoming the Freshmen the speaker pointed out to the others of the university, as well, what an enormous factor in itself the true spirit of loyalty could be in making of the University of California something larger and finer than anything which mere numbers could indicate.

Football coaches Andy Smith and Eddie Mahan were called upon to tell of the chances of the football team during the season. Both showed their ability as foretellers of the future by predicting a season not victorious

RAY BOGAROOM—YELL LEADER
LEM SANDERSON—ASSISTANT   BAT NELSON—ASSISTANT

FRESHMAN RALLY — FROSH BURN 1919 EFFIGY

but surely far from disastrous. F. W. Stewart '17, president of the A. S. U. C., spoke to the newcomers on behalf of the other three undergraduate classes, impressing on them the duties they owed as Californians.

PAJAMARINO RALLY — MARCHING TO THE GREEK

PAJAMARINO RALLY—SOPHOMORE STUNT

Finally, with the flames burning lower and lower but the spirit of the rally flaring ever higher, the classes serpentined to Harmon Gymnasium and a few moments later, with the closing strains of "All Hail" still sounding in the cool night air, 1920 went home, members of the university community and possessors of the true California Spirit.

Pajamarino Rally

IN MANY WAYS the Pajamarino Rally, which was held on the night of October 12, was a disappointment. Those who expected a brilliant display of university spirit were treated to a performance that was lacking in the essential characteristic of a successful rally. There was no enthusiasm in the pajama clad throng that filled the Greek Theatre to do homage at the shrine of athletic achievement. Perhaps there was too much similarity between the stunts and vaudeville exhibitions. Perhaps the speeches put a damper on any pep that may have intruded. Perhaps the night was too cold. Perhaps, after all, there was nothing to grow enthusiastic about.

As the flames curled over the pile of wood gathered by the Freshmen, the yell leaders, followed by the University Band, lead the serpentining classes into the theatre. The band struck up "The Golden Bear" and the hills rang with the sound of five thousand voices.

Professor Ira B. Cross represented the Faculty as the principal speaker. After looking forward to a successful athletic season, he told of the good things in store for the university in the future. In this regard he predicted the erection of a Students Union for the common meeting place of the Faculty, alumni and students.

Entertainment by the classes followed. The Freshmen depicted the sinking of the good ship "19" by the submarine "U-20" in five minutes of thundering fireworks. The Sophomores were more ambitious, and attempted to entertain with Oriental dancers that couldn't dance and speeches without a gem of wit.

North Hall in all its glory with the steps and the bench were the setting for a series of burlesques by the Juniors. Senior control formed the vehicle for impersonations, while a brawl on the miniature steps gave opportunity for an exposé of the "Peace Committee."

The Senior stunt showed the results of the heavy fall of the hand of the censor. The performance consisted of burial ceremonies for institutions that have been tried and abandoned.

A rally may be best judged by its ending, and from this criterion the rally was unsuccessful. The crowd walked out in silence. There was no big final "Oski." There was no serpentine. There was no evidence of a rally except in the fantastic garbs that reflected the dying embers of the fire.

Varsity Smoker Rally

AN ENTHUSIASTIC EXPRESSION of loyalty was the keynote of the Varsity Smoker from the uproar of the "Siren Oski" to the refrain of "All Hail" in the flickering light of the bonfire on the old baseball field.

Harmon Gymnasium was packed to the doors with lusty spirits all eager to have a part in expressing to the eleven men on the platform their optimistic faith in the outcome of the game. When the din had subsided, Forrest Stanton '09 addressed a few words to the audience concerning the return of the old game.

Professor Hildebrand was the speaker of the evening, introducing Andy Smith and explaining the methods and successes of the new coach. Professor Hildebrand reminded the rooters that it was as much their duty to

VARSITY ATTENDS THE PAJAMARINO

VARSITY SMOKER—HARMON GYMNASIUM

get behind the team and support it as it was the team's duty to fight out on the field.

When the chosen eleven filed out on the platform the roar shook the rafters of the gymnasium for fully ten minutes. "The Varsity has not forgotten the defeat at the hands of Washington last year," said Captain Montgomery. "The men have not forgotten about it since last November and everyone is going on the field determined to turn the tables."

Coach Andy Smith received a true California ovation. His talk was sincere, calculating and to the point, and everyone felt that he was expressing a rational judgment on the team's chances.

When Coach Smith had concluded, the serpentine wound its way out into the night and circled toward the huge bonfire.

The Axe Rally

THE STANFORD AXE came out of hiding for the annual rally, commemorating the stealing of the weapon from the Cardinal rooters, on the night of March 29. As Captain Sammy Adair walked into Harmon Gymnasium with the axe over his shoulder, the California rooters rose in pandemonium, as

"Give 'em the axe,
Give 'em the axe,
Give 'em the axe, Where?"

FRESHIE GLEE

1920

Harmon Gymnasium— March 9, 1917

PATRONS AND PATRONESSES

President and Mrs. Benjamin Ide Wheeler
Dean and Mrs. David Prescott Barrows
Professor and Mrs. Russell Tracy Crawford
Professor and Mrs. Joel Henry Hildebrand
Professor and Mrs. Frank Louis Kleeberger
Professor and Mrs. Edmund O'Neill
Doctor Romilda Paroni
Dean Lucy Ward Stebbins
Professor and Mrs. Leslie Morton Turner

Class President, Paul Bench Follett   General Chairman, St. Clair Garnett Cheney
Floor Manager, Karl Theodore Goeppert

RECEPTION COMMITTEE

Charles Hall Fishburn (Chairman)
Emma Madeline Becker
Lela Ewert
Margaret Eberts
Carmelita Parma

Mildred Spencer Ponting
Donald Clampett
Charles Crossen Dexter
Herbert Bonner Pawson
Irving Francis Toomey

DECORATION COMMITTEE

Gerville Mott (Chairman)
Mary Kathleen Cooper
Ruth Cooper
Florence Crellin
Laura de Veuve
Clarita Grace Nunan
Doris Peoples

Elizabeth Seymour
Marjorie Tuttle
James Edward Drew
Walter Ungerman Friedrichs
Norman Charles Heinz
Isaias Warren Hellman III
Alvin Davidson Hyman

Arthur Herbert Sinnock

ARRANGEMENTS COMMITTEE

Raybourne Wycoff Rinehart (Chairman)
Marian Louise Blankinship
Delight Brown
Marian Alice Black
Eleanor Ruth Gardner
Katherine Frothingham Haworth

Annette Emilie Ruggles
Helen Earle Sutherland
Katherine Amelia Towle
David Farragut Ashe
Edmund de Freitas
Britton Rey

Edward Albert Williams

SOPHOMORE HOP

1919
Harmon Gymnasium — October 20, 1916

PATRONS AND PATRONESSES
President and Mrs. Benjamin Ide Wheeler
Dean and Mrs. David Prescott Barrows
Dean and Mrs. Armin Otto Leuscher
Dean and Mrs. Thomas Milton Putnam
Dean Lucy Ward Stebbins
Professor and Mrs. Joel Henry Hildebrand
Major and Mrs. John Turrency Nance
Dr. and Mrs. Robert Thomas Legge
Professor and Mrs. Edmund O'Neill
Dr. Romulda Paroni
Professor Henry Morse Stephens

Class President, George Stocley Peterson   General Chairman, George John Atcheson
Floor Manager, Arthur Blair Cantwell

ARRANGEMENTS COMMITTEE
Bruce Howard (Chairman)
Madeline Macy Benedict
Helene Cowell
Juene Laura Fisk
Ruth Livingston Hammond
Mary Elizabeth Harrison
Stella Elizabeth Sharkey
Genevieve Spader   Jack Frederick White

Ruth Vincent
Gordon McCausland Boyes
Percy Osborne Brewer
Arthur Merrill Browne
Donald Leigh Leavitt
Walter Stewart McManus
Richard D. Perry
Fred Turner

DECORATION COMMITTEE
Earl Stanley Ward (Chairman)
Ella Cole Barrows
Truman Everett Boughton
Kenneth Sanborn Craft
Kathryn Cook
Angie Barbara Cowats
Catherine Holton Fletcher
Raymond Evan Gardner
Clifton Rogers Gordon
John Calvin Hickey
Anita Howard

Clara Gertrude Huffman
Gladys Amelia Hulting
Moreland Liethold
Ogle Charles Merwin
Helen Maclise
Constance Rogers
Margaret Rolph
William Samuel Rhea
Harry Allan Sproul
Clair Emanuel Woland
Carleton Gross Wells
Mary White

RECEPTION COMMITTEE
James Edward Holbrook (Chairman)
Helen Ruth Dotson
Margaret Forsyth
Sara Russell D'Ancona
Florence Amelia Hofer
Esther Margaret Langley
                Kenneth George Uhl

Frida Louise Leuschner
Charles Detoy
Alexander Blake Hill
Gerald Reid Johnson
Richard Holmes Kessler
George Garrison Mitchell

JUNIOR PROM

1918

Harmon Gymnasium — November 25, 1916

PATRONS AND PATRONESSES

President and Mrs. Benjamin Ide Wheeler
Dean and Mrs. David Prescott Barrows
Dean and Mrs. Thomas Forsyth Hunt
Dean Lucy Ward Stebbins
Professor and Mrs. Charles Mills Gayley
Professor and Mrs. William Bradbeck Herms
Professor and Mrs. Joel Henry Hildebrand
Professor and Mrs. Myer Edward Jaffa
Mr. and Mrs. Ralph Palmer Merritt
Mrs. and Mrs. Winfield Scott Thomas

Class President, Grant James Hunt General Chairman, William Hill Thomas
Floor Manager, Harvey Maher Kilburn

ARRANGEMENTS COMMITTEE
Chairman, Victor Lavenson Furth

Leslie Brown
Marian Brown
Estelle Eliza Cook
Valatee Scott Cowan
Margaret Wilson Honeywell

Margaret Eddy House
Ruth Benjamin Walker
George Magee Cunningham
Charles Franklin Harper
John Putnam Jackson

John O'Melveny
Edwin Sprague Pillsbury
John L. Keith
Albert Brodie Smith
Carroll Hutchinson Smith

DECORATION COMMITTEE
Chairman, Wymond Bradbury Garthwaite
Assistant, Thomas Carroll Winstead

Vera Lillian Christie
Frances Morris Cochrane
Blanche G. Coulter
Irene Ray
Catherine Helene Woolsey

Hollis Mansfield Black
Carroll Frances Dunshee
Charles Lawrence Frost
Fred Gray Gibbons
Eugene Pooler Hyatt
Heber Spencer Steen

Karl Eliot Kennedy
Frank Laub
Miles Way Middough
Lellier Bequette Miller
Leslie Scott Nelson
Cloyd Jonathan Sweigert

RECEPTION COMMITTEE
Chairman, Russell White Bell

Juliette Atwater
Bernice Hubbard
Helen Bailey Leete
Helen Matlock Olmstead

Helen Mary Rocth
Marjorie Isabel Stuart
Donald Laughlin Abshire
Robert Alston Brant

Thomas Arthur Gabbert
John Bentley Halbert
Russel Flavius Macdonald
Ray Rohwer

 # SENIOR BALL

1917
Hotel Oakland – May 14, 1917

PATRONS AND PATRONESSES
President and Mrs. Benjamin Ide Wheeler
Dean and Mrs. David Prescott Barrows
Dean and Mrs. William Carey Jones
Professor and Mrs. William Broderick Herms
Professor and Mrs. Charles Gilman Hyde
Professor and Mrs. Joel Henry Hildebrand
Professor Henry Morse Stephens
Professor Romalda Paroni
Mr. and Mrs. Ralph Palmer Merritt
Miss Lucy Ward Stebbins
Class President, George Washington Cohen
General Chairman Senior Week, Stephen Sears Barrows
General Chairman Senior Ball, Willis Guy Witter
Floor Manager, Luther Allen Nichols
Secretary Senior Ball Committees, James Benton Harvey

ARRANGEMENTS COMMITTEE
Thomas William Slaven, Chairman

Anna Frances Barrows	Elizabeth Mary Ruggles	Charles Stanley Dimm
Pauline Dillman	Leslie Underhill	Elbert Wilson Lockwood
Maud Carol Eberts	Dorothy Elizabeth Wetmore	Emery Herman Rogers
M'Louise Kevney	Harold Alfred Black	Chester Benson Tonkin
Natressa Pieda	Ernest Camper	Donald Clark Williams
	Charles Joseph Carey	

RECEPTION COMMITTEE
LeRoy Farnham Krusi, Chairman

Katherine van Dyke Bangs	Coe Elizabeth McCabe	Henry Raymond Hogaboom
Margaret Boveroux	Rosalinda Amelia Gleese	Charles David Lane
Tillie De Bernardi	Russelet Wallace	George Moore Lindsay
Alice Bunnell Elliott	Lewis Ryan Byington	Floyd Wane Stewart
Verna Maude Lane	Douglas Bray Cohen	John James Vandenburgh
	Edwin Madison Elam	

DECORATION COMMITTEE
Charles Knox, Chairman

Pauline Adams	Algeline Marlow	Norman Morris Lyon
Lois Bralyn Benton	Donna Moses	Alfred Leo Maguire
Barbara Burke	Mary Jane Sanderson	Joseph Nash Owen
Octavia Downie	Ruby Yoakum	Paul Weaver Penland
Elizabeth Frances Elliott	Raymond Karnaghan Bontz	Murrey Levering Royar
Dorothy Epping	Edward Brett	Hugh Fenimore Shippey
Dorothy Harriet Huggins	Wright Ethelbert D'Evelyn	Waite Henry Stephenson
	Lloyd William Goeppert	

1917

Harmon Gymnasium—March 30, 1917

PATRONS AND PATRONESSES

President and Mrs. Benjamin Ide Wheeler
Major and Mrs. John T. Nance
Dean and Mrs. David Prescott Barrows
Professor and Mrs. Joel H. Hildebrand
Professor and Mrs. John Galen Howard
Dean and Mrs. Thomas Forsyth Hunt
Professor and Mrs. Edmond O'Neill
Professor and Mrs. Frank L. Kleeberger
Professor and Mrs. Thomas M. Putnam
Professor and Mrs. Oliver M. Washburn

General Chairman, Captain John James Vandenbergh
Floor Manager, Henry Raymond Hogaboom

ARRANGEMENTS COMMITTEE

Captain Harold Putnam Detwiler, Chairman

Captain Carl George Hjelte	Corporal Clifton Rogers Gordon
Sergeant Arthur Wilson	Corporal Ross Jackson Wright

DECORATION COMMITTEE

Captain Gordon Fitzhugh Stephens, Chairman

Captain Edward Alexander Reinke	Sergeant Olin Wellborn III
Sergeant Harold Blackmer Reed	Corporal Matthews Maxwell Conley
Sergeant John Henry Spohn, Jr.	Corporal Miller Roe Huston
Sergeant Max Weston Thornburgh	Private Charles Francis Honeywell
Sergeant Howard Winthrop Turner	Private H. J. Hunter

RECEPTION COMMITTEE

Captain Floyd Theall McKune, Chairman

Captain Southall Rozelle Pfund	Corporal Lester Murta Johnson
Lieutenant Evans Ronald Foster	Corporal Kenneth King
Lieutenant M. J. Howell	Corporal George Garrison Mitchell
Sergeant John Walter Oakley	Private Elbridge Miles Cantelow

INFORMALS

Senior Assembly Committee
Hearst Hall—April 12, 1917

Clifford Bert Cole, Chairman

Marion Clarice Downie
Sadie Fredericks
Gertrude Frost
Kathryn Hubbard
Cora Floyd Keeler
Elizabeth Ermine Keith
Louise Kenn

Wiley Ross
Amy Waldon
Esther Louise Witter
Samuel Earl Breck
Vaughn Merwin Cobb
Cecil Amos Ditty
Lester Albert Fowler
Lawrence Frederick Knauer

Leslie Alphonse Isaacson
John Curtis Newton
Herbert Kuno Schulz
Raub Merrill Stafford
Gordon Fitzhugh Stephens
Floyd Wane Stewart
Whitney Braymer Wright

Junior Informal Committee
Hearst Hall—March 22, 1917

Albert Breslie Smith, Chairman

Addie Viola Babb
Rebecca Candelaria Borradaile
Evelyn Farrar
Beatrice Gerberding
Azile Howard
Margo Sheppa
Esther Sinclair

Myrtle Grace Taylor
Mildred Valeras
Edna Margaret Williams
Donald Laughlin Abshire
Howard Baldwin
George Williams Clark
Fuller Clarkson

Stanley Wallace Cosby
Henry Stephen Flock
Charles Lawrence Frost
Frank Lamb
Leo Roy Moody
Sydney Kinnear Smith
Catherine Helene Woolsey

Sophomore Informal Committee
Hearst Hall—March 23, 1917

Frank Foli Hargear, Chairman

Ella Cole Barrows
Ruth Adelaide Chrisman
Kathryn Cook
Margaret Forsyth
Vera Helen Gardiner
Mona Gardner
Maurine Elise Gilliam
Edith Caroline Horstman
Edith Marion McLenegan

Margaret Rolph
Ethelwynne Beth Sites
Mildred Swanson
Marjorie Waldron
Truman Everett Boudinot
Loys Melville Blakeley
Ralph Aldom Frost
Elliott Glen Hart
Alexander Blake Hill, Jr.

Edwyn Jolly
Harris Crozer Kirk
Donald Leigh Leavitt
Moreland Leithold
James Bandy Merritt
William Storey Nash
Eric Reynolds
Fred Turner
Florence Welch

ACTIVITIES

THE EUCALYPTUS GROVE

ACTIVITIES

MILIT4RY

Lieutenant Truman D. Thorpe

LIEUTENANT THORPE graduated from the United States Military Academy with the Class of 1907 and was assigned to duty with the Coast Artillery Corps at Key West, Florida. In January, 1909, he was retired on account of disability incurred in line of duty and two years later, in 1913, was detailed to the Wentworth Military Academy at Lexington, Missouri. Later, in 1914, he was transferred to Ohio State University to act as assistant to the commandant at that institution, serving there until July, 1916, when he came to the University of California as Assistant Professor in Military Science and Tactics. In addition to commanding the Third Battalion on the drill field he gives instruction in infantry problems to three sections of non-commissioned officers, courses which heretofore have been conducted by the commandant.

LIEUT. THORPE

Half-Day Drills

PROBABLY A LARGE SHARE of the benefit to be had from the military training at the University of California is that derived from the five or six half-day drills which are given each year. It is in the lesson gained from these marches that the students get a glimpse of real campaign conduct.

The object of these marches falls under three distinct heads. First is the idea of gaining security for an army while it is on the march. That this end may be accomplished, "points" must be sent ahead for advance reconnaissance, and patrols sent out to the flanks and to the rear to guard against hostile envelopment of the main body which may happen to show up.

The second phase of this drill is had in the sham battles which are worked out in the region bordering Cerritos Creek. One company of cadets is usually selected to outline the enemy and the rest of the regiment maneuvered against them. All these maneuvers are conducted by student officers supervised and umpired by competent men from the United States Army.

Finally the march discipline to which the students are subjected while on the road must be taken into account. For most of the unseasoned cadets the fourteen pound burden of rifle and equipment proves irksome before the ten-mile tramp is finished, and the self-restraint imposed is no small part of the benefit derived from the half-day's work.

From this it must be apparent that these week-end drills are of great value both in fitting a student to be of use to the Nation in time of need and as a means of disciplinary training invaluable in other walks of life.

The Summer Training Camps

EACH YEAR THE IMPORTANCE of the summer training camps of this country increases in a marked degree. These institutions have now become so well founded that this year will find a dozen well located and permanent camps distributed over the United States in place of the five or six imperfectly organized training places of last year. It is expected, moreover, that fully forty thousand men will be in attendance as compared with the twenty thousand of last summer and the two thousand of 1915. A Federal appropriation of two million dollars for the maintenance of these camps, and the consequent relief of the individual expense, will bring out the deep significance attached to them by the War Department.

COLORS PASSING THE PRESIDENT'S HOUSE

The organization of these institutions is of quite recent date. They had their beginning in two training camps for college students in 1913. The undertaking proved so popular and the result so satisfactory that the Federal authorities considered a repetition warranted in the summer of 1914. In evidence of their increased confidence, the following year, 1915, witnessed not only the continuation of the students' camps, but the installation of similarly conducted camps for business men. Last year the attendance increased 600 per cent. over that of 1915, and army officers are confident that the number this coming summer will fully double that of 1916.

For students at California the chief interest naturally centers about the camp situated in this state. Last year many university men were at the Monterey camp, and this year, with two camps at Santa Barbara, the attendance should be more than doubled. At Monterey last summer the chief instruction was directed toward infantry branches, which included such fundamentals as minor tactics, rifle practice, trench construction, and camp sanitation. Toward the close of the training period, when the "rookies" had become more seasoned, maneuvers involving the larger units were introduced, and the summer was closed with a blank cartridge battle involving one regiment of infantry and a battalion of artillery.

It may be said, then, that the chief aim of these camps is to prepare men to be of value on the firing line or as officers for the service of the country in time of war. The physical benefit, disciplinary training, and drill in team work are chief among the valuable assets derived.

SOME CALIFORNIA MEN AT MONTEREY MILITARY CAMP

Officers' Reserve Corps Training Association

ON THE THIRD OF JUNE, 1916, Congress passed an act "for making further and more effectual provisions for the national defense." Under this act the Officers' Reserve Corps has been created for the purpose of securing a reserve of trained men available for service as temporary officers in the regular army. Appointment of citizens as reserve officers is based upon physical and mental examination specially directed to ascertain the practical capacity of the applicant. The record of his previous service and training is considered a part of the examination.

It was with the idea of preparing members of the university and others of the community to take the examinations for reserve commissions that the University of California Officers' Reserve Corps Training Association was formed. The work of organization was undertaken by a committee of Faculty members headed by David P. Barrows, and thru their efforts a course of lectures on theoretical and general problems of army administration has been arranged for members of the association.

For those members desiring tactical instruction a provisional company of infantry has been organized. On the company roster may be found names of Faculty members, students, and men prominent in business in the community. Standard equipment, including shelter tents and escort wagon, was issued for the use of the company by order of General Bell, Commander of the Western Division, U. S. Army.

OFFICERS' RESERVE CORPS IN CAMP

Military Department

Commandant and professor of Military Science ... Major John T. Nance, U. S. Army (retired)
Assistant Commandant .... Lieutenant Truman D. Thorpe, U. S. Army (retired)
Instructor in Military Science ...... George E. Dickie, B. L., Lieutenant-Colonel U. C. Cadets
Assistant in Military Science .... Curtis O'Sullivan, Major U. C. Cadets
Assistant in Military Science and Director of Band .... Captain Herman Crutner, Jr.

Cadet Officers

STAFF

Captain and Adjutant .... J. J. Vandenburgh
Captain and Quartermaster .... F. T. McKune
Captain and Commissary .... L. W. Byington
First Lieutenant and Battalion Adjutant 1st Battalion .... L. W. Goeppert
First Lieutenant and Battalion Adjutant 2nd Battalion .... E. R. Foster
First Lieutenant and Battalion Adjutant 3rd Battalion .... G. L. Maxwell
Regimental Sergeant Major .... C. E. M. Bates
Regimental Commissary Sergeant .... K. B. Clark
Color Sergeant .... J. H. Mathews
Battalion Sergeant Major 1st Battalion .... F. C. Ransom
Battalion Sergeant Major 2nd Battalion .... J. T. Coulston
Battalion Sergeant Major 3rd Battalion .... H. C. Adler

OFFICERS

Company A
Captain .... G. P. Stephens
Lieutenant .... K. H. Schilling

Company H
Captain .... S. R. Pfaud
Lieutenant .... C. C. Harter
Lieutenant .... M. J. Howells

Company B
Captain .... W. C. Douglas
Lieutenant .... E. W. Andrews
Lieutenant .... C. B. Cole

Company I
Captain .... F. H. Cramer
Lieutenant .... C. R. F. Cramer

Company C
Captain .... W. N. Anderson
Lieutenant .... A. P. Conklin

Company K
Captain .... H. R. Weber
Lieutenant .... R. D. Sias

Company D
Captain .... G. Hjelte
Lieutenant .... R. N. Donaldson

Company L
Captain .... F. M. Ogden
Lieutenant .... B. Barthe

Company E
Captain .... H. P. Detwiler
Lieutenant .... W. S. Peterson

Company M
Captain .... C. D. Woehr
Lieutenant .... V. Hoffman

Company F
Captain .... A. L. Warren
Lieutenant .... M. B. Wiedenthal
Lieutenant .... M. A. Wright

Company N
Captain .... L. R. Penny
Lieutenant .... D. F. Bash

Company G
Captain .... F. M. Essig
Lieutenant .... J. T. Smith

Company O
Captain .... W. H. Thomas
Lieutenant .... F. B. McCullum

Company P
Captain .... E. A. Reinke
Lieutenant .... A. W. Mohr

University Cadet Band

Chief Musician and Captain.................................Henry Raymond Hogaboom '17
Principal Musician..Clarke Elmer Wayland '17
Principal Musician..Paul Raymond Brust '17
Drum Major...Glen Haydon '18

SERGEANTS

George B. Gleason '18
Elmore W. Roberts '18
Jay L. Ruddick '17
William C. Tesche '18
Claudius N. White '17

CORPORALS

Richard H. Behrens '19
Samuel T. De Remer '19
Llewellyn G. Haskell '19
Charles E. Marquis '18
James S. Mitchell '19
Joseph M. Reeves '19
Halley E. Stephenson '18
Monroe Sutter '19

PRIVATES

Albert G. Biehl '19
George E. Carson '18
Leo G. Cheim '19
Charles W. Day '19
Donald B. Fowler '20
Nathan Goldwater '19
James D. Graham '20
Walter W. Hadley '19
Reuben J. Irvin '20
Earl T. Jensen '19
Averill G. McAlpine '20
Edward C. McLaughlin '20
Julien J. Mathieu '19
John A. Merrill '19
Joseph T. Nakayama '20
Harold H. Plumer '20
Milton L. Roberts '19
Herbert H. Schultz '18
Walter H. Welch '20
William M. Welsh '20
Stephen N. Wilson '18

Trumpeters

CORPORAL
Joseph M. Reeves '19

PRIVATES

Dwight C. Bardwell '19
Milton T. Frumkin '19
Uno Lindstrand '19
William A. Martin '20

PUBLICATIONS

DAILY CALIFORNIAN

BLAKE　　　SEYMOUR　　　WILSON　　　MOULTON

IN SPITE OF SEVERAL FALSE STARTS many years ago, when the university was just large enough to enjoy a four-page monthly, the growth and development of the *Daily Californian* has been steady and has resulted in producing a paper which can be ranked along with the best of the college dailies. The *College Echo*, in 1868, was the foundation stone which in time gave rise to *The Berkeleyan*. In 1898 the *Daily Californian* appeared for the first time as Volume 10 of a second series of *Berkeleyans* which had been started in 1892. Rapid growth and marked changes have characterized the history of the paper from then on to the present year. In 1910 the Associated Students acquired the *Californian* and established it on its present sound financial basis.

This year, because of lack of space to care for the campus news the

CUNNINGHAM　　STEVENS　　CHAMPLIN　　MITCHELL　　FORTH　　WELLBORN

ASSOCIATE EDITORS
TOP ROW: RAPHAEL, DE FOY, GORDON, WARD, CHAPLIN
BOTTOM ROW: KITTREDGE, HOWARD, ATCHESON, TYNAN, PIERCE

sheet has been increased from six to eight columns in width and a proportionate amount in length. This permits a more efficient handling of the news by the editorial staff and also allows a greater variety in the "make-up" of the paper, adding to its attractiveness as well as its usefulness.

Through the "beat system" of handling stories the various departments of instruction and investigation have received publicity and the campus has become somewhat better acquainted with the work and activities of the technical and scientific branches.

A feature of the editorial columns has been the reappearance of "Little Bobbie" on several occasions when campus activities have tempted him to indite a letter to "Dere Freund Mike." Lastly, the editorials themselves have proven a factor in turning the minds of the students towards the more serious problems of college and outside life.

In the following statistics, the editors and managers of *The Berkeleyan* and *Daily Californian* have been tabulated since volume one. For the first nine volumes the paper was known as *The Berkeleyan*. Since that time it has been called *The Daily Californian*.

The Berkeleyan Statistics

Vol.	Year	Editor	Manager
1	1892	Jesse P. Soyte '93	Walter S. Braun '93
2	1893	Joseph C. Meyerstein '94	Harry W. Rhodes '94
3	1894	E. M. Wilder '94	Bernard P. Miller '97
4	1894	Will H. Gorrill '95	John G. Howell, Jr. '96
5	1895	Arthur W. North '95	John G. Howell, Jr. '96
6	1895	Harry B. Hirst '96	John G. Howell, Jr. '96
7	1896	Harry B. Hirst '96	John G. Howell, Jr. '96
8	1896	George H. Whipple '97	James M. Oliver, 98
9	1897	Charles A. Elston '97	Owen S. Case, 97

WOMEN'S STAFF

TOP ROW: GLADYS WINDHAM, DOROTHY STONER, FRANCES BROWN, MADELINE MULDOON
BOTTOM ROW: MARGARET HONEYWELL, LESLIE BROWN, MURIEL CAMERON, NAN BARROWS

Daily Californian Statistics

Vol	Year	Editor	Manager
10	1897	Allan M. Chickering '98	Irving J. Muma '00
11	1898	Wigginton E. Creed '98	Irving J. Muma '00
12	1898	Charles E. Thomas '99	Duncan McDuffie '99
13	1899	Harold Symmes '99	Duncan McDuffie '99
14	1899	Harrison S. Robinson '00	C. Duane Cobb '01
15	1900	Nathan M. Moran '01	J. W. S. Butler '01
16	1900	Edward A. Dickson '01	J. W. S. Butler '01
17	1901	Frederick M. Allen '02	Fred F. Reed '03
18	1901	George C. Mansfield '03	Fred F. Reed '03
19	1902	A. F. Leuthenger '03	Fred F. Reed '03
20	1902	J. A. Mcflarty '03	Fred F. Reed '03
21	1903	William L. Finley '03	Fred F. Reed '03
22	1903	Richard O'Connor '04	Eugene Halbert '05
23	1904	J. Gustave White '05	William C. Cavalier '06
24	1904	W. J. Hale '05	William C. Cavalier '06
25	1905	J. P. Loeb '05	H. L. Stoddard '06
26	1905	L. D. Bohnett '06	H. L. Stoddard '06
27	1906	Sam Hellman '08	J. J. Rhea '07
28	1906	Alfred C. B. Fletcher	J. J. Rhea '07
29	1907	John D. Van Becker	Van V. Phinney '08
30	1907	Lewis A. McArthur '08	Nion H. Tucker '09
31	1908	C. Kelley Hardenbrook '08	John J. McClellan '10
32	1908	George Bell '09	William J. Hayes '09
33	1909	William J. Hayes '09	S. W. Cunningham '10
34	1909	Chaffee E. Hall '10	Vernon Churchill '10
35	1910	Chaffee E. Hall '10	J. J. McLellan '10
36	1910	Dudley J. Caire '11	Roy L. Shurtleff '12
37	1911	Arthur C. Prendergast '11	Roy L. Shurtleff '12
38	1911	Edwin M. Einstein '12	Roy L. Shurtleff '12
39	1912	Morse A. Cartwright '12	Roy L. Shurtleff '12
40	1912	John L. Simpson '13	Francis Moulton '17
41	1913	H. Ray Randall '13	Francis Moulton '17
42	1913	Ralph M. Eaton '14	Earnest C. Brown '14
43	1914	J. H. Quire '14	Earnest C. Brown '14
44	1914	H. L. Dunne '15	Harry L. Jones '15
45	1915	Harvey Toney '15	Harvey L. Jones '15
46	1915	Philip Conley '16	F. G. Burland '16
47	1916	Osgood Murdock '16	F. G. Burland '16
48	1916	Robert Blake '17	F. S. Moulton '17
49	1917	Harry Seymour '17	F. S. Moulton '17

WITHIN THE LAST FEW YEARS the BLUE AND GOLD has come to represent far more than a record of the Junior Class of the university. It is an institution and an activity by itself. Simultaneously with the growth of the book, the difficulties and responsibilities of producing the annual have also increased.

The problem of keeping up the high standard set by previous classes in publishing their year books has been the greatest obstacle to the 1918 staff due to the increase in the cost of materials, with few means of increasing the income to meet these higher expenses.

As in the past two years, since the institution of the merit system by

EDITORIAL STAFF

COOLEY	THORNBURG	SUITS	STEEN	CAREY	SMITH
WILSON	WELLBORN	CUNNINGHAM	HONEYWELL	REITH	THOMAS
FURTH	MITCHELL	MASTERS	ROSENBLATT	CLARKSON	ISAACSON

MANAGERIAL STAFF

GRAY PISCHEL CHRISTIE MEYER McKEE PILLSBURY

the Blue and Gold Advisory Committee, men of the 1919 Class have materially aided both the editorial and managerial staffs.

A compiled list of the *Blue and Gold* editors and managers since the first book in 1874, follows:

Vol.	Class	Editor	Manager
1	1875	H. W. J. Dam	Arthur F. Lou
2	1876	C. B. Overacker	Myer Jacobs
3	1877	Peter T. Riley	Reg B. Webster
4	1878	Alex Morrison	Frank Easterby
5	1879	H. W. O'Melveny	J. Stern
6	1880	H. C. Perry	J. P. Gray
7	1881	Published by Zeta Psi Fraternity	
8	1882	J. B. Lincoln	R. D. Jackson
9	1883	Earle A. Walcott	E. C. Frick
10	1884	Charles S. Wheeler	Eugene Hoefer
11	1885	W. F. Cheney	W. A. Brewer
12	1886	Kimball C. Easton	Waldo S. Waterman
13	1887	W. C. Gregory	W. J. Bartlett
14	1888	Henry E. Monroe	James E. Beard
15	1889	H. A. Melvin	F. L. Wharff
16	1890	G. H. Stokes	E. W. Hill
17	1891	C. W. Merrill	Lester H. Jacobs
18	1892	Charles L. Turner	William H. Gentry
19	1893	J. D. Burke	E. J. Gates
20	1894	F. M. Todd	H. P. Benson
21	1895	Albert H. Houston	Herbert B. Lang
22	1896	Raymond J. Russ	Philip L. Bush
23	1897	Owen S. Case	Percy G. McDonnell
24	1898	Gilbert J. Rector	Leslie C. Mott
25	1899	Charles E. Fryer	Philip J. Franklin
26	1900	Stuart G. Masters	George O. Bruhns
27	1901	Paul A. Sinsheimer	Thomas N. Emerson
28	1902	J. Jewett Earle	Reuben G. Hunt
29	1903	Earle C. Anthony	Fred E. Reed
30	1904	Arthur L. Price	James L. Foxard
		Mary R. Rice	
		C. Roy Browning	
31	1905	Eugene M. Hallett	Mervyn J. Samuels
32	1906	Jackson Gregory	Prentiss Gray
33	1907	J. R. Gabbert	A. C. Hastings
34	1908	Maurice E. Harrison	J. D. Jenkins
35	1909	Clayton H. Shipway	Rossetter L. Mikes
36	1910	Alan C. Van Fleet	Herbert S. Johns
37	1911	Lorenzo L. Langstroth	John Pike
38	1912	Robert H. Clarke	Raymond C. Ingram
39	1913	Clara Morse Turney	R. W. Rust
40	1914	Frances Harrington Partridge	Maxwell Perry Griffiths
41	1915	Donovan O. Peters	Earl J. Fenstermacher
42	1916	Lloyd Nelson Hamilton	Percy Albert Mills
43	1917	Leroy Farnham Krusi	Floyd Wayne Stewart
44	1918	John L. Reith	Walson Meyer

OCCIDENT

BRUCE, EDITOR

MACDONALD, MANAGER

WITHOUT DEPENDING TOO MUCH upon the contributions of people well known to the university reading public, the *Occident* has forged ahead again in to the list of the first five magazines of college publications in the United States. The *Occident* has won this coveted position only through the conscientious and untiring efforts of the staff, who have striven unceasingly to maintain a high standard.

Vol	Year	Editor	Manager
1	1881	C. H. Oatman '82	A. M. Armstrong '82
2	1882	E. A. Walcott '83	A. M. Armstrong '82
3	1882	E. C. Sanford '83	H. F. F. Merrill '83
4	1883	E. C. Sanford '83	W. A. Beatty '84
5	1883	W. A. Beatty '84	H. E. C. Foster '85
6	1884	W. A. Beatty '84	David Lemsky '84
7	1884	F. W. Putnam '85	J. D. Murphy '86
8	1885	E. A. Howard '86	Charles L. Biedenbach '85
9	1885	Charles L. Biedenbach '86	John D. Murphy '87

Continued on next page

Occident Statistics—Continued

Vol	Year	Editor	Manager
10	1886	John D. Murphy '87	W. W. Sanderson '87
11-12	1886-87	W. W. Sanderson '87	G. A. Merrill '88
13	1887	E. R. Drew '88	F. L. Wharff '89
14	1888	D. Edelman '89	W. T. Craig '89
15	1888	L. Hutchinson '89	W. T. Craig '89
16	1889	W. L. Jepson '89	J. D. Halsted '89
17	1889	John D. Bicknell '89	V. K. Chesnut '90
18	1890	V. K. Chesnut '90	H. C. Head '91
19	1890	H. C. Head '91	F. L. McLean '91
20	1891	H. C. Head '91	Lee W. Lloyd '92
21	1891	Lee W. Lloyd '92	W. H. Gentry '92
22	1892	F. D. McLean '92	W. M. Carpenter '93
23	1892	W. M. Carpenter '93	J. P. Sayre '93
24	1893	C. L. Knight '93	Frank W. Bancroft '94
25	1893	Frank W. Bancroft '94	H. M. Anthony '95
26	1894	Frank W. Bancroft '94	Ralph Marshall '95
27	1894	H. M. Anthony '95	Wm. J. Drew '95
28	1895	E. T. Thurston, Jr '95	Wm. J. Drew '95
29	1895	M. C. Flaherty '96	A. McCulloch '96
30	1896	H. S. Phelps '97	A. McCulloch '96
31-32	1896-97	A. L. Weil '97	C. M. Dickerson '98
33	1897	J. Hopper '98	C. M. Dickerson '98
34	1898	J. Hopper '98	C. M. Dickerson '99
35	1898	Stuart G. Masters '99	Richard W. Tully '99
36	1899	Ira Abraham '99	Richard W. Tully '99
37	1899	Richard Walton Tully '01	Roy F. Dickerson '00
38	1900	Archibald J. Cloud '01	Ralph S. Perry '01
39	1900	Alexander Gordon Bex '01	Milton H. Schwartz '01
40	1901	Milton H. Schwartz '01	Monroe Deutsch '02
41	1901	Monroe Deutsch '02	James M. Koford '03
42	1902	Alexander Adler '02	E. L. Ming '03
43	1902	J. M. Koford '03	E. L. Ming '03
44	1903	Leslie M. Turner	N. N. Eddy '05
45	1903	Arthur L. Price '04	N. N. Eddy '05
46	1904	Hurt Greenfelder '04	George W. Lauder '05
47-48	1904-05	Gus Carter Keane '05	William Hussey Murray '05
49	1905	Joseph S. Koford '06	George Brown '07
50	1906	Edward Blackman '06	Warren A. Startsheimer
51	1906	Gordon Edwards '07	Bossiter L. Mikel '09
52	1907	John D. Fletcher '07	Bossiter L. Mikel '09
53	1907	David L. Levy '08	J. Harry Jenkins '08
54	1908	Philip Stoner Thatcher '08	J. Harry Jenkins '08
55	1908	Wm. S. Wells '09	Herbert S. Johns '10
56	1909	Richard S. Goldman '09	Albert J. Evers '11
57	1909	Francis B. Steele '10	Archer Bowden '10
58	1910	Wesley W. Kergan '10	Archer Bowden '10
59-60	1910-11	Robert W. Cross '11	Albert J. Evers 11
61	1911	Arne Rosholdt '12	Albert A. Hutchman, Jr '14
62	1912	Arne Rosholdt '12	Harold A. Fletcher '12
63-64	1912-13	Lloyd A. Myers '13	Austin Hamon Fobb '14
65-66	1913-14	Roswell G. Ham '14	Ben DeWitt Knapp '15
67-68	1914-15	Sidney Coe Howard '15	Howard Fletcher '15
69	1915-16	Hazel Havermale '16	John W. Benton
70-71	1916-17	John B. Bruce	Russell P. Macdonald

WILCOX   TAGGARD   STERN   ISAACS   O'MELVENY

MASLIN, EDITOR

BUXTON, MANAGER

SINCE THE YEAR 1914-15 the *Pelican* has held, with few exceptions, to its new policy of satiring "the crime as it appears in the species and not as it is circumstanced in the individual" with such success that future adherence to that principle is practically assured.

With this end in view the university's one comic magazine has followed the highest standards of humor and attempted to be a leader in the world of college lampoon periodicals, many of whom still cling to individual attacks for their fun.

The bounds of the campus have limited the field of production with the exception of some art work by students of San Francisco Institute of Art and the California School of Arts and Crafts.

The staff for 1916-17: Editor, Marshall Maslin '17; Associates: Dorothy Epping '17, Royal Baronidis '17, Elmer Wise '17, W. B. Garthwaite '18, C. W. Sweigert '18, G. J. Atcheson '19, Charles Miles '19 and

E. D. Bills '20; Manager, John Benton '17; Assistants: Glen Knight '17, Ronald Robinson '18, Ralph Bagley '18, Esmond Schapiro '18, Raymond Muenter '19, James Holbrook '19, Van Hartwell Steel '19, Mal Hook '20.

SWEIGERT   ATCHISON   BARONIDIS   KNIGHT
BILLS   EPPING   MILES   GARTHWAITE

California Law Review

WAHRHAFTIG, STUDENT EDITOR

HOLLINS, STUDENT MANAGER

FOUNDED IN THE BELIEF that "the life of law is certainly larger than the sum of law reports and statutes," and for the purpose of providing an organ for those who are interested in the subject to express their views thereon, the *California Law Review* has in the short period of its existence assumed a commanding position among the legal periodicals of the country. Dealing with a more restricted field than do the national legal periodicals, the *Law Review* is able to deal more intensively with the problems that come before it for discussion. It deals particularly with legal problems affecting the Pacific Coast states, and especially California law.

The *Review* is published bi-monthly by the faculty and students of the School of Jurisprudence of the University of California. The officers for the year 1916-1917 are:

Editor-in-chief, Orrin K. McMurray; Student Editor-in-chief, Matt Wahrhaftig '14; Business Manager, M. C. Lynch; Student Business Manager, S. F. Hollins '15; Secretary, Rosamond Parma '08.

Faculty Board of Editors: Wm. Carey Jones, A. M. Kidd, Wm. E. Colby, M. E. Harrison, A. P. Matthew, M. C. Lynch, J. U. Calkins, Jr.

Student Board of Editors: Jacob Goldberg '15, Wm. A. Sitton '15, Associate Editors, S. M. Arndt '16, E. W. Davis '16, R. E. Hoyt '15, L. N. Hamilton '16, H. A. Jones '15, J. L. Knowles '15, J. C. Nichols '16, O. C. Parkinson '15, Esther B. Phillips '09, Carol A. Rehfisch '15, J. B. Whitton '16, Frances H. Wilson '15.

The Journal of Agriculture

ALLIN, MANAGER

RYERSON, EDITOR

DEDICATED TO THE PURPOSE OF HELPING PEOPLE lead better, happier and more useful lives in the country, the fourth volume of the *University of California Journal of Agriculture* has made its monthly appearance this year in a new and larger form. The change to the large size, together with the additional illumination of the cover by means of an attractive series of color cuts, has made possible a wider field of activity, both in reading material and circulation.

A publication such as this serves a twofold purpose, first, that of uniting the students in the College of Agriculture to a common motive, and secondly, it is a factor in the dissemination of the influence of the college over the state and among the people who can profit by its messages. In so doing, the editors have selected material from the widest field possible, ranging from the concrete practical to more abstract social and economic problems of the country and written by experts of recognized authority.

The publication is entirely student-edited and managed. The personnel of the staff for the year 1916-17 is as follows:

Editor, Knowles A. Ryerson '16; Associate Editor, William C. Tesche '18; Manager, Geo. D. Allin '17; Assistant Manager, William V. Goin '19; Editorial Staff, J. E. Tippett '18, M. R. Huberty '18, J. L. Barter '19, L. R. Ward '19, L. W. Taylor '18, H. E. Drobish '17, O. Jenkinson '20, R. Jenkinson '18. Managerial Staff, W. C. Morrison '17, W. A. Degen '17, C. M. Seibert '18, C. J. Rolph, Jr. '18, F. O. Ballou '19, J. C. Gray '20, M. A. Soderberg '17.

The Alumni Fortnightly

ALTHOUGH THE CALIFORNIA ALUMNI ASSOCIATION has been an active factor in university life for a period of forty-five years, it was not until 1907 that an alumni publication devoted entirely to the interests of the graduates was brought to life. Prior to 1907 the *University of California Magazine* and the *Chronicle* at different times served in the capacity as the publication of the alumni. The experiment with periodicals partly devoted to alumni interests was hardly successful. As a result, in the administration of President James K. Moffitt '86, the *California Alumni Weekly* was established. The publication of the *Weekly* was continued without interruption for a period of eight years. In that time the prime importance of an alumni periodical was clearly obvious. In January, 1916, when the office of the association was reorganized, the *Weekly* was changed from the four-page newspaper form to a sixteen-page magazine, and the frequency of issue was altered from once a week to twice a month.

RONEY, EDITOR

It is too early to forecast the wisdom of the change. A few figures, perhaps, may be in point. For many years the former paper was published at an average loss of $500 a year; the present paper, in the opening term of its life, produced an approximate profit of $1,039.99. As to circulation, in the fall of 1915 the paid circulation of the *Weekly* was 834; at the end of the first year of the *Fortnightly*, the paid circulation was 2,624, with a guaranteed distribution of 3,150.

With the change in form came a change in policy. The printing of a detailed account of campus events gave way to an attempt at summarizing a series of events as they happen on the campus with the purpose of interpreting for the alumni the meaning of these happenings. Feature articles relating to the development of the university and the activity of the alumni in relation to the university have been secured from time to time. Among the contributors have been President Wheeler, Dean Burrows, James Hopper '98, Col. George C. Edwards '73, Paul A. Sinsheimer '01, George M. Stratton '88, Carleton H. Parker '04, William Nat Friend '96, and Prof. J. Loewenberg.

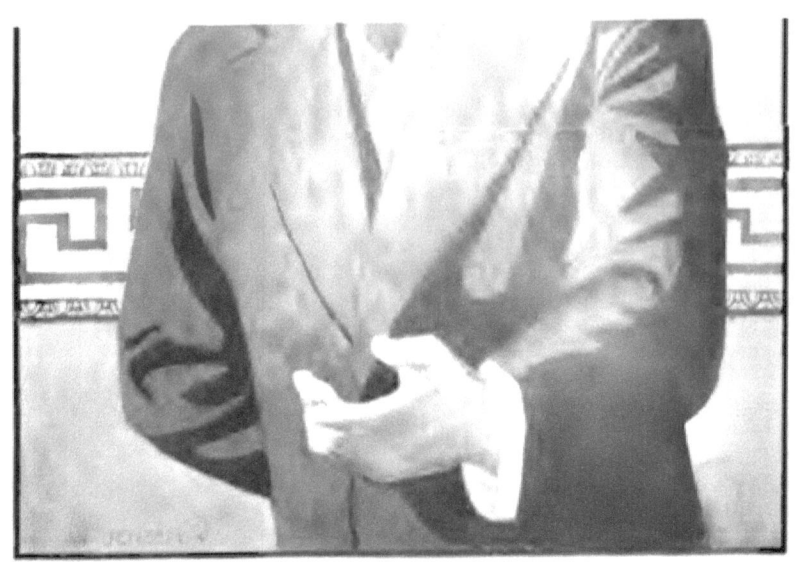

DEBATING

The Intercollegiate Debate
By Martin S. Rosenblatt

THE 1916 INTERCOLLEGIATE DEBATE with Stanford represented a departure from established debating procedure. No decision was rendered. There has always been considerable difficulty in securing judges, so this year the debate was undertaken without judges. This gave a new goal for the teams to strive for. Instead of satisfying two members of a highly intellectual board of judges, the speakers had to win the favor of an entire audience, for the only decision was to be the audience's unspoken opinion of the debate. Naturally, technicalities were to be avoided. To insure this the Stanford and California teams met early before the debate to agree upon an intrepretation of the question. Popular interest was guaranteed by choosing a preparedness question, the exact subject being "Resolved, That the United States Should Adopt a System of Compulsory Military Training Similar to that of Switzerland."

The debate was held at the Knights of Columbus Hall in San Francisco, November 24th, 1916, Professor Arthur U. Pope of California presiding. Although no decision was formally handed down, California was almost unanimously conceded the victory by the audience. Both teams strove to make their arguments clear-cut and orderly, but it is the common opinion that the California team was the more successful in this regard.

D. W. Evans '20 opened Stanford's argument in favor of the Swiss system. He pointed out the need for preparedness, indicating the perilous position of the United States due to her open-door policy in China, her adherence to the Monroe Doctrine, and the dangerous status of neutrals in the present war. C. J. Knight '19, Stanford's second speaker, devoted the major portion of his time to the contention that the volunteer system can never give this country the large army we need and that conscription is our only remedy. H. C. Blote '18, then concluded Stanford's argument with an attempt to show that the Swiss system will give the necessary army without bringing any evil consequences.

The negative argument was opened for California by M. S. Rosenblatt '18.

HYDE
INTERCOLLEGIATE AND CARNOT TEAMS

He first briefly indicated that the Swiss system of military training is universal, compulsory, and periodic. He then outlined the complete argument for the negative, characterizing the Swiss system as unnecessary, inadequate and highly dangerous. Unnecessary, because it would give the United States fourteen and a half million men; inadequate, because the men would have received only one hundred and sixty-five days' training scattered over a period of thirty years; dangerous, because it would lull the United States into a false sense of security. "The United States," he said, "doesn't need an army of fourteen and a half million men, and one hundred and sixty-five days' training scattered over a period of thirty years won't make an efficient soldier. The only system for the United States is that advocated by General Leonard Wood, a small army of highly trained soldiers such as can be secured by the volunteer system."

ROSENBLATT
INTERCOLLEGIATE AND CARNOT TEAMS

H. A. Hyde '17 retraced California's three-fold argument and laid special emphasis on the inadequacy of the short Swiss training. He pointed out that modern warfare is a battle of science and technical skill and that every soldier must receive intensive training for a period of not less than one year.

Ray Vandervoort '18 was the third speaker for the negative. His speech, like those of his team mates, covered all of California's three points. In this way the audience received the entire negative argument three distinct times. There was no chance for misunderstanding. Vandervoort showed rare skill in rebutting the affirmative arguments and in a humorous but forceful way put the last touches necessary to drive California's arguments home.

Hyde concluded for the negative with a seven-minute rebuttal. Philip Matthews '18 was alternate for the California team.

Freshman-Sophomore Debate

ACCORDING TO THE REGULAR CUSTOM, the annual Sophomore-Freshman debate took place this year upon the campus. The question which the two under classes had up for discussion was, "Resolved, That the Adamson Eight-hour Bill Should Be Repealed." The discussion took

VANDERVOORT
INTERCOLLEGIATE TEAM, CARNOT ALTERNATE

place on the evening of November 2. Class rivalry seemed to be more keen than usual in debating, for a large crowd of supporters of both sides turned out to back their respective favorites. The Sophomore team was composed of W. M. Green '19, L. H. Nuland '19, and H. A. Mazzera '19, while the first-year class was represented by L. L. Thornburg '20, R. N. Chase '20 and Ezra Shapeero '20.

The debate was interesting and from the standpoint of the audience was also exceedingly instructive. Every member of the teams showed that much conscientious and detailed study had been expended in the preparation of the topic. Although the decision was awarded to the Sophomores as upholding the affirmative of the question, nevertheless the first-year men were deserving of a great deal of credit for the excellent manner in which they put forth their first forensic efforts on the campus. Especially was the refutation of the 1920 debaters noticeable as representing clever arguing ability and the power to attack their opponent's points.

The judges for the discussion were: Professor W. A. Morris, Mr. J. R. Douglas and Mr. Paul Fussell.

Carnot Debate

In 1895 Baron de Coubertin inaugurated the annual Carnot debate between California and Stanford. The subject for the discussion must always be a French problem, and the method pursued in the contest is this: Early in the year a general topic is assigned; this year, "France's Policy of Reconstruction After the Present War." Two hours before the debate the three representatives of each college are given a specific resolution. Sides are chosen and the speakers then have two hours in which to prepare their arguments. The speeches are naturally extemporaneous, each contestant depending upon the information he has acquired in the months devoted to the study of the general topic. The medal, named after Carnot, martyr president of France, is awarded to the best individual debater as judged upon the merits of the contest.

The tryouts for the Carnot team are conducted much as the final debate. March 8, at 5 o'clock, the California debating aspirants were given the question, "Resolved, That of the Problems Which Will Confront France After the War, the Most Pressing Will Be Political Rather than Economic." Two hours and a half later the tryouts took place. Those selected for the team were S. K. Burke '17, H. A. Hyde '17, M. S. Rosenblatt '18, and Ray Vandervoort '18 alternate. Professors Flaherty, Wright and Mr. Leebrick acted as judges.

The final debate was scheduled for April 13 at Stanford, unfortunately too late to be reported in this section.

Intersociety Debates

This year has seen the institution of intersociety debates with Stanford. November 17, 1916, the Congress Debating Society represented by Abe Schmulowitz '18, T. C. Lawson '18, and W. M. Green '19, received a unanimous decision over the team of the Stanford Nestoria Debating Society. The Senate team, L. A. Cleary '18, P. H. Walker '18, and L. H. Nuland '19, was defeated by the Euphronia team in a close debate, the decision being two to one in favor of the Stanford society team. Both debates were on the Adamson Bill, and both discussions took place the same night, the Senate team remaining on the California campus, while the Congress team journeyed to Stanford.

These discussions are well received by the debating followers of both California and Stanford and it is hoped that they may be continued in the future. As well as furnishing an excellent channel for the furthering of practice in public speaking it also provides a means of bringing the two institutions of learning into closer touch with each other.

Upper Division Bonnheim Essay Contest

THE DEATH OF ALBERT BONNHEIM brings with it good cause to think of the many splendid things he has done for the university. Not least was his interest in forensics, in which field he provided two essay prizes, one for upper and one for lower division students.

This year the final discussion for the upper division contest was won by Calmur J. Struble '17 on the subject of "A Government Monoply of the Manufacture of Ammunition and Instruments of War."

BURKE CARNOT TEAM

DRAMATICS

Faculty Glade

DRAMATICS

Faculty Guide

Senior Extravaganzas

EXTRAVAGANZAS were introduced to the University's Commencement Week by Maida Castelhun (Mrs. Charles Darnton) and F. G. Burgess in 1894 when their work, "The Vehme Gericht" was produced. Illustrious graduates of the university are found in this field also. James Hopper wrote the 1898 Extravaganza, entitled, "Chinese Birthday Festival." Professor C. H. Parker, now head of the Economics Department at the University of Washington, wrote the 1904 Extravaganza, "Anyman Can't Graduate." In collaboration with D. L. Levy, Sam Hume, well-known for his work in pageantry in the East, wrote the 1908 Extravaganza, "The King and The Booster."

A list of the extravaganzas and their authors follows:

Year	Title	Author(s)
1894	*"The Vehme Gericht"	Miss Maida Castelhun (Mrs. Chas. Darnton) and F. G. Burgess
1895	*"Eleusnia," A Grecian Spectacle	Miss Gertrude Henderson and Walter H. Graves
1896	No performance	
1897	*"Aztec Funeral Rites"	Roger S. Phelps and Edward O. Allen
1898	"Chinese Birthday Festival"	James Hopper
1899	"Arabian Pageant" (otherwise called "A Persian Wedding")	David Raymond Curtis and Laura May Buffington (Mrs. Byron E. James)
1900	*"Quest of the Golden Fleece"	Miss Alice Humphreys
1901	"Pilgrimage to the Shrine of the Dragon Faculty"	Hugh McCaskey Love, Mr. Jewel Alexander and Herbert Meese
1902	"Robin Hood"	Miss Leta McKinne
1903	*"Knight of Ye Burnt Pretzel"	Earl Charles Anthony and James Mossin Koford
1904	"Anyman Can't Graduate"	Carleton Hubbell Parker and Arthur Lorenzo Price
1905	*"The Royal Road"	Bert Campbell, Augustine C. Keane and Joseph Philip Loeb
1906	No performance on account of the earthquake and fire	
1907	*"The Limit"	Harold Asa Clarke and Isabel McReynolds (Mrs. Gray)
1908	*"The King and the Booster"	David Livingston Levy and Sam J. Hume
1909	*"The Inferno Masculine"	Miss Christina Krysto
1910	*"The Chasers"	Nathaniel Schmulowitz
1911	"The Hop King"	Edwin Scott Walker
1912	*"Ephesian"	Camillus Nelson Hackett
1913	*"The Mischief-Makers"	Victor Chauncey Graves
1914	*"King Henry I"	Lawrence Livingston Levy
1915	*"Fiat Lux"	Frederick Schiller Faust and Sidney Coe Howard
1916	*"Absent on Leave"	Hazel H. Huyvetaugh and Roger Fulton Goss
1917	"Youth Comes Up"	Edson Marshall Maslin and John Roberts Bruce

*Manuscript in University Library Archives.

Junior Farces and Curtain Raisers

THE PRECEDENT THAT ESTABLISHED JUNIOR DAY on the California campus is of forty-two years standing. Away back in 1875, the Junior Class of 1876, spread the news throughout the university that on May 14 they would hold a "Junior Exhibition," or "Junior Exercises." These exercises began in the morning with a programme of poems, essays and orations. The afternoon was given over to dancing.

In 1891 the first Junior Farce was produced, entitled, "Hamlet At College." It was written by Burton L. Hall. No complete copy of this is extant.

Since Burton Hall's farce, California has come to have other noted playwrights in its lists. Frank Norris wrote the farce of the Class of 1892, entitled "Two Pair." In 1899 Richard Walton Tully wrote what is generally regarded as the most worth-while farce of all. He called it "James Wobberts, Freshman" but it has been taken onto the professional stage and is better known under the title "A Strenuous Life." Walter De Leon, who for several seasons played the lead in Ferris Hartman's musical company, wrote the 1906 farce and named it, "Just About Now."

The curtain raisers began in 1898 when Raymond Russ wrote "Seven Years After."

The following is a list of the farces and curtain raisers produced by the various classes, with their authors and co-authors:

Class	When Produced	Title	Author
1891	Dec. 14, 1889	"Hamlet at College"	Burton L. Hall
1892	Dec. 13, 1890	*"The Varsity of Samos"	F. M. Greene
1893	Feb. 13, 1892	No production.	
1894	Dec. 10, 1892	*"Two Pair"	B. Frank Norris
1895	Dec. 2, 1893	*"Menaur Reversed"	Maybelle Louise Feusier
1896	Dec. 1, 1894	*"An Olla Podrida"	Raymond J. Russ
1897	Nov. 30, 1895	*"Hence the Hatch"	Veda Louise Sherman and Lena M. Redington
1898	Dec. 5, 1896	"The Black Cat"	Walter A. Starr
		The first Curtain Raiser "Seven Years After"	R. J. Russ
1899	Dec. 4, 1897	"The Duke of Oldenburg"	Harrold S. Symmes
		Curtain Raiser, "A Fatal Revelation"	Margaret Webb
1900	Dec. 3, 1898	*"His Wife's Will"	Alice E. Duffy
		Curtain Raiser, "Fraternal Love"	Munroe R. Wilson (Mrs. William Olney)
1901	Dec. 9, 1899	"James Wobberts, Freshman"	
		*"A Strenuous Life"	Richard Walton Tully
		Curtain Raiser, "The Case of a Coach"	Milton H. Schwartz
1902	Dec. 8, 1900	*"Settled by Debate"	Ida McKinne
		Curtain Raiser, *"A Triumph of Science"	Robert W. Ritchie
1903	Nov. 29, 1901	*"Wing"	Bertha James (Mrs. A. M. Lopez)
		Curtain Raiser, "Cave Canem"	James M. Koford
1904	Nov. 28, 1902	* The Axe and the Pirate's Daughter"	Arthur L. Price
		Curtain Raiser, "The Rehearsal"	Virginia Whitehead
1905	Nov. 28, 1903	*"A Pair of Pajms"	Emil Kruschke
		Curtain Raiser, "A Record Proposal"	Mark H. Daniels
1906	Nov. 25, 1904	"Just About Now"	Walter DeLeon
		Curtain Raiser, "Some Idiots and Others"	Vance McCoy and Jackson Gregory
1907	Dec. 1, 1905	*"The Missing Miss Miller"	Harold A. Clarke
		Curtain Raiser, "Trouble With Docks"	Cornelia Stratton (Mrs. C. H. Parker)
1908	Nov. 30, 1906	"The Emeryville Ringer"	David L. Levy
		Curtain Raiser, "A Pelican's Daughter"	Julia Evans
1909	Nov. 29, 1907	*"The Wicked World"	Christina Krysto
		Curtain Raiser, * The Disgrace of Bingo"	Earle A. Snell
1910	Nov. 27, 1909	"His Father"	Nat Schmulowitz and F. J. Dergelich
		Curtain Raiser, * Escape of the Moon"	Margaret Bates Hunt
1911	Nov. 26, 1909	*"A Woman's Way"	Henry E. Mills, Jr.
		Curtain Raiser, *"Engaged"	Rose Gardner
1912	Nov. 25, 1910	"Two Brass Bands"	M. L. Dunkelspiel
		Curtain Raiser, *"Neophyte"	Caroline Nelson Hackett
1913	Dec. 1, 1911	*"Too Much Goat"	Victor Chauncey Gaines
		Curtain Raiser, *"Peach"	Roy Arthur Sclent
1914	Nov. 29, 1912	*"Engaged"	Clotilde Grunsky
		Curtain Raiser, "A Full House"	Kenneth Taylor Perkins and Norman Loyal McLaren
1915	Nov. 28, 1913	*"Jeannette's Way"	Sidney Coe Howard and Frederick Schiller Faust
		Curtain Raiser, "Plebang 'Pep' "	Theda Scucroft Cocheroft
1916	Nov. 27, 1914	*It Happened in Pottsville"	Herbert Edson Hall
		Curtain Raiser, *"O'Pillic"	Dorothy Woermer
1917	Nov. 26, 1915	* Thumbs Down"	Roy Edgar Belknap Bower
		Curtain Raiser, *"Caught in the Act"	Mabel Carol Elberts and Ruth Kinkead (Mrs. Fred S. Dohring)
1918	Nov. 25, 1916	*"Pin Pricks"	Edward Moss Jaffa and Camille Avna Pauly
		Curtain Raiser, *"The Trouble Track"	Leslie Brown

*Manuscript in University Library Archives.

"ANDROCLES AND THE LION"
DOROTHY RILEY, ALICE ELLIOT, JOE STURGIS, EARL WASHBURN, JOHN DAY

"Androcles and the Lion"

INCONGRUITY WAS THE KEYNOTE of "Androcles and the Lion," produced by the English Club, October 14, in the Greek Theatre. But the play, under George Bernard Shaw's able handling, was a comedy genuine enough to over-ride for all but the hypercritical spectator, the disturbing inharmonies. For such a person, the ponderous dignity of the Greek Theatre, with a curtain of Pacific fog hung above the footlights, stands in unseemly contrast to the performance of a Shavian satire, employing a Roman fable and a papier-mache lion with electric eyes.

The *Lion*, the last character the play might lose, is more than a mere half-title. There was a knowing subtlety about him, a prowling punctuality for his cue, too great a delight in his "velvet paws" to permit dramatic disregard for the beast. Herbert Hall '17, inclosed throughout the performance in beastly attire, portrayed as deep an insight into the anatomy and psychology of the kingly species as the play's author might desire.

The color and group arrangement of the mob scenes was one of the play's best features. Pageantry is a newly developed step in campus productions. We are finding that finesse alone will not carry a play on our stage. Our dramatic work needs bold, well-drawn lines and it was agreeable to note that the mob in "Androcles and the Lion" was more than convenient scenery for the leads. Each member of the mob seemed to live and act the spirit of the play.

Harold Black '17 made a composite tailor, Christian, hero and husband, who would have been more admirable if not so desirous of being so. He prepared to die well, and danced even better, but our sympathy for Andy was awakened not in his own acting but in Miss Wetmore's portrayal of *Megaera*, his shrewish wife. Indeed the necessary sympathy for *Androcles* was her only excuse for being.

Orville Caldwell '18 as *Ferrovius* played a part manifestly absurd and played it very well, that is to say, absurdly. Lacking the revelation from Shaw, nothing short of the omniscient assurance could have made an actor certain as to the interpretation of the character. Caldwell chose the simplest interpretation and made the best possible matter of a bad thing. In the role of the Emperor, E. S. Rosenthal '18 had an easier part, an emperor after our own hearts, admirably suited to the taming of two-legged

"ANDROCLES AND THE LION"

HAROLD BLACK   HERBERT HALL

lions and unkingly terrors. Alice Elliott's *Lavinia* was a woman of a single mood, obviously only one-half Shaw's *Lavinia*. Her natural loveliness and poise made a charming *Lavinia*.

The audience listened in vain for a note of sincerity under such lines as hers. Miss Elliott might have had the center of the stage. Hers were the real words of the play. Instead she chose to be merely one of many so-called Christians, albeit the most charming.

Lastly, we should like to discover the play's moral, whether a moral intended by Shaw or not. For the amateur critic, full of criticism for the amateur actor, there is a moral in Andy's anxious admonition as the zealous beast leaps at his prey.

So the critic, before he parts with that cheapest of all commodities, criticism, should remember in the future, before he multiplies his condemnation, this play's moral in our hero's warning, "Velvet Paws!"

THE CAST

Androcles	H. A. BLACK '17	Retiarius	D. S. JARVIS '18
The Lion	H. E. HALL '16	Secutor	J. R. EDWARDS '18
Ferrovius	O. R. CALDWELL '18	First Slave	R. J. BERNSTEIN '18
Caesar	E. S. ROSENTHAL '18	Second Slave	O. S. WATERS '18
Lentulus	W. B. STEPHENSON '18	Megaera	DOROTHY WETMORE '17
Metellus	C. S. EDWARDS '19	Lavinia	ALICE ELLIOTT '17
The Centurion	J. B. DAY '18	1st Christian Woman	MARIAN BLACK '20
Ox-Driver	H. S. STEEN '18	2nd Christian Woman	DOROTHY RIGBY '19
Spintho	A. E. WASHBURN '19	3rd Christian Woman	CLARITA NUNAN '20
The Editor	E. A. BREYMAN '17	4th Christian Woman	CARMELITA PARMA '20
The Menagerie Keeper	J. H. WEISE '18	5th Christian Woman	RUTH GOGGETT '19
The Call Boy	W. E. SAMPSON '19		

CHORUS FROM "WHAT NEXT"

"What Next"

A MUSICAL OPERA is a success if it makes the audience forget burdens and worries, to laugh and enjoy the gaiety and carefreeness of its songs and choruses. "What Next," written by I. B. Kornblum '17 and H. E. Kowalsky '17 and produced by Treble Clef Society, October 17, in the Oakland Civic Auditorium, was a success. The audience testified to this for they handclapped vigorously every one of the nineteen songs that were on the programme, and it was necessary to encore several two and three times. They appreciated the unusual situations in the plot and received the actors enthusiastically.

But the music deserves first consideration; it was the outstanding feature of the production. When the lyrics lacked punch, when the plot dragged, when the actors got excited and nervous and finesse in the dances was forgotten, the music came to the front and demanded applause. It was catchy and original, and time and again the audience showed their appreciation of its quality.

Of the lyrics "Two Thousand Years Ago," sung by Camille Purdy '18 and "It's Great to be a Potentate," by E. S. Ward '19 were perhaps the best.

They both were original and clever, but the popularity of their interpreters added much to their enjoyment. The first was sung by Camille Purdy '18 and was done in a finished style. She was backed by an original

"WHAT NEXT"
NELLIE WALKER AND ORVILLE CALDWELL

chorus and was encored time and again by the audience. It was the best song hit of the production. "It's Great to be a Potentate," by E. S. Ward '19, was appreciated more because of the style in which it was presented by Ward than because of any special inherent quality in the number. The piece was written for Ward and the author made no mistake in assigning it to him.

"Summer Girl" and "When I Dance With You" were two other numbers that deserve praise. The tunes were exceptionally catchy and original and rank well with the popular professional music of the day.

So if the fastidious critic found flaws in the staging, if the actors did not maintain a professional standard at all times, these weaknesses can be overlooked. E. S. Ward '19 in the role of *Dubs*, the stout waiter, was particularly jocose. He was suited to the part perfectly and if there was a star among the actors it was he. O. R. Caldwell '18 has had better parts than *Gerald Sherwood*, the rich son and hero of the play. But the role was difficult for this very reason and it is doubtful whether it could have been interpreted much different. W. F. Mayock '17 was well cast in the gruff, surly character of *Titus Sherwood*. Among the women characters Nellie Walker '19 was perhaps the most finished, and Sadie Fredericks '17 the most spontaneous.

Following is the cast of characters in the order of their appearance:

Mr. Titus Sherwood	W. F. MAYOCK '17	Selma Darewin	HAZEL HOLLINGSWORTH '17
Mrs. Sherwood	GOLDIE DE WOODWARD '16	Duke Robert McCarthy	E. A. BRENMAN '17
Dubs, the butler	E. S. WARD '19	Messenger	M. FELIX '20
Lois Manville	SADIE FREDERICKS '17	Squint	J. KENNETH MOODY '19
Marie, a French maid	MARIAN BAILEY '20	Red	G. E. GOMON '17
Gerald Sherwood	O. R. CALDWELL '18	Jack Wright	G. F. TAYLOR '17
Marcia Benson	NELLIE WALKER '19	Gladys Derby	KATHRYN COE '19
Charlie Owen	E. F. STEEN '18	Ambassador Price	H. S. STEEN '18
Jenny Brooks	CAMILLE PURDY '18		

"WHAT NEXT"

EUGENE BRENMAN   CAMILLE PURDY   KENNETH MOODY

GOLD DUST TWINS FROM THE JUNIOR FARCE
MARIE DAMIANAKES, NINA HALLOCK, MAUREEN SULLIVAN, DOROTHY COOPER, MARGARET POTTER, IRENE WYETH

The Curtain Raiser

A CURTAIN RAISER that fulfilled its every requirement, that knew its limitations and kept within them, that was original and entertaining, that was a definite dramatic accomplishment, was "The Trouble Track," the 1918 curtain raiser written by Leslie Brown. That was the unanimous opinion of all the critics.

"The Trouble Track" attempted to do nothing more than to fulfill its function. A curtain raiser is only the "key-noter" of the afternoon. It creates the atmosphere. And "The Trouble Track" put a refreshing taste in the mouths of the audience.

It was short but the plot action was rapid-fire. There were no lulls in the development of the threads of the story and the logical and probable complications produced laugh after laugh from the audience and worked up a spirit for the day.

But the merit of "The Trouble Track" lay in the fact that it was different. It was immune from over-worked phrases and situations. It got away from the commonplace but yet kept to the probable. It was unostentatious. It was genuine. It sets a high water mark for curtain raisers of the future.

The cast was not the best talent that was in the class. That was reserved for the farce. And so if it can be said that the curtain raiser succeeded in winning praise from the audience and critics that was unanimous, it is that much more of a compliment to the author.

And that is not to say that the acting was bad. It was not. But it showed lack of experience, and many times only the witty sayings and sudden, unexpected developments saved the plot. So it can be truly said that it was the real worth of the skit itself that scored.

But there was some finished acting. Catherine Woolsey mastered an extremely difficult part that required real dramatic ability to portray. And she did protray it well.

Lavinia Brown carried out the main thread of the sketch in a satisfactory manner. L. D. Sanderson was rather embarrassed and ill at ease in the leading man's role. The cast follows:

Helen Armstead			Lavinia Brown
Jim Trevor	L. D. Sanderson	Charles Jackson	D. C. Bell
Mrs. Armstead	Viola Lockhart	Blanche Harrison	Blanche Bouteiller
Dorothy Andrews	Catherine Woolsey	Jack Lane	L. W. Taylor
Marion Dumont	Marjorie Steart	Maid	Lucile Parr

JUNIOR FARCE
REBER STEEN, JESSIE TODHUNTER, MARJORIE LIDDLE

JOHN WEISSE   MINNIE SISSON   ED STEEN   CAMILLE PURDY   HOMER STEEN   DON SISSON

The Junior Farce

JUDGMENT ON A JUNIOR FARCE must be passed by the Junior Class. If the farce is entertaining to them, if it provokes laughs, if they approve it, even if that approval be only temporary, then it must be conceded to have achieved its purpose. And "Pin Pricks," by Camille Purdy and E. M. Jaffa, was voted a success by the Junior Class. They applauded it, and laughed, and were satisfied.

Perhaps the 1918 farce did not rank with "A Strenuous Life" or "Two Pair," its more illustrious predecessors, but then every class cannot boast a Richard Walton Tully or a Frank Norris. "Pin Pricks" scored, not because of its dramatic structure or dramatic action, in which particulars perhaps more could have been accomplished, but because it was appreciated by the Junior Class.

It was the cast and work of the coach that made the farce liked. The most popular and talented actors in the Junior Class carried the parts and their work, because it was well done and because they were all members of the class, was applauded and appreciated.

There were places in the development of the plot that could have been smoothed out a bit more, perhaps, situations and predicaments that would have been a bit more original, action that could have been faster, but there could not have been more made of the material in hand, there could not have been a better-cast group of actors chosen from the class, there could not have been better spirit and effort put forth than was given by Coach Carlysle in his endeavors to make the production a success.

So if the irrepressible critic must insist that "Pin Pricks" was not a farce in the true sense of the word, let him temper his censure with the thought that a Junior Farce is written for the express purpose of entertaining Juniors on Junior Day and if it escapes criticism from them, if it satisfies them, then it has served its function.

When an audience knows the capabilities of the actors, it is more prone to observe whether full advantage is being taken of the opportunities in each part than to watch for and criticise the shortcomings of the structure of the dramatic work itself. And that is what the 1918 Junior Farce audience did. It approved the play because the actors made the most of their chances. O. R. Caldwell, in the lead, as *Duke de Bunkville* showed why he has been rated the first actor in the class. His character work was careful and true. Beatrice Winder and Abe Schmulowitz, in their parts as proprietors of the tea garden, were spontaneous and clever. *Mlle. Sarah Divina*, as interpreted by Camille Purdy, was chic and charming. Her work was of a high order. Minnie Sisson was cast in a most difficult and illogical role, but made the most she could of the part under the circumstances. The cast for the farce was:

Bob Strong	A. B. SMITH
Tom Tyler	H. S. STEEN
Duke de Bunkville	O. R. CALDWELL
Sum, Manager of Tea Garden	ABE SCHMULOWITZ
Virginia Lee	MINNIE SISSON
Anne Adair	MARJORIE LIDDLE
Mlle. Sarah Divina	CAMILLE PURDY
Gladys Rayve	JESSIE TODHUNTER
Mauzie	BEATRICE WINDER

JUNIOR FARCE CAST

The Football Show

IN KEEPING WITH THE PRECEDENT begun last year the annual Football Show was staged in Harmon Gymnasium on the night of the Big Game. After two years trial the success of the move transplanting this event to the college campus might seriously be questioned, for while the Glee Club was singing its inimitable drinking songs the bulk of the campus population was hieing itself across the bay to the metropolis.

CAROL EBERTS AS HELENA IN
"HELENA'S HUSBAND"

The performance was presented before an audience of Berkeley citizens and empty sections reserved for the opposing varsities. There was not the semblance of an "Oski," not the vestige of an egg or the familiar carrot-top. The audience was not one of excited, overjoyed collegians and the casual wanderer who looked in on his way by never imagined that the event was in honor of a football team that had brought honor and glory to the Blue and Gold on the gridiron that afternoon.

The programme itself was a potpourri of choruses, character songs and sketches and musical numbers. Under the direction of Camille Purdy '18 an Oriental chorus gave a selection from "What Next," the Treble Clef Opera. The "Bellhop Chorus" from "Keeping It Dark," B. M. Melvin '17 and E. P. Hyatt '18 in songs and sketches, ensemble numbers by the Glee Club, and banjo and saxaphone numbers completed the bill. The show was managed by B. K. Vaughan '18.

The Mask and Dagger Plays
"The Bear"

THE FIRST SUCCESS of the production of four one-act plays by the Mask and Dagger Society, March 17, 1917, was in the choice of plays. Comedy raised the curtain in "The Bear," Maeterlinck's "Interior" followed in the swift vein of tragedy; "The Maker of Dreams" gave us the sentimental so dear to our fancy, while "Helena's Husband" suc-

"MAKER OF DREAMS"
HAROLD BLACK, MINNIE SISSON, BILL RAINEY

ceeded in satirizing not only its own but also all the preceding characters of the series. In such a manner, the group of plays became a unit.

"The Bear," played by Dorothy Wetmore '17, Paul Smith '17, and Orville Caldwell '18 came as a delightful surprise to an audience whose acquaintance with Russian literature and especially with Anton Chekoff, had tended to leave an impression of gloom. For two years Caldwell has done merited work in varied capacities but never before has his acting been so convincing or so finished. He had what is commonly supposed to be the impossible soliloquy, and proved how effective it may be made with good acting. He had what was perhaps more difficult, a twist of Slavic psychology to portray, a swift moment in which the "Bear" dives from towering rage to the depths of passionate love.

Miss Wetmore played the romantic woman, disguised in widow's weeds. The part did not allow her opportunity for vivid acting but she was acceptable in her straightaway work. P. D. Smith was pleasing in his role as the aged footman.

THE CAST

Elena Ivanovna Popova	Dorothy Wetmore '17
Gregory Stepanovitch Smirnov	Orville R. Caldwell '18
Luka, Popova's aged footman	Paul D. Smith '17

"The Interior"

Maeterlinck's "Interior," with its delicate symbolism, its absence of action, its weighty simplicity, was far more ambitious and doubly worthy of applause. Its theme is the mystery of life and death and its single important character begins to understand this mystery before our eyes. There are no high lights to portray, no splendid words to be said. Down to the curtain line the words were weighty with symbolism. The success of the play, therefore, was dependent on the acting in the part of *The Old Man*. Here again the long speech was even more dexterously handled with a fine knowledge of light and shade and the rising and falling tones of the voice. Beyond all the sureness of good technique displayed, the play convinced its audience, because of Ham's insight into *The Old Man's* discovery.

THE CAST

The Old Man	R. G. HAM '14
The Stranger	P. D. SMITH '17
Martha	CAROL EBERTS '17
Mary	CLAIRE TUCKER '16

"The Maker of Dreams"

"The Maker of Dreams," although we seldom admit it, was just what a college audience likes. W. S. Rainey liked it too and so did Minnie

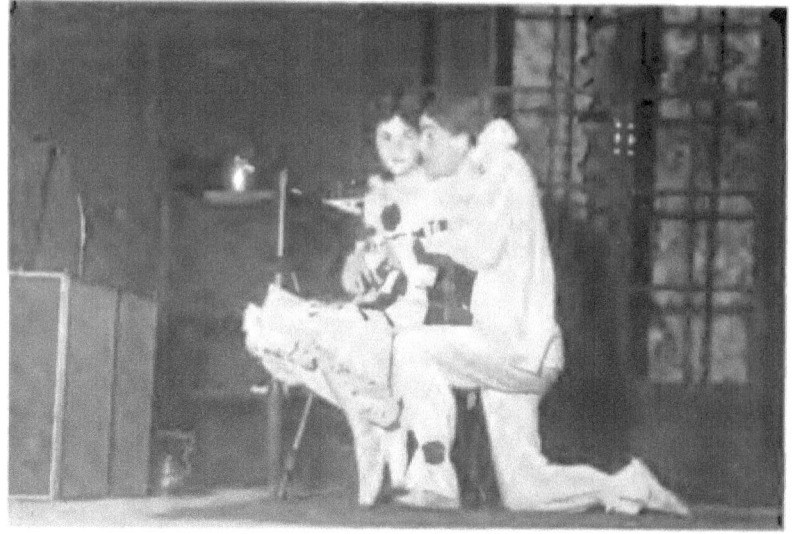

"THE MAKER OF DREAMS"
MINNIE SISSON AND BILL RAINEY

Sisson. Perhaps the secret of their acting lay there, and if this is true we cannot help wishing that Harold Black had liked it a little more.

"Oh, Baby don't cry for the moon, tra-la" and so it went. *Pierrette* put on the kettle in vain, warmed his slippers in vain, darned — yes darned his socks in vain. *Pierrot* just wouldn't be nice. Until the *Maker* came, and *Pierrette* admitted that "Love did make a difference." Then of course they changed blind *Pierrot*, caused a twitching in his shoulder blades, made him suddenly fond of the fender, and *Pierrette's* darning and *Pierrette* herself.

Rainey fitted the part without flaw. He was wistful, whitefaced, disarmingly gay, as *Pierrots* must be. The play went faster when he came in and flagged a little when he whisked himself off. It flagged perceptibly when the *Maker* came on, contrary to the intention of the *Maker's* lines. Without him the play would have been flat.

Minnie Sisson was charming enough to be *Pierrot's* counterpart in black and white which is very charming indeed — but a little too sad, and a little too sweet. This was a play admirably suited to both Miss Sisson and Rainey, and they did it pleasing justice.

"Helena's Husband"

The last of the quartette of plays succeeded in spite of its impersonators. Carol Eberts as *Helena* had splendid lines and all the pictorial qualities, but her acting lacked the finest part of good satire and good acting. *Helena* was too well assured of her ways to convince others of it. Claire Tucker was a pleasing contrast as a vivid character. Her lines had the quality of bringing a laugh after them. Bill Rainey as *Paris*, lent the professional flavor to the satire. Earl Washburn

"THE CANTERBURY PILGRIMS"
ORVILLE CALDWELL AND MINNIE SISSON

as *Analytikos* brought down the curtain with applause. His clever actions really bordered on hilarity.

THE CAST

Helena, the Queen	CAROL EBERTS '17
Tsunu, slave to Helena	CLAIRE TUCKER '17
Menelaus, the King	H. A. BLACK '17
Analytikos, the King's Librarian	A. E. WASHBURN '19
Paris, a Shepherd	W. S. RAINEY '16

"The Canterbury Pilgrims"

He must indeed be a surly theatre-goer who would not unbend to the wit and light-hearted sunshine of a fair presentation of Mr. MacKaye's "Canterbury Pilgrims." A college audience, particularly, opens its heart willingly to a well-done portrayal of youth and love and good-fellowship, and Mr. MacKaye has that indefinable touch of the artist to impress on his character portraits these high-lights which make them so likeable.

The characters impress one as being made of the stuff of which men and women are made, without falsifying England's first poet-laureate or the day in which he lived and wrote. His "Wife of Bath," his "Chaucer" as they are here, are Mr. MacKaye's own but they fit miraculously into the honest picture of the One-Nine-Pin Inn and the land of Robin Hood.

Indeed, the entire pageant — for it is scarcely more than a pageant — drips with the honey of realism. The author has even thickened the plot with a slight seasoning of the prodigious coarseness of that age and he shows a master-stroke in the delicacy with which he handles the indelicacy necessary to the realist in a setting in Olde Merrie England. Thus we may set aside any calumniations against him on that score; with all his apparent caricature and hidden satire, perhaps, he does not libel Chaucer, nor does Chaucer libel him.

The Canterbury Pilgrims themselves are the real excuses for the play's being, especially *Alisoun*, the jolly wife of Bath, one of the most delightful stage folk that has played behind campus footlights during the year. Personality with originality, to say the least, registers in her every action. A hail-fellow well met, a maiden with the heart of a man, the very first tomboy of literature we might say, she has a dash and a go of it that cannot help but endear her to the most conservative. And then set in a delightful background such as marked the day of Dick-of-the-Lion's-Heart when miller and friar and poet reveled together at the inn, drinking good brown ale served by buxom tap-maids, singing the archer's songs of the gray goose feather and the true yew-tree, she appeals to an audience as a reflection of the more human or Mr. Hyde side, perhaps, of its inner nature.

SCENE FROM "THE CANTERBURY PILGRIMS"

It is in her principally that Mr. MacKaye has proved himself the artist; by a less sure hand this merry widow of five might easily be a creature of hearty good-will and fellowship, yet not measure up to the criterion of refinement, but even with the somewhat too-Chaucerian lines which are frequently hers, she never oversteps the bounds. The cast was as follows:

Chaucer	O. R. Caldwell	Mistress of Tabard Inn	Louise Sheppy
Knight	A. E. Washburne	Tavern Maid	Mary Mae Catters
Squire	A. E. Brenman	Yeoman	P. J. Ritter
Friar	F. S. Rosenthal	Monk	A. B. Smith
Miller	R. W. Rhinehart	Merchant	H. A. Merril
Cook	Walter Sisson	Clerk	O. S. Waters
Shipman	J. H. Wiese	Franklin	G. E. Tays
Summoner	H. S. Sykes	Haberdasher	H. E. Miller
Pardoner	R. Bower	Carpenter	D. S. Jarvis
Host	H. H. Howard	Weaver	D. K. Poschel
Man of Law	B. F. Sisson	Dyer	Chas. Honeywell
Johanna	J. B. Robinson	Doctor	A. L. Mocks
Richard II	L. F. Logan	Parson	J. R. Edwards
John of Gaunt	W. B. Stephenson	Ploughman	W. Volberg
Wycliffe	V. E. Duffy	Manciple	W. Simpson
Archbishop of Canterbury	C. S. Edwards	Reeve	J. T. Cline
Wife of Bath	Ruth Wetmore	Canon's Yeoman	H. M. Berneman
Prioress	Minnie Sisson	Marcus	G. F. Taylor
Johanna	Marion Black		

"Youth's Adventure"

The Parthencia differs from other college dramatics in that the productions each year have been distinct contributions to creative California art, in literature, music and design. Sheldon Cheney, the author of "The New Movement in the Theatre," has referred to the Parthencia as "one of the few local expressions of dramatic enthusiasm that is deeply worth while. In originality of conception and in the actual achievement of visional beauty it stands well to the fore among American masques and pageants."

With the real purpose of the Parthencia thus in mind what shall be said of "Youth's Adventure" which was produced by the women of the university on April 13 in Faculty Glade?

The story of "Youth's Adventure" is of a young girl who dons knight's clothing and makes every effort to regain her father's sword which symbolizes the Ideal. As the action develops she not only wins the sword but also the love of a young knight.

The scene on the road to Camelot that formed the second episode was perhaps the most vulnerable point in the production. Beautiful in itself and serving well to make real the spirit of Arthurian days, nevertheless, it did not form an integral part of the masque as a whole. It did little to advance the action and as far as the dramatic construction was concerned might easily have been omitted. Its existence was justified, however, because it afforded a scene of shifting color, life and movement that was successful in producing that elusive quality called "atmosphere."

The music of "Youth's Adventure" deserves favorable comment. The use of adapted music which for a time was considered and would have been a backward step if carried out was happily averted through the efforts of Ruth Cornell and Sarah Unna '18. Their "The Dance of the Morning" and "The Dance of the Jewels," which was the finale, deserve special mention.

Dorothy Palmer '20, as "Beautiful Sin," the only solo dancing part this year, was a flame-colored sprite who flashed into the glade for a moment and then was gone.

Katherine Smith as *Alisande*, was charmingly youthful and loveable. The part of the young knight, *Sagramore*, was carefully interpreted by Ruth Jensen '19. Vera Morse '19 was a most haughty and disdainful enchantress. Doris McEntyre '17 was well suited to the part of *Romance*. Grace Ellis '20, as the ill-natured and malevolent dwarf, carried off a difficult part in a thoroughly satisfactory manner.

The production was ably coached by Porter Garnett, veteran of many previous productions.

"Youth Comes Up"

THE MOST DISCOURAGING ELEMENT about writing an extravaganza for the Class of 1917 was the obvious reflection that the preceding one, "Absent on Leave," set a high-water mark for all future ones. This year's authors developed a keen sympathy for those sons of famous men who support bravely a glorious but cumbrous heritage. And, after all, when ambitious Seniors have been writing extravaganzas since the Greek Theatre was Ben Weed's Amphitheatre, one feels that college life has been scrutinized to its far corners for every possible theme.

So the writers of "Youth Comes Up" grasped hungrily at the new type suggested in the 1916 extravaganza of Hazel Havermale and Roger Goss. What matter if their product did justify the remark of a Faculty member who still chuckles over the remembrance of Sam Hume naked in a barrel on the Greek Theatre stage? He said it was merely a Male Parthenein.

Of course a plot is not expected in an extravaganza. Artistically, however, this year's authors thought its inclusion in the show would be a rather interesting experiment. And so they slouched down before a fireplace and searched the flames for an appealing theme. It came—the delightfully original design of placing on a South Sea island a young woman who had never seen a man. It was a brilliant idea, and the authors saw visions of tropic maidens, soft music, starry skies, dense shrubbery, and all the rest of the theatrical staffage. They had gleams of a wonderful second act dominated by an enormous ruined idol and suffused with the glow of the Southern Cross and the glamour of youthful love. That was easy; the rest was the difficult part—the necessary mechanics of creating for the heroine a father and a mother and a lover. She was to be the

DOROTHY PALMER AS "BEAUTIFUL SIN"

THE PARTHENEIA
DORIS MCENTYRE AS "ROMANCE"

daughter of two professors who had become estranged some score of years before—back in civilization. The mother has taken the child and founded a university for dissatisfied women on this island. During the intervening years the father professor has sat lonely, heartsick, patient, at home, longing, longing . . . . . At this point the hero is created, obviously a student friend of the professor who is asked to find the daughter and bring her home. This is the method of bringing Him and Her together.

Bruce invented the characters, *Love* and *Adventure*, to clear out the channel and aid the course of true love; and Maslin created a devil-may-care character named *Pococurante*, to oppose *Puppy Love* with *Passion*, aided by his followers, *Luck*, *Temptation*, *Satan* and *Crust*. Here is the skeleton, not very carefully articulated, but strong enough to justify further progress. But the skeleton was put in the closet and forgotten for two months until one fine day, uncomfortably close to the date when manuscripts were to be submitted, he was dragged out and work started again.

Bruce did all the dialogue and put the flesh on the characters; Maslin wrote most of the songs. Bruce had a dictionary and Roget's Thesaurus; Maslin owned a volume of love poetry, Esenwein on versification, and a book of *vers de societe*. Bruce was a conscientious word-artist; Maslin, an artisan, creating mosaic-poetry from anthologies.

THE PARTHENEIA
THE MOONBEAM CHORUS

Authors and Co-Authors

"Youth Comes Up"
By JOHN R. BRUCE and E. MARSHALL MASLIN

FOR THE THIRD CONSECUTIVE TIME the Senior Extravaganza has been the work of the editors of the *Pelican* and *Occident* as co-authors. This year's production, "Youth Comes Up," has for its authors J. R. Bruce, skipper of the *Occident*, and E. M. Maslin, who trims the feathers of the *Pelican*. Bruce admits to the dialogue and shaping of the play, while Maslin is responsible for the lyrics and ballads. The play takes its place among the greatest of extravaganzas ever submitted, in fact, so well has it been received that it has been copyrighted by the 1917 Class.

"Pin Pricks"
By EDWARD M. JAFFA and CAMILLE PURDY

It has often been said that the dark horse is usually the winning writer of the Junior Farce. This year there were two dark horses in the persons of E. M. Jaffa and Camille Purdy. By being the successful co-authors of the Junior Play these two writers make their initial appearance on the campus as dramatic producers. The farce was pleasing and well received by the Junior Class. Although not a masterpiece of modern playwriting it served its purpose and the authors are to be commended upon their work.

MARSHALL MASLIN

JOHN BRUCE

ISIDORE KOENIGSMAN

CAMILLE PURDY

EDWARD JAFFA

LESLIE BROWN

"The Trouble Track"
By LESLIE BROWN

Leslie Brown, the author of "The Trouble Track," the 1918 curtain raiser, won for herself an enviable reputation for dramatic writing from all critics. "The Trouble Track" was liked because it was not portentous and did not claim to be more than it was. It was simple, witty, original and enjoyable and is ranked among the top-notch curtain raisers of any previous Junior Day. Like the authors of the farce Miss Brown is new to dramatic writing and this production was her first to appear on the campus.

"What Next"
By I. B. KORNBLUM and H. E. KOWALSKY

It is a hard task for students to write a successful musical comedy, for the audience not only criticizes the airs and choruses but scrutinizes the originality of the production, the dialogue, the lyrics and the staging. When the production is pronounced a success, then, all the more credit is due to the authors. And "What Next" was voted worth while. The authors of this year's Treble Clef production were I. B. Kornblum '17 and H. E. Kowalsky '17. Kornblum wrote the music and Kowalsky contributed the lyrics. The book was written by E. S. Rosenblatt '18.

ORGANIZATIONS

Founder's Rock

ORGANIZATION

For Sam's Book

STUDENT BODY ORGANIZATIONS

The Associated Students

WITH THE SETTLEMENT of the intercollegiate athletic relations, the final adoption of the new constitution and the placing of all athletic activities on a definite basis, the year 1916-1917 has run as smoothly as could be wished. No troublesome questions of a serious nature have arisen, such as the break in intercollegiate relations with Stanford or the changing to American football from the old Rugby game.

The first semester's test of the new constitution showed beyond a doubt its advantages over the old one. But one small defect has shown itself in its operation — this was concerning the election of the two mid-year members of the Executive Committee from the Junior Class. As adopted, the constitution provided simply for the election of two members of the Junior Class. But to avoid the possibility of the pooling of votes for one of the candidates and the election of the other on a minority vote, an amendment was proposed and carried providing that the two should be designated as "Candidate One" and "Candidate Two."

STEWART A. S. U. C. PRESIDENT

Another move which has proved its worth after a year of trial is the selling of A. S. U. C. cards for the whole year at $5.00 with a rebate of $2.50 to those who do not return in the spring semester. Card sales this year amounted to $4,214.00 with $712.50 refunded.

Following is the financial report of the graduate manager as given January 1, 1917:

	Disbursements	Receipts
Football	$34,129.96	$36,418.75
Student Body	6,313.47	19,988.54
Track	2,017.57	1,563.45
Daily Californian	99.00	660.35
Crew	1,224.31	393.15
Tennis	154.54	151.66
Baseball	1,527.15	73.21
Soccer	134.58	71.95
Basket-ball	338.59	22.10
Labor Day	5.42	6.00
Debating	38.55	4.40
Chess	5.25	3.50
Loans	....	6,000.00
Interest	259.05	....
Loans repaid	....	17,000.00
Overdraft June 1, 1916	730.13	....
Totals	$64,067.57	$65,357.10

Executive Committee

As was the case with the Associated Student Body as a whole, the Executive Committee has found itself confronted with no problems of extreme difficulty. Practically the whole of its work has been the granting of dates, the hiring of coaches, and the general administration of the Student Body affairs.

Following the break in athletic relations with Stanford, more interest was taken in contests with other Pacific Coast universities. The result of this was the formation of the Pacific Coast Conference, composed of the University of Washington, Washington State College, the University of Oregon, Oregon Agriculture College, the University of California; and, after the Student Body had accepted the Freshman rule, Stanford University. The University of Southern California has also made application for admission to the Conference, and will probably be granted membership at the next meeting of the governing body of the Conference.

Among the most important minor changes was the institution of a uniform system of caring for the troublesome matter of class finances. To guard against the misuse of or unnecessary expenditure of class funds, it was proposed that each class treasurer work in conjunction with the graduate manager's office; that the books be always kept there for inspection; and that every expenditure be approved by that office before the money was actually paid out. In order to accomplish this, no check on a

STROUD — GRADUATE MANAGER

class fund was to be valid unless countersigned by the graduate manager or by his secretary. Any class might overrule a veto of this office by a majority vote, however. A charge of $12.50 per class per semester was to be levied for the payment of the extra clerical work involved. The plan was accepted by the Seniors and two lower classes in November, and by the Junior Class after the final Junior Day report had been rendered.

Beginning the fall semester of 1916, the publication of *Brass Tacks* was discontinued, it being evident that there was no need for such a publication on the campus.

Andrew Smith of Pennsylvania was hired as football coach for the spring and fall of 1916. At the close of the season a contract for three years further service as head coach was signed with him. A. B. Ziegler was hired to assist him for the year, and P Elliott was chosen to coach the Freshman team. Contracts with Carl Shafor and Carl Zamloch were signed for the coaching of the soccer and baseball teams respectively. Ben Wallis, who voluntarily gave his services as crew coach in 1916 was retained, and a salary voted him for this year.

Much misunderstanding concerning the granting of letters and numerals has been cleared up by the adoption of definite rules covering practically every case which might arise.

Student Committees

Though routine work has composed the duty of nearly every student committee this year, one of the most active, and the one which produced probably the most far-reaching effects is the Students Union Committee.

Feeling increasingly the need of such an institution as a Students Union, the

HARPER — A. S. U. C. SECRETARY

committee appointed last year spent its whole time in determining just what were the needs of the campus to be satisfied by the new building.

The committee this year has, using the work of the preceding body as a foundation, advanced the plans until a Students Union Building is now an assured proposition.

As planned, the first unit of the building will be placed between Harmon Gymnasium and Sather Gate. When the Gymnasium is removed, additions extending over the ground now occupied by it will be constructed. Provision is made for space in the building for the students' store, a cafeteria, the offices of the various campus publications, a dormitory at which visiting teams may stay, or where our own training table may be held, lounging rooms, A. W. S. rooms, banquet halls and accommodations for visiting alumni.

Sufficient funds for the commencement of the construction are now available; and it is planned to raise the rest on the outside, and, by extending the period of the debt over twenty-five years, to let the store and cafeteria pay off both the principal and interest.

Every organization on the campus has been touched in the publicity campaign of the committee, and every one is enthusiastic in its support of the plan. A modern Students Union therefore will be a reality in the very near future.

The Executive Committee membership is as follows:

President, F. W. Stewart '17
Vice-President, W. G. Witter '17
Secretary, C. F. Harper '18
Anna Barrows '17

Faculty Representative, Professor M. C. Lynch
Graduate Manager, J. A. Stroud, Jr. '13
Alumni Representative, C. E. Hall '10
J. N. Owen '17

First Semester
Carol Eberts '17
H. A. Hyde '17

Second Semester
Vera Christie '18
G. W. Clark '18

Following are the standing Student Committees:

Governors of Senior Hall—A. T. LaPrade '17, E. P. Pfingst '17.

Intercollegiate Agreement Committee—D. B. Cohen '17, J. A. Stroud, Jr. '13, F. P. Griffith '06.

Football Rules Committee—J. A. Stroud, Jr. '13, Chairman; W. R. Montgomery '17.

Rally Committee—L. R. Byington '17, Chairman; H. R. Hogaboom '17, E. M. Elam '17, J. C. Newton '17, T. W. Slaven '17, J. S. Candee '17, C. F. Roeth '17, E. S. Pillsbury '18, E. C. Sutton '18, W. J. Hulting '18, Pierce Works '18, L. S. Nelson '18, L. D. Sanderson '18, Howard Baldwin '18, Bruce Howard '19, A. B. Cantwell '19, R. D. Perry '19.

Intercollegiate Debating Council—*Fall Semester:* D. S. Shattuck '17, Chairman; H. A. Black '17, G. W. Cohen '17, S. S. Barrows '17, M. S. Rosenblatt '18,

EXECUTIVE COMMITTEE IN SESSION
LEFT TO RIGHT: CLARK, OWEN, HARPER (SECRETARY), STEWART (PRESIDENT),
WITTER, STROUD, BARROWS, CHRISTIE, LYNCH

C. S. Brown '18. *Spring Semester:* D. S. Shattuck '17, Chairman; H. A. Black '17, M. S. Rosenblatt '18, C. S. Brown '18.

Students Union Committee—G. W. Cohen '17, Chairman; F. T. Elliott '17, Secretary; D. S. Shattuck '17, W. F. Mayock '17, R. K. Bontz '17, R. S. Mayock '17, A. L. Dunn '17, G. L. Maxwell '17, C. G. Hjelte '17, V. L. Furth '18, G. M. Cunningham '18, L. D. Sanderson '18, C. L. Isaacson '18, H. S. Steen '18, R. F. Macdonald '18, H. A. Sproul '19, H. W. Sayre '20.

Students Affairs Committee—F. W. Stewart '17, Chairman; S. S. Barrows '17, Secretary; L. F. Krusi '17, H. A. Black '17, L. A. Nichols '17.

Students Welfare Committee—E. W. Lockwood '17, Chairman; M. L. Royar '17, R. L. Ryan '17, E. L. Garthwaite '17, R. W. Bell '18, W. B. Garthwaite '18, R. E. Gimbal '17, W. B. Norton '17. *Spring Semester:* E. W. Lockwood '17, Chairman; M. L. Royar '17, R. L. Ryan '17, R. W. Bell '18, W. B. Garthwaite '18, Ray Vandervoort '18, H. A. Sproul '19, L. M. Gimball '19, R. W. Rinehart '20.

Associated Students Store Committee—Professor M. C. Lynch, Chairman; Professor C. C. Plehn, J. A. Stroud, Jr. '13, H. F. Shippey '17, F. W. Stewart '17, J. R. McKee '18, B. K. Vaughan '18, E. F. Steen '18.

Blue and Gold Advisory Committee—L. F. Krusi '17, Chairman; F. W. Stewart '17, A. R. Eimer '17, P. W. Clark '17, A. V. Saph '17, J. L. Reith '18, Wilson Meyer '18.

University Meeting Committee—A. L. Dunn '17, Chairman; W. H. Thomas '18, H. M. Black '18.

LEILA BERRY—PRESIDENT   ESTHER SINCLAIR—SECRETARY

The Associated Women Students

THE ASSOCIATED WOMEN STUDENTS, formed in 1894 for the purpose of directing the activities in which the women primarily are interested, includes all women students who are members of the Associated Students of the University of California. All activities and interests of the women are controlled by the organization through its executive committee and the following affiliations: Prytanean, Sports and Pastimes Association, Treble Clef Society, Art History Circle, Iota Sigma Pi, Mandolin and Guitar Club, Delta Epsilon, Istyc California Club, Women's "C" Society and Nu Sigma Si.

In addition to the supervision of all social and athletic events, the A. W. S. directs certain independent institutions for the women. A loan fund is maintained to provide emergency loans. The "Counter" provides sandwiches and chocolate. The Parthencia, an annual masque produced by the women, is given under the auspices of A. W. S.

For 1916-1917 the officers were: President, Leila Berry '17; Vice President, Bertha Galloway '17; Athletic Manager, Alberta McNeeley '17; Treasurer, Marian Brown '18; Secretary, Esther Sinclair '18.

The executive committee was composed of the officers of the association and the following: Dean of Women, Miss Lucy Ward Stebbins; Woman's Editor, *Daily Californian*, (August-December, '16); Representative A. S. U. C. Executive Committee, Anna Barrows '17; Woman's Editor *Daily Californian* (January-May, '17) Frances Brown; Parthencia Manager, Dorothy Wetmore '17; Representative A. S. U. C. Executive Committee (August-December, '16); Carol Eberts '17; Representative A. S. U. C. Executive Committee (January-May, '17), Vera Christie '18.

ATHLETIC ORGANIZATIONS

BIG "C" SOCIETY

Officers *Fall Semester:*
President, L. A. Nichols '17.
Vice-Pres., Ernest Camper '17.
Secretary, W. A. Russell '17.
Treasurer, E. M. Rogers '17.
Sergeant-at-arms,
    C. C. Gildersleeve '18.

Spring Semester:
President, F. T. Brooks '18.
Vice-Pres., P. A. Embury '18.
Secretary, W. A. Russell '17.
Treasurer, E. M. Rogers '17.
Sergeant-at-arms,
    C. C. Gildersleeve '18.

CIRCLE "C" SOCIETY

Officers *Fall Semester,*
President, R. L. Shearman '17.
Vice-Pres., K. B. Clark '18.
Sec.-Treas., J. W. Coulter '18.

Spring Semester:
President, J. W. Coulter '18.
Vice-Pres., E. G. Schlapp '18.
Sec.-Treas., N. M. Lyon '17.

GYMNASIUM CLUB

Officers:
President, O. E. Snyder '19.
Director, F. B. McCollom '17.

Secretary, V. B. Davis '19.
Manager, G. W. Clark '18.

RIFLE CLUB

Officers:
President, C. I. Howell '18.
Secretary, E. K. Schultz '18.

Vice-Pres., G. A. Patterson '18.
Treasurer, E. M. Atchison '18.

ALUMNI ORGANIZATIONS

Alumni Association

FOR THE CALIFORNIA ALUMNI ASSOCIATION the past year has been a period of intensive preparation. The management of the secretary's office has been reorganized, the publication of the association has been remodelled into the *California Alumni Fortnightly*, the active enrollment has been tripled, the fourth edition of the *Directory of Graduates* has been compiled, and a plan has been set in motion to replace the dormant alumni clubs with energetic units in the numerous centers throughout the country. The value of the preparation will be determined, naturally, as the individual purposes are carried to completion.

There is a total number of living alumni of 11,826. Of these at least 6,000 names should be actively enrolled in the association. In June, 1915, there were 1,302 members; in June, 1916, there were 2,905 enrolled.

A word on the present income of the association may have a bearing on the possibilities of the future. The collections are confined to a two-dollar yearly assessment, covering membership and subscription. A summary which shows, by a comparison of each month, the collections during the fiscal years since 1910-11, is noteworthy in several particulars. In 1910-11 the total income was $1,246; in the next year, $1,208; in 1912-13 it was $1,099; in the next, $1,232; in the last year, $1,546; and in the current year (to May 30) it was $4,624.18. In connection with this an interesting feature is the collections during the month of May, 1916. Between 1910 and 1915 the collections for the May month averaged $127. The total receipts for May, 1916, were $2,179.97.

The treasurer's report shows that the amount of the expenditures for the year has been exceptional. But the money, for the most part, has been put into permanent things. The effort in this direction has been aided materially through the generous financial co-operation of the Regents of the university. For the development of the association the Regents appropriated $3,000 in 1915-16, and have included in the 1916-17 budget a like amount.

A committee is at work on the proposal to establish an information and employment exchange in connection with the general offices of the association. This bureau, if the appropriate plans are devised, will be the medium through which the employers may reach the graduates as they leave the university and through which the graduates may be brought in touch with prospective occupations. The service which a bureau of this type will give is a service which the association must perform.

The *Directory of Graduates*, for which the compilation is complete, is the preparation for the district council plan. When all the graduates and the majority of the former students are accurately located the state-wide organization into local districts will be perfected. Each district is to have a council dependent on the central council, which meets every three weeks at the university. The district council scheme has been submitted to several localities and has been received with enthusiasm. The details of the plan are attractive and offer a solution to the problem that is ever-present in the administration of the local independent clubs. For example, San Joaquin County, San Diego County, Marin County, Solano County, and Los Angeles have been visited in the interest of the district scheme. When there is work to do there is active organization. The framework of organization is being built because there are great tasks ahead.

The custom for the Bay counties alumni to hold a Charter Day dinner was inaugurated last March, when 350 men and women were hosts to President Vincent, of Minnesota, the Charter Day speaker. The usual rally banquets were held on the eve of the Big Game. The women met in Berkeley; the men, numbering 320, dined in San Francisco. On Commencement Day the customary luncheon was given in Faculty Glade. Over 480 alumni were present. The policy for making the influence of alumni organization felt in the state at large brought out a plan to hold the 1916 annual meeting of the association at Kearney Park, the university estate in Fresno County, on June 3. A special Pullman train carried the Bay counties' delegation of 150 persons to the festivities, while a total of nearly 1,000 alumni registered at the park. The officers of the association for the year of 1916-17, elected at the annual meeting, are: President, Oscar Sutro '94; First Vice-President, W. E. Creed '98; Second Vice-President, S. M. Haskins '93; Secretary, Harvey Roney '15; Treasurer, R. F. Sproul '13. The Councilors are: Frank Otis '73, S. L. Rawlins '99, M. C. Lynch '06, C. E. Hall '10, Douglas Brookman '10, S. C. Irving '79, C. W. Merrill '91, W. H. Waste '91, Miss Margaret Hayne '08, and Mrs. Rose Gardner Marx '11. For the two places on the Board of Administration of the LeConte Memorial Fellowship, T. M. Putnam '97, vice W. E. Ritter, resigned, and F. P. Griffiths '06, vice C. S. Greene '86, whose term expired June 30, 1916, were elected. J. N. LeConte, whose term expired June 30, 1916, was re-elected.

··· RELIGIOUS ···
ORGANIZATIONS

The University Y. M. C. A.

THE PROGRAM of the University Young Men's Christian Association for the year has been built around a twofold purpose; namely, to meet the need existing in a state university for religious education, and to give practical expression to the spirit of service.

In the field of service the Freshman Class was welcomed at the beginning of the year; employment has been secured for more than three hundred students; and more than one thousand dollars raised for the support of the work of Roy Service '02, secretary of the Y. M. C. A. in San Chuan Province, China.

The officers are: President, G. L. Maxwell '17; Vice-President, W. D. Norton '17; Recording Secretary, L. B. Sharp '17; Corresponding Secretary, K. L. Hanson '18; Treasurer, George Hjelte '17; Secretaries, B. M. Cherrington, E. L. Devendorf, H. C. Kingman, G. L. Collins '15 and Gail Cleland '07.

Y. M. C. A. CABINET

The University Y. W. C. A.

WITH AN INCREASED MEMBERSHIP of 530 as against 350 for last year, and with general progress showing up from all angles, the Young Women's Christian Association of the University of California finishes this year of its work with accomplishing great strides in the fundamental purpose of the organization. Under the leadership of Inra Wann '17, the Y. W. C. A. has been brought into closer touch with the real needs of such a body on the Campus, not only in the furthering of social interest, but also along the lines of bringing the girls of the university into more intimate and closer touch with each other.

Many new and original methods have been tried out by the Cabinet this last year with remarkable success. Chief among these were the institution of "Friendship Luncheons." So important did these luncheons become that it was found necessary to add a new member to the Cabinet for the sole purpose of handling them.

In order to bring the members into closer touch with the inner workings of the organization and to afford a sort of calendar of coming events a weekly paper called the *Record* has been printed. The editors for the past year have been Bernice Hubbard '18, and Algeline Marlow '17.

The officers for the year 1916-1917 were: President, Inra Wann '17; Vice-President, Freda Bayley '17; Treasurer, Louise Keen '18; Secretarys, Josephine Parks '19, Laurnne Mattern '19, and Margaret Sherman; Annual Member, Margaret Marchant '17. For the 1917-1918 are: President, Marian Brown '18; Vice-President, Marion Pears '18; Treasurer, Mary Lee '18; Secretarys, Pauline Whittlesley '20 and Margaret Sherman; Annual Member, Virginia Baldwin '18.

Christian Science Society of the U. of C.

CHRISTIAN SCIENCE societies exist at the universities of California, Chicago, Columbia, Cornell, Harvard, Illinois, Leland Stanford Junior, Michigan, Minnesota, Nebraska and Wisconsin, and at Simmons, Smith, and Wellesley colleges. The Manual of The Mother Church, The First Church of Christ, Scientist, in Boston, Massachusetts, authorizes members of the Faculty and students, who are members in good standing with The Mother Church, to establish and conduct Christian Science organizations in universities and colleges where religious organizations are permitted. Under this provision Christian Science Society of the University of California was organized in 1907.

The society holds meetings on the first Tuesday evening after registration, and on alternate Tuesdays thereafter during the regular and summer sessions of the university. Selections from the Bible are read, followed by correlative passages from the Christian Science text-book, "Science and Health with Key to the Scriptures," by Mary Baker Eddy. Experiences, testimonies of healing and remarks on Christian Science are also given.

Authorized lectures are delivered by members of the Board of Lectureship of The Mother Church. The purpose of these lectures is to present a clear, definite statement of Christian Science, and to correct prevalent misconceptions concerning its teaching, and the life and works of its discoverer and founder, Mary Baker Eddy.

A reception is held in the fall to welcome those interested in Christian Science, and to explain the purpose of the organization.

In the Doe Library are found all the works of Mrs. Eddy, with the concordances thereto, translations in German, with parallel pages in English, of "Science and Health," and the authentic "Life of Mary Baker Eddy" by Sibyl Wilbur. The Periodical Room contains the *Christian Science Journal,* the official organ of The Mother Church; the *Christian Science Sentinel,* a weekly; the *Christian Science Quarterly Bible Lessons, Der Herold der Christian Science* and the *Christian Science Monitor.* The *Journal, Sentinel* and *Der Herold* always contain signed testimonies of healing. Authorized literature on Christian Science is also available to students in the Free Reading Room in the Berkeley Bank Building, maintained by the Churches of Christ, Scientist, of Berkeley.

The purpose of the society is to afford all in the university who so desire, an opportunity to gain an understanding of Christian Science as taught in the Christian Science text-book. Members of the Faculty and students, of present and former classes of this university, are invited to these testimonial meetings, receptions and lectures.

The Newman Club

During the year the Newman Club has enlarged its activities to keep pace with the growth of the university.

In addition to the courses in scripture and ethics given by Rev. Thomas Lantry O'Neill, Ph. D. and Rev. Clarence E. Woodman, Ph. D., who have charge of the religious work for Catholic students of the university, the club has offered, this year, a course in scholastic philosophy by Dr. Charles R. Baschab.

Though the primary purpose of the association is to secure for Catholic students opportunities for religious instruction and worship, it contributes to the social and intellectual life of the university by the many public lectures, receptions, and entertainments given under its auspices.

The lectures and other activities are held in Newman Hall, a large, well-appointed, English gothic building situated on the north side of the university campus near Founders' Rock Entrance, at the corner of Ridge Road and La Loma Avenue. It contains a chapel, reading room, library, and recreation rooms.

OFFICERS: President, Dwight E. Eveleth '16; First Vice-President, Allan Peter Lindsay '18; Second Vice-President, Alice A. Griffin, '17; Corresponding Secretary, Flora M. Wilson, '17; Recording Secretary, Rebecca Borrodaile '18; Treasurer (*Fall Semester*), William F. Carroll '18; (*Spring Semester*), Charles E. Rhein '17

HEADS OF STANDING COMMITTEES: *Executive*, Nicholas J. Scorsur '17; *Social*, Katherine F. Quinn '17; *Women's Membership*, Madeline A. Muldoon, '18; *Men's Membership*, Mervyn T. Prindiville '19, and William V. Coin '19.

St. Mark's Club

THE ST. MARK'S CLUB affords Episcopal students in the university an opportunity of meeting together for discussions of religious activity, hearing talks by members of the Faculty, or for social recreation. Its members meet each Sunday evening at the St. Mark's Parish House.

In addition to the regular weekly meetings the organization has charge of the Sunday school of St. Mark's Church. Boys' clubs, gymnasium classes and other forms of social service work are conducted by the club in West Berkeley. Various other kinds of service are undertaken by the club during the year with the idea of supplying the less fortunate people of the Bay region with the necessities of life.

The officers of the club for the Fall Semester were: President, John Lawton '17; First Vice-President, E. W. Jacobsen '17; Second Vice-President, Marion Underwood '18; Secretary, Margaret Lawton '19; Treasurer, Bruce Jameyson '17. For the Spring Semester they were: President, E. W. Jacobsen '17; First Vice-President, Marion L. Underwood '18; Second Vice-President, Margaret Lawton '19; Secretary, Dorothy Lilly '19; Treasurer, R. H. Young '19.

DEBATING SOCIETIES

Senate Debating Society

OFFICERS—*Fall Semester:*
President, S. S. Barrows '17
Vice-Pres., E. S. Pillsbury '18
Secretary, H. S. Flock '18
Treasurer, Ray Vandervoort '18

EXECUTIVE COMMITTEE:
E. S. Pillsbury '18, Chairman
H. A. Black '17
L. B. Schlingheyde '18

Spring Semester:
President, H. A. Black '17
Vice-Pres., H. S. Flock '18
Secretary, J. H. Weise '18
Treasurer, D. L. Abshire '18

EXECUTIVE COMMITTEE:
H. S. Flock '18, Chairman
D. F. Bush '17
L. B. Schlingheyde '18

Congress Debating Society

OFFICERS—*Fall Semester:*
Speaker, G. W. Cohen '17
Speaker protem, E. F. Coe '17
Clerk, J. J. Posner '19

EXECUTIVE COMMITTEE:
R. I. Daley '16
G. L. Maxwell '17

Spring Semester:
Speaker, D. S. Shattuck '17
Speaker protem, R. I. Daley '16
Clerk, W. M. Green '19

EXECUTIVE COMMITTEE:
M. S. Rosenblatt '18
E. F. Coe '17
T. C. Lawson '18

Freshman Debating Society

OFFICERS:
President, W. S. Fortson
Vice-Pres., Max. Felix

OFFICERS:
Secretary, G. P. Hammond
Treasurer, D. G. Montell

Forum Debating Society

OFFICERS—*Fall Semester:*
President, Baptiste Barthe '17
Vice-Pres., E. S. Leslie '19
Sec.-Treas., E. C. Ward '19

EXECUTIVE COMMITTEE:
E. S. Leslie '19
C. S. Brown '18

Spring Semester:
President, C. S. Brown '18
Vice-Pres., R. A. Way '20
Sec.-Treas., Julian Pardini '19

EXECUTIVE COMMITTEE:
R. A. Way '20
M. O. Olson '19
E. C. Ward '19

Debating Council

Fall Semester:
D. S. Shattuck '17 (Congress), Chairman
S. S. Barrows '17 (Senate)
G. W. Cohen '17 (Congress)
Baptiste Barthe '17 (Forum)

FACULTY REPRESENTATIVES:
Prof. M. C. Flaherty
Newton B. Drury

Spring Semester:
D. S. Shattuck '17 (Congress), Chairman
H. A. Black '17 (Senate)
M. S. Rosenblatt '18 (Congress)
C. S. Brown '18 (Forum)

FACULTY REPRESENTATIVES:
Prof. M. C. Flaherty
Newton B. Drury

Women's Parlimentary Society

OFFICERS:
President, Helen Harris '19
Vice-Pres., Helen Rocca '19

Secretary, Stella Ajamian '20
Treasurer, Frances Stranahan '18

DEPARTMENTAL ORGANIZATIONS

Agriculture Club

OFFICERS —*Fall Semester:*
President, W. D. Norton '17
Vice-Pres., L. S. Hadley '17
Secretary, T. O. Sprague '18
Treasurer, E. J. Tippet '18
Sergeant-at-arms, L. E. Williams '18

Spring Semester:
President, Verne Hoffman '17
Vice-Pres., E. J. Tippett '18
Secretary, Frank Wood '17
Treasurer, J. L. Barter '19
Sergeant-at-arms, M. E. McCollum '17

Journal of Agriculture

Editor, Knowles Ryerson '16
Manager, G. A. Allin '17

Editor, Knowles Ryerson '16
Manager, G. A. Allin '17

Architectural Association

OFFICERS—*Fall Semester:*
President, J. C. Clowdsley '17
Secretary, Pauline Chamberlain '17
Treasurer, C. B. Roeth '17

Spring Semester:
President, E. F. Kaufman '17
Vice-Pres., Jeanette Dyer '17
Secretary, Myrtle Henrici '15
Treasurer, H. C. Collins '17

Art History Circle

OFFICERS:
President, Camilla Clark '17

Sec. Treas., Leona Jones '17

Associated Electrical and Mechanical Engineers

OFFICERS—*Fall Semester:*
President, Graydon Oliver '17
Vice-Pres., R. W. Lingle '17
Secretary, C. E. Wayland '17
Treasurer, Thomas Spencer '17

Spring Semester:
President, W. K. Potts '17
Vice-Pres., T. L. Nudd '17
Secretary, R. D. Berst '17
Treasurer, E. R. Foster '17

Associated Pre-Medical Students

OFFICERS:
President, R. L. Ring '17
Vice-Pres., Agnes Wood '19
Secretary and Treasurer,
  M. F. Desmond '18

EXECUTIVE COMMITTEE:
R. L. Ring '17
Agnes Wood '18
M. F. Desmond '18
D. K. Pischell '18

Le Cercle Français

OFFICERS — *Fall Semester:*
President, Jenny Fayard '18
Vice-Pres., L. L. Pavid '16
Secretary, Simone Brangier '17
Treasurer, Esmond Schapiro '18

Spring Semester:
President, Simone Brangier '17
Vice-Pres., H. J. Howells '19
Secretary, Alma Berude '19
Treasurer, Esmond Schapiro '18

Il Circulo Italiano

OFFICERS:
President, Priscilla Cavagnaro '17
Secretary, J. A. Pardini '18

Vice-Pres., I. A. Cereghino '19
Treasurer, F. G. Casella '20

Civil Engineering Association

OFFICERS — *Fall Semester:*
President, R. L. Ryan '17
Vice-Pres., A. V. Saph '17
Secretary, S. C. King '17
Treasurer, F. J. McKune '17
Librarian, A. M. Jensen '17
Sergeant-at-arms, C. W. Jones '17

Spring Semester:
President, A. M. Jensen '17
Vice-Pres., J. W. Oakley '17
Secretary, L. F. Krusi '17
Treasurer, E. E. Blackie '17
Librarian, H. Latson '17
Sergeant-at-arms, R. B. Hansen '17

Commerce Club

OFFICERS — *Fall Semester:*
President, Prosper Reiter '17
Vice-Pres., C. J. Felt '17
Sec.-Treas., R. B. Wheeler '18

Spring Semester:
President, E. H. Tucker '17
Vice-Pres., F. A. Buckingham '17
Sec. Treas., S. C. Goth '18

Cosmopolitan Club

OFFICERS:
President, A. E. Lundkvist '16
Secretary, V. S. Ram '17
Treasurer, S. Y. Kiang '19

EXECUTIVE COMMITTEE:
Surendra Karr
H. F. Rakshit
Abraham Schwartz

Deutscher Kranzchen

OFFICERS — *Fall Semester:*
President, Fannie Granger '17
Vice-Pres., B. P. Puckett '19
Secretary, W. L. Montgomery '19
Treasurer, R. C. Kissling '18

Spring Semester:
President, Fannie Granger '17
Vice-Pres., Frances Porter '20
Secretary, Amelia Johnson '19
Treasurer, R. C. Kissling '18

Deutscher Verein

OFFICERS — *Fall Semester:*
President, Jenny Schwab '15
Secretary, Sarah Olsen '16
Treasurer, Mariza Clow '16

Spring Semester:
President, E. G. Gudde '17
Secretary, Sarah Olsen '16
Treasurer, Mariza Clow '16

Deutscher Zirkel

OFFICERS—*Fall Semester:*
President, Edna Stut '18
Vice-Pres., Vera Crispin '18
Sec. Treas., Elizabeth Johnson '17

Spring Semester:
President, Vera Crispin '18
Vice-Pres., Vera Bhend '18
Sec. Treas., E. R. Higgins '19

Die Plaudertasche

OFFICERS—*Fall Semester:*
President, M. H. Olender '18
Vice-Pres., Genevieve Mott '17
Secretary, Clyffice Nevin '18
Treasurer, V. L. Gavin '18

Spring Semester:
President, Hazel Katzenstein '17
Vice-Pres., Esther Siemens '18
Secretary, Dorothy Hooper '17
Treasurer, E. E. Nichols '18

Education Club

President, Robert Daly '17

Secretary-Treasurer, Robert Sturgis

Forestry Club

OFFICERS—*Fall Semester:*
President, Murrell Warren '17
Vice-Pres., Charles Van Riper '19
Secretary, H. L. Hansen '17
Sergeant-at-arms, Professor D. Bruce

Spring Semester:
President, F. N. Aylward '17
Vice-Pres., V. B. Davis '19
Secretary, George Byrne '18
Sergeant-at-arms, Prof. Walter Mulford

Humboldt Club

OFFICERS:
President, F. K. Haight '17
Secretary, Ruth Horel '17

Vice-Pres., Mary Hamilton '18
Treasurer, L. H. Nielson '19

Konversationsklub

OFFICERS—*Fall Semester:*
President, L. S. Rosenbaum '17
Vice-Pres., Louise Ploeger '18
Secretary, Sylvia Volmer '17
Treasurer, Helen Smith '19

Spring Semester:
President, Sylvia Vollmer '17
Vice-Pres., Grace Arlett '20
Secretary, Lucille Murphy '17
Treasurer, F. D. Kent '20

Law Association

OFFICERS:
President, T. G. Chamberlain '15
Vice-President, Rosamond Parma '08
Secretary, W. G. Witter '17

BOARD OF GOVERNORS:
Forrest Cobb '15
Herbert Hall '16
C. J. Carey '17

Lodi Club

OFFICERS:
President, R. L. Johns '17
Sec.-Treas., Adelaide Weihe '18

Vice-Pres., Hazel Tindell '15

Menorah Society

OFFICERS:
President, B. F. Rabinowitz '17
Vice-Pres., Rose Horwitz '17
Secretary, S. A. Coblentz '17
Treasurers, Irene Mosbacher '17
M. H. Olender '18

STUDENT EXECUTIVE COMMITTEE:
G. W. Cohen '17
Fanny Juda '18
F. J. Jonas '17

GRADUATE EXECUTIVE COMMITTEE:
S. M. Arndt '16
M. M. Friedman '16
Jeanette Harber '16

Mining Association

OFFICERS—*Fall Semester:*
President, M. H. Knowles '16
Vice-Pres., C. R. Knox '18
Secretary, H. T. Helgesson '17
Treasurer, A. C. Kroeger '17
Librarian, C. N. Schuette '17
Sergeant-at-arms, J. Denbo '17
Senior Alumni Sec., W. E. Inman '17
Junior Alumni Sec., J. Deane '18

EXECUTIVE COMMITTEE:
J. L. Bennett '18
R. Starbird '17
G. Gray '16

Spring Semester:
President, C. N. Schuette '17
Vice-Pres., H. B. Barkis '17
Secretary, H. I. Altshuler '19
Treasurer, J. L. Bennett '18
Librarian, R. C. Kerr '19
Sergeant-at-arms, L. C. Mekler '17
Senior Alumni Sec., W. E. Inman '17
Junior Alumni Sec., J. Deane '18

EXECUTIVE COMMITTEE:
E. Wisser '17
G. Coffey '17
W. Sprague '17

Philhellenon Hetairia

OFFICERS—*Fall Semester:*
President, G. F. Stephens '17
Vice-Pres., H. V. White '15
Secretary, Elizabeth Burnham '18
Treasurer, Catherine Delamere '19

Spring Semester:
President, R. A. Way '19
Vice-Pres., Joseph McMorrow '18
Secretary, Louise Ploeger '18
Treasurer, Catherine Delamere '19

Pre-Legal Association

OFFICERS:
President, Ralph A. Frost '19
Vice-Pres., Fay Christie '20
Girls' Vice-Pres., Dorris Peoples '20

Treasurer, Max C. Baugh '19
Secretary, George R. Miller '19

Scandinavian Club

OFFICERS:
President, M. A. Soderberg '17
Vice-Pres., Gerda Frederiksen '19

Secretary, Bertha Nielsen '19
Treasurer, G. O. Sagen '17

Siskiyou Club

OFFICERS—*Fall Semester:*
President, D. L. Abshire '18
Vice-Pres., Dorothy Hancock '19
Sec.-Treas., O. C. Wilson '19

Spring Semester:
President, Ralph Albee '18
Vice-Pres., Helene Hooper '17
Sec.-Treas., A. C. Rowe '20

Slavic Society

OFFICERS—*Fall Semester:*
President, J. L. Seymour '17
Vice-Pres., Zdenka Buben '17
Advising Vice-Pres.,
 Prof. G. R. Noyes
Secretary, Clara Winslow '95
Treasurer, Jane Campbell '18

Spring Semester:
President, Zdenka Buben '17
Vice-Pres., J. L. Seymour '17
Advising Vice-Pres.,
 Prof. G. R. Noyes
Secretary, Dorothea Prall '10
Treasurer, Melicia Medigovich '19

Ellen Wilson Chapter of the Southern Club

OFFICERS—*Fall Semester:*
President, Gladys Reston '17
Vice-Pres., Amrah Smith '17
Secretary, Blanche Lucas '19
Treasurer, Marion Tilton '19

Spring Semester:
President, Gladys Reston '17
Vice-Pres., Amrah Smith '17
Secretary, May Carter '18
Treasurer, Marion Tilton '18

Southern Mines Club

OFFICERS:
President, Phyllis Bates '18

Sec.-Treas., I. M. Bromley '20

Spanish Club Officers

OFFICERS—*First Term:*
President, Alberto O. Montijo '18
Vice-Pres., Rebecca Borrakaile '18
Secretary, Mason Johnston '17
Treasurer, Anne Jenkins '16

Second Term:
President, Luis B. Tagorda '18
Vice-Pres., Constance Edmunds '16
Secretary, William G. Lopez '18
Treasurer, Marian Sutton '19

Sprechverband

OFFICERS—*Fall Semester:*
President, Beatrice Swan '19
Vice-Pres., Charles Rugh '19
Secretary, Margaret Martin '19
Treasurer, Ellen Deruchie '19

Spring Semester:
President, Beatrice Swan '19
Vice-Pres., Ellen Deruchie '19
Secretary, Margaret Martin '19
Treasurer, Mary Buhler '20

American Society of Mechanical Engineers
University of California Branch Established 1912

HONORARY CHAIRMAN   Prof. Herbert Bamford Langille
CHAIRMEN   Herman Charles Greenwood
    William Kenneth Potts
VICE-CHAIRMAN   Howard Stewart Bean
SECRETARY   John Herman Fenton
TREASURER   Herman Graydon Oliver

ASSOCIATE MEMBERS
Prof. Herbert Bamford Langille
Prof. Joseph Nisbet LeConte
Prof. B. F. Raber
Prof. Reuben Simpkin Tour
B. R. Vanleer

SENIORS
Gaston Bolado Ashe   Frank Le Roy Hill
Howard Stewart Bean   Henry Raymond Hogaboom
Llewellyn M. K. Boelter   Matthew Hall Jones
James Edmund Currens   Cyril Philip Kenville
Robert Dean Easton   Alexander H. Munro
John Herman Fenton   Herman Graydon Oliver
Evans Ronald Foster   William Kenneth Potts
Herman Charles Greenwood   Thomas Spencer
Clarke Elmer Wayland

JUNIORS
John Louis Cooley   Harold Wadsworth Kidwell
Francis Christopher Holman   Frank Laub
Ernest Kalisch Schulze

MUSIC

Glee Club

Officers—Fall Semester:
President, G. Edward Gordon '17
Secretary, Walter S. McManus '19
Manager, B. Kendrick Vaughan '18
Director, Clinton R. Morse '06

Spring Semester:
President, C. Stanley Dimm '17
Secretary, Myron E. Etienne '19
Manager, B. Kendrick Vaughan '18
Director, Clinton R. Morse '06

FIRST TENORS

Edward C. Brett '17
Edwin D. Bronson '17
Roy D. Sifford '17
Whitney B. Wright '17
Shirley C. Horseley '17
Axel B. Gravens '18
Eugene Lamb '18
M. Way Mablough '18
Freeman A. Reed '18

Rodney S. Spring '18
Edwyn F. Steen '18
Walter S. McManus '19
Ataullo Medina '19
Edgar D. Boal '19
Alfred A. Gropp '19
Louis A. Bagley '20
Alven K. House '20
Emery Lovett '20

SECOND TENORS

Clifford B. Cole '17
Frederick F. Janney '17
Richard G. Martens '17
Benjamin H. Ormand '17
Gilbert L. Patteson '17
Fletcher H. Dutton '18
Thomas A. Gisbert '18
Fred G. Gibbons '18
Cyrus L. Howell '18
Herbert D. Langhorne '18
B. Kendrick Vaughan '18
Frank R. Beese '19
Arpad Braun '20

Charles S. Edwards '19
Ronald W. Hunt '19
Moreland Leithold '19
John K. Moody '19
Kenneth M. Morse '19
William S. Nash '19
George J. O'Brien '19
Charles E. Pardon '19
George E. Smith '19
Charles W. Whitmore '19
Archibald S. MacDonald '20
Harry A. Schatz '20
Harford C. Sharon '20

FIRST BASS

Henry B. Barkis, Jr. '17
C. Stanley Dimm '17
F. Thomas Elliott '17
G. Edward Gordon '17
Bradford M. Melvin '17
Donald L. Abshire '18
Orville B. Caldwell '18
George E. Goodall '18
George M. Parrish '18
Wayne H. Stephenson '18
Kenneth S. Craft '19

Myron E. Etienne '19
Edwin J. Jolly '19
Edward B. Kennedy '19
Almer J. Norton '19
Percy H. Ward '19
Harold E. Williams '19
John Gifford '20
Howard H. McCreaty '20
Joseph H. Maddux '20
Ralph W. Nicholson '20
Edward A. Williams '20

SECOND BASS

Harry V. Adams '16
Hugh N. Herrick '17
Harold A. Morse '17
Fred H. Reynolds '17
Harry H. Scherling '17
Edward R. Shaw '17
Thomas Spencer '17
Charles R. Knox '17
George W. Clark '18
Eugene P. Hyatt '18
Philip W. Janney '18
Harvey M. Kilburn '18

Helmet S. Steen '18
John T. Donnellan '19
Maurice C. Gibbon '19
James S. Taylor '19
Clair E. Woland '19
John H. Duhring '20
Charles F. Honeywell '20
Sumner N. Mevius '20
Leon J. Le Tourneau '20
Walter S. Lewis '20
Frank A. Morgan '20
Andrew M. Moore '20

ASSOCIATE MEMBERS

George W. Baker '16
Leslie H. Bingham '16
H. Syril Duerstery '17
Isadore B. Kornblum '17
J. Harold Barker '18
Thomas M. Benson '18
Wymond R. Garthwaite '18
Carl A. Goldsmeyer '18
Malin T. Langstroth '18

Frank C. Bassets '18
Elmore Roberts '18
James A. Taylor '18
Lawrence J. Eade '19
Oren C. Hyde '19
Harold E. McGowan '19
Lee B. Milbank '19
Milton J. Frumkin '19
Rumun H. Landsberger '20

University of California Orchestra

DIRECTOR	Paul Steindorff
PRESIDENT	Glen Haydon '18
SECRETARY-TREASURER	William C. Tesche '18
LIBRARIAN	Charles S. Edwards '19

FIRST VIOLINS

Milton J. Frumkin '19	George P. Soups '20
John Gifford '20	Hermann J. Stern '20
Herbert L. James '20	William C. Tesche '18
Hermann Kohlmoos '19	Clarence W. Wagner '19
DeWitt L. Lee '19	Melville E. Wank '19

SECOND VIOLINS

John R. Edwards '18	Frank A. Morgan '20
Parker L. Hall '19	Sidney H. Samuels '19
Cyril P. Kenville '17	Kenyon J. Scudder '17
Myron E. Lackey '20	Melvin Solomon '18

VIOLA
Harry E. White '20

CELLOS

Charles S. Edwards '19	Arthur W. Mohr '17
H. H. Burska '20	Richard G. Montgomery '19

FLUTES

Herbert H. Schultz '19	Burford C. Sharon '20

CLARINETS

Glen Haydon '18	Edwin P. Tiffany '20

CORNETS

Donald C. DeWitt '20	Jay L. Ruddick '17
Charles E. Marquis '18	Alfred E. Wollitz '20

Averill G. McAlpine '20

HORN
James D. Graham '20

TROMBONES

J. C. Jurgenson	Edward C. McLaughlin '20

BASSOON
Alfred P. Solomon '20

Mandolin Club

Officers—Fall Semester:
President, John C. Sammi '19
Vice-Pres., Norman S. Hamilton '19
Secretary, Harry E. Peet '18
Manager, Frank C. Ransom '18

Spring Semester:
President, William A. Elliott '18
Vice-Pres., Leslie B. Simpson '20
Secretary, Eric H. Sargeant '18
Manager, Harry E. Peet '18

Director, Richard J. Carpenter

FIRST MANDOLINS

James R. Carpenter '18
Donald S. Deskey '19
William A. Elliott '18
Leslie B. Simpson '20
Dudley W. Steeves '19
Raymond L. Suppes '18
John C. Sammi '19

SECOND MANDOLINS

Charles B. Carkeek '18
Pryon F. Grimmer '17
Charles W. Jones '17
Wilber A. Green '20
Max M. Herrerias '20
Eric H. Sargeant '18
Dean G. Searls '20

GUITARS

Norman S. Hamilton '19
Albert J. Hodges '19
Harry E. Peet '18

MANDOLA

Frank C. Ransom '18

PIANO

Eldon B. Spofford '18

ASSOCIATE MEMBERSHIP

Emmet J. Allen '18
William Bigelow '18
Earl D. Davis '18
Arnold Poppic '19
Frank C. Ransom '18

Treble Clef

Officers—Fall Semester:
President, Elfrida Steindorff '17
Vice-President, Camille Abbay '17
Secretary, Evelyn Farrar '18
Treasurer, Hazel Hollingsworth '17

Spring Semester:
Elfrida Steindorff '17
Virginia Baldwin '18
Helen Smith '18
Hazel Hollingsworth '17

Executive Committee:
Helen Smith '18
Helen McGee '18
Hilda Johe '17

Executive Committee:
Margaret House '18
Elizabeth Elliott '17
Iuene Wylie '18

FIRST SOPRANOS

Lois Baker '17
Elizabeth Elliott '17
Hilda Johe '17
Alice Noble '17
Elfrida Steindorff '17
Alice Eastwood '18
Helen Smythe '18

Alpha Bonney '19
Helen Hambly '19
Lucille Nichols '19
Maude Ellis '19
Frances Blair '20
Gwen Howe '20
Dorothy Hanna '20

Frances McCullom '20
Ethel McMurchie '20
Lorene Mellon '20
Florence Cole '20
Constance Reston '20
Margaret Steiger '17

SECOND SOPRANOS

Sadie Fredericks '17
Hazel Hollingsworth '17
Virginia Baldwin '18
Reyna Berka '18

Margaret House '18
Camille Purdy '18
Helen Leithold '19
Dixie Ritchie '19

Marion Bailey '20
Narcissa Cerini '20
Leone Clark '20
Harriett Crabtree '20
Alice Madeley '20

FIRST ALTOS

Evelyn Farrar '18
Esther Ireland '18
Beatrice Winder '18

Dorothy Kirkland '19
Esther Sittig '19
Marguerite Templeton '19

Nydia Corcoran '20
Mildred Estabrook '20
Lela Ewert '20
Consuelo Julian '20

SECOND ALTOS

Gladys Wright '18
Geraldine Pratt '20

Margaret Seligman '19
Ruth Vincent '19

Maurine Gilliam '19
Helen Whiting '19

Women's Mandolin and Guitar Club

OFFICERS

PRESIDENT	Ruby Campbell '17
VICE-PRESIDENT	Genevieve Kilpatrick '18
SECRETARY	Lenore Doran '18
TREASURER	Lucille Parr '18
MANAGER	Camille Abbay '17
DIRECTOR	Professor R. J. Carpenter

FIRST MANDOLINS

Clara Gregory '19
Genevieve Kilpatrick '19
Lucille Parr '18
Ruby Campbell '17

SECOND MANDOLINS

Virginia Green '18
Dorothy Munro '19
Vera Van Kirk '20
Vera Chatfield '20
Flora Yesberg '20
May Campbell '20

BANJO

Camille Abbay '17

GUITARS

Ruth Mallock '16
Aileen Reynolds '20
Helen Whistler '20

CELLO

Ruth Persons '20

PIANO

Alice Clemo '20

Ukulele Club

Officers—First Semester:
President, Ruth Walker '18
Manager, Margaret Carter '19
Treasurer, Norene Howe '18

Second Semester:
Florence Denham '19
Vice-President, Norene Howe '18
Treasurer, Gayle Partridge '18
Manager, Gladys Basye '18

Gladys Basye '18
Beatrice Blanchard '20
Alpha Bonney '19
Lenora Clark '20
Lylia Dougherty '20
Louise Ellinger '18
Pearl Gisney '20
Katherine Green
Lois Harding '18
Bertha Haskett '17
Norene Howe '18
Irene Hund '17
Ruth Le Have '20

Mildred Kenworthy '19
Adele Leslaine '19
Mabel McGrath '19
Lorene Mellon '20
Ruth Monroe '16
Margaret Murdock '18
Lucile Nichols '19
Gayle Partridge '18
Constance Renton '20
Dorothy Shade '17
Mary Smith '20
Harriett Teter '20
Ada Thompson '18

Ruth Walker '18

HONOR SOCIETIES

HEARST MEMORIAL MINING BUILDING

HONOR SOCIETIES

Blaise Montana, Sister Brennan

Phi Beta Kappa

Founded at William and Mary College, Williamsburg, Va., in 1776.
Alpha of California—Established in 1898.

FACULTY

George Plimpton Adams
Robert Grant Aitken
Albert Henry Allen
James Turney Allen
Arthur Carl Alvarez
Annie Dale Biddle Andrews
Ernest Brown Babcock
Albert Lloyd Barrows
David Prescott Barrows
Louis Bartlett
Charles Barrows Bennett
Benjamin Abram Bernstein
Walter Charles Blasdale
George Henry Boke
Herbert Eugene Bolton
Cornelius Beach Bradley
Charles Edward Brooks
Harold Lawton Bruce
William Fitch Cheney, Jr.
Edward Bull Clapp
John Taggart Clark
Beatrice Quijada Cornish
William Walter Cort
Russell Tracy Crawford
Ira Brown Cross

Arnold Abraham D'Ancona
John Franklin Daniel
Charles Derleth, Jr.
Monroe Emanuel Deutsch
Adolphus James Eddy
Bernard Alfred Etcheverry
Herbert McLean Evans
Percival Bradshaw Fay
Isaac Flagg
Martin Charles Flaherty
Charles Mills Gayley
Walter Morris Hart
Mellen Woodman Haskell
Henry Rand Hatfield
Victor Hendricks Henderson
Joel Henry Hildebrand
Dennis Robert Hoagland
Samuel Jackson Holmes
John Galen Howard
Lincoln Hutchinson
Frank Irwin
Willis Linn Jepson
William Carey Jones
Eugene Jurgensen

Charles Atwood Kofoid
Alexis Frederick Lange
Joseph Nisbet LeConte
Derrick Norman Lehmer
Atughis Otto Leuschner
Exum Percival Lewis
Gilbert Newton Lewis
Ivan Mortimer Linforth
George Davis Louderback
David Townsend Mason
John Brenne McDonald
Orrin Kip McMurray
Henry Albright Mattill
William Augustus Merrill
Martin Abraham Meyer
Ralph Smith Minor
Herbert Charles Moffitt
Agnes Fay Morgan
Sylvanus Griswold Morley
William Alfred Morris
Bernard Moses
Charles Albert Noble
George Rapall Noyes
Herbert Chester Nutting

Leonard Outhwaite
Louis John Paetow
Jessica Blanche Peixotto
Torsten Peterson
Carl Copping Plehn
William James Raymond
Leon Joseph Richardson
Charles Henry Rieber
William Emerson Ritter
Charles Edward Rugh
Arthur William Ryder
Rudolph Schevill
Franz Schneider
Rorland Frederick Schols
William Albert Setchell
Charles C. Staehling
Henry Morse Stephens
George Malcolm Stratton
Francis Battelle Sumner
James Sutton
Chauncey Wetmore Wells
Benjamin Ide Wheeler
Arthur Robinson Williams
Rosalind Wulzen

GRADUATE STUDENTS

Constance B. Abbott
Phyllis Ackerman
Elda Olga Braccs
William Byron Brown
Margaret Buckham
Leslie Gale Burgevin
Asa Leonard Caulkins
Corinne Crouse
Pine Davidson

Jeanette Ralph Dyer
Elisabeth Janet Easton
Paul Longstreth Fussell
Helen Marian Goodall
Lloyd Nelson Hamilton
Kathleen Harnett
Robert Willard Hodgson
Maybelle Lena Hudson
Freda Rose Meyer

Sarah Elizabeth Olsen
Curtis Dion O'Sullivan
Oscar Charles Parkinson
Caroline Rehbuch
Alveeda Elva Roische
Esther Roth
Marie Ruth Salwiman
Jennie Altgeld Schwals
Charles Donald Slinne

Hiram Franklin Sheldon
William Ashley Sitton
James Wallace Spofford
Wilford Ebenezer Talbert
James Sturdevant Taylor
Matt Wahyhading
Selman Abraham Wakesman
Dorothy Wormser

SENIORS

Flossie Banks
Ina Weatherman Berthold
Harold Alfred Black
Frances Leslie Brown
Nancy Irena Brown
Barrett Nelson Coates
George Wesley Coffey
John Peter Conrad
Mildred Crane
Thomas Willard Dahlquist
Doris Alden Daniels

Jean Marjorie Deming
Octavia Thorne
Alice Bonnell Elliot
Frederick Monroe Essig
Elizabeth VanEverest Ferguson
Myrtle Viola Futchen
Gregory Alexander Harrison
Irene Estelle Hurley
Harold Anthony Hyde
Lucy Hoge Kuchlem

Gladys May Kraemer
Anita Duncan Latou
Doris Elizabeth McEntyre
Elise Jeanette McFarland
Ivander MacIver
George Lawrence Maxwell, Jr.
David Robert Merrill
Rosa Maria Pfund
Eugene Mitchell Prince
Bert Franklin Rabinowitz

Harry Boyd Seymour
John Laurence Seymour
Ruth Sherman
Harry Pratt Smith
Robert Lacy Smyth
Marian Shaw Stayner
Avery Tompkins
Elmer Horton Tucker
Ethel Pearl Walther
Frank Howard Wilcox

JUNIORS

Julia Wilson Cairs
Eleanor Kenyon Jennings

Ruth Raymond Lane

Leslie Bernard Schlingheyde Ray Vanderveenet

OFFICERS 1916-1917

President .... Charles Henry Rieber
1st Vice-President .... Charles Albert Noble
2nd Vice-President .... George Rapall Noyes
3rd Vice-President .... Orrin Kip McMurray
Secretary-Treasurer ...... Percival Bradshaw Fay

Counsellors
{ Lincoln Hutchinson
Charles Atwood Kofoid
Ivan Mortimer Linforth
Paul Longstreth Fussell
Curtis Dion O'Sullivan
David Robert Merrill

Golden Bear

Senior Honor Society—Organized in 1901.

HONORARY

Benjamin Ide Wheeler
John A. Britton

Arthur W. Foster
Hiram Warren Johnston
William Carey Jones

William W. Morrow
Chester H. Rowell

FACULTY

Clarence Linus Cory
Charles Derleth Jr.

Charles Mills Gayley
Henry Morse Stephens

Chauncey Wetmore Wells
Edward James Wickson

ALUMNI MEMBERS
(Associated with the University)

David Prescott Barrows
Monroe Emanuel Deutsch
Newton Bishop Drury
George Cunningham Edwards
Martin Charles Flaherty
Maurice Edward Harrison
Victor Hendricks Henderson
Alexander Marsden Kidd

Frank Louis Kleeberger
Karl C. Leebrick
Matthew Christopher Lynch
Orrin Kip McMurray
Charles W. Merrill
Ralph Palmer Merritt
James Kennedy Moffitt

Herbert Charles Moffitt
Thomas Milton Putnam
Harvey Roney
Francis William Rubke
Robert Gordon Sproul
John Allen Stroud
Oscar Sutro
James Sutton

GRADUATES

Samuel Adair
Elmer Granville Burland
Thomas Gossner Chamberlain
Paul Longstreth Fussell

Waldemar A. Falck
Howard W. Fleming
Lloyd Nelson Hamilton

Donovan Otto Peters
William Sears Rainey
Herman Adolph Spindt
John Boardman Whitton

SENIORS

Stephen Sears Barrows
Robert Blake
Raymond Karnaghan Bonta
John Robert Bruce
Charles Joseph Carey
Douglas Bray Cohen
George Washington Cohen
Albert Laurence Dunn
Daniel Parsons Foster

Edwin Lowell Garthwaite
James Benton Harvey
Henry Raymond Hogaboom
Harold Anthony Hyde
Le Roy Farnham Krusi
Travis Pollard Lane
Edwin Marshall Maslin
Willis Robert Montgomery
Claude Earn Monlux
Luther Allen Nichols

Warren Dexter Norton
Louis Hubbard Penney
Emery Herman Rogers
William Alexander Russell
Harry Boyd Seymour
Leroy Bassett Sharp
Floyd Wayne Stewart
John James Vandenburg
Willis Guy Witter

Winged Helmet
Junior Honor Society—Organized in 1901

FACULTY

Benjamin Ide Wheeler
James Turney Allen
Leonard Bacon
David Prescott Barrows
Walter Christie
Ben Mark Cherrington
Edward Bull Clapp
Herbert Ellsworth Cory

Newton Bishop Drury
James K. Fisk
Farnham P. Griffiths
Maurice Edward Harrison
Joel Henry Hildebrand
Charles Gilman Hyde
Arman Otto Leuschner
Matthew Christopher Lynch

Ralph Palmer Merritt
Thomas Milton Putnam
Leon Josiah Richardson
Richard Frederick Scholz
William Albert Setchell
Henry Morse Stephens
James Sutton
Charles Volz
Chauncey Wetmore Wells

GRADUATES

Samuel Adair
Elmer Granville Burland
Thomas Gassner Chamberlain
Randall Males Dorton
Victor Hugo Doyle

Archibald Munroe Edwards
Waldemar Adolph Falck
Herbert Edwin Hall
Lloyd Nelson Hamilton
Donovan Otto Peters

William Sears Rainey
Harvey Roney
Herman Adolph Spindt
Milton William Vedder
John Boardman Whitton

SENIORS

Stephen Sears Barrows
Robert Blake
Raymond Kanaghan Bouts
John Robert Bruce
Lewis Ryan Byington
Ernest Camper
James Somers Candee
Charles Joseph Carey
Douglas Bray Cedern
Albert Laurence Dunn

Edwin Madison Elam
Frank Thomas Elliot
Edwin Lowell Garthwaite
Ronald Dalzell Gibbs
Henry Raymond Hogaboom
LeRoy Farnham Krusi
Charles David Lane
Alfred Leo Maguire
Edwin Marshall Maslin

Willis Robert Montgomery
Luther Allen Nichols
Warren Dexter Norton
Louis Hubbard Penney
William Alexander Russell
Harry Boyd Seymour
Leroy Bassett Sharp
Floyd Wayne Stewart
John James Vandenburgh
John Stewart Weeks

JUNIORS

Russell White Bell
William Lee Bender
Hollis Mansfield Black
Fred Thomas Brooks
John Louis Cooley
George Magee Cunningham
Harold Edwin Dimock
Philip Albert Embury
Victor Lavenson Furth
Wynonah Bradbury Garthwaite
Fred Gray Giddens

Carleton Carlyle Gildersleeve
Charles Franklin Harper
George Marco Hicks
Grant James Hunt
Chester Leroy Isaacson
Harvey Maher Kilburn
Frank Lamb
Harry Bluett Liveredge
John O'Melveny
Russell Flavius Macdonald
Wilson Meyer
Pierce Works

John L. Reith
Claude Rohwer
Ray Rohwer
Lemuel Dalton Sanderson
Carroll Hutchinson Smith
Darwin Jackson Smith
William Hall Thomas
Max Weston Thornburg
Ray Vandevoort
Otis Wellborn III
Arthur Reid Wilson

Skull and Key
Organized in 1892

HONORARY

David Prescott Barrows
John Peter Buwalda
James Kenneth Fisk
Martin Charles Flaherty
Stanley Barron Freeborn
Lincoln Hutchinson

Matthew Christopher Lynch
Walter Edmund Magee
Edmond O'Neill
Carleton Hubbell Parker
Thomas Milton Putnam

Thomas Frederick Sanford
James Garfield Schaeffer
William Albert Setchell
George Arnold Smithson
Henry Morse Stephens
Benjamin Ide Wheeler

GRADUATES

James Townsend Barstow
Elmer Granville Burland

Thomas Gassner Chamberlain

Merritt Barton Curtis
Aloysius Ignatius Diepenbrock

SENIORS

Samuel Adair
Ben Alexander
George Washington Baker, Jr.
Leslie Hollis Brigham
Ernest Camper
James Somers Cauder
Warner Sabin Chadbourne
Douglas Bray Cohen
John Bradford Crow
Charles Stanley Dimm
Edwin Madison Flinn
Waldemar A. Falck

Theodore Randolph Finley, Jr.
Benjamin Blackwood Foster
Rudolph Leonard Gianelli
Lyman Dunlap Heacock
Frederic Fuller Janney
Charles David Lane
Travis Pollard Lane
Marshall Pierce Madison
Richard Ashe McLaren
Bradford Morse Melvin
Kenneth Monteagle
Willis Robin Montgomery
Willis Guy Witter

J. R. Murray, Jr.
Luther Allen Nichols
Henry Augustus Ruffo
Harry Hall Scheeline
Harry Boyd Seymour
Albert Carnahan Simonds
Floyd Wayne Stewart
Elmer Ellsworth Stone
Chester Benson Tonkin
John Stewart Weeks
Harry Kirk White
John Bandini Winston, Jr.

JUNIORS

Hollis Mansfield Black
Fred Thomas Brooks
Edward Porter Bruck
Fred Gray Gibbons
Charles Franklin Harper

William Knox Holt
Walter John Hulting
Grant James Hunt
Harry Bluett Liverselge
Russell Flavius Macdonald
George Washington Young

Merwin Louis McCabe
John O'Melveny
John L. Reith
Ray Rohwer
Pierce Works

Tau Beta Pi
[Technical and Scientific.]

Founded at Lehigh University in 1885.
California Chapter—Established in 1906.

FACULTY

Raymond Barrington Abbott
Arthur Carl Alvarez
Clarence Linus Cory
Elmer Fred Davis
Charles Derleth, Jr.
Adolphus James Eddy
Bernard Alfred Etcheverry
Harmon Francis Fisher

Francis Seeley Foote, Jr.
Ernest Albion Hersam
John Galen Howard
Charles Gilman Hyde
Andrew Cowper Lawson
Joseph Nisbet LeConte
George Davis Louderback
Baldwin Munger Woods

GRADUATE
Ephraim Field

SENIORS

Frank Cover Bell
Edwin Earle Blackie
Carroll Clark
George Wesley Coffey
Austin Robert Eimer
George Adair Fleming
Evans Ronald Foster
Hugh Nathan Herrick

Frank LeRoy Hill
Kenneth Ward Houston
Henry Temple Howard
Andrew Martin Jensen
LeRoy Farnham Krusi
Vsevolod Lankovsky
Harley Latson
William Leslie McCabe
Roy Starbird

John Ignatius McVey
Arthur Raymond May
Glenn Kendall Morrison
Samuel James Ogilvie
William Simon Peterson
Walter Ruppel
Augustus Victor Saph
Albert Henry Siemer

JUNIORS

Carl William Appleford
Frank Edwin Baxter
Bradley Belknap Brown

John Louis Cooley
Daniel McLean Duncan
Melvyn Lloyd Frandy
William Wilson Wurster

Arthur Worcester Kidder
Clarence John Nobmann
Loyal Walter Whitton

Alpha Zeta
[Agriculture]

Founded at the Ohio State University in 1897.
California Chapter—Established 1909.

FACULTY

Ernest Brown Babcock
Curtis P. Clausen
Roy Elwood Clausen
J. Eliot Coit
Bertram Hanford Crocheron
Jay Brownlee Davidson
Bernard Alfred Etcheverry
William Frederick Gericke
John Washington Gilmore
Clarence Melvin Haring
Arthur Howard Hendrickson
William Brodbeck Herms

William Titus Horne
Thomas Forsythe Hunt
Meyer Edward Jaffa
Charles Bernard Lipman
Robert Hills Loughridge
Robert Frederick Miller
David Naffziger
Walter Mulford
Walter Eugene Packard
William Robert Ralston
Henry Josef Quayle
Chester Linwood Roadhouse
W. W. Wobus

William Albert Setchell
Leslie Theodore Sharp
Charles Frederick Shaw
Ralph Eliot Smith
Thomas F. Tavernetti
Ralph Hawley Taylor
John Irwin Thompson
Gordon Haines True
Hubert Everett Van Norman
Edwin Coblentz Voorhies
Herbert John Webber
Edward James Wickson

GRADUATES

Paul Carle
Clarence V. Castle

Robert Willard Hudgson
Donald E. Martin
Harold A. Wadsworth

Knowles Augustus Ryerson
William L. Sweet

SENIORS

John Willis Adriance
George Donald Allin
John M. Coffeen
John P. Conrad
Frederick Carrington Corey
Sydney Harold Davidson
Harold Putnam Detwiler
Harry Everett Drobish
Arthur Folger
Ronald Dolizell Gibbs
William Alexander Graham

Ansel F. Hall
Kessler Gilbert Hammond
Paul James Hartley
Laurence Emerson Haseltine
Verne W. Hoffman
Louis William Jongeneel
William G. Kretsinger
Perry Eugene Lantz
Eugene Thomas Laugenour
Carrol Theodore Land
Roy Drummond McCallum

Millard Earl McCollam
William Alfred McCutchan
James McVicar Mills
Warren Dexter Norton
Raub Merrill Stafford
Frank Gile Tiffany
Ralph Mervin Walker
Fred Ernest Weidenmuller
Frank Wosel
Harold Evans Woodworth
Carol Willard Wright

JUNIORS

Clyde C. Barnum
Earl Murray Blair

Martin Richard Huberty
Guilford Fuller Meredith
Joseph Ellsworth Tippett

Laurence Wilson Taylor
William Carl Tesche

Phi Lambda Upsilon

[Chemistry]

Founded at the University of Illinois in 1899.
Mim Kaph Mim Chapter—Established in 1913.

FACULTY

Benjamin Ide Wheeler
Elliot Quincy Adams
William Lind Argo
Charles Barrows Bennett
Henry Chalmers Biddle
Walter Charles Blasdale
Edward Booth
Gerald Eyre Kirkwood Branch
William Vere Cruess
George Ernest Gibson
Reuben Simpkin Tour

Ernest Albion Hersam
Joel Henry Hildebrand
Myer Edward Jaffa
Frank Louis Kleeberger
Andrew Cowper Lawson
Gilbert Newton Lewis
George Davis Louderback
Edmond O'Neill
Merle Randall
Thorburn Brailsford Robertson

GRADUATES

Charles Stewart Bisson
Parry Borgstrom
Craig Miller Bouton
Thomas Bow Brighton
Asa Leonard Caulkins
Arthur W. Christie
Tenney Lombard Davis
Ernon Dwight Eastman
William Grenville Horsch
Donald Babcock Keyes

Julius Alexander Willi Lack
John Merritt McGee
Axel Ragnar Olson
George Sutton Parks
Worth Huff Rodebush
Charles Caeser Scalione
Ewing Carruth Scott
Yu Hwa Twan
Dean David Waynick
John T. Winkler

SENIORS

Angier Hobbs Foster
William Henry Hampton

Henry Theodore Hedgsson
David Robert Merrill

JUNIORS

John Whitney Elmore
Claude Williams Howse

Carl Iddings
Reginald Bryant Rule

Theta Tau

[Engineering]

Founded at University of Minnesota in 1904
Epsilon Chapter—Established in 1911

FACULTY

John Peter Buwalda
Elmer Fred Davis
Merwin Guy Edwards
Ernest Albion Hersam
George Davis Louderback
Lester Charles Uren

GRADUATES

Clifton Wirt Clark
Frank Samuel Hudson
Wm. Stephen Webster Kew
Charles Richardson Knox
Clarence Lemuel Moody
Roy Robert Morse
Chester Stock
Nicholas Lloyd Taliaferro
Francis Edward Vaughan

SENIORS

George Chesley Coffey
John Marshal Dento
Wright Ethelbert D'Evelyn
Arthur Raymond May
Samuel James Ogilvie
Karl Howard Schilling
Roy Starbird
Whitney Braymer Wright

JUNIORS

Joseph Tenison Deane
Philip Albert Embury

Beta Gamma Sigma
[Economics]
Organized in 1913

ASSOCIATE MEMBERS

David Prescott Barrows
Charles E. Brooks
Ira Brown Cross
Stuart Daggett
Newton Bishop Drury
John Franklin Forbes

Henry Rand Hatfield
Lincoln Hutchinson
Frederick Robertson Macaulay
Father T. H. O'Neill
Carl Copping Plehn
Charles C. Staehling

GRADUATE
Stanley Morris Arndt

SENIORS

Barrett Nelson Coates
Raymond Williams Crook
Charles Stanley Dimm
William McCalla Irvine
James Kenneth Lochead
Ferris S. Moulton
Hilmer Oehlmann

Prosper Reiter, Jr.
Nicholas James Scorsur
George Francis Taylor
William Hill Thomas
Elmer Hill Tucker
Howard Edward Webber
Claudius Nelson White

JUNIORS

Arthur Robert Bradford
Victor William Galvin

Sophus Carl Goth
Donald Hardy Packer

Prytanean
Organized in 1901

FACULTY

Edith J. Claypole
Maude Cleveland
Mary Blossom Davidson
Katherine Jewell Everts
Romilda Paroni

Mary F. Patterson
Jessica Blanche Peixotto
Aurelia H. Reinhardt
Ethel Sherman
Lucy Ward Stebbins

GRADUATES

Ruth Ransom Calden
Dorothy Crofts
Mariquita de Laguna
Lura Dell Dinsmore

Sarah Elizabeth Olsen
Caroline Louise Sheppa
Margaretha Pauline Suermondt
Dorothy Wormser

SENIORS

Anna Frances Barrows
Freda Cadell Bayley
Lelia Baldwin Berry
Harriett Louise Bowman
Frances Leslie Brown
Majorie S. Carlton
Anna Breckinridge Carter
Octavia Downie
M. Carol Eberts
Bertha Mabel Galloway
Ruth Marian Heynemann
Hazel Helen Hollingsworth

Louise Egerton Keen
Esther Laurilla King
Coe Elizabeth McCabe
Doris Elizabeth McEntyre
Alberta McNeely
Margaret Marchant
Maude Marion Meagher
Donna Moses
Elizabeth Mary Ruggles
Mary Jane Sanderson
Leslie Underhill
Imra Margaret Wann

Anne Radford Wharton

JUNIORS

Marian Brown
Vera Lillian Christie

Alice Dorothea de Wit
Esther Sinclair

Iota Sigma Phi
[Chemistry]
Organized in 1900.

HONORARY

Mrs. William Lind Argo
Mrs. Walter Charles Blasdale
Mrs. Edward Booth
Mrs. Gerald Eyre Branch
Mrs. William Crowell Bray
Mrs. Joel Henry Hildebrand
Mrs. Ruliff Stephen Holway
Mrs. Gilbert Newton Lewis

FACULTY

Kate Gompertz
Agnes Fay Morgan
Romilda Paroni
Ruth Risdon
May Searls

GRADUATES

Helen Czarnecki
Alice Duschak
Anna MacKenzie
Isita Girdler Morse
Vera Lynn Whipple
Leona Young

SENIORS

Doris Alden Daniels
Ellen Douglas
Esther Kittridge
Coe Elizabeth McCabe
Carey Dunlap Miller
Alice Eleanor Schlots
Imogene Willard

JUNIORS

Inno Pearl Baughman
Helen Emelyn Dana
Martha Fibush
Paula Schoenholz
Pearl Willson

ENGLISH CLUB

(Literary)
Organized in 1906.

HONORARY MEMBERS

James Turney Allen
William Dallam Armes
Leonard Bacon
Frederic Thomas Blanchard
Carlos Bransby
Warren Cheney
Herbert Ellsworth Cory
Robert Dupuncy
James Kenneth Fisk
Martin Charles Flaherty
Charles Mills Gayley
Charles S. Greene

Farnham Pond Griffiths
Walter Morris Hart
Victor Hendricks Henderson
Charles Keeler
Alexander Marsden Kidd
Benjamin Putnam Kurtz
J. B. Landfield
Alexis Frederick Lange
Orrin Kipp McMurray
George Rupert MacMinn
Lucy Sprague Mitchell
Eleanor Gates More

Arthur Upham Pope
William Popper
Arthur William Ryder
Millicent Shinn
George Arnold Smithson
Henry Morse Stephens
E. G. Stricklen
Mrs. H. B. Torrey
Richard Walton Tully
Charles Don von Neumayer
Earle A. Walcott
Chauncey Wetmore Wells

GRADUATES

Richard Henry Chamberlain
Deborah Dyer Calkins
Paul Longstreth Fussell

Herbert Edwin Hall
Roswell Gray Ham
Lloyd Nelson Hamilton

Donovan Otto Peters
William Sears Rainey
Harvey Roney

SENIORS

Anna Frances Barrows
Harold Alfred Black
Robert Blake
Roy Bower
John Robert Bruce

George Washington Cohen
Maud Carol Eberts
Alice Bunnell Elliot
Dorothy Epping
LeRoy Farnham Krusi

Edwin Marshall Maslin
Maude Marion Meagher
Harry Boyd Seymour
Norman Benjamin Stern
Frank Howard Wilcox

JUNIORS

Leslie Brown
Orville Robert Caldwell

Florence Isaacs
John L. Reith

Minnie Mae Sisson
Genevieve Taggard

Mask and Dagger
[Dramatics]
Organized in 1908

FACULTY
Roswell Gray Ham

GRADUATES
Richard Henry Chamberlain, Jr. William Sears Rainey
Claire Althea Tucker

SENIORS
Harold Alfred Black Alice Bunnell Elliot
Maud Carol Eberts Dorothy Wetmore

JUNIORS
Orville Robert Caldwell Minnie Mae Sisson

PRESS CLUB

[Journalism]
Organized in 1914.

HONORARY
David Prescott Barrows Victor Hendricks Henderson
Charles Henry Rieber

GRADUATES
Elmer Granville Burland Lloyd Nelson Hamilton

SENIORS
Robert Blake Edwin Madison Elam
Raymond Karnaghan Bontz Edwin Marshall Maslin
John Robert Bruce Ferris S. Moulton
Charles Joseph Carey Harry Boyd Seymour
Norman Benjamin Stern

JUNIORS
Walter Budd Champlin John O'Melveny
George Magee Cunningham John L. Reith
Victor Lavenson Furth Olin Wellborn III
Anthony Laurence Mitchell Arthur Reihl Wilson

'Η ΣΦΙΓΣ

Sphinx
[Philosophical]

Organized in 1911.

FACULTY

George Plimpton Adams
Leonard Bacon
Albert Lloyd Barrows
Harold L. Bruce
Herbert Ellsworth Cory
Ira Brown Cross

Newton Bishop Drury
Roswell Gray Ham
Richard Frederick Scholz
Charles Louis Seeger
Arthur Upham Pope
Chauncey Wetmore Wells

GRADUATES

Adolph Edmund Anderson
Chandler Parks Barton
Leslie Gale Burgevin
Ben Mark Cherrington

George Winthrop Fish
Sidney David Gamble
Curtis Dion O'Sullivan
John Boardman Whitton

SENIORS

Stephen Sears Barrows
Raymond Karnaghan Bentz
John Robert Bruce
Charles Josef Carey
George Washington Cohen
Robert Campbell Clark
Gregory Alexander Harrison
George Henry Hotaling
Harold Anthony Hyde

Edwin Marshall Muslin
Ferris S. Moulton
Warren Lee Pierson
Harry Boyd Seymour
David Stoddart Shattuck
Gordon Fitzhugh Stephens
Norman Benjamin Stern
Marshall Taylor
Frank Howard Wilcox

JUNIORS

Philip Strong Mathews
John O'Melveny

John L. Reith
Max Weston Thornburg

Phrontisterion
(History)

Organized in 1915.

HONORARY MEMBER
Benjamin Ide Wheeler

ASSOCIATE MEMBERS
The Faculty of the History Department

GRADUATES

Charles Wilson Hackett	Curtis Dion O'Sullivan
Herbert Edwin Hall	William Henry Poytress
Karl Clayton Leebrick	Francis William Rubke
John Lloyd Mecham	Joseph Marius Scammel
Charles Solomon Mitrani	Herman Adolph Spindt

Arthur Pryer Watts

SENIORS

Robert Blake	Warren Lee Pierson
George Henry Hotaling	Eugene Mitchell Prince
Harold Anthony Hyde	Robert Lacy Smyth

JUNIORS

John O'Melveny	Joseph Louis Zimmerman

Beta Beta
Organized in 1914.

GRADUATES

Samuel Adair
George Washington Baker, Jr.
James Clark Bequette
Darrell Joseph Bogardus
Leslie Hollis Brigham
John Stewart Brown
Merritt Barton Curtis
Thomas Snell Dinsmore
William J. Duddleson
James Kenneth Fiske
Rudolph Leonard Ginnelli
Richard Morris Lyman, Jr.
William Sears Rainey
Charles Edward Street, Jr.

SENIORS

Ben Alexander
Stephen Sears Barrows
Charles Houghton Bayley
Edward Duerdin Bronson
Lewis Ryan Byington
Ernest Camper
James Somers Candee
Clifford Bert Cole
Fred Edward Delger
Charles Stanley Dinan
Albert Laurence Dunn
Edwin Madison Flom, Jr.
Frank Thomas Elliott
Theodore Randolph Finley, Jr.
Benjamin Blackwood Foster
Raynor Eugene Gimbal
Lloyd William Goeppert
Frederic Fuller Janney
Laurence Frederick Knauer
Charles Richardson Knox
Charles David Lane
George Moore Lindsay
Alfred Leo Maguire
Luther Allen Nichols
Emery Herman Rogers
Henry Augusto Ruffo
Harry Hall Schesline
Hugh Fenimore Shippey
Albert Carnahan Simonds
Floyd Wayne Stewart
James Herbert Tietzen
Chester Benson Tonkin
John Stewart Weeks
Willie Coy Witter

U. N. X.
Organized 1911.

HONORARY

James Kenneth Fiske
Stanley B. Freeborn

Matthew Christopher Lynch
Andrew L. Smith
Carl Zamlock

George Arnold Smithson
Charles R. Volz

GRADUATES

Guy Webb Adriance
James Townsend Barstow

Chandler Parks Barton
Merritt Barton Curtis
Nicholas Lloyd Taliaferro

Aloysius Ignatius Diepenbrock
Henry Chapman Dodge

SENIORS

Samuel Adair
Harry Vaughn Adams
Benjamin Alexander
Henry Bruce Barkis, Jr.
William Henry Bingaman
Lewis Ryan Byington
Ernest B. Camper
James Somers Candee
Warner Sabin Chadbourne
Charles Lester Clark
Douglas Bray Cohen
Clifford Bert Cole
John Bradford Crow
John Marshall Denbo

Charles Stanley Diman
Waldemar A. Falck
Theodore Randolph Finley, Jr.
George Winthrop Fish
Benjamin Blackwood Foster
Lester Albert Fowler
Rudolph Leonard Gianelli
Robert Leroy Graves
Andrew McDonald Hazzard
Frederick Sidney Jones
Charles Richardson Knox
Charles David Lane
Richard Ashe McLaren

Marshall Pierce Madison
Alfred Leo Maguire
Willis Robert Montgomery
Floyd Erle Onyett
James Brayton Philbrook
Emery Herman Rogers
Henry Augusto Ruffo
William Alexander Russell
Manley William Sahlberg
Harry Hall Scheeline
Harry Boyd Seymour
James Herbert Tietzen
John Stewart Weeks
Willis Gay Witter

JUNIORS

Charles Houghton Bayly
Thomas Mardenbro Benson
Nicholas Kittle Boyd
Robert Alston Brant
Edward Porter Brock
Fred Thomas Brooks
John O'Neil Ciprico
Thomas Arthur Gabbert

Charles Franklin Harper
William Knox Holt
Walter John Helting
Grant James Hunt
Harry Bluett Liversedge
Mervyn Louis McCabe
Paul Wilbur Masters
John O'Melveny

Marshall William Paxton
John L. Reith
Elmore Williams Roberts
Albert Dunnedin Shaw
Benjamin Kendrick Vaughan
Morrell Emerie Vecki
Arthur Reihl Wilson
George Washington Young

Betta Kappa Alpha
(Biology)

Organized 1911.

FACULTY

Ernest Babcock Babcock
Albert Lloyd Barrows
Harold C. Bryant
Theodore Cecil Burnett
John Peter Buwalda
Bruce Lawrence Clark
Roy Elwood Clausen
George Washington Corner
William W. Cort
Ruby Lacy Cunningham
John Frank Daniel
Edward Oliver Essig

Herbert McLean Evans
Stanley Barron Freeborn
Frederick Parker Gay
Thomas Harper Goodspeed
Harley N. Gould
Grace Florence Griffiths
Joseph Grinnell
Ivan C. Hall
William Brodbeck Herms
Samuel Jackson Holmes
Charles Atwood Kofoid
Joseph Abraham Long

Samuel Stern Maxwell
John Campbell Merriam
Robert Orton Moody
Thoburn Bradford Robertson
Katherine J. Scott
H. H. P. Severin
Philip Edward Smith
Ralph Elliot Smith
Olive Swezy
Edwin Cooper Van Dyke
Charles William Woodruff
Rosalind Wulzen

GRADUATES

Dorothy Atkinson
Margaret Isabel Beattie
Robert W. Berkley
William Charles Boeck
Dolores Elizabeth Bradley
Edwin Linus Bruck
Etta May Conkie
Pirie Davidson
A. Dunter Drew
Charles Clarke Hall
Homer H. Hitchcock
Robert Willard Hodgson
John Henry Burns
John Norman Kendall
William Stephen Webster Kew

Charles Edward Locke, Jr.
Frederic G. Maggs
Robert Carson Martin
John G. McQuarrie
Isaac Borden McRoberts
Swarns Kumer Mitra
Freda Meyer
Clarence Moody
Lilian Moore
Lois Pendleton
Robert Larimore Pendleton
Sidney Olsen
Elizabeth Heald Purington
Ralph Rolonowsta
Alverda Elva Rouche

Robert C. Rhodes
Homer Roberts
Cecil Rowe
Carl L. A. Schmidt
George Embry Shunji
Harry Pratt Smith
Ida May Stevens
Chester Stock
Tracy Irwin Storer
Noble McMurray Stover
Charles Vincent Taylor
Theodore H. Taylor
Frances Amelia Torrey
Dean David Waymack
LeGrand Wesley
Harry Barclay Yocum

SENIORS

Leland Morrison Bell
Coleman C. Bestwick
Morrison Hugo Childress
Granville Sinclair Delamere
Elizabeth Ferguson

Daniel Parsons Foster
Dolores Gibson
Hubbard Spencer Hoyt
George Ira

Armistead C. Leigh, Jr.
William Henry Stalder
Homer Sussdorf
Pearl Walther
Arthur La Mayette Warren

JUNIORS

Nelson Caryl Davis
Winnifred Eldred

Lillian M. Jordan
Eschscholtzia Lichthardt

Monroe Sutter
Pierre Jaques Walker

Epsilon Alpha
[Dentistry]

Organized in 1916

FACULTY

Frank C. Bettencourt
Henry Benjamin Carey
Harold C. Kausen
Benjamin F. Loveall

Edwin Henry Mauk
Harry J. Mathieu
Guy Stillman Millberry
James Graham Sharp

William Fuller Sharp
Francis Vance Simonton
George W. Simonton
Frederick Wolfsohn

GRADUATES

T. C. Bender
Leslie R. Cesloni
Fayne L. Hill

John E. Kennedy
Conrad C. Kohmler
John A. Marshall
Thomas R. Sweet

George J. Rau
Allen E. Scott
Walter S. Smith

SENIORS

John Oliver Armistead
Eddy Tallman Bender
Ralph Perry Chessall
Carl Nichols Dorman
F. Clifton Elzea

Renwick William Genley
James Raymond Griffiths
Charles Dudley Guinn
Howard Milne Johnston

Charles Schiller Lipp
Adrian Lewis Morin
Percy Ansley Steeves
Homer Clinton Tollefson
John Wakefield

JUNIORS

Elmer Holmes Berryman
Ward Glenn Cadwallader
Charles Westley Craig
James Stewart Craig

Paul Ehorn
Francis Wayland Epley
William Howard Huskins

Otto Richard Jungerman
Philip Thomas Lynch
Leon Westley Marshall
Carl Paul Rapp

Delta Epsilon

[Art Honor Society for Women]

Organized in 1914.

HONORARY

Mary F. Patterson
Grace Y. Weeks
Gertrude E. Comfort
Olympia Goldarceena

GRADUATES

Alice Gertrude Plummer
Jean Myrtle Williamson
Caroline Louise Sheppa
Dorothy Wormser
Marguerite Cordell

SENIORS

Cleo Theodora Damianakes
Simone Martha Brangier
Dorothy Epping
Martha Jensen

JUNIOR

Jessie-Lee Fairfax Decker

SOPHOMORE

Flora Lucie Rouleau

FRESHMEN

Edna Sawyer McGill
Ruth Ethel Wetmore

Sigma Kappa Alpha
[History Honor Society for Women]
Organized in 1915.

HONORARY

Mrs. William Alfred Morris
Jessica Blanche Piexotto
Mrs. Richard Frederick Scholz

Henry Morse Stephens
Mrs. Benjamin Ide Wheeler
Mary Floyd Williams

ASSOCIATE

Helen Marian Goodall

Helen Hathaway

Anita Moffett

GRADUATES

Ruth Ransom Calden

Kathleen Harnett

Olive Kuntz

SENIORS

Barbara Burke
Mary Fundenberg

Frances Caroline Lowell
Florence Mary Macaulay

JUNIORS

Alice Irene Baucom
Doris West Bepler
Vera Bullwinkel

Marjorie Clothilde La Grave
Eva Smith Pressley
Marion L. Underwood

Nu Sigma Psi
(Physical Education)

Organized in 1916.

HONORARY

Marjorie John Armour
Maude Cleveland
Ruth Elliott

Signe E. Hagelthorn
Mildred Lemon
Edna Lee Roof

GRADUATE
Mabel Anne Council

SENIORS

Mildred Adams
Ruth Emma Goodsell

Alberta McNeely
Helen Emma Rosenberg

Margaret Anne McDermed

JUNIORS

Marion Avery
Mary Alice Barnes
Elinor Benedick
Doris West Bepler
Louise Mortimer Chandler
Doris Dee Cooper
Freddie Alice Cowan
Ethel Blanche Craig
Dorothy Flynn
Elinor Durbrow
Mira Mae Foster
Ruth Ada Gardner

Daphne Esko Gerry
Edith Rodgers Harshberger
Marguerite Johnson
Claire Marie Johnston
Ida Muller
Helen Janet Nutting
Marian Tuber Sanderson
Emma Skaale
Marion Elizabeth Tiffany
Helen Barton Smyth
Edith Ueland
Helen Lucile Wirt

SOPHOMORES

Elizabeth Beall
Jessie Caroline Boies
Helen Gertrude Halliday
Hazel Pearl Neely
Dorothy Cornelia Riedy

Doris Margaret Sherman
Helen Ward Spencer
Grace Cotes Stearns
Carolyn Steel
Portia Faye Wagenet

Eta Kappa Nu
[Electrical Engineering]
Organized in 1915.

FACULTY

Clarence Linus Cory
George Lothaine Greves
Frederick Eugene Pernot
Baldwin Munger Woods

GRADUATE
Alfred Nigel D'Oyly

SENIORS

Frank Couver Bell
Russell Dolman Berst
Willard Franklin Burke
Carl Torrey Dixon
Stephen E. Dunn
H. Syril Dusenbery
George Adair Fleming
Nathan Hugh Herrick
Kenneth Ward Houston
Warren Runyon Kemper
Ralph Waldo Linge
William Leslie McCabe
Glenn Kendall Morrison
William Simon Peterson
Thompson Price
Samson H. Rosenblatt

Arthur J. Swank

JUNIORS

Bradley Belknap Brown
Harold Edwin Fielder
Charles Wiles Robbins

Torch and Shield
Founded in 1907 — Re-organized in 1915.

GRADUATE
Grace Van Dyke Bird

SENIORS

Frances Leslie Brown
Maud Carol Eberts
Esther Laurilla King
Coe Elizabeth McCabe

Algeline Marlow
Dorothy Elizabeth Wetmore
Anne Redford Wharton
Elizabeth Louise Witter

JUNIORS

Leslie Brown

Margaret Eddy House

Madeline Ann Muldoon

Economics Club
Organized in 1917.

FACULTY

Mrs. Ira B. Cross

Miss Lucy Ward Stebbins

GRADUATES

Dulce de la Cuesta

Lura Dell Dinsmore

Margaretha Pauline Suermondt

SENIORS

Helen Trexler Baer
Emily Harriet Huntington
Leona Jones
Grace Eleanor Kimble

Donna Moses
Rosalinda Amelia Olcese
Mary Jane Sanderson
Ruth Allison Turner

Gertrude Lucy Young

JUNIORS

Marian Lovina Chandler
Alice Dorothea de Wit

Mrs. W. French
Edith Craig Owen

Alice Sheridan Towle

Alpha Nu
[Nutrition]

Organized in 1916.

FACULTY

Josephine E. Davis
Agnes F. Morgan

GRADUATES

Ilma Lotta Badgley
Edith Louisa Brown
Dorothy Ede Bulson
Jean Whitcher Christie
Anna Field
Nellie Adele Hermle
Alice Helen Metcalf
Agnes Sophia Pearson
Pearl Pemberton
Vera Lynn Whipple

SENIORS

Carlotta Beshlitch
Doris Alden Daniels
Mildred Jessup
Norah McKenzie
Carey Dunlap Miller
Erminie Ursula Sala
Gertrude Nancy Whitton

Istyc
[Women's Journalistic Honor Society]

Organized in 1916.

GRADUATES

Grace Van Dyke Bird
Caroline Louise Sheppa

SENIORS

Anna Frances Barrows
Frances Leslie Brown
Maud Carol Eberts
Dorothy Epping
Esther Kittredge
Algeline Marlow
Elsie Catherine McCormick
Anne Radford Wharton

JUNIORS

Leslie Brown
Muriel Margaret Cameron
Margaret Wilson Honeywell
Bernice Hubbard
Madeline Ann Muldoon
Dorothy Stoner
Genevieve Taggard
Gladys Mary Windham

Sigma Iota Phi
(Civil Engineering)

Organized in 1912.

FACULTY

Charles Derleth, Jr.
Adolphus James Eddy
Charles Gilman Hyde
Bernard Alfred Etcheverry
Francis Seeley Foote, Jr.

SENIORS

Austin Robert Cimer
Andrew Martin Jensen
LeRoy Farnham Krusi
Floyd Theall McKune
Robert Lawrence Ryan
Augustus Victor Saph
John James Vandenburgh
John Stewart Weeks

JUNIORS

George Magee Cunningham
Arthur Worcester Kidder
John Walter Oakley
Max Weston Thornburg

Dyslyt
(Women's Literary)

Organized in 1916.

GRADUATES

Helen Lucile Henry
Elizabeth Hoyt
Clara Estelle Mortenson
Frances Hamrick Wilson
May Sarah Preuss
Hazel Odette Thompson
Jean O. Watson

SENIORS

Frances Leslie Brown
Ruth Frances Horel
Anne Radford Wharton
Algeline Marlow
Sepha Dohrmann Pischel

JUNIORS

Lillian Thekla Stephany
Genevieve Taggard

ATHLETICS

The Campus
Mount Tamalpais in the Distance

ATHLETICS

*The Games,
Most Dangerous to the Players.*

FOOTBALL

FOOTBALL

CAPTAIN MONTGOMERY   CAPTAIN-ELECT BROOKS

Preliminary Season

EIGHTY-FIVE CANDIDATES for the California Varsity football team reported for the season of 1916 when Coach Andy Smith sounded the first call on September 1. While the majority of the men had one year's experience in the American game, they were still lacking in a knowledge of the essential rudiments of the code and were devoid of that "football instinct" which comes to players only after years of long and patient practice. So the task that confronted the coaching staff at the beginning of the season was to first ground the recruits in the fundamentals of the American game and then teach the Varsity squad technical and scientific football and the intricate and complicated plays.

California entered the season better equipped in the coaching department than ever before. From all parts of the East the best coaches had been gathered during the summer to whip the Varsity into shape. Andy Smith, former head coach at Purdue, had been selected the previous spring to take charge of the California Varsity. With his colleague, Pete Vaughn

ANDY SMITH HEAD COACH

also of Purdue, he held spring practice and drilled a squad of sixty men in tackling and blocking. But when the season opened in the fall Vaughn was on the Mexican border as a lieutenant in the Illinois National Guard, and A. B. Ziegler, line coach at Pennsylvania State, was selected to take charge of the linemen. Ziegler was for four years a Varsity lineman and the last two years of his undergraduate days he was chosen as All-American guard. Eddie Mahan, captain of the Harvard eleven in 1915 and All-American fullback for four years, was chosen as backfield coach. Ben Cherrington, former University of Nebraska player, was appointed to coach the Reserves.

Coach Smith laid out a strenuous campaign of work for the squad. He was found to be a tireless worker, an exacting master and a man of system. He insisted that no football play was perfect until every man in the opposition was accounted for and unless he had a man on his own team who was always free to dispose of a loose opponent.

A. B. ZIEGLER — LINE COACH

A great deal of new equipment was purchased and many improvements made on California Field for the convenience of the squad. Two gridirons were laid out and three tackling dummies put up. The season's work started with practice in tackling the dummy and in blocking. The linemen and the backs were immediately segregated and put in charge of Ziegler and Mahan, while Coach Smith took general oversight of the entire squad.

After a week of preliminary training to work the soreness out of their muscles, the squad was divided into Varsity and Reserves and a number of scrimmages were held between these two teams before the Varsity was given competition by an outside eleven. Never before in the history of football at California had a squad been worked so hard. Every afternoon from 4 o'clock until 7 o'clock the coaches drilled the men. California Field was lighted with seventeen large incandescent lamps, which made it possible to practice long after sundown with the whitewashed "ghost ball."

The Varsity went on the training table on October 7, six weeks before the Washington game — the longest training table period in the history of athletics in the university. From a large number of fraternity and club houses offered, the Zeta Psi and Phi Gamma Delta houses were chosen. The first three weeks were spent at the Zeta Psi house and the remainder of the season at Phi Gamma Delta.

Coach Smith had advised the long period on the training table in order to have an opportunity to keep the men together for the purpose of teaching them scientific football. The task of keeping the men from going stale under the strain of the long season was a hard one. Numerous remedies were tried for this. Sudden changes in schedule were sprung and entertainers were brought in after dinner. One afternoon the entire squad was loaded into a "rubberneck" touring car and taken to a suburban lot near Richmond where they held signal practice.

The schedule for the season marked a new era in California's athletic relations. Besides the usual games with the athletic club teams from Oakland and San Francisco, three new teams— Oregon, Whittier and Occidental—were pitted against the Varsity for the first time.

EDDIE MAHAN - BACKFIELD COACH

Eleven games were played during the season. Six were won, four lost and one tied. Of the nine games played during the preliminary season California won seven and lost two. In only one, the Oregon defeat, was California outplayed, as the Occidental game was lost at the last minute through carelessness and poor field generalship.

The season was opened on September 16 with a victory over the Olympic Club eleven by a score of 23 to 0. The minute the ball was snapped from center to the quarterback for the first time, it was apparent that the Varsity was one hundred per cent better than last season. Coach Smith did not have his men use any fancy football. It was plain, determined line plunging that won the game. Brooks made two touchdowns and Wells one, Montgomery kicking two of the goals. Graf made

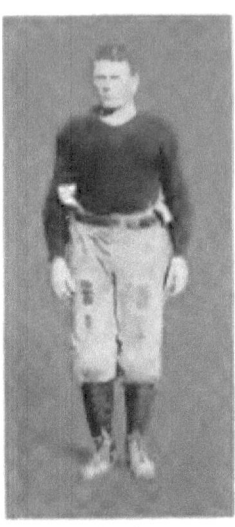

BELL—GUARD

one field goal. The poor condition of the club men aided the Varisty in piling up a big score.

The following week the Oakland Originals were defeated by a score of 23 to 0. The Varsity showed a big improvement in line smashing and in handling the forward double pass successfully. In the first quarter Montgomery scored three points by a field goal. No scores were made in the second quarter, but in the third Brooks and Sharp each went across the line. Montgomery kicked one of the goals. The last touchdown was made by Wells in the fourth quarter.

On September 30 the Olympic Club players staged a come-back while the Varsity took a slump and neither team was able to score a single point. A wet and muddy field precluded the possibility of any open field play and straight football of necessity predominated. As a result punting was resorted to quite frequently, Brooks and Daly furnishing a pretty exhibition of kicking which was the principal feature of the game.

COFFEN—END

In the final contest against a club team the Varsity defeated the Oakland Originals, on October 7, by a score of 13 to 0. Sharp was the stellar performer of the day, making both touchdowns and several long runs. One of the most spectacular plays seen during the preliminary season was when Sharp received a kick-off on California's fifteen-yard line and ran eighty-three yards through a broken field, being downed only on the two-yard line. Both touchdowns were made the first quarter. Montgomery kicked one of the goals.

COFFEN—END

California 21   Whittier 17

Whittier opened the college season against the Varsity in the most sensational pre-season game seen on California Field. The brilliant forward passing of the visitors and the dogged, determined play of the Blue and Gold featured the game. Whittier scored eleven points on a field goal and a touchdown in the first half. Touchdowns were made for California by Wells and Foster. Montgomery kicking both goals. A fifty-yard run gave Whittier another touchdown in the second half. California was on the short end of the score until three minutes before the end of the game when Fred Brooks intercepted a forward pass and ran twenty-five yards to a touchdown. Montgomery kicked the goal and changed a 17 to 14 defeat into a 21 to 17 victory.

GIMBAL—QUARTERBACK

FOSTER—FULLBACK

California 14   Oregon 39

The Varsity suffered its first defeat of the season on October 21 at the hands of the veteran University of Oregon eleven by a score of 39 to 14. Oregon played its shifting, smashing game, while California relied on short, snappy forward passes and trick plays to gain ground. It was the first time during the season that California had been pitted against an experienced eleven. The Varsity showed its real strength and played the best game of the season to date, but was beaten by a more experienced and better team.

California made the first touchdown on short forward passes from Brooks to Sharp and line

CONGDON—GUARD

plunging by Brooks and Wells. Wells went over the line and Montgomery kicked the goal. Oregon scored one touchdown in each of the first, second and fourth quarters and two in the third. California made its second touchdown in the fourth quarter. Oregon was penalized thirty yards, which put the ball on its one-yard line. From there Wells bucked it over and Montgomery kicked the goal.

California 13   Occidental 14

Costly errors in generalship and loose play on the part of the Varsity lost the second successive game to Occidental College by a score of 14 to 13. Forward passes and line bucks by Brooks, Foster and Sharp resulted in a touchdown for California the first quarter. Gimbal dropped the kickout from Sharp and the opportunity to try for the goal was lost. Occidental took the lead a few minutes later when Perkins intercepted a forward pass and ran to a touchdown. In the second quarter Brooks scored another touchdown and Montgomery kicked the goal. Then California's heretofore invincible line crumbled and the visitors marched the entire length of the field to the one-yard line. California fought desperately, but on the fourth down the ball was over and a few seconds later the goal was kicked that won the game.

This defeat undoubtedly did the California players more good than if they had won, for it taught them the consequences of carelessness and how easily a victory may be turned into defeat,

GORDON—TACKLE

HICKS—QUARTERBACK

JOHNSON—TACKLE

California 27   U. S. C. 0

The Varsity showed its true form in the next game when it hammered the University of Southern California eleven into submission by a score of 27 to 0 on the Los Angeles gridiron. California was slow to get started, the first half ending without a score; but in the second half the Blue and Gold opened with a terrific attack, scoring one touchdown in the third quarter and three in the fourth. Foster bucked the ball over the first time, and Sharp, Wells and Maguire followed in succession. Montgomery kicked three out of the four goals. Captain Montgomery responded in fine form.

LANE HALFBACK

LEGGETT—END

California 48   St. Mary's 6

In the last preliminary game of the season the Varsity defeated St. Mary's by a score of 48 to 6. After the first half only second-string men were used by Coach Smith. The Oakland collegians were helpless and the Blue and Gold scored almost at will.

California unloosed a variety of plays which completely bewildered the inexperienced St. Mary's players. It was distinctly a practice game, the Varsity running through its signals with a finished speed and precision. The "end around" runs of Cohen who came out of the line and took the ball from the quarter, were the features of the game. In the first quarter touchdowns were made by Cohen and Brooks, Montgomery kicking both goals. Another touchdown

LIVERSEDGE—GUARD

was made by Brooks in the second quarter. In the third quarter one touchdown was made by Cohen, and Montgomery fell on a blocked kick for another. Montgomery kicked both goals. In the final quarter Foster made one touchdown, Montgomery kicking the goal and Graf made another, Wells kicking the goal. Olsen scored St. Mary's only points in the same period.

First Washington Game

A sun of burnished gold sinking before the bronzed Berkeley hills cast a purple glow over California Field. The shimmering green carpet, gridironed with white battle-scarred bars where the sons of Washington and California had just ended their struggle for glory and the upholding of collegiate tradition, caressed the serried ranks of some sixteen thousand standing spectators massed in the great bleachers reaching up on all sides, who had come to see the supreme athletic struggle of the West, and rested significantly on the big black scoreboard at the south end of the picture where hung the figures, Washington 13, California 3.

There never was a brighter, snappier, more ideal football day. Fleecy, white clouds scudded overhead, while an autumn sun took just enough chill out of the air to make wraps unnecessary. And it was one of the greatest Big Games that ever thrilled the red heart of fan. From the drab and unemotional affair of the year before it emerged with all its radiance to twang the throat till the heart tightened and send the

MADISON—TACKLE

MAGUIRE—HALFBACK

McCULLOUGH—TACKLE

ripples and quivers down one's spine. The spirit, the glamour, the clutch returned with all its vigor and held the crowd with gripping uncertainty till the very end.

And grim was the battle and great were the feats thereof! During the entire contest the Blue and Gold rooting section was hopeful that Washington's string of victories would be broken. But with the lowering sun a shadow crept across the field from the Washington side on the west. It was a portentous shadow, and, as with the succeeding periods of play, it moved slowly but surely toward the eastern side, hope died in the hearts of the Californians massed there, and the Purple flush of victory mounted higher and higher.

PAXTON—TACKLE

MOXLEY—GUARD

But it was not until the final gun that the Varsity or the rooters gave up hope, for California always had a chance to win. It was an even struggle, far more evenly disputed than the 13 to 3 score would indicate. The Varsity waged a bitter fight before it conceded victory to the visitors. The men played with every ounce of energy they possessed and bowed only to Experience as their master.

Washington played straight, hard football, and attempted only one forward pass. On the other hand California made its gains on sensational forward passes and a great variety of trick plays, which brought the bleachers to their feet time and again. The Varsity's defense was a revelation. A new formation, which brought the backs in the form of a hollow square directly behind the

RUSSELL—CENTER

SEWELL—TACKLE

SHARP—HALFBACK

WELLS—FULLBACK

first line of defense, proved to be a severe stumbling block for the smashing Northmen. Washington's line held slightly better than did California's. On the other hand, Brooks had the edge on Morrison in punting. Washington scored two touchdowns from one of which a goal was kicked. California made its points from a field goal kicked from a difficult angle by Captain Montgomery.

It was 2:33 o'clock when the game started. Washington won the toss and chose to defend the south goal. Fred Brooks adjusted the ball on the little mound in the middle of the field, stepped back and waited. Captain Montgomery and Captain Seagrave answered referee Varnell's call of "ready," the Blue and Gold charged down the field under Brooks' long, high kick, and the game was on. Hainsworth took the ball on his own ten-yard line and ran it back to California's twenty-five yard line. It was Washington's ball.

Then came the tensest moment of the game. Johnson, the Purple and Gold quarter, spoke a few words to his backs and then began to snap the signals. Could the California line h o l d? The question was in the mind of every spectator who remembered the 72 to 0 score of the year before when Washington never failed to make its yards. The teams lined up; the ball was snapped from center directly into the waiting hands of "Cy" Noble, veteran of four seasons and kingpin of the Washington team. The six-feet-three of bone and sinew hurled himself against right tackle. Not an inch was gained. The line held!

WHITE TACKLE

			American		
Year	S.	C.	Captain	Manager	Head Coach
1892	14	10	Foulks	Gallagher	None
1892	10	10	Hunt	Brann	McClung
1893	6	6	Benson	Deaman	Heffelfinger
1894	6	0	Benson	Lang	Heffelfinger
1895	6	6	Sherman	Lang	Butterworth
1896	20	0	Ransome	Rheinhart	Butterworth
1897	28	0	Hall	Brown	Nott
1898	0	22	Hall	Brown	Cochran
1899	0	30	Whipple	Muma	Cochran
1900	5	0	Pringle	Hutcheson	Kelly
1901	0	2	Womble	Drento	Simpson
1902	0	16	Albertson	Drento	Whipple
1903	6	6	Overall	Drento	Whipple
1904	18	0	H. Stroud	Drento	Hopper
1905	12	5	Force	Drento	Nobles
			Rugby		
1906	6	3	Hadry	Snedigar	Taylor
1907	24	11	Toller	Snedigar	Taylor
1908	12	3	Butler	Merritt	Taylor
1909	13	10	Cerf	Merritt	Schaeffer
1910	6	25	Deggins	Farmer	Schaeffer
1911	3	21	Elliott	Farmer	Schaeffer
1912	3	3	J. Stroud	Donald	Schaeffer
1913	13	8	Pearl	Donald	Schaeffer
1914	26	8	McKim	Stroud	Schaeffer
			American		
Year	W.	C.	Captain	Manager	Head Coach
1915	72	0	Canfield	Stroud	Schaeffer
	13	7			
1916	13	3	Montgomery	Stroud	Smith
	19	7			

Twice more did the smashing Washington backs try to make gains, and when on the third down the ball was still on the twenty-five-yard line Morrison was forced to punt.

California's first play was an attempted forward pass which failed. A punting duel followed, and then a penalty gave California the ball on Washington's thirty-yard line. The Blue and Gold started its real attack. Sharp caught a beautiful forward pass from Brooks and carried the ball to Washington's twenty-yard line. A second forward pass thrown by Sharp was missed by Brooks because the sun was in his eyes, and it cost California a touchdown for there was no one between Brooks and the goal line, five yards distant. It was California's quarter at the beginning but Washington's at the end. Unable to make yards, Brooks kicked and then Johnson skirted California's left end for thirty-seven yards, which put the ball on California's ten-yard line. A series of bucks, and Murphy was forced over for the first score. Faulck failed to kick the goal.

The second period was only five minutes old when California scored. With the ball on his own twenty-yard line Johnson punted to Sharp on the second down. Brooks and Foster gained five yards on bucks through center. Then Hicks called for a forward pass. Brooks passed the ball to Montgomery who was far out at the right and the captain made twenty-two yards before he was stopped. Sharp was then called upon and he wriggled through a cloud of interference for twenty yards. The ball

FIRST BIG GAME. NOBLE RECOVERS LOST BALL

stopped at the ten-yard line, well out to the side. A touchdown would have tied the score. Two forward passes failed and Hicks knew better than to try the Washington line in such a crucial position. Then Sharp flattened himself out on the ground. Montgomery stepped back and measured the distance with his eye. Was it possible to kick a goal from such an angle? It was a long chance. Russell shot the ball out from center. Montgomery swung and the ball slipped through the goal posts for California's only points. The half ended with the score 6 to 3.

An uncanny quirk in luck in the way of a blocked kick in the third quarter, paved the way for Washington's second touchdown. Neither

Big Game Line-up

CALIFORNIA								WASHINGTON
Player	Age	Wt.	Ht.	Pos'n	Ht.	Wt.	Age	Player
Cohen	24	170	6 0	L. E.	5 10	168	22	Faulck
Madison	21	201	6 1	L. T.	5 11	195	20	Grimm
Bell	24	185	5 9	L. G.	5 8	182	24	Morrison
Russell	22	176	5 9	C.	5 11	178	24	L. Smith
Monlux	22	190	6 2	R. G.	6 2	185	24	(C) Seagrave
Gordon	22	174	6 0	R. T.	6 2	186	22	Murphy
Montgomery (C)	22	171	6 0	R. E.	6 0	165	22	G. Smith
Hicks	22	152	5 8	Q.	5 9	154	21	Johnson
Sharp	21	148	5 7	L. H.	6 1	170	23	Noble
Foster	24	175	5 11	F.	6 2	164	19	Briggs
Brooks	22	176	5 9	R. H.	5 10	170	20	Hainsworth

SUBSTITUTES

California—Johnson for Cohen; Cohen for Johnson; Coffen for Cohen; Paxton for Coffen (left end); McCullough for Madison; Madison for McCullough; White for Madison; Sewell for White (left tackle); Compton for Monlux (right guard); Gimbal for Hicks (quarterback); Wells for Foster, (fullback). (*Washington*—Wiet for Seagrave, (right guard); Calhou for Mayheid, (right tackle).

Touchdowns—Murphy, Hainsworth.   *Umpire*—A. E. Stow.
Goals Kicked—Faulck.   *Head Linesman*—Ben Cherrington.
Field Goal—Montgomery.   *Assistant Linesman*—John Fancher
Referee—George Varnell.   *Timekeepers*—Loftus and O'Dea.

FIRST BIG GAME—RETURNING FOR THE SECOND HALF

FIRST BIG GAME—BROOKS MAKING LINE PLUNGE.

FIRST BIG GAME—CAPTAIN MONTGOMERY TACKLES CY NOBLE.

FIRST BIG GAME—NOBLE PLOUGHING THROUGH CALIFORNIA'S LINE.

VARSITY AT THE ZETE HOUSE

team could make any appreciable gains and both were forced to resort to punts. Finally Washington punted to California's ten-yard line. Not since the first half had the Blue and Gold been in such a dangerous position. Hicks attempted to punt for safety but the Washington forwards rose in a mass and blocked the kick, recovering the ball on California's three-yard

JOHNNIE BECKETT—CAPTAIN TACKLE
HAYWARD—TRAINER   HUGO BEZDEK—COACH

California Season Scores

Date		Score	Opponent	Opp.
Sept.	16	Varsity 23	Olympic Club	0
Sept.	23	Varsity 23	Original Club	0
Sept.	30	Varsity 0	Olympic Club	0
Oct.	7	Varsity 13	Original Club	0
Oct.	14	Varsity 21	Whittier	17
Oct.	21	Varsity 14	Oregon State	39
Oct.	28	Varsity 13	Occidental	14
Nov.	4	Varsity 27	U. S. C.	0
Nov.	11	Varsity 48	St. Mary's	6
Nov.	18	Varsity 3	Washington	13
Nov.	30	Varsity 7	Washington	14
		Varsity 191	Opponents	103

FIRST BIG GAME—AN EXCITING MOMENT

line. Three downs and Hainsworth was shot over for the final score. Faulek kicked the goal.

In the last quarter honors were even. Neither team made any big gains and both resorted to punting, with Washington trying to kill time. The game ended with the ball on Washington's forty-yard line.

Line-Up of Second Washington Game

California	Position	Washington	California	Position	Washington
Cohen	L. E.	Faulek	Montgomery	R. E.	Abel
Johnson	L. T.	Tidball	Hicks	Q.	Johnson
Bell	L. G.	Caulkins	Wells	F. H.	Noble
Russell	C.	Wick	Sharp	L.	Hainsworth
Monlux	R. G.	Seagrave	Brooks	R. H.	Murphy
Gordon	R. T.	Morrison			

SUMMARY: Touchdowns—Johnson, Faulek, Wells. Goals after Touchdown—Faulek 2, Montgomery. SUBSTITUTES: Washington—Briggs for Hainsworth. California—Maguire for Brooks, Coffeen for Cohen, Loveridge for Bell, McCullough for Johnson, Law for Maguire, Leggett for Coffeen, Mathews for Gordon, Gimbal for Hicks. Referee—George Varnell. Umpire—Plowden Stott. Head Linesman—Henderson.

FIRST BIG GAME—WASHINGTON HALF BACK BREAKING THRU DEFENSE

SECOND BIG GAME— SHARP TACKLING MORRISON

In the interval between the two Big Games the California coaches built up the weak side of the line and new plays were learned, while Washington went through a stormy week of controversy when the players threatened to call the game off after the Faculty disqualified one of the Varsity. As a result the Blue and Gold went North for the Thanksgiving Day game, confident that they could break the Purple and Gold's nine years of consecutive victories.

If the first game was hard fought, the second was harder; if the first was sensational, the second was more so. Every yard gained was the result of gruelling battle and desperate struggle. California went against the Northmen with a feeling of confidence. The line held as it never held before; the backs were swift and sure, but that inexperience that dogged them throughout the season coupled with the fate that guards the uncanny Dobie lost the second game, 14 to 7.

In the first five minutes California had Washington on the defensive and battling desperately to prevent a score. Following the kick-off by California, Washington was unable to make its yards and Morrison kicked to Hicks in midfield. California's heady little quarter made a fair catch and prepared for a kick. But instead of sending a long punt he booted a short onside kick, which Wells caught on Washington's thirty-yard line. A forward pass, Brooks

ON THE SIDE LINES

SECOND BIG GAME—BROOKS IN CHARACTERISTIC PLUNGE

to Montgomery, gained ten yards and a buck by Wells three more. But on the new play Johnson intercepted a forward pass on his own five-yard line and prevented a score. Throughout the remainder of the period the play was constantly in the vicinity of Washington's thirty-yard line but the Northmen fought desperately and California was unable to get closer.

In the second quarter Washington made its yards for the first time. A series of line bucks brought the ball to California's twenty-five yard line. Here Faulck tried for a goal but missed. During the entire quarter the ball was in the Varsity's territory but Washington was held at a safe distance from the goal line. Thus, California's dashing, overhead play of the first quarter was offset by the smashing line plunging of the Washington backs in the second, and the half ended with the score 0 to 0 and anybody's game.

Shortly after the second half opened Brooks and Noble had a collision and for the first time in his collegiate football career the Blue and Gold star had to be removed from the game. Brooks' loss was a severe blow to

SECOND BIG GAME—BRIGGS RUNNING IN OPEN FIELD

SECOND BIG GAME. COHEN EXECUTING TRICK PLAY

California's chances as he was the kingpin of the backfield. Besides doing the kicking and passing for the team he was a tower of strength on the secondary defense. Washington had already started its plunging tactics. Hainsworth, Noble and Murphy carried the ball to California's twenty-five yard line. Johnson took the ball on the next play, and after wriggling through the line, ran twenty-five yards for a touchdown. Faulck kicked the goal and the score was, Washington 7, California 0.

An intercepted forward pass on California's forty-yard line shortly after the opening of the final period, which was carried by Briggs to California's twenty-yard line, gave Washington its chance for the second score. The ball was worked to the seven-yard line by bucks and then a forward pass, Noble to Faulck, scored a touchdown. Faulck kicked the goal making the score 14 to 0.

The game was over. California had made two unsuccessful attempts to fall the mighty Dobie, but the memory of that spirit which lived through the just ended season will live forever in the hearts of loyal Californians.

Freshman Football

One week after the Varsity started practice, one hundred and fourteen Freshmen reported to Pat Elliott, former University of Chicago star, to vie for places on the baby eleven. One week later Elliott made a cut in the squad so he might concentrate his instructions upon fewer men.

Of the nine games played during the season the Freshmen lost but two and played one tie. They piled up a total of 257 points against 25 for their opponents.

Freshman Season Scores

Date			Opponent	Score
Sept. 23	Freshmen	0	Olympic Club	6
Sept. 30	Freshmen	33	Sacramento High	0
Oct. 7	Freshmen	3	Olympic Club	7
Oct. 14	Freshmen	6	Davis State Farm	6
Oct. 21	Freshmen	34	Nevada	0
Oct. 28	Freshmen	25	Sacramento High	0
Nov. 4	Freshmen	26	U. S. C. Freshmen	6
Nov. 11	Freshmen	36	Nevada (at Reno)	0
Nov. 30	Freshmen	3	Davis State Farm (at Davis)	0
Totals:	Freshmen	257	Opponents	25

PAT ELLIOTT
FRESHMAN COACH

TOP ROW—FOWLER, DI COUDRES, TALBOT, BOUCHER, TOOMEY, GUILFORD, WRAITH, STEBBINS, ROWE
BOTTOM ROW—FLORY, SHARON, PARLY, HUSON, KNUKEL, RILEY

BIG FRESHMAN GAME TALBOT MAKES FIRST TOUCHDOWN

The big game for the baby team was played on November 4th, against the University of Southern California Freshmen. The Blue and Gold first year men won by a score of 21 to 6. The game was played in a heavy rain which made the field and ball slippery and slowed the play considerably.

Toomey and Stebbins were the stars for the Freshmen, the former making two of the three touchdowns and converting all three of them.

California–U. S. C. Freshmen Line-up

U. C. Freshmen	Position	U. S. C. Freshmen
Riley	(L) End (R)	Hamilton
DeCoudres	(L) Tackle (R)	McMillan
Boyd	(L) Guard (R)	Dahlgren
Fowler	Center	Hester
Wraith	(R) Guard (L)	Smith
Boucher	(R) Tackle (L)	Parrett
Parot	(R) End (L)	Joslyn
Sharon	Quarter	Jaques
Toomey	(L) Half (R)	Packer
Stebbins	Full	Eartley
Talbot	(R) Half (L)	Mueller

Substitutes: California—McKay for Riley, Gifford for McKay, Koi Koo for Boucher, Higginson for Parot, Flory for Toomey, Howe for Talbot.

U. S. C. Freshmen—Wilcox for Joslyn, Anderson for Wilcox, Lenox for Smith, Voss for Jaques, Hunter for Eartley, Thomas for Packer.

Touchdowns—California:—Toomey (2) and Stebbins. U. S. C.: Voss. Goals—Toomey (3).

The Reserves

Following out Andy Smith's suggestion the 1915 Goofs became the Reserves in 1916, and under the coaching of Ben Cherrington had a very successful season. This team, composed of men who as yet did not have experience enough for Varsity places, gave invaluable service toward perfecting the first team.

There are two fundamental ideas behind the Reserve system. The first is the development of men for the Varsity team and the second is to give the Varsity opposition in scrimmage practice. It was the task of the Reserves to work up the different styles of offense used by Oregon, Washington, and U. S. C., in order that the Varsity might be prepared to meet the attacks.

Hansen, Shaw and McCullough were "graduated" from the Reserves to the Varsity squad soon after the season started, having shown that they were promising Varsity material.

Those who made up the Reserves and stayed out the entire season with Coach Cherrington are: Nudd, Coulson, Alford, Bradley, Brown, Chambers, Dahlem, Easton, Enderly, Hansen, Hill, Huston, McCullough, Miller, Moses, Pennycook, Price, Shaw, Shultz, Slater, Snook, Spear, Weeks and Young.

TOP ROW—MILLER, PRICE, HILL, PENNYCOOK, ALFORD, ENDERLY, WEEKS, SPEAR.
BOTTOM ROW—NUDD, COULSTON, SCHULTZ, BRADLEY, SNOOK, SLATER.

Interclass Football

In a series that took four games to decide the winner, the Sophomores annexed the interclass football title for the season of 1916, by victories over the teams entered from the Junior and Freshman classes.

The series proved the worth of the annual interclass contests. As exhibitions of the American game they ranked with the best of the preliminary season and exceeded all in point of interest. At each game the contesting classes organized rooting sections. Each team had a coach and spent several days preparing for the contests before they took the field.

In the first match the Seniors and Juniors battled to a scoreless tie. While the Juniors had the advantage in practically all stages of the game, the fourth year men showed ability to hold the line at critical times and thus prevented a score. The second time the two teams met the Juniors won a closely contested game by a score of 7 to 6. Shaw's long punts featured this contest.

The Sophomores nosed out the Freshmen in the last minute of play when Skin Brewer booted a field goal, giving his team a victory by a score of 3 to 0.

This qualified the Sophomores to meet the Juniors for the championship. In the final game the 1919 men won a decisive 13 to 0 victory over the third year eleven. Symes of the 1919 team was the individual star, scoring both touchdowns. Jones kicked one of the goals.

JUNIOR FOOTBALL TEAM

BASKETBALL

BASKETBALL

CAPTAIN SHARPCAPTAIN-ELECT EMBURY

Varsity Season

THE VARSITY BASKETBALL TEAM made the best record in the history of the sport at California during the 1916-1917 season. It won fifteen out of the sixteen games played, taking the annual series from Stanford in two straight games, tieing for the championship of the Pacific Coast Conference with Washington State College and piling up a total of 697 points against 304 for its opponents. The only defeat was suffered at the hands of the Washington State five, the score of 32 to 29 being the closest of the season.

CHERRINGTON—COACH

The Varsity squad reported for practice immediately after the close of the football season in late November. Ben Cherrington was named as coach. During the Christmas vacation the team toured the southern part of the state, winning games from San Jose Y. M. C. A., Asilomar All-Stars, Watsonville, Los Angeles Y. M. C. A., Los Angeles Athletic Club, Long Beach Y. M. C. A., Whittier and the University of Southern California. After the spring semester opened, the Berkeley high school team was defeated in the first practice game, and then the college season was opened on the new Harmon Gymnasium court with a victory 42 to 18 over the University of Southern California five.

The Pacific Coast Conference season started with the Washington State College quintet, which opposed the Varsity on February 2 and 3. Both contests were hard fought, the speed and aggressiveness of the California players being pitted against the accurate long distance basket shooting of the visitors. The Blue and Gold team won the first game, 28 to 20, but lost the second 32 to 29.

California had to win both games with the Oregon Agricultural College to tie with Washington State for the conference title. The first game was played on September 20 and resulted in a 28 to 24 victory for California after an additional five minutes had been played to determine the result. At the end of the second half the score was 24 all but in the five minute period Hjelte scored two field baskets which gave California the game. California won the second game, 20 to 11. The first half ended with the score 5 to 4 in favor of the Varsity.

The first game against Stanford was played on the Harmon Gymnasium court on February 14 and resulted in a win for California, 20 to 14.

SPENCER—FORWARD FLODBERG—FORWARD WORKS—CENTER HJELTE—CENTER

The second game was played on February 15 at Stanford and the Blue and Gold again triumphed over the Cardinal, this time, 29 to 20. Neither of the games were as fast as the other conference contests, due mainly to the fact that both teams adopted strong defensive tactics.

Following are the individual scores for the conference games:

Field goals—Hjelte 22, Embury 14, Sharp (captain) 10, Flodberg 7, Spencer 4, Sandner 4, Works 3. Free goals from foul—Sharp 17 out of 27, Sandner 9 out of 13.

The Season's Score

California	80—San Jose Y. M. C. A.	16
California	79—Asilomar All-Stars	8
California	73—Watsonville	16
California	39—Los Angeles Y. M. C. A.	16
California	44—L. A. A. C.	12
California	69—Long Beach Y. M. C. A.	36
California	27—U. S. C.	15
California	40—Whittier	30
California	50—Berkeley High	16
California	42—U. S. C.	18
California	28—Washington State	20
California	29—Washington State	32
California	20—Stanford	14
California	29—Stanford	20
California	28—O. A. C.	24
California	20—O. A. C.	11
Total	697—Total	304

Interclass Basketball

THE ANNUAL INTERCLASS BASKETBALL SERIES, which was held in December, was won by the Junior team when they defeated the Seniors 23 to 13 in the final game of the tournament. Six games were played in three days in the series. The Seniors defeated the Sophomores, the Juniors won from the Freshmen, the Juniors from the Sophomores, the Freshmen from the Seniors, the Sophomores from the Freshmen, and the Juniors from the Seniors. These games resulted in a total of three victories for the Juniors and one victory and two defeats for each of the other three classes.

The Junior team was composed of: Zolot and Newlands, forwards; Gibbons, center; Salmina and Bourne, guards.

The Reserves

THE SECOND STRING VARSITY MEN constituted the Reserve team. Besides affording competition for the Varsity five the Reserves were entered in the California-Nevada league and played a number of games. In practice games they defeated the Berkeley High School, 44 to 11, and the Davis State Farm team, 32 to 28. They won from the College of Pacific, 49 to 10; from St. Ignatius, 40 to 25, and from the University of Nevada, 53 to 23.

The men who played with the Reserves are: Forwards: Spencer, Munro, Sangmaster, Flodberg, Middough. Center: Works and Symes (captain). Guards: Rugh, Anderson, R. Rohwer and Brooks.

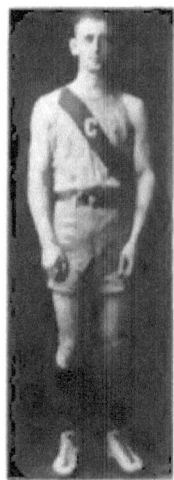
ROHWER—GUARD

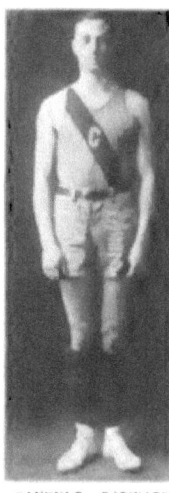
SANDNER—FORWARD

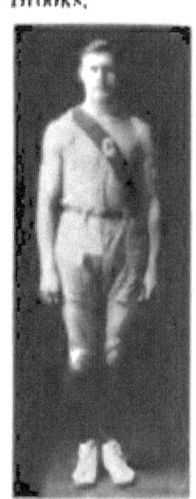
FOSTER—GUARD

The Freshman Season

OUT OF A SQUAD OF MEDIOCRE PLAYERS Coach W. D. Norton '17 succeeded in developing a Freshman team that won the annual series against the Stanford first-year men. Out of the ten games played during the season six were won and four lost. The final line-up was: Forwards, Toomey and Beresford; center, Greene; guards, Paret and Grul.

Season's Scores

Date	Freshmen		Opponents	
Dec. 10	Freshmen	45	Plymouth Center	16
Dec. 14	Freshmen	35	Berkeley Y. M. C. A.	25
Dec. 21	Freshmen	21	Berkeley Y. M. C. A.	20
Jan. 20	Freshmen	12	Berkeley Y. M. C. A.	20
Jan. 23	Freshmen	12	Berkeley High	19
Feb. 3	Freshmen	16	Woodland High	17
Feb. 8	Freshmen	17	Oakland High	22
Feb. 12	Freshmen	18	Berkeley High	13
Feb. 16	Freshmen	34	Stanford Freshmen	27
Feb. 23	Freshmen	19	Stanford Freshmen	18
Total		229	Total	197

TOP ROW — CUTLE, MANHARDT, TUCKER, WRAITH, SAYRE, SHARP.
BOTTOM ROW — PARET, TOOMEY, GREENE (CAPTAIN), BERESFORD, GRUL

BASEBALL

BASEBALL

CAPTAIN ADAIR

CAPTAIN-ELECT ROHWER

The Preliminary Season

BECAUSE OF AN EXCEPTIONALLY DRY SPRING the baseball season of 1917 started fully two weeks earlier than usual, a squad of thirty players reporting to Coach Carl Zamloch for first practice on January 22. With nine veterans of the previous year, including Captain Adair, who was kept out of the Stanford series in 1916 with a broken ankle, prospects to repeat the victories of the past three years against Stanford were exceedingly bright.

Only two places on the team had to be filled. Gimbal, who had caught in the Oregon games, took his place behind the bat and Hudson the other new man was put on second, Claude Rowher being shifted to the vacancy at short.

More preliminary games were played than ever before, the Varsity averaging three a week. Most of them were with the semi-professional teams around the Bay, but St. Mary's, the Olympic Club and Oakland Coast League teams were also included. Of the seventeen games played before the first contest with Stanford, California won nine, lost seven and tied one.

Instead of the usual three-game series with Stanford it was arranged to have a five-game series, the first team to annex three games to be declared the winner.

HEAD COACH ZAMLOCH

It was thought that by this means there would be no shadow of a doubt as to which university had the better team. In previous years the two nines had been very evenly matched with one run deciding the first two games, each side having one game to its credit, and the final game being won after a fourteenth inning rally, and the series going to the lucky team. "Baseball luck" could therefore decide the fate of the series and it was thought a good plan to do away with the possibility of having any such thing occur again.

First Stanford Game

The "inside baseball," which had been drilled into them by Coach Carl Zamloch coupled with the ability of the Varsity to lay down bunts in the pinch, and Ray Rohwer's terrific hitting won the first of the five-game series, which was played on the Stanford diamond on March 24.

With the score standing 2 to 1 against California, Ray Rohwer started a ninth inning rally with a smashing three-bagger to right field. Works went out, but Starbird laid down a perfect bunt and Rohwer slid across the plate with the run that tied the game, and paved the way for the victory in the tenth.

In that inning Hudsen walked and Dimock was safe on an error. Morse sacrificed both runners — Hudson squeezed in from third when Adair bunted, reaching first safely. Claude Rohwer went out and Ray Rohwer scored Dimock and Adair on a single.

CALIFORNIA	AB.	R.	H	SB	PO.	A.	E.
Smith, 3b	3	0	0	0	0	0	0
Adair, c. f	3	1	0	1	2	0	0
C. Rohwer, s	4	0	0	0	1	1	0
R. Rohwer, l. f	4	1	2	0	0	0	0
Works, r. f	5	0	0	0	3	0	0
Starbird, 1b	2	1	0	1	10	0	0
Gimbal, c	4	0	0	0	11	0	0
Hudson, 2b	2	1	0	1	2	5	0
Dimock, p	4	1	1	0	0	1	0
Morse, 3b	0	0	0	0	1	0	0
Totals	31	5	4	4	30	7	0

STANFORD	AB.	R.	H	SB	PO	A.	E.
Cowan, s	5	0	0	0	4	3	3
Mitchell, r. f	4	0	0	0	1	0	0
Hayes, 1b	4	0	1	1	13	1	2
Lilly, c. f	4	0	0	0	2	0	0
Braden, 2b	4	0	0	2	2	4	0
Dickey, l. f	4	0	1	0	3	0	0
Stevens, 3b	4	1	1	0	2	1	0
Campbell, c	3	1	2	1	3	0	0
Mattes, p	3	0	1	0	0	5	0
*Wilson	0	0	0	0	0	0	0
**Reagan	1	0	0	0	0	0	0
Totals	36	2	6	3	30	15	5

*Wilson batted for Mattes in tenth inning.
**Reagan batted for Mitchell in tenth inning.

Score by Innings
California 0 0 0 1 0 0 0 1 3—5
Base hits   0 0 0 2 0 0 0 1 1—4
Stanford   0 0 0 0 0 0 2 0 0 0—2
Base hits   0 1 0 0 2 1 2 0 0 0—6

Summary
Home run — Campbell. Three-base hit — R. Rohwer. Two-base hits — Starbird, Stevens. Sacrifice hits — C. Rohwer, Starbird, Morse, Adair. Double plays — Hayes to Stevens. Base on balls — off Dimock 2, off Mattes 4. Struck out — By Dimock 11. Runs responsible for — Dimock 2, Mattes 2. Left on bases — California 6, Stanford 6. Umpire — George Hildebrand. Time of game — 2h. 10m.

FIRST STANFORD GAME — DIMOCK ATTEMPTS TO CATCH CAMPBELL OFF FIRST

Second Stanford Game

Facing Mattei and Draper as nonchalantly as if they were merely second rate pitchers of a practice outfit and swatting them accordingly, the Varsity won the second game of the series played on California Field on March 31 with conspicuous ease by a score of 16 to 2. With one exception it was the largest score ever registered in a game between the two universities.

The victory was as clean-cut as the size of the score was surprising. The bombardment started in the first inning and did not end until the last man was out in the ninth. California registered a home run, a three-bagger, a brace of doubles and numerous singles. The dejection of the Cardinal was intensified by seven errors, while Dimock's foxy flinging allowed them but four scattered hits. California ran wild on the bases, Works even stealing home.

C. ROHWER (SHORTSTOP)   R. ROHWER (LEFT FIELD)   MORSE (THIRD BASE)   WORKS (RIGHT FIELD)

HUDSON (SECOND BASE)   DIMOCK (PITCHER)   GEMMNE (CATCHER)   STANBERY (FIRST BASE)

Varsity vs. University of Southern California

FRESH FROM THEIR 16 to 2 VICTORY over Stanford, the Varsity again reached the high water mark on April 3, when the University of Southern California Law School was defeated by a score of 16 to 4 on California Field. The California batters started in the first inning when they knocked Schmitz, the southern pitcher, from the box, and forced six runs across the plate.

The Varsity made runs at regular intervals, forcing Spiess, the second pitcher, from the box in the seventh. The day before U. S. C. defeated the second Varsity with Ball in the box by a score of 3 to 1.

SMITH (THIRD BASE)   BALL (PITCHER)

Third Stanford Game

STANFORD STAGED a come-back the following Saturday and defeated California on the Palo Alto diamond by a score of 3 to 1. Hoever, on the mound for the Cardinal, pitched a great game, allowing the Blue and Gold but three scattered hits. McCabe hurled for California and was touched for seven safeties. The Varsity played errorless ball for the third straight game.

Stanford scored in the first inning when Mitchell was given a life on a passed ball and scored on Shriver's triple. In the second frame Campbell singled, stole second and scored on Cowan's hit to left. California made its run in the fourth when Starbird walked, stole second and scored on Gimbal's double. The Cardinal scored again in the eighth when Shriver walked and scored on Hayes' three-bagger.

SECOND STANFORD GAME — RAY ROHWER CROSSING PLATE FOR HOME RUN

Fourth Stanford Game

With Dimock on the mound pitching no-hit, no-run ball California took the fourth and deciding game of the series played on California Field, April 14, by a score of 4 to 0.

The Blue and Gold won the game in the second inning. Ray Rohwer started the fun with a two-bagger. Works singled, and both scored on Vecki's two-cushion swat. Vecki scored when Cowan let Smith's grounder go between his legs. The final tally came in the seventh when Claude Rohwer singled, stole second, went to third on Ray Rohwer's bunt and scored while the Stanford infielders were trying to catch his brother between first and second.

Captain Adair and second baseman Hudson were both confined in the Infirmary with measles and unable to be in the game.

SECOND STANFORD GAME — CAPTAIN SAMMY ADAIR BEATS OUT INFIELD HIT

The Season's Scores

Jan. 30	Varsity ... 2	Maxwell Hardware ... 5	Mar. 10	Varsity ... 6	Olympic Club ... 3
Feb. 3	Varsity ... 2	Commercial Club ... 6	Mar. 14	Varsity ... 4	St. Mary's ... 2
Feb. 10	Varsity ... 9	Standard Oil ... 8	Mar. 16	Varsity ... 0	Oakland Coast League ... 6
Feb. 12	Varsity ... 9	First National Bank ... 3	Mar. 17	Varsity ... 4	Oakland Coast League ... 9
Feb. 17	Varsity ... 2	Standard Oil ... 5	Mar. 24	Varsity ... 4	St. Mary's ... 2
Mar. 1	Varsity ... 3	Maxwell Hardware ... 0	Mar. 24	Varsity ... 5	Stanford ... 2
Mar. 3	Varsity ... 4	Olympic Club ... 5	Mar. 31	Varsity ... 10	Stanford ... 2
Mar. 6	Varsity ... 4	Maxwell Hardware ... 3	April 5	Varsity ... 16	U S C ... 4
Mar. 7	Varsity ... 7	Agnew's Sanitarium ... 0	April 7	Varsity ... 1	Stanford ... 3
Mar. 8	Varsity ... 2	Commercial Club ... 2	April 14	Varsity ... 4	Stanford ... 4
Mar. 9	Varsity ... 1	Oakland Coast League ... 5			

Intercollegiate Baseball Series and California Captains

Year	Captain	California	Stanford	Year	Captain	California	Stanford
1892	Simpson	0	2	1905	Heitmuller	2	0
1893	Simpson	0	3	1906	Gillis	1	1
1894	Goslinsky	0	2	1907	Sweesy	1	2
1895	Bond	0	2	1908	Jordan	2	1
1896	Johnson	1	2	1909	Stoath	2	1
1897	Elston	2	1	1910	Lewis	1	2
1898	Hoag	1	2	1911	Greenham	2	0
1899	McLaren	2	0	1912	Allen	2	0
1900	Kaarsberg	2	1	1913	Coone	0	2
1901	Hunter	2	1	1914	Ruleke	2	1
1902	Hatelin	2	0	1915	Dodson	2	0
1903	McKeown	2	0	1916	Adur	2	0
1904	Adams	2	1	1917	Adur	3	1

Series won: California 16, Stanford 9. Series tied, 1.

Freshman Baseball

IT WAS AN EXCEPTIONALLY successful year for the Freshman baseball team. The team won fifteen out of its eighteen preliminary games against the high schools and clubs around the Bay and then took the annual series from the Stanford 1920 men in two straight games. Harold Dexter, who had played consistent ball both in right field and behind the bat was chosen captain.

In the first Stanford game, played at Palo Alto, on March 31, the Freshmen won, 4 to 0. McClain pitched a remarkable game, allowing but one hit. California scored three runs in the third and one in the ninth. The game was played in a drizzling rain.

The second Stanford game, played on California Field, April 6, was close. It was not until the ninth inning that California changed a 4 to 3 score into a 5 to 4 victory. Two walks, an error by Stanford's third-sacker and a sacrifice fly by Dexter brought in the winning run. Ellison pitched the first five innings and McClain four.

The Freshman lineup for the Stanford games was: Crystal, r. f.; Hyman, c. f.; Dexter, l. f.; Davidson, s. s.; Tooney, c.; Stephens, 1b., Welch, 2b; Luddy, 3b; Orchison, r. f.; McClain and Ellison, p.

Freshman Intercollegiate Baseball Scores

1912	California	5	U S C	4	1916	California	7	Stanford	0
1913	California	3	U S C	4		California	5	Stanford	4
1914	California	6	U S C	4	1917	California	4	Stanford	0
1915	California	2	U S C	0		California	4	Stanford	3

Series won: California 5; opponents 1.

1920 FRESHMAN BASEBALL TEAM
TOP ROW: COZENS (COACH), ELLIS (ASST. COACH), LUDDY, WELCH, DEXTER, STEPHENS, MCCLAIN, ELLISON
BOTTOM ROW: TOOMEY, DAVIDSON, TREFTS, HYMAN, CRYSTAL, ORCHISON

PACIFIC COAST INTERCOLLEGIATE CHAMPIONS, 1919
TOP ROW: BEQUETTE, SMITH, WORKS, C. ROHWER, DIMOCK, R. ROHWER, ZAMLOCH (COACH), ADAIR (CAPTAIN)
BOTTOM ROW: MASTERS, PARRISH, MCFADDEN (SCORER), STARBIRD, YOUNG, GIMBAL

Pacific Coast Championship Series

For the first time since 1912 California played for and won the championship of the Pacific Coast in intercollegiate baseball following the Stanford series in the spring of 1916. The Oregon Agricultural nine, champions of the Northwest were brought to Berkeley and defeated in a three-game series by scores of 5 to 2, 10 to 3 and 9 to 0. The games were played on California Field. The Blue and Gold outclassed the visitors in every department of the game, hitting the Oregon pitchers hard and running wild on the bases. Holmes, McCabe and Dimock worked for California in the order named.

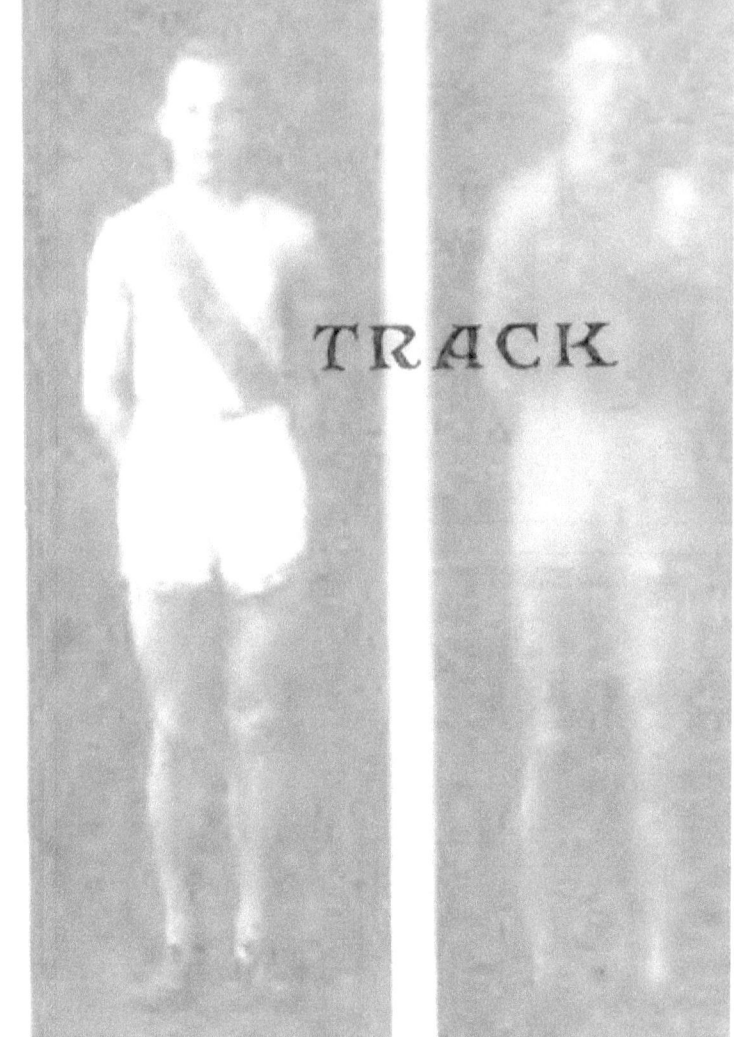

TRACK

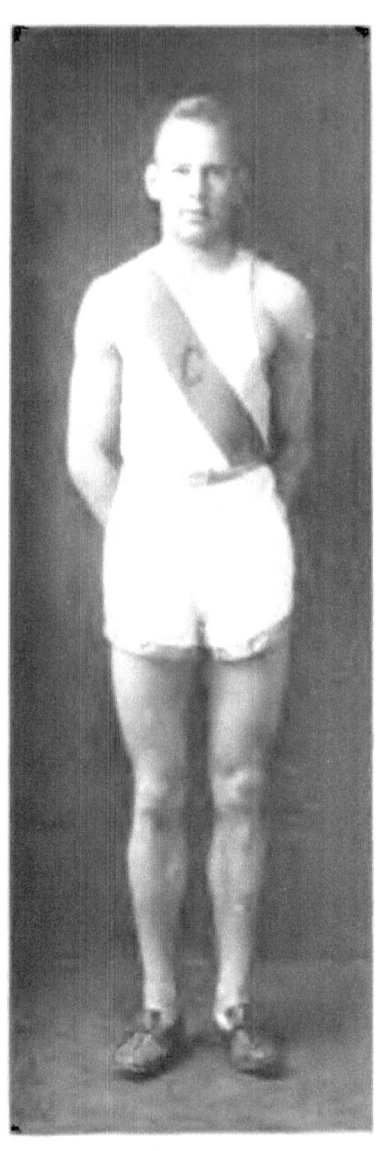 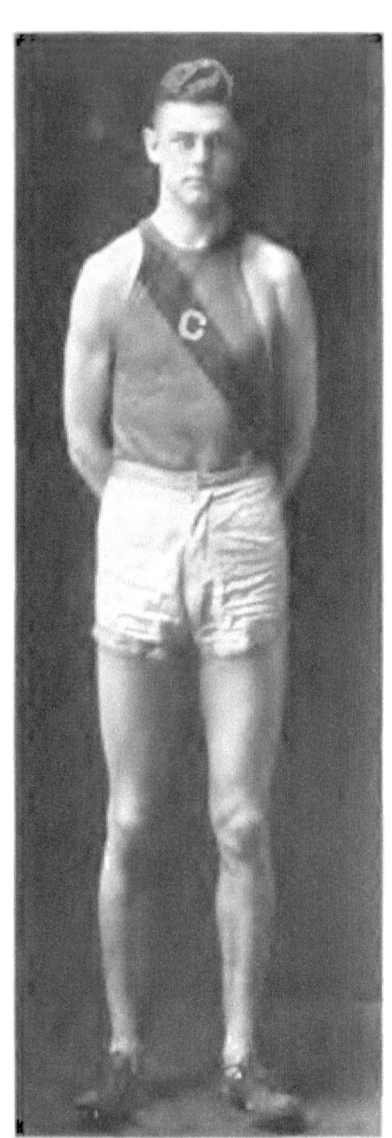

CAPTAIN NICHOLS   CAPTAIN-ELECT JACKSON

P. A. A. Meet

CALIFORNIA WON THE ANNUAL P. A. A. track and field meet held on California Oval, April 22, 1916, with a score of 89 points, 28 points ahead of Stanford, her closest competitor. The Olympic Club finished third with 31 points, the Caledonian Club fourth with 10, Visitacion Valley fifth with 5, while an unattached entry captured sixth place with three points.

One world's record was equalled and two new P. A. A. marks set up. Fred Murray, of Stanford tied Fred Kelly's and Forrest Smithson's record of 15 flat for the high hurdles. "Skin" Wilson of Stanford set a new P. A. A. mark in the mile, running it in 4:25 and Frank Maker, of California, set a new mark in the broad jump, leaping 23 ft. 1½ inches. Harry Liversedge defeated Caughey of Stanford in the shot with a heave of 45 feet 9½ inches. Liversedge also captured first in the javelin and second in the discus throw, for a total of 13 points. Nichols was the heaviest point winner for the Blue and Gold with 14. He captured first place in the hop, step and jump, and second in the high jump, broad jump and pole vault. Frisbie of California won the vault at 12 feet ½ inch.

COACH WALTER CHRISTIE

Fall Training Season

INSPIRED BY THE SUCCESSFUL competition against the Eastern athletes, the California track men returned to the campus in the fall of 1916 with fresh inspiration and a determination to break Stanford's winning streak of the four previous seasons. The entire fall training period was taken up by Coach Walter Christie in teaching the men the fundamentals of track competition and the correct running form. No meets against outside teams were scheduled, but a number of inter-class and intra-college meets were run. Del Rey won the annual interclub meet and Sigma Phi Epsilon the annual inter-fraternity meet.

Favored by good weather the greater part of the time and plenty of competition the spring track season of 1917 was all that Coach Walter Christie could ask. A squad of more than one hundred Varsity and Freshmen signed up at the annual spring track rally held on February 13, although work had been in progress since January 24, the first week of the semester, which opened January 15.

To limber the muscles of the athletes and get ready for the season's grind, Coach Christie inaugurated a series of Saturday hikes through the Berkeley hills. Eight and ten miles were covered each week-end for the first three weeks. During the week days the squad worked out on the track, Coach Christie correcting faults and developing the correct track form.

The crunching of spikes into the cinders and the crack of the starter's pistol announced the opening of the season of competition on February 17, with the annual Novice Meet. Few Varsity stars were entered, but uniformly good times and good distances were made.

The annual interclass held on March 3, brought out strong competition, and was won by the Seniors, with $59\frac{1}{4}$ points. The Juniors took second with 57 and the Sophomores third with $56\frac{3}{4}$. The Freshmen did not enter a team, as the 1920 class had had a meet with Lowell High School in the morning. Nichols of the Senior class was the individual star, capturing first place in the broad jump, high jump and pole vault. Clark's mark of :10-2 in the hundred, Sullivan's 4:42-3 in the mile, Johnson's :22-3 in the 220-yard dash and Nichol's 22 feet $8\frac{1}{2}$ inches in the broad jump, Liversedge's 46 feet 4 inches in the shot put and Richardson's 162 feet in the hammer throw were the best. C. E. Sullivan captained the Seniors, J. P. Jackson the Juniors and J. K. Moody the Sophs.

The Varsity handicap meet was held on March 10. A cold wind and a wet track hindered the competition, but despite these drawbacks several good times were made. Blanchard won the 880-yard dash in 1:57-2 and Purnell won the 220-yard dash in :22-3.

The last meet without outside competition was the Intercollege meet on March 24, which was won by Letters and Science with a score of 57 points. Agriculture followed with 51, and then came: Pre-Legal 24, Engineering colleges 9, and Chemistry 9. Sullivan of Agriculture won the mile in 4:40, Goeppert of Letters and Science, won the 440-yard dash in :51-2, Liversedge put the shot 46 feet 6 inches and Richardson threw the hammer 160 feet 3 inches. Nichols was the heaviest point winner, annexing the high jump, broad jump and pole vault. Liversedge captained Agriculture; Gibbons, Commerce; Ross, Pre-Legal; and Raisner, Letters and Science.

California vs. Pomona

THE FIRST MEET of the season against outside competition was with Pomona College on March 14. California won by a score of $80\frac{1}{2}$ to $50\frac{1}{2}$. The Southern athletes furnished the Blue and Gold strong competition on the track but in the field events the Varsity annexed 46 out of a possible 54 points. Captain Nichols was the individual star, taking first place in each of his favorite events—high jump, broad jump and pole vault.

In the field events the Blue and Gold athletes merely had an afternoon of practice. The Southern men seemed to have no entries in the weights and jumps.

Although a heavy rain the day before had softened the track, good times were made in almost every event. Adkinson of Pomona broke the Southern California record in the half mile by running it in 1:56, with Blanchard close at his heels. Moody and the Pomona sprinter, King, furnished keen competition in the 440-yard dash and relay, the California man winning both events by inches.

California vs. University of Southern California

THE FOLLOWING SATURDAY, March 17, the Varsity defeated the University of Southern California, $86\frac{1}{2}$ to $44\frac{1}{2}$. California scored 43 points on the track and $43\frac{1}{2}$ in the field, as compared with U. S. C.'s 34 on the track and $10\frac{1}{2}$ in the field. Nichols, Richardson, Grunsky and Jackson were the heaviest point winners for the Blue and Gold. Nichol's 12 feet 1 inch in the pole vault was the best performance of the day.

Moody lead a fast field of quarter-milers and Grunsky scored a double win in the hurdles. Sullivan won the mile and Lloyd the two-mile with little competition. Wadsworth and Gildersleeve, who was sick, did not make the trip south.

Intercollegiate Track Meets and California Captains

Year	Captain	California	Stanford	Year	Captain	California	Stanford
1893	W. H. Henry	91	45	1906	Geo. Stoddard	No meet	
1894	A. W. North	90	38	1907	N. J. Weeks	57	63
1895	F. W. Koch	67	45	1908	F. Stanton	$63\frac{1}{2}$	$58\frac{1}{2}$
1896	L. T. Merson	56	56	1909	R. Cooley	56	66
1897	F. J. Brown	$62\frac{1}{2}$	$59\frac{1}{2}$	1910	H. S. Edner	$55\frac{1}{2}$	$66\frac{1}{2}$
1898	L. J. Brown	88	38	1911	*W. G. Donald	87	44
1899	J. D. Hoffman	74	43	1912	G. Kneeinger	80	$41\frac{1}{2}$
1900	W. P. Drum	84	48	1913	H. H. Wood	$60\frac{1}{2}$	$61\frac{1}{2}$
1901	E. M. Hussey	85	32	1914	**J. R. Crabbe	$55\frac{1}{2}$	$66\frac{1}{2}$
1902	A. M. Walsh	$78\frac{1}{2}$	$43\frac{1}{2}$	1915	E. Stanton	60	62
1903	A. G. Cadogan	$58\frac{1}{2}$	$63\frac{1}{2}$	1916	T. Preble	53	69
1904	A. M. Cooley	53	69	1917	L. A. Nichols	55	67
1905	M. O. Barkley	$72\frac{1}{2}$	$49\frac{1}{2}$				

*W. A. Edwards elected captain but left the university before next track season.
**G. D. Wood elected captain but left the university before the next track season.
Meets won: California, 14; Stanford, 10; tie meets, 1.

California vs. Olympic Club

IN THE LAST COMPETITION before the Big Meet with Stanford, the Olympic Club was defeated by the Varsity on April 7 by a score of 70 to 47. California took nine first places and the Olympic Club six, all on the track.

The best race of the day was between Blanchard of the Varsity and Stout of the Olympic Club. Stout won by inches in the time of 1:59. Vlught, Olympics, won the two-mile in 9:50 1-5. Jackson cleared 23 feet 3¼ inches in the broad jump and 6 feet 2½ inches in the high jump.

California vs. Southern California All-Stars

THE VARSITY DEFEATED the Southern California All-Stars on March 31 by a score of 78½ to 38½. Fast times and good distances were registered in all events, but the showing of the All-Stars was disappointing. With the exception of the hurdles and sprints and one or two field events they rarely pressed the Blue and Gold entrants. On the field California annexed 35 out of a possible 45 points.

The best performance of the day was Grunsky's win in the high hurdles over Fred Kelly, former world's record holder, in the fast time of :15-1. He also won the low hurdles in :24-4. Sullivan won the mile but was disqualified on a foul. Purnell won the 200-yard dash in 23 flat and came second in the 100-yard dash. Moody romped home in the quarter in :51-2, with Pitts and Kerr second and third. Blanchard won the half in 2 minutes flat. Lamport of the All-Stars won the broad jump with a leap of 22 feet 2 inches. Maurer's tie with Nichols in the pole vault was the only first place taken by the visitors.

After the meet was over, Captain Nichols cleared 6 feet 3 inches in the high jump, and Liversedge put the shot 46 feet 9 inches, in exhibitions in their events.

Varsity vs. Southern All-Stars

Event	Points C	Points A-S	Result	Winner	Second	Third
100-yard	3	6	:10-2	H. Lamport (A-S)	Purnell (C)	Kelly (A-S)
220-yard	5	4	:23	Purnell (C)	Kelly (A-S)	Johnson (A-S)
440-yard	9	0	:51-2	Moody (C)	Pitts (C)	Kerr (C)
880-yard	6	3	2:00	Blanchard (C)	George (A-S)	Ruisner (C)
Mile	1	8	4:43	Miller (A-S)	Crippen (A-S)	Hjelte (C)
2-Mile	9	0	10:10-1	Lloyd (C)	Humphreys (C)	Olfield (C)
120 hurdle	5½	3½	:15-1	Grunsky (C)	Kelly (A-S)	Cameron (A-S), Kiessig (C)
220 hurdle	5	1	:24-4	Grunsky (C)	Cameron (A-S)	Lamport (A-S)
Broad	1	5	22' 2"	H. Lamport (A-S)	Jackson (C)	Jackson (C)
High	9	0	5' 8"	Nichols (C)	Jackson (C)	Taylor (C) - tied
Vault	4	5	11' 6"	Nichols (C)	Maurer (A-S) - tied	Watkins (A-S)
Shot	9	0	45' 8"	Liversedge (C)	Richardson (C)	McCutcheon (C)
Hammer	9	0	133' 10"	Richardson (C)	Holley (C)	Gildersleeve (C)
Javelin	9	0	165' 1"	Liversedge (C)	Hirschfelder (C)	McCutcheon (C)
Discus	9	0	115' 1½"	Moulux (C)	Richardson (C)	Johnson (C)
Total	78½	38½				

Comparative Records

Event	Stanford	California	I C A A A A	World's Record
100-yard	10 Cadogan (C) 1911; Meeker (S) 1911; Stockett (C) 1914; Meeker (S) 1914	10 Scragum (C) 1905; Cadogan 1911; Meeker 1912; Snedigar 1916	9.4 Wefers (Georgetown) 1896; Craig (Michigan) 1911; Patterson (Penn) 1913	9.3 Drew 1914
220-yard	21-3 Murray (S) 1916	22 E. Stanton 1914	21-1 Craig (Michigan) 1900; Lippincott (Penn) 1913	21-1 Wefers 1896; Craig 1910; Lippincott 1913
440-yard	50 Wyman (S) 1905	50-1 Todd 1913; Clark 1913	47-2 Meredith (Penn) 1916	47-2 Meredith 1916 (Penn)
880-yard	1.54-3 Nobbett (S) 1911	1.58-1 Dowd 1911	1.53 Meredith (Penn) 1916	1.52-3 Meredith 1912 (U.S.A.)
Mile	4.20-1 Wilson (S) 1911	4.21-3 H. Wood 1914	4.11-2 Jones (Cornell) 1913	4.12-3 Taber 1915 (U.S.A.)
2-Mile	9.54 Crabbe (C) 1913	9.42-3 H. Wood 1913	9.23-4 Hoffmire (Cor.) 1914	9.18-3 Shrubb 1904 (England)
120-yd. h.	15-1 Whittell (S) 1913; Grunsky (C) 1917	15-1 Edwards 1909; Grunsky 1917	15-1 Shaw (Dartmouth) 1908	14-3 Simpson 1916 (U.S.A.)
220-yd. h.	24-1 Norton (S) 1916; Horst (S) 1917	24-4 Johns 1909	23-3 Kraenzlein (Penn) 1898; Wendell (Wesleyan) 1913	23-1 Kraenzlein 1898 (U.S.A.)
Broad jump	23' 7.25" Jackson (C) 1917	23' 7.92" Snedigar 1915	24' 4.5" Kraenzlein (Penn) 1899	24' 11.25" O'Connor 1901 (England)
High jump	6' 4.75" Maker (C) 1916	6' 5.5" Brown 1913	6' 4.5" Oler (Yale) 1915	6' 7.5" Brown 1914 (U.S.A.)
Pole vault	12' 6" Krohn (S) 1914	12' 4" Nichols 1914; Gish 1914	13' 1" Gardner (Yale) 1912	13' 2.5" Wright 1912 (U.S.A.)
Shot	46' 7.5" Hohmann (S) 1917	47' 3.5" Loveridge 1916	48' 10.5" Beatty (Colum.) 1912	51' Rose U.S.A. 1909
Hammer	175' 10" Shattuck (C) 1913	175' 10" Shattuck 1913	185' 4.5" Bailey (Maine) 1913	189' 6.5" Ryan U.S.A. 1913

CALIFORNIA-SOUTHERN ALL-STAR MEET — GRUNSKY BEATING FRED KELLY IN 220-YARD LOW HURDLES

Stanford-California Meet

By a score of 67 to 55 Stanford won its fifth straight cinder-path victory in the annual track and field meet held on California oval on April 14. The date was originally set for April 21, but it became necessary to bring it forward a week following the declaration of war with Germany. Practically every member of Stanford's track team and a large number of the Blue and Gold athletes were members of the Officers Reserve Training Corps and were ordered to be ready to report for duty at any time.

Stanford displayed unusual strength in the field and may attribute her victory to an unexpected eight points in the shot-put, when Liversedge had a reversal of form and lost to Bihlman and Caughey, and first and second places in the pole vault. The Cardinal scored 42 points on the track to California's 30, and 21 points in the field to the Varsity's 25. The calculations were upset in many events on both track and field.

Two California-Stanford records were broken and two more were tied, despite the fact that the track was slowed up to some extent by a heavy shower in the morning. J. P. Jackson of California bettered the broad jump record made by Dawson of Stanford in 1913 by one inch when he leaped 23 feet 8½ inches. Bihlman of Stanford broke the shot-put record when he heaved the lead 47 feet 8¾ inches. The former record of 46 feet

100-YARD DASH, SECOND HEAT
PURSELL (C), FIRST; BOWEN (C), THIRD; LACHMUND (S), SECOND; CLARK (C) FOURTH

WADSWORTH   SULLIVAN   KIESSIG

JACKSON   LIVERSEDGE   LLOYD

PURNELL   BLANCHARD   GRUNSKY

RICHARDSON   MOODY   GILDERSLEEVE

120-YARD HURDLES — KIESSIG (C), SECOND; GRUNSKY (C), FIRST; WILLIAMS (S); HALSTEAD (S), THIRD

7¾ inches was made by Rice of California in 1912. When Grunsky took the high hurdles in :15-4 he equalled the record set by Whitted and Murray of the Cardinal, and when House won the low hurdles in :24-1 he equalled the record set by Norton of Stanford the year before.

The highest individual point-winner of the day was Meredith House of Stanford, who won the low hurdles and the 100-yard dash. Grunsky of California was second and the highest point winner for the Blue and Gold with first in the high hurdles and second in the low sticks. Captain Nichols took seven points with first in the high jump, and thirds in the pole vault and broad jump.

440-YARD DASH — DIEVENDORF (S), THIRD; ROGERS (S), SECOND; MOODY (C), FIRST

220-YARD HURDLES, FINALS
GRUNSKY (C), SECOND; WRIGHT (C); HOUSE (S), FIRST; HALSTEAD (S), THIRD; HIRSCHFELDER (C)

The quarter-mile was one of the feature events of the day, with Moody of California and Rogers of Stanford contenders. Moody drew the inside lane and took the pole from the start with a fine burst of speed. On the backstretch Rogers challenged him but the Blue and Gold star had plenty of reserve power and held the inside on the second turn where he gained two yards. He increased his lead to four yards, finishing in :50-3.

Purnell furnished a thrill in the 220-yard dash when he crossed the finis a fraction of an inch ahead of Lachmund of Stanford.

Honors were divided in the distances. Chapman of Stanford took the mile with Aupperle of Stanford second. But in the two-mile Lloyd of

100-YARD DASH, FINALS
LACHMUND (S), SECOND; HOUSE (S), FIRST; WADSWORTH (C); BOWEN (C); PURNELL (C), THIRD

220-YARD DASH (FINALS). PURNELL (C), FIRST; WADSWORTH (C), THIRD; LACHMUND (S), SECOND

LIONS (C) LEADING FIELD IN TWO-MILE

WILLIAMS (S) AND GRUNSKY (C) VIEING FOR FIRST IN HIGH HURDLE HEATS

CAPTAIN NICHOLS   SCHNELL (S) WINNING HALF-MILE; BLANCHARD (C), THIRD

California outran his old rival and crossed the finish 35 yards ahead of Chapman. Schnell of Stanford won the half. Blanchard of California took the lead for the first quarter but on the last stretch Schnell forged into the lead. Aupperle of Stanford made a great finish and just nosed out Blanchard for second place.

The relay furnished a multitude of thrills. Jackson of California and Hertel of Stanford ran a dead heat in the first quarter in :52-3. Kerr of California and Kegley of Stanford also ran neck and neck in the second lap and when the batons were given to Dievendorf of the Cardinal and

The Summary

Event	Points C	Points S	Result	Winner	Second	Third
100-yard	1	8	:10 1	House (S)	Lachmund (S)	Purnell (C)
220-yard	6	3	:23 1	Purnell (C)	Lachmund (S)	Wadsworth (C)
440-yard	5	4	:50	Moody (C)	Rogers (S)	Dievendorf (S)
880-yard	1	8	1:58 4	Schnell (S)	Aupperle (S)	Blanchard (C)
Mile	1	8	4:43.2	Chapman (S)	Aupperle (S)	Sullivan (C)
2-Mile	5	4	10:30.1	Lloyd (C)	Chapman (S)	Wilson (S)
120-hurdle	8	1	:15 1	Ginocks (C)	Krissig (C)	Hulstud (S)
220-hurdle	3	6	:25 1	Houge (S)	Grinsky (C)	Hulstud (S)
Relay	0	5	3:40.1	Stanford		
Broad	9	0	23' 8½"	Jackson (C)	Stirling (C)	Nichols (C)
High	6	3	6' 1¼"	Nichols (C)	Templeton (S)	Jackson (C)
Vault	1	8	12'	Wilson (S)	Gross (S)	Nichols (C)
Shot	1	8	47' 8¼"	Balentine (S)	Coughey (S)	Liversedge (C)
Hammer	8	1	161' 9"	Richardson (C)	Goldeneyer (C)	Miller (S)
Total	55	62				

Pitts of California the runners were even. But here the tables turned. The Cardinal runner gained twelve yards and although Rogers had Moody to reckon with in the last lap the margin was too great, and Rogers broke the tape a good ten yards ahead.

Freshman Preliminary Season

AFTER A MONTH AND A HALF of preliminary training at the hands of Coach Walter Christie, during which time the Freshmen were taught the fundamentals of running and the correct track form, the 1920 men were plunged into competition with outside teams on March 3, when they met Lowell and Berkeley high schools in a triangular meet. Despite the fact that the Freshmen had only one man entered in each event they took every first place in the field and broke the tape in all but two of the track events. The score was: Freshmen 62; Lowell 59; Berkeley 26.

This meet gave Coach Christie a chance to see what track possibilities the babes had and the next few days were spent in weeding out those who showed unusual promise in the Tri-angular Meet in order that time might be concentrated upon them for their big meet with the Stanford Freshmen.

In the next meet with Lowell High the Freshmen allowed their opponents only one first place. The score was $95\frac{1}{2}$ to $26\frac{1}{2}$. In the last preliminary meet the Freshmen defeated the Alameda County All-Stars, $85\frac{1}{2}$ to $31\frac{1}{2}$. The babes made a clean sweep of first places in both track and field.

FRESHMAN MEET—100-YARD DASH—FIRST HEAT. DINKELSPIEL (S), CALDEN (C), LYON (S)

Freshman Track Meet

THE CALIFORNIA FRESHMEN won the annual track and field meet with Stanford by a score of 68 to 54, on the Stanford oval, April 7. The meet was close and the result was in doubt until the finals of the 220-yard dash were run. The Blue and Gold swept the field in that event and clinched the meet. Two Freshman intercollegiate records were smashed and one was tied. Carl Goeppert of California won the 440-yard dash in :50 4-5, better by a second than the mark set by Wyman of Stanford in 1908. Colglazier, of Stanford, ran the mile in 4:37, Boysdon of California having set the mark at 4:38 4-5 in 1908. Calden of California equalled Scott's time of :10 1-5 made by the Stanford man in 1907.

Goeppert was the star of the day. The feature race was the 440-yard dash in which Goeppert and Frank Sloman, holder of the world's intercollegiate record for the quarter-mile straightaway, were pitted against each other. The old rivals ran neck and neck to the first curve, Goeppert gained a yard on the back stretch, lengthened his lead to another yard on the final turn and came home an easy ten yard to the good. His record of :50 4-5 was all the more remarkable, as both runners were set back one yard for a false start. Goeppert also won the 880-yard dash by thirty-five yards.

Goeppert's performances were rivaled by Calden in the sprints who did :10 1-5 in the 100-yard dash and :22 1-5 in the 220-yard dash, after running heats.

Freshmen Track Meet Results

Year	California	Stanford	Year	California	A. S. C.
1906	73½	48½	1913	42⅔	79⅓
1907	67½	54½	1914	54⅓	66⅔
1908	81⅔	40⅓	1915	73	49
1909	79	43		California	Stanford
1910	84	38	1916	65⅓	59⅔
			1917	68	54

Meets won: California 8, Opponents 2.

Summary of California-Stanford Freshman Meet

Event	Points C. '20	Points S. '20	Result	Winner	Second	Third
100-yard	5	4	:10.1	Calden (C)	Johnson (C)	Wells (S)
220-yard	9	0	:22.1	Calden (C)	Johnson (C)	Cantelow (C)
440-yard	5	4	:50.4	Goeppert (C)	Sloman (S)	Watters (C)
880-yard	6	3	2:02.1	Goeppert (C)	Maynard (S)	Wentworth (C)
Mile	1	8	4:37	Colglazier (S)	Satow (S)	Fredericks (C)
2-mile	4	5	10:36.2	Westwick (S)	Richards (C)	Houser (C)
120 h.	6	3	:16.1	McKenzie (C)	Davis (S)	Drew (C)
220 h.	4	0	:25.3	Wells (S)	Graves (C)	Davis (S)
Relay	0	5	3:32.2	Stanford		
Broad	3	6	21' 3½"	Nagel (S)	Calden (C)	Lyon (S)
High	4	5	5' 10"	Heath (S)	Siebert C/Sharon C/Young C tied	
Vault	8	1	11'	Sissle (C)	Peterson (C)	Davis (S)
Shot	9	0	38' 10¼"	Bluett (C)	Miller (C)	Wrublet (C)
Hammer	1	8	112' 4½"	Scott (S)	Cooper (S)	Freloni (C)
Javelin	9	0	142'	Bluett (C)	Jones	Felix
Discus	9	0	110' 2"	Bluett (C)	Miller (C)	Bowen (C)
Total	68	54				

GOEPPERT WINNING 880

FRESHMAN MEET
SLOMAN FINISHING RELAY

Western Conference

BECAUSE THEY HAD COMPETED for an athletic club in the Panama-Pacific International Exposition games the year before, Captain-elect Nichols and Harry Liversedge were disqualified in the Western Conference track meet held at Chicago on June 3, after they had won first places in the high jump and shot-put, and third in the javelin. The rule deprived California of twelve points, which would have given the Blue and Gold third place with 24 points. As it was the Varsity took fifth place with 12 points.

Wisconsin won the meet with 49 points, Illinois took second with $35\frac{3}{4}$, Chicago third with $20\frac{3}{4}$, Missouri fourth with $20\frac{1}{4}$, and California fifth with 12. Purdue, Mississippi, Miss. Ag., Kansas, Notre Dame, Minnesota, Oberlin, Northwestern, Indiana, Ohio and Ames followed in the order named.

Liversedge broke the Conference record in the shot-put, held by Ralph Rose, with a put of 47 feet 5 inches, and took third in the javelin. Nichols won the high jump at 6 feet $1\frac{1}{2}$ inches. Gildersleeve won the hammer-throw with a throw of 153 feet 8 inches; with Monlux second; Jackson took third in the high jump and Lockhart took third in the broad jump.

The men who went on the Eastern trip were: Captain Preble, Captain-elect Nichols, Jackson, Lockhart, Maker, Liversedge, Richardson, Gildersleeve, Monlux, Frisbie and Young.

Summary of Western Conference Meet

Event	Points C	Result	Winner	Second	Third	Fourth
100-yard		:10	Smith (W)	Hohman (I)	Peterson (W)	Barker (N)
220-yard		:21.3	Smith (W)	Hohman (I)	Carter (W)	Peterson (W)
440-yard		**:47.2	Diamond (Ch.)	Williams (W)	Daggy (Mo.)	Spink (I)
880-yard		1:53	Scott (M.A.)	Harvey (W)	Von Askent (P)	Huget (Minn.)
Mile		4:28.1	Mason (I)	Palin (I)	Schardt (W)	Campbell (P)
2-mile		*9:29.4	Stout (Ch.)	Bende (W)	Atkins (P)	Mason (I)
120 h.		§:14.3	Simpson (Mo.)	Ames (I)	Bush (I)	Heintzen (W)
220 h.		:23.4	Simpson (Mo.)	Renick (Mo.)	Ames (I)	Parker (A)
Relay		3.23.2	Wisconsin	Chicago	Missouri	Illinois
Broad	2	23' ½'	Pogue (I)	Smith (W)	Lockhard (C)	Grotamacher (K), Simpson (Mo.) tied, Webster (I)
High	2	6'1½'	Nichols (C) ‡	Fisher (Ch.)	Jackson (C)	James (N), tied Treweeke (K)
Vault		12'	Culp (I), Fisher, Liversedge (C)	(Ch.), Broc (Minn.)	Powell (Mo.) tied	
Shot		47'5'	Liversedge (C)	Mucks (W)	Reber (K)	Husted (I)
Hammer		138'8'	Gildersleeve (C)	Menken (C)	Mueller (Ind.)	Bennett (I)
Javelin		*172'	Arbuckle (P)	Kruez (W)	Liversedge (C) ‡	Vogel (N.D)
Discus		*155'2'	Mucks (W)	Husted (I)	Bachman (N.D.)	Rankin (O.S.)
Total	12					

‡Nichols and Liversedge disqualified
§World's record. **Two intercollegiate record *New Conference record †Ties Conference record.
Abbreviations—A, Ames; C, California; Ch., Chicago; I, Illinois; Ind., Indiana; K, Kansas; Minn., Minnesota; Mo., Missouri; M.A., Mississippi Aggies; N.D., Notre Dame; N, Northwestern; O, Oberlin; O.S., Ohio State; P, Purdue; W, Wisconsin.

I. C. A. A. A. A. Meet

CALIFORNIA SCORED twenty-two points and tied for third place with Stanford University in the annual I. C. A. A. A. A. meet held in the Harvard stadium on May 27, 1916. Cornell won the meet with 44 points, while Yale was second with 29. With only a small but select team the Varsity was able to outrank Pennsylvania with 18 points, Dartmouth with 14, Michigan with 13, Harvard with 11 and Princeton with 10. Bowdoin, Syracuse, Penn. State and Massachusetts followed in the order named.

The Blue and Gold placed in five events, taking two firsts, one second, two thirds and one fourth. Liversedge won the shot with a heave of 46 feet 2½ inches and Gildersleeve won the hammer throw with a throw of 155 feet 1 inch. Richardson took third in the hammer. Maker took second in the high jump, which was won at 6 feet 2¼ inches and was fourth in the broad jump. Preble took third in the high hurdles.

Two intercollegiate records and one world's record were broken. Meredith of Pennsylvania broke the world's record in the 440 by running it in :47 2-5. He also broke the intercollegiate half-mile record in 1:53. Murray of Stanford made a new intercollegiate record in the high hurdles of 15 flat.

The meet furnished strong competition in every event and records were threatened or tied in practically every instance where they were not actually broken. The cream of the country's athletes were entered and Harvard stadium was crowded with spectators to see the contests.

It was the third time that California had sent a track team east to compete in the I. C. A. A. A. A. After the Big Meet with Stanford a campaign was started to raise the money to defray expenses on the trip. A tag day and dance informal netted nearly $2,000.

The Blue and Gold did not send a team East during the 1917 season as both the I. C. A. A. A. A. and Western Conference meets were cancelled following the declaration of war by the United States against Germany.

Summary of I. C. A. A. A. A. Meet

Event	Points		Record	Winner	Second	Third	Fourth	Fifth
	C	S						
100 yard			:10	Smith Mich.	Moore P.	Teschner H.	Van Winkle Cor.	Troutman Y.
220 yard			:21 3	Moore P.	Smith Mich.	Van Winkle Cor.	Troutman Y.	Kaufman P. S.
440 yard	*3		:47 2	Maxwell Penn	Rice D.	Christ Cor.	Mahan H.	Richardson P.
880 yard	6		1:54	Maxwell Penn	Bingham H.	Strebler Penn	Taylor Cor.	Peterson Syr.
Mile		2	4:18	Watchman Cor.	Carter Mich.	Overton Y.	Mahan S.	Brown M. I. T.
2 mile			9:42 1	Potter Cor.	H. Power Cor.	Lucy Cor.	Carroll Cor.	Putnam Y.
120 h	3	7	:15	Manes S.	Gale Cor.	Preble C.	Norton S.	Farrell Y.
220 h			:24 1	Mattis S.	Clrens Y.	Norton S.	Bonn P.	Savage Bow.
Broad	2	3	23' 5¼"	Worthington D.	Oler Y.	Slaney S.	Maker C.	Hampton Y.
High	1		6' 2¼"	Oler Y.	Maker C.	Richards Cor.	Johnson H.	Gifford S. and
Vault			12' 8"	Foss Cor.	Newcomer Penn	Sewell Princ.	Curtis Syr.	Black Y. Nurss Y. tied
Shot	5	2	16' 2½"	Loveredge Cor.	Swan D.	Richards Cor.	Caughey S.	Braden S.
Hammer			155' 1"	Goldemonds Cor.	Lea Bletter Bow.	Richardson Cor.	Hagemann Cor.	Padrath D.
Total	22	22						

*New record—intercollegiate.
†New world's record.
Abbreviations: Bow. Bowdoin, C. California Cor. Cornell D. Dartmouth, H. Harvard, M. I. T. Massachusetts Institute of Technology, Mich. Michigan, P. Princeton Penn. University of Pennsylvania, P. S. Pennsylvania State, S. Stanford Syr. Syracuse, Y. Yale

TRACK TEAM IN HARVARD YARD
TOP ROW: MONEUX, FRISBIE, GILDERSLEEVE, PREBLE (CAPTAIN), LINDERSEDGE, RICHARDSON, JACKSON
BOTTOM ROW: YOUNG, NICHOLS, MAKER, LOCKARD, CHRISTIE (COACH)

CREW

CREW

CAPTAIN PENNEY   CAPTAIN-ELECT STEBBINS

1916 Washington Regatta

AFTER THE CLOSE of the spring semester in 1916 the Varsity eight went north for a return regatta with the University of Washington on May 21. Choppy water on the afternoon of the regatta prevented fast time, but did not prevent the Washington men from winning from California by nine lengths. The Varsity made a better showing against Coach Conibear's men than did Stanford, which was defeated over the same course by twelve lengths a few weeks before.

The men left Berkeley on May 12 and had a week's workout before the regatta.

The California crew was seated as follows: Bow, De Mund; No. 2, Ebner; No. 3, Black; No. 4, Hardy; No. 5, Lamb; No. 6, Congdon; No. 7, Penney; Stroke, Falck (captain); Coxswain, Gale. Coach Ben Wallis, Hogaboom and Clune also made the trip.

In the evening after the regatta the crew gathered at one of the Seattle cafes where they unanimously elected L. H. Penney '17 captain for the season of 1917.

Interclass Crew

ROWING ON a rough estuary the second Freshman crew won the annual interclass regatta held on the Oakland Estuary on the morning of February 24, crossing the finish two and one half lengths ahead of the Senior boat. The Sophomores finished third and the Juniors fourth.

The winning Freshman boat was seated as follows: Bow, Spear; No. 2, Lyons; No. 3, Tegner; No. 4, Hinsdale; No. 5, Wight; No. 6, Anderson; Stroke, Montgomery; Coxswain, Hubbard.

COACH BEN WALLIS

Varsity Season

WITH THE BENEFIT OF ONE YEAR of the new coaching system inaugurated by Ben Wallis, the 1917 crew season opened with brighter prospects for a winning eight than for a number of seasons. But after the spring semester opened the fate that continually hovers over the sport bobbed up again. Black and Lamb, both members of last year's eight were declared ineligible; the coaching launch, sent by freight, became lost and did not arrive until three weeks before the race, and finally the new shell, "California," purchased in January, was wrecked the week before the regatta.

Coach Wallis had three veterans—Captain Penney, ex-captain Falck and Congdon—and practically all of last season's victorious Freshmen crew as a nucleus. For the first time the crew was provided with separate training quarters, built beneath the west side bleachers of California Oval. The rowing machines were moved out of Harmon Gymnasium and all work done in the new quarters. Fall training started the week after the opening of the semester with more than one hundred out. Freshmen and new men worked on the rowing machines while all Varsity candidates who had had previous experience worked on the estuary in pair oars four afternoons a week.

FRESHMAN AND VARSITY CREWS WORKING OUT ON OAKLAND ESTUARY

CREW TRAINING TABLE AT THE DELTA UPSILON HOUSE.

The spring crew rally was held on January 16 and on January 22 the crews were out for their first spin on the water. The training table was opened at the Delta Upsilon house on March 17. The following were on the table:

Thomas, Penney, Falck, Congdon, Dykes, Stebbins, Jones, Reed, Gardner, Donnellan, Spear, Carter, Swank, Black, Tilden, Okell, Brown, Anderson, Kemp, Nelson, Johnson, Lyons, Wagy, Edwards, Martin and Hinsdale. Coxswains did not go on the training table as in previous years.

California Crew Records

Year	Captain	Winner	Second	Third	Lengths
1903	Bonnell	Washington	California		2
1904	Bonnell	California	Stanford	Washington	1½
1905	Bannister	California	Stanford	Washington	4
1906	Jones	No race			
1907	McKilbean	Washington	Stanford	California	2
1908	Witter	California	Stanford		4
1909	Ball	Stanford	California		3½
1910	Ashley	Stanford	California		3
1911	Davidson	Stanford	California		½
1912	Maynard	Stanford	Washington	California	1
1913	Eaton	Washington	Stanford	California	12
1914	Shaw	Washington	Stanford	California	2
1915	Merritt	Stanford	Washington	California	½
1916	Falck	Stanford	California		4
1917	Penney	Washington	Stanford	California	4

Regattas won: California, 3; Washington, 5; Stanford, 6.

Pacific Coast Regatta

Rowing with machine-like precision and unison, their White-tipped oar blades flashing back defiance to the Red of Stanford and the Blue of California, Washington's powerful Varsity eight flashed across the finish line with irritating ease, four lengths ahead of the Stanford boat, which led California by three lengths, in the annual regatta held on Oakland Estuary on the morning of April 14. A stiff gale blowing diagonally across the course kicked up a choppy sea of small whitecaps, a strong ebb was flowing and rain started to fall before the race was finished, which made fast time impossible.

Washington drew the inside course, Stanford the middle and California the outside. Up to the first mile California led Washington by half a length with Stanford third, but from that point on the powerful, well-timed sweep of the Northerners took them gradually away from their straining rivals. Washington covered the course in 16 min. 32 sec., Stanford in 16 min. 57 sec., and California in 17 min. 14 sec.

So rough had the water become at the finish of the Varsity event that it was decided to row the Freshman race up stream from the Webster Street bridge to the Park Street bridge. The steady business-like stroke of Washington took them past the finish two lengths ahead of the Blue and Gold, who had an advantage over Stanford of five lengths.

1920 FRESHMAN CREW
HINSDALE, MARTIN, EDWARDS, KEMP, OKELL, JOHNSON, ANDERSON, WAGY AND HOUSTON (COXSWAIN)

The Crews

CALIFORNIA	VARSITIES				Position			FRESHMEN	CALIFORNIA
	Height	Weight	Age	Year		Age	Weight	Height	
Thomas, W. P., '16	5' 10½"	157	20	First	Stroke	18	165	5' 10"	Hinsdale, G. S.
Penney, L. H. (C) '17	5' 11"	181	22	Fourth	7	17	175	6' 1½"	Marvin, W. A.
Tobin, Chas., '18	6'	176	21	First	6	19	178	6'	Edwards, Neville
Dykes, J. R., '18	6' 1"	185	20	First	5	18	190	6' ¾"	Kemp, J. J.
Stebbins, H. Y., '19	5' 10½"	186	21	First	4	18	174	6' 1"	eka, Jack
Falk, W. A., '17	6' 1½"	168	21	Fourth	3	19	175	5' 9"	Johnson, H. B.
Jones, Webb, '19	6'	175	22	First	2	18	172	6'	Anderson, S. A.
Rossi, F. A. '18	5' 10"	164	21	First	Bow	20	164	5' 10"	Waggs, J. H.
Average	5' 11½"	174	22			18	174	5' 11½"	Average
Gale, Guy, '17	5' 7"	110	23	Fifth	Coxswain	19	104	5' 6"	Hoepton, A. J.
WASHINGTON									**WASHINGTON**
Kamen, Ward (C), '17	6'	168	21	Fourth	Stroke	18	155	5' 8½"	Foreman, Byron (C)
Rogstron, Alison, '19	6' 3"	182	21	Second	7	19	169	6' 1"	Gonzales, Stewart
Newton, Chas., '17	6' 2"	188	20	Third	6	19	174	6' 1"	Copeland, Harold
Simmons, Wilbert '17	6' 2"	189	20	First	5	20	177	6' 2"	Harper, Paul
Briggs, Fred, '18	5' 10½"	170	21	Third	4	19	169	5' 10"	Smith, Bronson
McConlee, Paul, '17	5' 11"	171	24	Fourth	3	18	164	5' 11"	Mocnynera, John
Brandenthaler, A., '17	6' 1"	168	20	First	2	21	165	5' 10"	Crutch, Isaac
Whitney, Carey, '18	6' ¼"	175	22	First	Bow	17	155	5' 11"	Saunders, Edward
Average	6'					19	165	5' 11½"	Average
Ebright, C. M., '17	5' 8"	115	23	Third	Coxswain	17	105	5' 4"	Crawford, Randall
STANFORD									**STANFORD**
King, R.	6'	178	21	Fourth	Stroke	18	152	6'	Stump, W.
Watts, F. A.	6' 1½"	178	20	First	7	18	166	5' 10½"	McCormack, D. F.
Rogers, L.	6' 4"	188	25	Third	6	20	178	6' 1"	McCabe, H. C.
McEuen, A. H.	6' 1"	188	25	Third	5	20	189	6' 2"	Tilton, L. F.
LaForge, E. C.	6' 3"	174	22	Second	4	19	171	6'	Davis, C. S.
Russell, J.	6' 3½"	170	22	First	3	19	173	6' 2"	McGilvray, H.
Mauer, B. (C)	5' 11½"	174	22	Fourth	2	20	166	5' 11"	Fauser, C.
Taylor, P. H.	5' 11"	168	21	First	Bow	19	164	6'	Swift, T. R.
Average	6'	174	22			19	169	6' ½"	Average
Lyon, L. S.	5' 4"	112	21	Third	Coxswain	18	112	5' 8"	Schellenback, H. C.

START OF VARSITY CREW RACE — CALIFORNIA, STANFORD, WASHINGTON

TENNIS

TENNIS

CAPTAIN ROGERS

CAPTAIN-ELECT GRAHAM

The Varsity Season

THE VARSITY TENNIS SQUAD went through one of the most successful seasons in the history of the sport at California. All of the prominent tennis players of the Bay region appeared on the Varsity courts, and the Blue and Gold racquet wielders either defeated or broke even with every team played with the exception of Johnston and Strachan—the strongest doubles combination in the United States at present.

A new system of selecting players was introduced by Captain E. H. Rogers in the fall. Ten men were ranked numerically by the captain. Each man was open to challenge by the man immediately below him, and if defeated had to change places with the victor. The system is continuous, and afforded a definite system for picking the men who would meet the Cardinal. The system provides that the first three men on the list shall play the singles in the intercollegiate tournament. The same method applied to the Freshman team.

A tennis rally was held for the first time, in the history of the university on February 1. Thirty-five men signed up. During all the preliminary season the men played matches with each other, paying more attention to form and stroke than to winning the match.

ROGERS (CAPTAIN)   VARSITY DOUBLES TEAM   GRAVEM

EMERY ROGERS, CAPTAIN

In two tournaments with Gardner and Strachan, the Varsity composed of Rogers and Gravem, broke even. In the first one Gardner and Strachan defeated California two sets to one, and in the second the Blue and Gold defeated the visitors two sets to one.

The Varsity also broke even in its tournaments with Davis and Roberts, losing the first, two sets to one, and winning the second by the same score. The Blue and Gold team defeated Gardner and Roberts three sets to none; Marcus and Whelan five sets to none; Whelan and Holmes two sets to one; and Gardner and Holmes four sets to one.

The Varsity proved its right to be ranked among the best doubles team on the Coast when it defeated Fred Alexander and Carl Gardner in straight sets, 7-5, 7-5, and 5-2. This team had defeated Johnston and Strachan the week before. A few days later the Varsity met Johnston and Strachan in a fast exhibition, only losing after playing five sets. The Blue and Gold won the first two, 7-5 and 6-4, lost the second two 6-4 and 7-5, and lost the match with the fifth set by 6-3.

Southern Trip

Rogers and Gravem made a clean sweep of their matches against Pomona and the University of Southern California when they invaded the South on March 16. Out of ninety-eight games played they lost but twenty-five, and were not defeated in a single set. At Pomona, Rogers and Gravem defeated Jones and Peterson 6-2, 6-3. Rogers defeated Peterson, 6-2, 6-2; Gravem defeated Jones 6-0, 7-5.

At U. S. C. Rogers and Gravem defeated Sindorf and Godshall, 6-2, 6-1; Gravem defeated Sindorf 6-2, 6-1; Rogers defeated Godshall 6-3, 6-3.

The following week U. S. C. played a return tournament on the California courts. The results follow:

Singles—Rogers (C) defeated Sinsheimer (U. S. C.), 6-2, 6-4. Clark (C) defeated Godshall (U. S. C.), 6-4, 4-6, 6-4. Stanwood (U. S. C.) defeated Stich (C), 2-6, 7-5, 6-2.
Doubles—Sinsheimer and Godshall (U. S. C.) defeated Clark and Simard (C), 6-0, 4-6, 6-4. Rogers and Stich (C) defeated Stanwood and Nathan (U. S. C.), 6-2, 6-2.

Stanford Series

WITH THE RESULT of the tournament hanging on the outcome of the first doubles, Rogers and Gravem of California won a hard-fought match from Barber and Johns of Stanford, 6-2, 6-0, 5-7, 6-1, and brought another tennis victory to California on April 13. The tournament was played on the California courts. Captain Rogers was defeated in the first singles after a hard match, but Gravem played brilliant tennis and won the second singles. In the first doubles the two stars played bang-up tennis. The results:

First Singles—Barber (S) defeated Rogers (C), 10-8, 6-2.
Second Singles—Gravem (C) defeated Johns (S), 6-2, 7-5.
Third Singles—Wolford (S) defeated Simard (C), 6-4, 6-4.
First Doubles—Rogers and Gravem (C) defeated Barber and Johns (S) 6-2, 6-0, 5-7, 6-1.
Second Doubles—Clark and Stich (C) defeated Chapman and Holman (S) 6-2, 6-1, 6-3.

Freshman Tennis Season

THE FRESHMAN SQUAD also went through a successful season. The first-year men played a number of matches with high school teams around the Bay and with the Varsity during the preliminary season. They met the Stanford Freshmen April 7 on the Cardinal courts and defeated them easily. Stanford won only two of the eight sets played. The scores:

Danehey (C) defeated Burrill (S), 4-6, 6-2, 6-3.
Cheney (C) defeated Barry (S), 7-5, 6-4.
Cheney and Norris (C) defeated Barry and Burrill (S), 2-6, 7-5, 6-2.

AXEL GRAVEM

Record of Intercollegiate Tennis Tournaments

Year	*Captain	California	Stanford	Year	*Captain	California	Stanford
1892		4	5	1905		3	0
1893	To Stanford by default			1906	No tournament		
1894		5	1	1907		1	2
1895		5	1	1908		3	0
1896		1	5	1909		3	0
1897		5	3	1910	M. H. Long	5	0
1898	E. A. Stone	3	0	1911	B. M. Frees	4	1
1899	P. Selby	1	2	1912	H. N. Rogers	2	3
1900	P. Selby	1	2	1913	C. A. Rogers	4	1
1901	R. G. Hunt	3	0	1914	V. E. Breeden	5	0
1902		3	0	1915	H. C. Breck	5	0
1903		3	0	1916	R. L. Lipman	4	1
1904		2	1	1917	E. H. Rogers	3	2

Tournaments won: California 18, Stanford 6.
*Records do not give names of any captain until 1910. For four years (1898 to 1901) managers were elected who acted as captains.

FRESHMAN TENNIS TEAM
DUNSHEE   CHESLEY   NORRIS   BENSON

WEARERS OF THE C

Track

Elbert Willard Davis '16
Melton Watson Nesbier '16
Lee Ansdre Woltsworth '16
William Earl Bowen '17
Ronald Dalzell Gibbs '17
Claude Lars Morden '17
Luther Allen Nichols '17
George Tugger Swaim '17
Fred Gray Caldison '18
Carlton Carlyle Caldenderver '18

John Putnam Jackson III '18
Willam Frederick Koenig '18
Harry Hayes Loveridge '18
Eugene Char Lloyd '18
Darcy Harden Richardson '18
Eldridge Houghton Blanchard '19
Carroll Cello Cerauska '19
John Kenneth Moody '19
Lee Julius Pinsell '19
Matthew Williams Starling '19

Football

Travis Pollard Lane '16
Charles Robert Bell '17
Douglas Bryn Cohen '17
Daniel Parsons Foster '17
Ronald Dalzell Gibbs '17
Walter Harold Johnson '17
Marshall Pierce Mechem '17
Frank Dole McCulloch '17
Claude Lars Morden '17
Willie Robert Montgomery '17

Williams Alexander Russell '17
Lewis Bassett Sharp '17
Henry Burke White '17
William Lee Bender '18
Fred Thomas Brooks '18
Walter Arthur Gordon '18
George Myers Hicks '18
Harry Hayes Loveridge '18
Charles Lee Tilden '18
Chariton Grose Wells '19

Baseball

Samuel Asher '16
Wayne Rozencer Ball '17
Logan Crosby Edwards '17
Raymer Eugene Gordon '17
Harold A. Mets '17
Roy Strobart '17
Harold Edwin Dunock '18

Melwyn Louis McCabe '18
George McKinley Puttuth '18
Claude Holmes '18
Ray Holmes '18
Verrell Hutchinson Smith '18
Pierce Works '18
James William Hudson '19

Crew

Waldemar A. Fleck '16
Guy Harrison Gair '16
Ernest Camper '17
Edward Pearse Congdon '17
Henry Raymond Hopkinson '17
Logan Huldvard Penney '17
Hollis Mansfield Black '18

Leonard Roland Dykes '18
Frank Jacob '18
Freehorn Albert Reed '18
Charles Lee Tildon '18
Martin Webster Jones '19
Harry Young Stebbins '19
William Paul Thomas '19

Basketball

Daniel Parsons Foster '17
Carl Gunter Hyche '17
Warren Dexter Norton '17
Lewis Bassett Sharp '17

Eldridge Tod Spencer '17
Philip Albert Finhuty '18
Fred William Fiselberg '18
Herbert William Santner '18

Pierce Works

Tennis

Robert Campbell Clark '17
Emery Herman Rogers '17

William Joseph Stoh '17
Axel Berg Graven '18

Cyril Thomas Simard '18

MINOR SPORTS

Cross-Country

FOR THE FIRST TIME in the history of the sport, a dual cross-country race took place between California and Stanford this year. Heretofore Stanford had refused to enter a team against the Blue and Gold on some pretense or other but finally after several years of parleying and persuasion the Cardinal distance runners were induced to race a California team for the sake of the training that it would give the distance and middle distance men for the spring track season.

The race was held on the Stanford Campus on the afternoon of November 17. The course lay over four miles of Stanford foothills stretching in and out of the rolling knolls which are so characteristic of the Cardinal Campus.

It was decided that each team should consist of fifteen men. For the purpose of choosing these fifteen, a sort of tryout in the shape of an interclass was held on November 6, and the first fifteen in these tryouts were chosen to represent California against Stanford.

The manner of deciding the cross-country race was to take the first five men of each team who finished first and add up the points which corresponded to the place in which they finished. The team having the least number of points was the winner. Contrary to all previous "dope" the Stanford team won the race by a score of 26-29.

VARSITY CROSS-COUNTRY TEAM
D'EVELYN, HUMPHREYS, SHEARMAN, CHRISTIE (COACH), RAISNER, HOWARD

Soccer

FOR THE FIRST TIME in the history of soccer at California the U. C. team was returned a winner over our Cardinal rivals. The season started with prospects very bright. C. G. Shafor, captain during 1915, was chosen to coach the team, and succeeded in developing a team the equal of which would be hard to find among the colleges of the United States.

CAPT. HARDING

Playing in the university and club soccer league, the team got off to a bad start, being defeated by the strong combinations of the Olympic Club and the Barbarian Club, however these defeats were more than wiped out in the victories over these clubs later in the season when the men first played as a team.

The finish of the season, however, is what most pleases all those who have ever played soccer at California. After meeting defeat at the hands of the Stanford red by a score of 3-1 on November 18, the team journeyed to Stanford the following week, November 25 and there administered the long promised drubbing, coming out on the long end of a 3-2 score.

After the final game E. G. Schlapp '18 was elected to lead the team during the 1917 season, to succeed H. E. Harding '17. Schlapp hails from Australia and since coming to California he has developed into the best fullback on the Pacific Coast. The team lined up as follows:

J. B. McKinley '18	Outside Right
J. W. Coulter '18	Inside Right
J. L. Webster '17	Center Forward
L. S. Spigelman '18	Inside Left
O. A. Wilson '18	Outside Left
G. O. Sagen '17	Right Halfback
H. E. Harding '17 (Captain)	Center Halfback
H. L. Reich '17	Left Halfback
W. R. Lockwood '17	Right Fullback
E. G. Schlapp (Captain elect)	Left Fullback
J. Stockton '18	Goal Fullback

SUBSTITUTES: F. K. Carey '18, E. G. Hart '19, L. H. Nolands '19, L. W. Hahn '19, T. H. Corcoran '19.

SOCCER TEAM

TOP ROW: C. G. SHAFOR (COACH), J. B. McKINLAY, W. R. LOCKWOOD, J. L. WEBSTER, L. W. HAHN
SECOND ROW: L. L. SPIEGELMAN, GEO. O. SAGEN, T. H. CORCORAN, L. H. NULAND, E. G. SCHAPP
FRONT ROW: J. W. COULTER, O. A. WILSON, R. F. HARDING (CAPTAIN), H. L. REICH, H. K. CAREY

Swimming

CALIFORNIA'S SUCCESS IN SWIMMING was more than evident during the spring semester of 1916 and a continued success is expected throughout their entire 1917 season. The work of Ludy Langer, captain of the 1916 team, was the sensation of last year's team, Langer having set several new world's records in intercollegiate and open swims.

Stanford fell before the Blue and Gold attack in their meet last year, the final score being California 41, Stanford 27. Lindsay of California won the fifty-yard swim in 28 seconds; Pedley of Stanford the 100-yard breast stroke in 1:22 4-5 seconds and the 100-yard back stroke in 1:26 seconds; Langer won both the 100 and 220 yard swims in 1:02$\frac{1}{2}$ and 3:31 respectively, while Lyon of California won the distance plunge with a mark of 71 feet. Kahle of Stanford took the fancy dive while California won the relay with a team composed of Lewis, Langer, Lindsay and McElroy.

This meet was exceptionally noteworthy because each event was finished in times and distances setting new intercollegiate records.

The present season started with a meet against the Piedmont swimmers, California losing 44 to 22. The only facts of note in this match were Lindsay's time in the 100-yard swim, the California captain covering the distance in the fast time of 1:00 2-5 and Lyon, also of California, making a plunge of 66 feet 5 inches.

In the season's second meet, California took but 3 points. This match, the P. A. A., brought together the best swimmers in amateur ranks and Lindsay brought California to the front by finishing third in the 100-yard championship swim, his time being 1:00 1-5 seconds. In the relay California finished third, being nosed out by Piedmont for second place.

The Varsity had a full schedule for the season just closed, meets being held on March 30 with the Los Angeles Athletic Club at Los Angeles, with the San Diego Athletic Club at San Diego the following night and with Stanford on April 20. A return meet with Piedmont was held during the latter part of the season and meets with the Olympic Club were fitted in to offer competition for the Varsity.

Prospects for a successful team in 1918 are bright because there will be a loss of but two men, Lindsay and Lyon.

VARSITY SWIMMING TEAM
STANDING: KIDDER, THOMAS, CAMPBELL
SITTING: O'BRIEN, LINDSAY (CAPTAIN), LYON, MCQUESTON

UNIVERSITY OF CALIFORNIA GYM CLUB

VARSITY ICE HOCKEY TEAM
STANDING: TURNER, YOUNG, TAYLOR, STEBBINS, McKIM, RADU, HOWARD, HOLM
KNEELING: MADDOX, FAWCETT

Ice Hockey

ICE HOCKEY appeared as an innovation in the field of minor athletics this year and California celebrated the beginning of intercollegiate competition in this sport by defeating Stanford in the first series. The Cardinal was the only rival college to have an ice hockey team but with the interest aroused a full schedule is expected next season.

The first match was held on February 16 at the Winter Garden Rink in San Francisco and California took this game by a 4 to 1 score, starting with a rush and scoring two goals early in the match when McKim placed the puck between the Stanford net. Two more scores were made near the end of the third period by Fawcett. Purdy, of Stanford, was the only scorer for the Cardinals.

California won the intercollegiate title on March 2 when they again defeated Stanford, this time by a 3 to 0 score. The game was much cleaner and showed that California was superior to Stanford in speed and fight but lacked the team play of the Farm men. Sayre of Stanford was responsible for the low California score by his steady game at goal.

Although a third game was played it was not decisive, California having won two straight. However, the rivalry and spirit displayed in the first games was not lacking in the last match and the teams were forced to play fifteen minutes additional in an effort to break a 1 to 1 tie. The game finally ended a tie and closed the first ice hockey season.

From the interest shown and from conditions which prevail in Eastern colleges, it is probable that this sport will be ranked among those awarded circle "C's." Over 1,000 spectators were present at each of the three games and heated rivalry was shown. In all Eastern colleges where ice hockey is played, it is considered a major sport and is classed along with football, track, baseball and basketball.

Considerable credit for the starting of this sport belongs to Captain George Young. Young captained and managed the team and secured the sanction of the university to organize a team to represent California, yet receiving no aid from the university. The team was equipped and kept up by the men themselves.

The teams lined up for the first game with Stebbins at goal, Taylor and Radil at point, Young at cover point, McKim at rover, Fawcett at center, Holm and Turner at right wing, and Maddox at left wing, but in the second game some changes were made, Maddox being placed at rover, Holm and Turner at left wing and McKim at right wing. In the final game Brown replaced Stebbins at goal while Young went in at point and McKim at cover point and Maddox at rover. Turner played left wing and Holm right wing.

Rifle Shooting

ACTIVITY ON THE RIFLE RANGE has been particularly successful this year in spite of the fact that some have tried to have the sport withdrawn from the list of minor sports. As a result of this agitation a campaign was launched to incite more interest in the pastime and the response was so gratifying that it is hoped that this activity may be allowed to retain its former status.

A great deal more shooting has been done on the ranges, both short and long distance, this spring than ever before. Those of the Rifle Club who have shown any interest at all have entered into it whole-heartedly and consequently the result of such active participation in practices has raised the standard of the team.

In competition with all the larger universities of the country this year the California team finished in sixth place. This is the first time that a Blue and Gold rifle team has placed anywhere near the front at all since the instigation of the activity. With this advance in the quality of the men's work so much in one term, it is expected that they will finish up nearer the top next year.

The national indoor intercollegiate contests have taken up most of the spring competition and the California teams have done remarkably well in these contests, having won more than three-fourths of them.

RIFLE TEAM
STANDING: BOUDINOT, DETWILER, HOWELL, SCHATTENBURG, ATCHISON
SITTING: PUCKETT, WHITTON, CLARK, SARGENT, SCHULZE

WEARERS OF THE C

SWIMMING

Marston Campbell Jr. '18
Arthur W. Kidder '18
George M. Lindsay '17

Norman M. Lyon '17
Jacques F. Resleure '15
William H. Thomas '18

CROSS-COUNTRY

Elbert W. Davis '16
Wright E. D'Evelyn '17
Enville D. Howard '17
Hiram H. Humphrey '18

Wilbur Raisner '17
Raymond L. Shearman '17
H. A. Spindt '16
Milton W. Vedder '16

BASKETBALL
(Now awarded Big "C")

Philip A. Embury '18
Daniel P. Foster '17
Frank M. House '15

Benjamin B. Logan '17
Warren D. Norton '16
Leroy B. Sharp '17

GOLF

Marshall P. Madison '17
Eberhardt G. Schlapp '18

Henry R. Schlapp '18

SOCCER

Francis K. Carey '18
Thomas F. Corcoran '19
John W. Coulter '18
Elliot G. Hart '19
George H. Hotaling '17
Walter R. Lockwood '17
John B. McKinlay '18
Lester H. Nuland '19

Henry L. Reich '17
Edward A. Reinke '17
George O. Sagen '17
Louis S. Spiegelman '18
Francis H. Stewart '17
J. D. Stockton
Jackson L. Webster '17
Omi A. Wilson '18

WRESTLING

Ernest R. DeChenne '15
George S. Ikt '17

Ernest E. Schmitt

RIFLE
(No longer awarded Circle "C")

Karl B. Clark '18
Harvey Hardison '18
Cletus I. Howell '18

Matthew H. Jones '16
Ernest R. Schulze '18
Loyal W. Whitton '18

WOMEN'S ATHLETICS

Rowing

THE SPRING OF 1917 has seen unprecedented activity in women's rowing. One hundred and fifty girls have manifested keen interest in the sport and have faithfully wielded their oars throughout the season under the direction of Coach Maude Cleveland, head of the Physical Education Department. Practice has been held regularly on Lake Merritt in the navy cutters which carry a crew of twelve rowers, a pilot and a coxswain. This spring the Seniors had one crew on the water, the Juniors and Sophomores each two, and the Freshmen four.

For the first time in the history of the sport, the season opened with a month's indoor practice on rowing machines, the property of the A. S. U. C. On the lake the result of this practice showed itself in more efficient blade work and a lengthened stroke. Two new sets of oars were bought by Sports and Pastimes, as the result of the sale of two unused rowboats. The five sets of oars which the university owns were given a bright coat of California blue paint, the blade tipped off with a gold "C." A new locker for these oars was built and installed at the Municipal Boat House.

The crowning event of the season was the first annual regatta held at Lake Merritt on the morning of April 7. Here interclass races were held amid waving of pennants, the playing of the University Cadet Band, and the lively interest of the spectators.

Crew managers of this season were:

Mary L. Kleinecke, Manager   Edna L. Brown, Assistant Manager

CLASS MANAGERS
- Seniors—Hazel Katzenstein '17
- Sophomores—Ruth Ware '19
- Juniors—Marian Chandler '18
- Freshmen—Anna-Gay Doolittle '20

WOMEN'S CREW ON LAKE MERRITT

Hockey

THE FALL OF 1916 saw the end of hockey's second successful season in the history of the sport at California. The season began early with more girls signed up for each sport than ever before, approximating about one hundred and forty girls. The sport was new to a great many of these girls but, in spite of the handicap, perseverance won out and before the end of the season everyone had an intelligent grasp of the game.

About the first of October the first and second class teams were picked and a round-robin series of games followed. These games were spread over a period of three weeks, during which time both teams kept training according to rules drawn up by Sports and Pastimes. During this time class spirit was at its highest pitch. There was a great deal of enthusiastic rivalry and the competition between all classes was good. The Sophomores carried off the honors of the season by defeating all of the other three classes. On Saturday morning, November 25, the date of the Women's Fall Athletic Day, an exhibition game was played on Hearst Field between the Sophomore and Freshman teams—the Sophomores again coming out victorious.

No outside games were played, all attention and effort being given by Miss Elliott, the coach, and Evelyn Petch, the manager, to the development of four good class teams. Numerals were given to all those who made the first team and who faithfully kept training. In addition, an all-star team was picked by Miss Elliott and each member was given an emblem characteristic of the sport. Those who made the all-star team were:

Carolyn Steel	Center Forward	Alice De Witt	Right Half
Helen Rosenberg	Right Inside	Helen Spencer	Left Half
Claire Johnston	Left Inside	Anna Carter	Right Fullback
Alberta McNeely	Right Wing	Ruby Yoakum	Left Fullback
Evelyn Petch	Left Wing	Ruth Merrill	Goal
	Caroline Neill	Center Half	

PLAYING HOCKEY ON WOMEN'S ATHLETIC FIELD

FENCERS IN ACTION

Fencing

ALTHO, AS A SPORT AMONG WOMEN, fencing can never rank as high in popularity or numbers as such activities as basketball and hockey, nevertheless it has continued to hold its own during the past year.

The sport took a new start in the fall when Mr. Miller, an expert fencer and formerly coach at Columbia University, was secured to coach the girls. During the fall semester an average of from forty to fifty girls turned out and were drilled in the rudiments of the sport in preparation for the interclass and Varsity contests which were held this spring.

In the spring semester the girls were organized in classes under class captains and assigned definite hours of practice, Edith Logan '17 and Mr. Miller acting as coaches as before. The class teams were chosen the last week in March, each team having three members and one substitute. After three weeks of training and hard practice the interclass series was fenced during the third week in April.

On April 21, Women's Athletic Day, the Varsity team, consisting of five girls and a substitute, met the Stanford team in Hearst Hall, in competition for the possession of the large silver loving cup, given by Mrs. Lathrop of Stanford and awarded to the team winning the contest.

It is hoped that next year many more girls will become interested in the sport as it provides mild exercise for those who are too busy to go out for some heavier activity.

VARSITY TENNIS TEAM

Tennis

THE TENNIS SEASON FOR 1916 and 1917 has been a peculiarly successful one from the standpoint of competition. During the first semester tryouts were carried on and twenty girls picked—five on each class team—to represent California in the interclass-intercollegiate matches with Stanford. These matches proved very successful and California won by large scores.

The second semester Miss Miriam Hall, one of the finest coaches in the Bay region, was obtained to coach a large Varsity squad and develop material for this year's team as well as next year's.

On March 31 U. S. C. played California on the home courts and a great deal of interest was taken in the matches. Just two weeks later, April 14, four girls—Claire Tucker '16, Anna Carter '17, (captain and manager) Beatrice Gerberding '18, and Elizabeth Beall '19—journeyed south to Los Angeles where matches were played with U. S. C. and Occidental.

On April 21 the big Women's Spring Sports Day, the All-California tennis team was announced, and gold tennis racket pins, the All-California emblem, were awarded.

No review of tennis is complete without mentioning the splendid aid and co-operation of the physical education department. In every way they were always ready to help, and great thanks is due them for their untiring efforts in teaching the girls the fundamentals of the game as well as starting out the novices.

Swimming

SWIMMING AS A WOMEN'S SPORT has made vast strides since the opening of the Hearst Pool in the spring of 1915. The beginning of the fall term of 1916 found the tank filled to its capacity every day, both with those receiving their first instructions in swimming and diving and also by those who were more advanced along those lines. Sixty girls signed up for swimming this year as their choice for a sport. Organized into classes, these girls with the help of two very competent coaches, Miss Armour, of the Physical Education Department, and Miss Anderson, the life-guard, were taught correct forms of diving and stroking, as well as practical life-saving.

Interclass meets were held each Friday afternoon. From the best of these swimmers of each class seven were chosen to represent their respective classes in the final interclass meet held on Fall Sports Day. As a result of this meet all those who competed on their first-class teams were awarded numerals. An All-California team, picked by the coaches from the five best swimmers, received medals in the shape of small gold life-preservers. The girls receiving these medals were Ruth Heynemann '17, Jane Halbert '17, Gladys Basye '18, Mary Heger '19 and Portia Wagenet '19.

Water-polo was added this spring to the already large list of women's sports. Goals were placed in the tank for the use of the water-poloists and from the enthusiastic turn-out for the first practice the new sport looks as though it is here to stay.

Preparations are already being made in the tank for the increased number of swimmers which is expected to turn out next year.

CAUGHT BY THE CAMERA

Baseball

BASEBALL STARTED THIS YEAR as an organized sport among women, under the management of Helen E. Rosenberg '17. The game is played under regulation rules, although the field is not of regulation size.

Among the fifty girls, who turned out for regular practice, there was exceptionally good material and under the able coaching of Miss Edna Roof of the Physical Education Department, the girls learned the rudiments of our national game, at the same time becoming deeply interested in the sport.

There were not enough girls out for class teams, but Upper Division and Lower Division teams were chosen. The girls making these teams were awarded their numerals. A preliminary game between teams representing the "even" and "odd" classes, was played, in which the odds were victorious, 13-9. The final game between the Upper and Lower teams was played on the Women's Spring Athletic Day.

This is the first season that baseball has been an organized sport and judging from the number of girls who turned out, and from the interest shown, the selection of an All-California team next season is assured. It is hoped that by next year, there will be increased facilities for women's baseball in the shape of one or more fields of regulation size. Much difficulty was experienced this year on account of the limited ground on which to play. Consequently the progress of the sport was greatly hindered.

A HEALTHY SWING

SENIOR WOMEN'S CREW

VARSITY TENNIS DOUBLES TEAM

ANNA CARTER   ELIZABETH BEAL

WEARERS OF THE WOMEN'S C

The award of a "C" to women athletes has undergone a change during the past year and the discrimination of sports has been discarded to be replaced by a general standard decided upon by managers of sports, various coaches and members of the Sports and Pastimes Society. Good scholarship enters into the new award, especially in physical education subjects, and the candidate must live up to training rules, have a good posture and carriage. She must be sportsman-like in spirit and must be efficient in at least two sports. No Freshman woman can receive a "C," and candidates have opportunities to compete in athletic events in the interclass and intercollegiate matches with Stanford and on the two women's field days.

GRADUATES

Maude Cleveland
Ruth Elliott
Helen Hopkins
Caroline Louise Tucker
Claire Althea

SENIORS

Anna Breckinridge Carter
Margaret Calder Hayes
Ruth Marian Heynemann
Esther Laurilla King
Mary Louise Kleineeke
Edith Harriet Logan
Alberta McNeely
Caroline Neill
Myrtle Evelyn Petch
Rose Maria Pfund
Gladys Isabel Reston
Ruby Yoakum

JUNIORS

Clarascott Goodloe
Margo Sheppa

THE CLASSES

The 1910 Senior Class Bridge

THE CLASSES

The 1910 Senior Class Banner

SENIOR CLASS

TOM SLAVEN

GEORGE COHEN

OFFICERS

First Semester
President, Thomas William Slaven
Vice-President, Coe Elizabeth McCabe
Secretary, Charles Elroy Rhein
Treasurer, Frank Thomas Elliott
Sergeant-at-arms, Edwin Harold Hesselberg
Yell Leader, Erwin Herbert Hirschfelder

Second Semester
President, George Washington Cohen
Vice-President, Margaret Marchant
Secretary, William Ross McKay
Treasurer, Frank Thomas Elliott
Sergeant-at-arms, Edwin Harold Hesselberg
Yell Leader, Erwin Herbert Hirschfelder

Undergraduate Reminiscences
By HAROLD A. BLACK '17

HIS SOUL IS DEAD INDEED, who can look forward to the setting of our sun without a little pang of regret along with the keen anticipation of the burst of glory with which we make our triumphant exit from California. A Senior is a pretty sentimental soul, if you can get him to stop a moment to think about it and what it all means; parting overnight with all these bosom friends that it took four years to acquire; laying down our scepters as kings of this little world of ours to become vassals once again in the real world outside.

It is only in the last few weeks that we realize that Father Time has been playing tricks on us. We certainly had no thought for anything but the living present back in 1913 when we jostled our seventeen hundred odd associates about California Hall, wrestling with the red-tape of registration. It was then that we met our friends, the enemy, in the persons of the Sophomores, to whose attentions we took anything but kindly and ever brooded unchristian revenge. We had our opportunity a week after registration. We assembled in front of the gym and after being baptized in venomous green paint, vowed to teach 1916 something about the game of push-ball. We did—to the tune of three to nothing—and as we returned across the campus almost sans clothing, each one of us realized that 1917 had found itself.

At the Freshman Rally when Henry Morse Stephens told us we were "not a class, but a mob," we listened respectfully but we didn't agree with him. During the year we demonstrated rare prowess on the athletic field; we lost to U. S. C. in football 6-0, but we beat them in tennis and in baseball. We won the interclass regatta, and in the track meet against U. S. C., we ran up a bigger score than did the Varsity two weeks before.

Most of us survived the ravages of the recorder's office, and returned in the fall of 1914, to become proud possessors of racy looking pipes and racier caps. We battled with the Freshmen to a tie that year in push-ball, but afterwards looked after their welfare with tender solicitude and prevented them from breaking sacred campus traditions. This was the year of the threatened invasion of the campus by the hated Red from down at the farm, and as custodians of the crucial point of attack - the Big "C", we Sophomores had a peculiar responsibility. So much enthusiasm was engendered that year that it seemed as though we could not lose in football, but we were opposing too good a team. Nevertheless the 8 to 26 score does not indicate how hard fought the game was.

The spring semester brought retribution in the shape of a baseball victory. But epochal events happened that term—California Day, on which occasion four thousand Californians returned to their Alma Mater to renew old acquaintances, was a gala event. But perhaps of greater interest to the undergraduate was the break with Stanford. Rugby was thrown into the scrap-heap and a new and strange foe, Washington, was talked about.

Potentate clad in regal splendor never sat upon his throne with more satisfaction than we Juniors, when, resplendent in corduroys, we sank into the Upper Class Bench. Apparently we were not very energetic politicians for we couldn't even scare up a competitor for Tom Elliott for Junior "Prex." But we did care about having a good time on Junior Day—we had the most glorious Prom ever staged and as for the financial side, it was worth it! We mourned over the Washington disaster and rejoiced in the remarkable 8-13 "come-back" a week later.

The second semester came around with the class under the leadership of Imra Wann. Labor Day proved the event of the term. Floyd Stewart was chosen A. S. U. C. president by a large majority and Anna Barrows and Carol Eberts defeated their male opponents for places on the Executive Committee, which had been re-created by a revision of the constitution. We gloried in another baseball victory, but again admitted defeat in a track meet. We congratulated Krusi and Stewart on their success in editing and managing our *Blue and Gold*.

We found the reins of government as Seniors not too difficult to manage, and under Tom Slaven began our routine of control. Weekly the men and women met in their Senior halls and discussed affairs of state. A Senior endowment plan was evolved which, modeled after those followed in Eastern universities, should be successful because simple.

By this means we are enabled to have a permanent class organization, through which we may remain intact in years after graduation.

We started our last semester, and looked about for candidates for our president, not only for the last term but also for our graduate years. We nominated George Cohen and Harold Hyde, and, after a spirited contest, the former won by a narrow margin.

And when we don the cap and gown and step upon the stage to receive the coveted parchment, not one of us can forget the debt of gratitude we owe our Alma Mater; not one can forget those who made possible our coming here, the friends we have made, or our professors who have labored earnestly and not altogether in vain we trust, to give us some idea of the meaning of a university course of study.

Nineteen Seventeen—Freshmen yesterday, Seniors to-day, Alumni tomorrow—says *"ave atque vale."* May she ever render good service to her university, to her state and to her country!

SENIOR RECORDS

CAMILLE LEONIE ABBAY — Berkeley
Letters and Science — Women's Mandolin and Guitar Club (1), (2), (3), Manager (4); Treble Clef (2), (3), (4); Cast of 1917 Junior Farce "Thumbs Down"; Cast "Julius Caesar"; Staff of 1917 Blue and Gold; Senior Advisory Committee; Senior Women's Banquet Committee; Cast of 1917 Senior Extravaganza.

JOSEPH LEONARD ABREAN — Oakland
Pharmacy.

MILDRED ADAMS — Berkeley
Letters and Science. Nu Sigma Psi.

PAULINE ADAMS — Oakland
Letters and Science. Kappa Alpha Theta.

WINOLA ADAMS — Los Angeles
Letters and Science.

JOHN WILLIS ADRIANCE — Napa
Agriculture — Alpha Zeta.

FRANCES NORENE AHL — Santa Rosa
Letters and Science — Y. W. C. A.; Le Cercle Francais; Women's Parliamentary Society; Sophomore Informal Committee; Junior Election Committee.

EDWARD ALBERT — Alameda
Letters and Science

HENRY ALBERTSON — San Francisco
Letters and Science.

IRVING G. ALGER — Berkeley
Letters and Science.

JOSEPHINE EDDY ALGER — Berkeley
Letters and Science.

HARRIET OZENA ALLEN — Riverside
Letters and Science.

MARY ELIZABETH ALLEN — Pasadena
Letters and Science.

GEORGE DONALD ALLIN — Pasadena
Agriculture — Grand Club; Alpha Zeta; Manager Journal of Agriculture (4); Senior Week Program Committee; Undergraduate Students Welfare Committee (4).

ROSABELLE AMES — Berkeley
Letters and Science. Women's Parliamentary Society; Konversationsklub; Deutscher Zirkel.

WALTER NELS ANDERSON — San Diego
Letters and Science (Jurisprudence) — Cadet Military Officers' Club (4); Captain Company "C" (4); Congress Debating Society (4); Rifle Club (4); Scandinavian Club (4); Treasurer Labor Club (4); Law Association.

ANTON BENNET ANDRADE — Hayward
Letters and Science

STELLA CLARE ANDRES — Los Angeles
Letters and Science — Phi Mu.

EDMUND WARD ANDREWS — Jackson
Letters and Science — Member Assembly Debating Team, Assembly versus Senate Debate 1915, (3); First Lieutenant, Company "B," California Cadets (4).

ALEXANDER NIKOLAOS ANGELOF — Monastir, Macedonia
Letters and Science — Sociology Club.

ELLSWORTH MYRL APPERLY — Modesto
Pharmacy.

ROBERT JAMES ARCHIBALD — Wheeling, W. Va.
Agriculture.

JOHN O. ARMISTEAD — Newman
Dentistry — Phi Kappa Psi; Delta Sigma Delta; Epsilon Alpha.

ELWYN A. ARNOLD — Oakland
Letters and Science.

GASTON BOLADO ASHE — San Francisco
Mechanics — A. S. M. E.; A. E. M. E.

HOMER LUCIAN ASSELIN — San Jose
Pharmacy — Phi Delta Chi.

SHARON MARION ATKINS — Virginia (State)
Medical — Phi Alpha Gamma; Sigma Alpha Beta; U. Orchestra; Class V-President (3); Class Secretary (4); Manager Pericope (4).

LLOYD CROCKETT AUSTIN — Fresno
Dentistry — Delta Sigma Delta

BEATRICE AVERILL — Berkeley
Letters and Science.

MIRIAM NEIL HAYNES BABBIT — Berkeley
Commerce.

MARION BACHMAN — Berkeley
Letters and Science — Alpha Omicron Pi.

HELEN TRENKLER BAER — Berkeley
Letters and Science — La Rapiere; Economics Club; Secretary-Treasurer (3); Parliamentary (4); Partheneia (3); Senior Advisory Committee (4); Women's Labor Day Committee (3); Women's Class Hockey Team (4).

CRYSTAL ESTELLA BAILEY — Susanville
Letters and Science.

MYRTLE THERESA BAILEY — San Pablo
Letters and Science.

OSCAR BAILEY — San Diego
Dentistry; Sigma Phi Sigma; Editor Dentistry Division 1917 Blue and Gold.

MARY LOIS BAKER — South Pasadena
Letters and Science—Mekatina Club; Treble Clef.

GEORGE GALE BAKEWELL — Riverside
Mechanics.

JOHN KNOX BALLANTINE — Los Angeles
Letters and Science—Alpha Tau Omega; Junior Farce "Prunella"; Senior Permanent Organizing Committee; Treasurer Architecture Association (4).

FREDERICK HERBERT BALLOU — Tempe, Ariz.
Letters and Science.

KATHARINE VAN DYKE BANGS — Oakland
Letters and Science—Kappa Alpha Theta; Staff 1917 Blue and Gold; Decoration Committee, Junior Prom; Students Union Committee; Reception Committee, Senior Ball; Reunion Committee; Permanent Memorial Committee; Senior Advisory Committee.

IRVING HALSEY BANKER — Berkeley
Letters and Science.

FLOSSIE BANKS — Ukiah
Letters and Science—Norroena.

SISTER MARY BARBARA — Oakland
Letters and Science.

HENRY BRUCE BARKIS — Lodi
Mining—Bachelordon; U. N. X. Glee Club; De Koven Club; Mining Association; Vice-President, Mining Association, Spring, 1917.

JESSE WRIGHT BARNES — Mobile, Alabama
Letters and Science—Alpha Chi Sigma; Chess Team (2).

MARY ALICE BARNES — Santa Barbara
Letters and Science—To Graduate December, 1917. Nu Sigma Psi; Basketball (2); Swimming Team (3).

RUTH LILLIAN BARNES — Long Beach
Letters and Science—Alpha Delta Pi.

MARIE RICHMOND BARNEY — Anderson
Letters and Science—Senior Advisory Committee.

WILLIAM GORDON BARNUM — Oakland
Dentistry.

DOROTHY EARLE BARONIDIS — Berkeley
Fine Arts—Delta Kappa Delta; Vice-President (2); "Xmas Jinks" Decorative Committee (1), (2); Winner Kyoto Museum Fine Arts and Designs Prize, 1916.

THE "FAT BOY" AT THE AFFILIATED

ROYAL ROHAN BARONIDIS — Berkeley
Medical; Phi Alpha Gamma; Sigma Alpha Beta; U. Orchestra (3), (4); Class President (3); Associate Editor Pelican (3), (4); Blue and Gold Staff (3), (4); Cosmopoli Club; Assistant Manager of Pericope (4).

HELEN ALICE BARR — Los Angeles
Letters and Science—Women's Crew; (3); Parthenia (4); "Julius Caesar" Cast (3); Banquet Committee (4).

ANNA FRANCES BARROWS — Berkeley
Letters and Science—Alpha Phi; Prytanean; English Club; Istyc; Treasurer A. W. S. (3); Executive Committee (3), (4); A. S. U. C. Executive Board (4); Daily Californian Editorial Staff (2), (4); Women's Editor (4); Managerial Staff 1917 Blue and Gold; Senior Advisory Committee (3); Parthenia (1), (2); 1917 Crew (2); Reception Committee Freshie Glee; Reception Committee Sophomore Hop; Decoration Committee Junior Prom; Arrangements Senior Ball; General Senior Week Committee; 1917 Reunion Committee; 1917 Permanent Organizations Committee; Students Union Committee; President Prytanean (4).

STEPHEN SEARS BARROWS — Berkeley
Letters and Science—Beta Beta; Golden Bear; Winged Helmet; Sphinx; Y. M. C. A. Cabinet (3),(4); Labor Day Committee (3); Assistant Editor Blue and Gold (3); Students Welfare Committee; Students Affairs Committee (3); Secretary (4); Senate Debating Society; President (3); General Chairman Senior Week; Honor System Committee (4).

BAPTISTE BARTHE — Livermore
Commerce; Tilicum; Lieutenant; President of Forum Debating Society (4); President of Cercle Francais (2).

WALTER H. BARTHEL — Berkeley
Mining—Chi Phi; Freshman Football Team.

RICHARD BARTHOLOMEW — Denver, Colo.
Agriculture—Beta Theta Pi (Denver); Transfer from Stanford in Junior Year.

PEARL C. BAUGHMAN — Seattle, Wash.
Letters and Science.

LORETTA BAUM — San Francisco
Letters and Science.

REPUBLICAN REPENTANCE

TIRED BUSINESS MEN

FREDA CADELL BAYLEY   OAKLAND
Letters and Science — Alpha Xi Delta; Prytanean; Blue and Gold Editorial Staff (3); Y. W. C. A. Cabinet (2), (3), (4); Y. W. C. A. Vice-President (4); Chairman Women's Welfare Committee; Senior Pilgrimage Committee; Senior Advisory Committee.

CHARLES H. BAYLY   LOS ANGELES
Letters and Science — Phi Upsilon; U. N. X.; Beta Beta.

MARY ISABEL BEAN   SAN JOSE
Letters and Science.

ANGENETTA IDELL BEASLEY   CLOVERDALE
Letters and Science — Alpha Delta Pi; Le Cercle Francais, Parliamentary Society; Partheneia (2), (3); Junior Farce; Y. W. C. A. Membership and Social Committee.

CLARENCE WALTER BEEBE   BERKELEY
Chemistry.

CHARLES ROBERT BELL   KINSLEY, KANS.
Agriculture — Acacia; Varsity Football Team (4).

FRANK COLVER BELL   OAKLAND
Mechanics — Sigma Nu; Tau Beta Pi; Eta Kappa Nu; A. I. E. E., A. E. and M. E.; Freshman Interfraternity Committee; Delegate, Eta Kappa Nu Convention (4); Senior Pilgrimage Committee.

LELAND MORRISON BELL   SACRAMENTO
Agriculture — Acacia; Beta Kappa Alpha; Class President (1); Junior Prom Committee.

JOHN WILLIAM BENTON   REDDING
Letters and Science — Sigma Phi Epsilon; Freshman Track Team (1); Varsity Track Team (2); Senior Football Team (4); Manager of The Occident (4); Manager Pelican (4); Chairman of Senior Permanent Organization Committee (4); Track Team East Committee (3); Assistant Manager Blue and Gold (3); Class Rally Committee (2), (3); Labor Day Implement Committee (3); California Day Committee.

LOIS BRULYN BENTON   RENO, NEVADA
Letters and Science — Delta Delta Delta; Senior Assembly Committee; Senior Endowment Committee; Senior Ball Committee; Senior Extravaganza.

EDWARD WILLIAM BERG   KINGSBURG
Agriculture.

JAMES BOURLAND BERGER   BERKELEY
Pharmacy.

ROBERT ELLIS BERING   SAN FRANCISCO
Agriculture — Delta Sigma Phi.

LEILA BALDWIN BERRY   BERKELEY
Letters and Science — Kappa Kappa Gamma; Prytanean, President A. W. S. (4); Students Union Committee (4); Member General Senior Week Committee.

RUSSELL DOLMAN BERST   PORTLAND, ORE.
Mechanics — Electrical Engineering; Eta Kappa Nu; Sigma Xi.

ELISE CAROLYN BERTHEAU   SAN FRANCISCO
Letters and Science — Kappa Alpha Theta; Deutscher Verein, Senior Adviser.

INA WEATHERWAX BERTHOLF   BERKELEY
Letters and Social Science — Phi Beta Kappa.

CHARLES COLEMAN BERWICK   BERKELEY
Letters and Science (Medicine) — Sigma Phi Epsilon, Alpha Kappa, Beta Kappa Alpha; President Associated Pre-Medical Students (3).

CARLOTTA BESHLICH   OAKLAND
Letters and Science Alpha Nu.

WILLIAM CAMPBELL BINKLEY   SANTA ANA
Letters and Science — Phi Delta Kappa; Associate Editor Daily Californian (2).

ALIEDA BIRCH   SANTA ROSA
Fine Arts — Delta Kappa Delta; Honorary Member P. C. B. L.; Christmas Jinks Entertainment Committee (1), (2), (3); Captain, Girls' Baseball Team (3).

IRENE WINIFRED BIXBY   LOS ANGELES
Letters and Science — Senior Adviser (4); Senior Women's Banquet Committee (4).

EDITH VIRGINIA BLACK   FELLOWS
Letters and Science.

HAROLD ALFRED BLACK   SAN FRANCISCO
Letters and Science (Jurisprudence) — Kappa Sigma; Phi Beta Kappa, Phi Delta Phi, English Club, Mask and Dagger, President of Senate (4); Debating Council (4); Undergraduate Students Affairs Committee (4); Arrangements Committee Senior Ball; Senior Peace Committee; Editorial 1917 Blue and Gold; Rally Committee (3); Junior Prom Committee; Cast "Richelieu"; "Prunella"; Junior Curtain Raiser; "Devil's Disciple"; "Julius Caesar"; "Androcles and the Lion"; "Helena's Husband", "The Maker of Dreams"; Commencement Speaker.

NELLIE ESTELLA BLACK   SANTA MARIA
Letters and Science.

EDWIN EARLE BLACKIE   LINCOLN
Civil Engineering.

ROBERT BLAKE   BERKELEY
Letters and Science — Golden Bear; Winged Helmet; English Club; Phrontisterion; Daily Californian Staff (1), (2), (3), (4); Editor Fall Semester 1916.

JOHN PHILLIP BLANK   LOS ANGELES
Commerce.

WILLIAM WALLACE BLISS   BERKELEY
Mechanics.

OWEN ROBERTSON BLOIS   DINUBA
Agriculture — Pi Kappa Alpha.

CLIFFORD ARTHUR BLY   LOS ANGELES
Agriculture — Tilicum.

JOHN GILBERT BOARDMAN   LINDSAY
Agriculture — Delta Sigma Phi.

FREDERICK KARL JOHAN BOCK   GIESSEN, GERMANY
Pharmacy.

LLEWELLYN M. K. BOELTER   LATAH, WASH.
Mechanics.

CLARENCE CARL BOHNHOFF   LOS ANGELES
Mechanics.

BERT ALLISON BONE   SAN DIEGO
Civil Engineering — Tilicum.

BEATRICE LOUISE BONNER — FRESNO
Letters and Science—Delta Delta Delta; Organization Committee Parthenon (3); Chairman Book Exchange (4); Class Basketball Team (1), (2), (3); Varsity Basketball (1).

RAYMOND KARNAGHAN BONTZ — SACRAMENTO
Letters and Science—Beta Theta Pi; Golden Bear; Winged Helmet; Sphinx; Press Club; Daily Californian (1), (2), (3); Blue and Gold Staff (1); Rally Committee (2); Junior Prom Committee (3); Permanent Organization Committee (4).

FRANKLIN OTIS BOOTH — LOS ANGELES
Agriculture.

BENJAMIN BORCHARDT — SAN FRANCISCO
Letters and Science.

BRADFORD WALSWORTH BOSLEY — BERKELEY
Letters and Science—Delta Chi.

MARGRET BOVEROUX — OAKLAND
Letters and Science—Gamma Phi Beta.

WILLIAM EARL BOWEN — OAKLAND
Mechanics—Theta Chi.

ROY BOWER — BERKELEY
Letters and Science.

BENNETT HART BOWLEY — SAN FRANCISCO
Civil Engineering.

HARRIETT LOUISE BOWMAN — SPOKANE, WASH.
Letters and Science—Manager A. W. S. Counter; Senior Women's Banquet Committee; Parthenon (3), (4).

EDDY TALLMAN BOYD — NAPA
Dentistry—Delta Sigma Delta; Epsilon Alpha.

RUTH ESTELLA BOYER — BERKELEY
Letters and Science.

ROSAMOND JORDAN BRADBURY — SANTA BARBARA
Letters and Science—Pi Beta Phi; Blue and Gold Staff.

CHARLES DUSTIN BRADLEY — SPRECKELS
Dentistry—Sigma Pi; Delta Sigma Delta.

LLOYD PAYNE BRADLEY — BERKELEY
Agriculture—Agriculture Club.

MABEL BRADWAY — HOLLYWOOD
Letters and Science.

SIMONE MARTHA BRANGIER — AGNEW
Letters and Science—Le Cercle Francais; President (4), Treasurer (3), Secretary (4); Delta Epsilon; Ambulance Committee.

RICHARD ROY BRAVIN — RENO, NEVADA
Pharmacy—Phi Delta Chi.

HELEN LUCILLE BRAYTON — LONG BEACH
Letters and Science—Sigma Kappa.

EDWARD C. N. BRETT — LOS ANGELES
Letters and Science—Delta Tau Delta.

FRANCIS THORBURN BREWSTER — BERKELEY
Letters and Science—Editor Student Opinion (3) (Pilot); Captain Quartermaster of Cadets, 4.

EUGENE ARTHUR BREYMAN — SAN FRANCISCO
Letters and Science—Dwight Club; Carl English Club "Prunella," "Julius Caesar," "Androcles and the Lion," "Canterbury Pilgrims" Extravaganza; Mask and Dagger; "Devil's Disciple," Treble Clef Opera "What Next," Senate Debating Society; Z.O.L.; Treasurer (3); Senior Reunion Committee, Secretary.

BARBARA BRIDGE — MILL VALLEY
Letters and Science.

HENRY SPENCER BRINK — BIGGS
Commerce—Pi Kappa Phi.

SAMUEL BRODIE — BERKELEY
Letters and Science.

SAMUEL BRODSKY — NEW YORK, N. Y.
Letters and Science—Member of the Menorah Society.

EDWARD DUERDIN BRONSON — OAKLAND
Letters and Science—Beta Beta, Senate; Glee Club, Secretary (2), 1917 Blue and Gold.

CHARLES THOMAS BROOKS — OAKLAND
Commerce—Abracadabra; Y. M. C. A. Cabinet.

EDNA LOUISA BROWN — BOISE, IDAHO
Letters and Science—Sophomore Crew, Junior Crew; All California Crew 1916, Assistant Rowing Manager 1917.

FRANCES LESLIE BROWN — PETALUMA
Letters and Science—Delta Zeta; Prytanean; Phi Beta Kappa; Deskri; Ivy; Torch and Shield, Editorial Staff Daily Californian (3); Women's Edited (4); A. W. S. Executive Committee (4); Class Vice-President (4); Parthenon Publicity Committee (3); News Editor 1917 Record (3); Cast of Junior Curtain Raiser; Senior Advisory Committee; Senior Endowment Committee; Toastmistress Senior Women's Banquet.

IDA LOUISE BROWN — OAKLAND
Letters and Science—French Club, 1916; Treble Clef Club.

JOHN HERBERT BROWN — LOS ANGELES
Letters and Science—Phi Kappa Sigma; Sophomore and Senior Crews; Chairman Decoration Committee, Sophomore Hop; Member Senior Finance Committee; Secretary American Ambulance Corps Committee.

BEFORE THE SHOW

STUDYING AT THE FARM

RALPH MERCER BROWN SAN FRANCISCO
Commerce.

HAROLD HENDERSON BROWNE BERKELEY
Chemistry.

HENRY JOHN BRU OAKLAND
Letters and Science.

JOHN H. BRUCE SAN FRANCISCO
Letters and Science—Chi Psi; Golden Bear, Winged Helmet, Sphinx, English Club, Press Club; Associate Editor Occident (2), (3), Editor (4); Editor Josh Department 1917 Blue and Gold, Co-author 1917 Extravaganza; Junior Farce Committee; Senior Extravaganza Committee, Stunt Committee Big "C" Sirkus (4); Publicity Committee Labor Day, 1916.

PAUL RAYMOND BRUNT SAN DIEGO
Letters and Science—Librarian U. C. Orchestra 1914, 1915; Principal Musician Band, 1917; First Lieutenant U. C. Cadets (4).

ZDENKA BUBEN ALAMEDA
Letters and Science—Parthencia (2); Slavic Society, President (4).

FISHER AURELIUS BUCKINGHAM SAN FRANCISCO
Commerce—Senoyanh Club; Class Constitution Committee (4); Cosmopolitan Club (2), (3); Congress Debating Society (2), (3), (4); Commerce Club (2), (3), (4), Vice-President (4).

WALTER GEORGE BUELL SOLANO
Letters and Science.

BARBARA BURKE BERKELEY
Letters and Science—Kappa Alpha Theta, Sigma Kappa Alpha; Freshman Glee Decoration Committee; Senior Ball Decoration Committee; Senior Reunion Committee, Senior Advisory Committee (3), (4).

SHERMAN KENNEDY BURKE BERKELEY
Letters and Science — Phi Kappa Sigma; Phi Delta Phi; Intercollegiate Debating Team (3); Carnot Debating Team (3), (4).

ELLA MAY BURT PRINCETON
Letters and Science.

DAVID FRAZER BUSH MARTINEZ
Letters and Science (Jurisprudence)—Dahlonega; Senate, Class Crew (4); Senior Pilgrimage Committee; Senior Permanent Organization Committee; Cadet Lieutenant.

LEILA ELLA BUTLER BOISE, IDAHO
Letters and Science.

MARY DOREAS BUTMAN WHITTIER
Letters and Science—Alpha Delta Pi.

LEWIS RYAN BYINGTON HEALDSBURG
Letters and Science (Jurisprudence)—Phi Sigma Kappa; Phi Delta Phi; Winged Helmet, Chairman Rally Committee (4), (4); Rally Committee (3), (4); Varsity Track Team (2), (3), (4); Freshman Baseball Team; Student Manager A. S. U. C. (4); Chairman A. S. U. C. Card Sale Committee (3); Constitution Revision Committee (4); Beta Beta, U. N. X; Cadet Captain; Senior Ball Committee; General Committee Junior Prom.

HELEN DOUGLAS CAMPBELL VANCOUVER, B. C.
Letters and Science.

JOHN LOCKHART CAMPBELL PACIFIC GROVE
Dentistry.

RUBY CATHERINE CAMPBELL ORANGE
Letters and Science — Phi Mu; Treasurer Women's Mandolin and Guitar Club (3), President (4); Stunt Committee, Women's Day Dance (4); Transfer from Pomona (3).

ERNEST CAMPER BERKELEY
Letters and Science — Sigma Alpha Epsilon; Skull and Key; Winged Helmet, U. N. X; Beta Beta; Omicron Delta; Big "C" Society; Freshman Crew; Varsity Crew (4); Mandolin Club (1), (2). Sophomore Hop Committee (2); Junior Banquet Committee (3); Senior Ball Committee (4).

JAMES SOMERS CANDEE HUNTINGTON PARK
Letters and Science—Phi Delta Theta; Winged Helmet; Skull and Key; U. N. X; Beta Beta; Glee Club; Chairman Arrangements Committee Freshie Glee; Chairman Arrangements Committee Junior Prom; Lead in Senior Extravaganza, De Koven Club; Rally Committee (4).

GRAY AT SUMMER SCHOOL

CHARLES JOSEF CAREY SACRAMENTO
Jurisprudence—Delta Upsilon; Phi Delta Phi; Winged Helmet; Golden Bear; Press Club; Sphinx; Senate; Sophomore-Freshman Debate (2); General Chairman Junior Day (3); Chairman Students Welfare Committee (4); Chairman Senior Peace Committee (4); Toastmaster Sophomore Banquet (2); Toastmaster Senior Banquet (4); Publicity Committee Labor Day (3); Publicity Committee Senior Week (4); Arrangements Committee Senior Ball (4); General Committee Senior Week (4); Bonnheim Scholar; Bonnheim Lower Division Essay Winner (1); Bonnheim Upper Division Essay Winner (1), (2); Secretary Honor System Committee (3); Senior Hall Pilgrimage Speaker; Cast Senior Extravaganza; Board of Governors Senior Hall.

MARJORIE S. CARLTON BERKELEY
Letters and Science—Prytanean; Junior Prom Committee; Labor Day Committee (3); Partheneia Executive Committee (2), (3); Chairman (4); Senior Advisory Committee (3), (4); Senior Women's Banquet Committee (4).

IRENE CARMICHAEL LIVINGSTON
Letters and Social Science—Alpha Gamma Delta.

HAROLD CHESTER CARNIGLIA SAN FRANCISCO
Civil Engineering.

IRENE CARPENTER BERKELEY
Letters and Science.

GEORGE JAMES CARR CAMBRIDGE
Letters and Science—Sigma Nu; Cadet Band (1), (2); Associate Editor Daily Californian (2); Editor of Department of Activities, 1917 Blue and Gold.

ZELMA ALICE CARROLL ELKO, NEVADA
Letters and Science.

HAVE YOU HEARD THIS ONE?

ANNA BRECKINRIDGE CARTER RIVERSIDE
Letters and Science—Prytanean; Women's Big "C" Society; Sports and Pastimes Society; Transfer from Occidental College (1); Varsity Tennis Team (1), (2), (3), (4); Varsity Basketball Team (1); Class Tennis Team (2), (3), (4); Captain (1); Class Hockey Team (3), (4); All-Star Hockey Team (4); Labor Day Committee (3); Captain and Manager Tennis Team (4).

ANTONIO L. DEL CASTILLO CUBA
Medical II—Class Treasurer (3).

JULIA W. CATES BERKELEY
Letters and Science—Phi Beta Kappa.

PRISCILLA ANASTASIA CAVAGNARO OAKLAND
Letters and Science—Newman Club; Italian Club; Women's Class Crew (2); Honorable Mention Partheneia Contest, Jeanne d'Arc 1916; Welfare Committee (4); Students Affairs Committee (4); Chairman Constitutional Revision Committee A. W. S. (4); Pilgrimage Committee (4); Ambulance Committee (4); President Italian Club (4); Senior Advisory Committee (4).

WARNER SABIN CHADBOURNE SUISUN
Agriculture—Kappa Alpha; U. N. X. 2; Skull and Key (3); Rally Committee (3).

PAULINE CHAMBERLAIN BERKELEY
Letters and Science—Pi Beta Phi; Ukulele Club; Treble Clef; Reviews of Construction Committee of A. S. U. C. 1914; Chairman of Final Arrangements Committee Partheneia 1917; Partheneia 1914 and 1915; Extravaganza 1917.

HOWARD FRANCIS CHAPPELL LOS BANOS
Agricultural Education.

RALPH PERRY CHESSAL UKIAH
Dentistry—Xi Psi Phi; Epsilon Alpha; Class Vice-President (4); 1917 Dance Committee.

ROSE CHEW OAKLAND
Letters and Science.

LOIS LIZZIE CHILCOTE BERKELEY
Letters and Science.

MARMION HUGO CHILDRESS BERKELEY
Medicine—Phi Chi; Beta Kappa Alpha; Lieutenant in Band; Chairman Executive Committee (4); Associated Pre-Medical Students.

MARY MARGARET CHILSON BERKELEY
Letters and Science—Zeta Tau Alpha.

SARAH MU JIN CHING BERKELEY
Letters and Science.

WINOS

LABOR DAY AT THE AFFILIATED COLLEGES

MARIAN ELIZABETH CHRISTENSEN San Rafael
Letters and Science—Kappa Alpha Theta; Senior Advisor.

ARTHUR LEO CLARK Fresno
Letters and Science (Jurisprudence).

CARROLL CLARK Oakland
Letters and Science.

CHARLES LESTER CLARK Berkeley
Letters and Science.

ROBERT CAMPBELL CLARK Berkeley
Letters and Science — Phi Kappa Sigma; Chi Beta Sigma; Sphinx; Athletic Editor Daily Californian; Athletic Editor 1917 Blue and Gold; Editor California Section "American Collegiate Athletic History," in charge Campus Publicity Senior Week; in Charge Senior Week Printing Master; Chairman Senior Week Programme Committee; General Committee Senior Week; Freshman Tennis Team.

ZELL FAVEL CLARK Berkeley
Letters and Science.

CAMILLA DOROTHEA CLARKE Pasadena
Letters and Science—Kappa Kappa Gamma; Partheneia (2), (3), (4); Junior Farce; Senior Extravaganza; Y. W. C. A. Committees (Permanent) (3), (4); Art History Circle, Secretary-Treasurer (3); President (4); Prytanean Fete Committee; Partheneia Costume Committee.

ROBERTA CARRICK CLARKE Tulare
Letters and Science.

HARRY ERVING CLAUDES Porterville
Pharmacy.

THOMAS HUBBARD CLEMENTS Los Angeles
Chemistry.

RUTH ALICE CLIFFORD Lindsay
Letters and Science.

WILLIAM THOMAS CLOW Berkeley
Agriculture—Cadet Captain.

JOHN UPTON CLOWDSLEY Stockton
Letters and Science, (Architecture)—Architectural Association; Freshman Track Team; Varsity Track Team (3).

HELEN WHEELER CLOWES Stockton
Letters and Science—Alpha Omicron Pi.

BARRETT NELSON COATES Sacramento
Commerce—Phi Beta Kappa, Beta Tau Sigma.

VAUGHN MERWIN COBB Los Angeles
Commerce—A. S. U. C. Finance Reorganization Committee (4); Senior Jolly-up Committee (4); Endowment Fund Committee (4).

STANTON ARTHUR COBLENTZ Stockton
Letters and Science — Varsity Chess Team, President (3 and 4); Associate Editor Student Opinion (3); Congress, Treasurer (3); Menorah, Secretary (4); University Chess Secretary (4).

ZACH BENJAMIN COBLENTZ Santa Maria
Medicine.

LEONARD AVON COBURN Visalia
Civil Engineering.

HUGH McCAULEY COCHRAN San Francisco
Mechanics.

CORA EDITH CODY San Jose
Letters and Science.

ELMON FRANK COE Mesa, Arizona
Letters and Science—Alpha Kappa Lambda; Congress Speaker Protem (4); Senior Pilgrimage Committee.

JOHN M. COFFEEN Pasadena
Agriculture—Beta Theta Pi, Alpha Zeta, Big "C" Society, Varsity Football (4).

GEORGE WESLEY COFFEY Oakland
Mining—Theta Tau, Tau Beta Pi, Phi Beta Kappa, Sigma Xi.

DOUGLAS BRAY COHEN Oakland
Agriculture—Chi Phi, Golden Bear, Winged Helmet, Big "C" Society, Omicron Delta, U. N. X., T. N. E., Skull and Keys; Chairman Decoration Committee Freshie Glee; Decoration Committee Soph Hop; Floor Manager Junior Prom; Reception Committee Senior Ball; Varsity Football Team (2), (4); Chairman Intercollegiate Agreement Committee (4); Freshman Track Team; Varsity Track Team (3).

GEORGE WASHINGTON COHEN Los Angeles
Letters and Science — Golden Bear, Phi Delta Phi, English Club, Sphinx, Congress, Speaker (4); Senior Class President; Chairman of Students Union Committee (4); Carnot Debating Team, Medalist (3); Junior Prom Committee.

MILTON HAROLD COHN San Francisco
Letters and Science (Jurisprudence)—Orchestra (1), (2), (3), (4).

CLIFFORD BERT COLE Oakland
Letters and Science — Delta Tau Delta; Beta Beta; U. N. X. Freshman Track Team; Labor Day Committee; Students Union Committee; Assistant Trainer (1), (2), (3); Assistant Coach Freshman Track Team (4).

SUNDAY MORNING, D. K. E.'S PREPARE FOR WAR

HENRY CHARLES COLLINS — SAN FRANCISCO
Letters and Science

JULIUS LLOYD COLLINS — BERKELEY
Agriculture

ERNEST FLEMING COLVIN — FLEMING, OREGON
Dentistry—Pre Owen

MADISON HENRY COMPTON — LOS ANGELES
Letters and Science

ALVAH PUTNAM CONKLIN — BERKELEY
Letters and Science, (Pre-Agriculture)

EDITH MARION CONNELL — BERKELEY
Letters and Science

JOHN P. CONRAD — SAN BERNARDINO
Agriculture; Alpha Zeta, Phi Beta Kappa

CORBIN CORBIN — SANTA MONICA
Letters and Science (Pre-Legal); Theta Delta Chi

FREDERICK CARRINGTON COREY — LA JOLLA
Agriculture; Pi Kappa Alpha, Alpha Zeta, Decoration Committee Sophomore Hop, Freshman Crew

HARRY BEAUMONT CORLETT — NAPA
Civil Engineering

BROTHER FIDELIS CORNELIUS — OAKLAND
Letters and Science

WILLIAM DARREL COUGHLAN — NEVADA CITY
Letters and Science—Phi Lambda Upsilon

MARIE COVINGTON — FORT SMITH, ARKANSAS
Letters and Science; Zeta Tau Alpha

JOHN GARDNER CRAFTS — OAKLAND
Pre-Medical

CHESTER RUDOLPH FRANCIS CRAMER — SAN FRANCISCO
Agriculture; Sigma Phi Sigma; Vice-President Agriculture Club (4); Vice-President Davis Agriculture Club (3); Chairman Agriculture Dance (4); First Lieutenant of Cadets, (4);

ON AN OUTING

MILDRED CRANE — SACRAMENTO
Letters and Science; Phi Beta Kappa; Class Crew (2), (3)

ALICE BEULAH CRANSTON — SANTA ANA
Letters and Science; Alpha Omicron Pi; Senior Assembly Committee; Permanent Organization Committee

HELEN CRAWFORD — TOPEKA, KANSAS
Letters and Science; Kappa Alpha Theta; Deutscher Verein; Senior Printing Committee

JAMES McNEITH CRAWFORD — ANTIOCH
Agriculture; Alpha Sigma Phi; Ag Club

LOUIS ANTONIO CRIBARI — SAN JOSE
Letters and Science (Medicine)

RAYMOND WILLIAMS CROOK — SAN FRANCISCO
Commerce; Commerce Club; Beta Gamma Sigma

BRADFORD J. CROW — BERKELEY
Letters and Science; Phi Gamma Delta; Skull and Keys; U. N. X.; Omicron Delta; Freshman Baseball Team; Junior Men's Banquet Committee

DENNIS JAMES HYACINTH CROWLEY — PORT COSTA
Letters and Science

WINNIFRED CUMMINGS — SALT LAKE CITY, UTAH
Letters and Science; Delta Zeta; Captain Partheneia Properties Committees, (3 and 4)

JAMES EDMUND CHESTER CURRENS — BERKELEY
Mechanics

ELOISE BOSTWICK CUSHING — OAKLAND
Letters and Science (Jurisprudence)

LOUISE LUTZ DAHL — SAN FRANCISCO
Fine Arts; Delta Kappa Delta; Christmas Jinks Decorations Committee (1), (2), (3), (4); Dance Committee (1), (2);

OSCAR EDWIN DAHLEN — STOCKHOLM, SWEDEN
Medical—Orchestra (3), (4)

THOMAS W. DAHLQUIST — SALT LAKE CITY, UTAH
Letters and Science—Pi Kappa Alpha; Phi Beta Kappa

CLEO THEODORA DAMIANAKES — OAKLAND
Letters and Science—Delta Epsilon; Junior Prom Committee; Chorus, Junior Farce; Partheneia (2), (3); Women's Interclass Track Team (1), (2), (3); Partheneia Costume Designing Committee (3), (4);

KEROSENING THE YAHOO BIRD BEFORE TOUCHING A MATCH

KIEFER AND HIS HEIFER

DORIS ALDEN DANIELS   Monrovia
Letters and Science—Iota Sigma Pi; Alpha Nu; French Circle.

VERNA MAY DARROW   Oakland
Letters and Science.

SIDNEY HAROLD DAVIDSON   Los Angeles
Agriculture.

CLINTON GEORGE DAVIES   Modesto
Pharmacy.

CYRIL ALFRED DAVIS   San Francisco
Mechanics.

HELEN MARGARET DAVIS   Berkeley
Letters and Science.

MARY FAYE CAULKINS DAVIS   Ceres
Letters and Science.

FRANCES DOROTHY DAY   Los Angeles
Letters and Science.

JNANENDRA KRISHNA DEB   Calcutta, India
Commerce—Nalanda Club, President; Cosmopolitan Club, Secretary.

TILLIE de BERNARDIE   Santa Rosa
Letters and Science—Treble Clef (1), (2); Ukulele Club (1), (2), (3); Swimming Captain (3); Junior Prom Committee on Arrangements; Senior Ball Reception Committee; Cast Senior Extravaganza; Senior Endowment Committee.

WILLIAM AUGUST DEGEN   Alameda
Agriculture.

GRANVILLE SINCLAIR DELAMERE   Berkeley
Letters and Science—Sequoyah Club; Phi Chi.

JEAN MARJORIE DEMING   Auburn
Letters and Science—Phi Beta Kappa.

JOHN MARSHALL DENBO   Lafayette, La.
Mining—Sigma Alpha Epsilon.

MYRTLE VALENTINE DENNET   San Francisco
Letters and Science.

WRIGHT ETHELBERT D'EVELYN   San Francisco
Mining—Chi Phi; Theta Tau; Varsity Track Team (3); Cross-Country Team (4); Circle "C" Society (4).

MARGARETTE ADAH DERMONT   Williams, Ariz.
Letters and Science—Kappa Kappa Gamma.

RAY ORREN DIETHER   Hollywood
Letters and Science—Alpha Kappa Lambda; Phi Delta Kappa; Education Club; Sociology Club.

HAROLD PUTNAM DETWILER   El Paso, Texas
Agriculture—Abracadabra; Alpha Zeta; Rifle Team (2), (4); Class Football Team (3), (4); Varsity Football Squad (3); Cadet Captain (4); Military Ball Committee (4); Senior Week Committee.

PAULINE DILLMAN   Sacramento
Letters and Science—Kappa Alpha Theta; Parthenia (2), (3); Parthenia Costume Designing Committee (3), (4); Chairman Second Semester (4); Labor Day Entertainment Committee (3); California Day Refreshment Committee (3); Senior Permanent Organization Committee; Senior Advisory Committee; Senior Week Arrangements Committee; Undergraduate Women's Welfare Committee (4); Transfer from Mills College (2).

CHARLES STANLEY DIMM   Berkeley
Commerce—Delta Tau Delta; Beta Gamma Sigma; Skull and Key; Beta Beta; U. N. X.; De Koven Club; President Glee Club (4); Chairman, Junior Informals (3); Chairman, Sophomore Charter Day Festivities; Senior Ball Arrangements Committee.

SOPHIA DINSDALE   Woodland
Letters and Science.

WILLIAM DINSMORE   Marysville
Letters and Science—Sigma Phi Sigma.

CECIL A. DITTY   Pomona
Commerce—Sigma Pi; Commerce Club (3), (4); Senior Assembly Committee.

CARL TORREY DIXON   San Diego
Mechanics—Tilicum; Eta Kappa Nu; A. I. E. E.

ELLEN AUGUSTA ERIKA DOMINIQUE   Santa Barbara
Letters and Science.

GEORGE TURNER DONALDSON   Liberty, Mo.
Pharmacy.

ROBERT NELSON DONALDSON   Berkeley
Chemistry—Alpha Chi Sigma; Cadet Lieutenant.

LOUISE AGNES DORAN   Healdsburg
Letters and Science.

CARL NICHOLS DORMAN   Sacramento
Dental—Delta Sigma Delta.

HUGH FREDERICK DORMODY   Placerville
Letters and Science.

ROBERT EARLE DORTON   Kansas City, Mo.
Letters and Science—Dwight Club; Senate Debating Society.

NEIL FRANCIS DOUGHERTY   Los Angeles
Agriculture.

ELIZABETH ELLEN DOUGLAS   Berkeley
Letters and Science—Iota Sigma Pi.

Mrs. HENRIETTA L. DOUGLAS RED BLUFF
Letters and Science.

WILLIAM CRUMBAUGH DOUGLAS RED BLUFF
Commerce Commerce Club; Officers Club; Cadet Captain (4).

MARION CLARICE DOWNEY MODESTO
Letters and Science Pi Beta Phi; Junior Informal Committee; Blue and Gold Staff (3); Senior Assembly Committee (4).

OCTAVIA DOWNIE BERKELEY
Letters and Science Pi Beta Phi; Phi Beta Kappa; Prytanean.

JAMES PAUL DOYLE SAN FRANCISCO
Pharmacy.

CLAUDE WILLIAM DRAKE ALHAMBRA
Mechanics.

JAMES SHIELDS DRAPER COLORADO SPRINGS, COLORADO
Mechanics —A. E. M. E.

HARRY E. DROBISH RIVERSIDE
Agriculture Alpha Kappa Lambda; Alpha Zeta; Y. M. C. A. Cabinet (3), (4); U. C. Farm Picnic Publicity Chairman (4); Journal of Agriculture (3), (4); Agricultural Club (3), (4);

ALBERT LAURENCE DUNN LONG BEACH
Letters and Science —Phi Kappa Psi; Golden Bear; Winged Helmet; Beta Beta; Blue and Gold, (2), Assistant Editor (3); Crew Informal Chairman (3); Junior Informal, Chairman; Treasurer Y. M. C. A. (4); Students Union Committee, (2), (4); Rally Committee (3); University Meetings Committee, Chairman (4); Class Finance Committee (4).

M. SYRIL DUSENBERY SAN FRANCISCO
Mechanics Eta Kappa Nu; A. E. and M. E.; Mathematics Club; American Institution of Electrical Engineers, Glee Club, (2), (3), (4); Camera Club (2), (3); Radio Club, (3), (4); Chief Electrician Big "C" Sirkus.

ROBERT DEAN EASTON SACRAMENTO
Mechanics —Sigma Alpha Epsilon; A. S. M. E.; Freshman Poster Committee; Senior Informal Committee; Senior Permanent Organization Fund Committee; A. S. M. E. Banquet Committee.

MAUD CAROL EBERTS OAKLAND
Letters and Science —Delta Gamma; English Club; Mask and Dagger; Issue, Torch and Shield; Prytanean; Co-author of Junior Farce; Executive Committee A. S. U. C.; Executive Committee A. W. S.; Assistant Editor 1917 *Blue and Gold*; Big "C" Sirkus Committee (4), (4); Freshie Glee Committee; Chairman Junior Farce Committee; Cast Senior Extravaganza, "Countess Cathleen", "Richelieu", "You Never Can Tell"; "Helena's Husband"; Junior Farce; Parthenia (3).

MIRIAM ECKART MARYSVILLE
Letters and Science —Delta Delta Delta.

CECIL ELI EDGAR SANGER
Letters and Science.

MARJORIE GWENDOLINE EDWARDS PASADENA
Letters and Science.

PAUL DUNCAN EDWARDS VISALIA
Letters and Science —Theta Chi; Mandolin Club (1), (2), (3).

ANNA ELIZA EHLERS WHITTIER
Letters and Science —Transfer from Nebraska State University.

EDWIN MADISON ELAM BERKELEY
Letters and Science Phi Gamma Delta; Phi Delta Phi; Beta Beta; Winged Helmet; Skull and Key; Press Club; *Daily Californian* Staff (1), (2), (3); Senate Debating Society (2); Assistant Yell Leader (3); 1917 *Blue and Gold* Staff.

ALICE BUNNELL ELLIOT OAKLAND
Letters and Science Delta Delta Delta; Phi Beta Kappa; English Club; Mask and Dagger; Freshie Glee Committee; Sophomore Hop Committee; Junior Prom Committee; Secretary of English Club (3); Junior Farce; Cast of Parthenia (2), (3); "Much Ado About Nothing," "Richelieu," "You Never Can Tell," "The Devil's Disciple," "Keeping It Dark," "Androcles and the Lion."

ELIZABETH FRANCES ELLIOTT BERKELEY
Letters and Science Alpha Omicron Pi; Treble Clef; Senior Week Committee.

FRANK THOMAS ELLIOTT VISALIA
Commerce Phi Gamma Delta; Omicron Delta; Beta Beta; Winged Helmet; General Chairman Freshie Glee; Glee Club; Students Union Committee (1), (2), (3), (4); Sophomore Hop Committee; Belgian Relief Committee; Class President (3); Chairman Junior Peace Committee (3); California Day Committee (2); Labor Day Committee (3); Senior Peace Committee; Senior Adviser; Senior Endowment Committee; Class Treasurer (4); Permanent Class Treasurer; Senior Week Finance Committee; Senior Ball Committee; Cast Senior Extravaganza.

AUSTIN ROBERT EMBER ALAMEDA
Civil Engineering Beta Theta Pi; Tau Beta Pi; Sigma Iota Phi; Glee Club; Assistant Editor *Blue and Gold* (3); *Blue and Gold* Advisory Committee (4); Cross Country (3); Extravaganza Committee (4); Labor Day Committee (4).

KOSHIRO ENDO SENDAI, JAPAN
Agriculture

DOROTHY EPPING HOOD RIVER, OREGON
Letters and Science Delta Gamma

FREDERICK MONROE ESSIG SHIVELY
Letters and Science —Phi Beta Kappa; Military Captain (4).

JOHN MANDERSON EVANS WOODLAND
Agriculture.

MARION EVANS SAN FRANCISCO
Letters and Science —Alpha Xi Delta.

DEPUE FALCK OGDEN, UTAH
Agriculture.

WALDEMAR A. FALCK LOS ANGELES
Letters and Science Bachelordon; Golden Bear; Winged Helmet; U. N. X.; Skull and Key; Big "C" Society; Varsity Crew (1), (2), (3), (4), Captain (4); Captain Class Crew (2); Glee Club.

KAPPA CONTRIBUTION

BONES

DONALD GUY FARNEMAN LOS ANGELES
Commerce

EBNER DWIGHT FARRINGTON EL MONTE
Letters and Science — Phi Chi.

OLIVETTA FAULKNER ABERDEEN, WASH.
Letters and Science — Kappa Alpha Theta; Partheneia Properties Committee (2), (3), (4).

JENNIE LOUISE FAYARD SAN JOSE
Letters and Science.

JULIAN FEINBERG NEW YORK, N. Y.
Mining.

ALOIS HUBERT FELCHLIN STOCKTON
Letters and Science.

CLARENCE JAMES FELT BERKELEY
Commerce — Commerce Club, Vice-President (4); Class Football Team (1).

JOHN HERMAN FENTON SACRAMENTO
Mechanics.

ELIZABETH VAN EVEREN FERGUSON BOLSA
Letters and Science — Delta Delta Delta; Phi Beta Kappa; Beta Kappa Alpha (4); Transfer from Brown University; Senior Advisory Committee.

EDNA FIRKIN RIVERSIDE
Letters and Science — Phi Mu; Women's Mandolin and Guitar Club (2), (3); Ukulele Club (3); Senior Extravaganza (4).

THEODORE RANDOLPH FINLEY, JR.
 SANTA MARIA
Letters and Science — Zeta Psi; Omicron Delta; U. N. X.; Skull and Key.

MARGUERITA MARIE FISCHER SAN FRANCISCO
Dentistry.

GEORGE WINTHROP FISH LOS ANGELES
Letters and Science — Delta Kappa Epsilon; T. N. E.; O. A. U. N. X.; Sphinx; Freshman and Varsity Football Teams (1); Varsity (2); Varsity Swimming Team (4).

RAY WALL FISHER OAKLAND
Agriculture.

MYRTLE VIOLA FITSCHEN SAN FRANCISCO
Letters and Science — Delta Delta Delta; Phi Beta Kappa; Partheneia Cast (2); Speechwerkband (3); Pyramiding Fete Committee (3), (4); Ukulele Club (4).

ARTHUR GERALD FITZGERALD BERKELEY
Letters and Science.

GEORGE ADAIR FLEMING SAN DIEGO
Mechanics — Delta Sigma Phi; Sigma Xi; Tau Beta Pi; Eta Kappa Nu; A. I. E. E.; A. E. M. E.; Freshman Track Team; Cross-Country Track Team (2), (3); Senior Assessment Committee.

MARJORIE FLYNN BERKELEY
Letters and Science — Alpha Gamma Delta; Senior Advisory Committee.

ARTHUR HERBERT FOLGER MILL VALLEY
Agriculture — Alpha Zeta.

ANGIER H. FOSTER EL PASO, TEXAS
Chemistry — Alpha Chi Sigma; Phi Lambda Upsilon; Rifle Team (2), (3).

DANIEL PARSONS FOSTER PORTLAND, OREGON
Letters and Science — Chi Psi; Nu Sigma Nu; Golden Bear; Big "C" Society; Circle "C" Society; Beta Kappa Alpha; Basketball Team (1), (2), (3), (4); Varsity Football Team (2), (3), (4); Glee Club (1), (2), (3), (4).

CAUGHT IN THE ACT

three hundred and eighteen

EVANS RONALD FOSTER — EAST AUBURN
Mechanics—Mineralogists; Tau Beta Pi; A. I. M. E.; Treasurer (4) A. S. M. E.; Y. M. C. A. Cabinet (3); Cadet Captain (4); Military Ball Committee (4); Senior Permanent Organizations Fund Committee.

VALERIE MILENE FOVEAUX — ALAMEDA
Letters and Science — Delta Delta Delta.

LESTER ALBERT FOWLER — LOS ANGELES
Civil Engineering.

RAY FOX — GLENN
Letters and Science.

OLGA FOYLE — OAKLAND
Letters and Science — Zeta Tau Alpha.

MARIUS ANDRE FRANCOZ — SAN FRANCISCO
Medical — Phi Alpha Gamma; II Class President (4); II College Orchestra (1), (2), (3), (4); Chairman Entertainment Committee (3), (2), (3), (4).

ANNA ROSALIND FRANK — LOS ANGELES
Letters and Science.

SADIE FREDERICKS — OAKLAND
Letters and Science; Zeta Tau Alpha; Treble Clef; Senior Assembly Committee; Senior Endowment Fund Committee.

HELEN STANSBURY FREELAND — EAST ORANGE, NEW JERSEY
Letters and Science.

MARGARETTA JOSEPHINE FRENCH — WATSONVILLE
Letters and Science.

JOHN FROBERG — BERKELEY
Commerce.

GERTRUDE DE FROST — SHANGHAI, CHINA
Letters and Science.

KENGO FUJIMORI — LOS ANGELES
Letters and Science; Japanese Student Club.

ME AND "THE QUEEN"

SWEET MEMORIES

MARY LOUISE FUNDENBERG — PASADENA
Letters and Science.

MARGUERITE FURLONG — REDONDO BEACH
Letters and Science.

JOHN DOYLE GALLAGHER — BERKELEY
Civil Engineering.

BERTHA MABEL GALLOWAY — BERKELEY
Letters and Science; Alpha Chi Omega; Prytanean; Cast "Prunella," Cast "Julius Caesar"; Mandolin and Guitar Club (1), (2), (3); Class Secretary (3); Vice-President A. W. S. (4); Students Affairs Committee (4); Students Union Committee (4); General Committee Senior Week; Finance Committee Senior Week; Reunion Committee; Women Chairman of Ambulance Field Service Committee.

MARGARET C. GALLUP — SANTA ANA
Letters and Science — Der Deutscher Zirkel (2); Deutscher Verein (4); Wander Vogel (4).

VIVIEN GARDNER — HOLLYWOOD
Letters and Science; Sudwiva Club; Sophomore Informal Committee; A. W. S. Finance Committee (3); (4); Parthenon Property Committee (4); Senior Advisory Committee.

EDWIN LOWELL GARTHWAITE — OAKLAND
Agriculture — Chi Psi; Golden Bear; Winged Helmet; Freshman Football Team (1); Freshman Track Team (1); "Big C" Sirkus" Committee (2); California Day Committee (2); Labor Day Committee (3); Welfare Committee (2), (3); Chairman "Track Team East" Committee, 1917 Permanent Organization Committee; 1917 Farm Picnic Committee.

VERNON GEORGE GARRETT — MEDFORD, OREGON
Letters and Science — Santa Na; Transfer from University of Oregon; Senior Football Team Coach.

RENWICK WILLIAM GEALEY — OAKLAND
Dentistry.

WILLIAM ALLAN GEE — OAKLAND
Agriculture.

LLOYD WILLIAM GOEPPERT — SAN FRANCISCO
Commerce — Alpha Tau Omega; Beta Beta; Officers' Club; Commerce Club; Chairman Junior A. S. U. C. Card Committee 1916; First Lieutenant and Battalion Adjutant U. C. Cadets; Staff 1917 Blue and Gold; Senior Ball Committee, Cast of "Prunella"; Pageantising Rally Committees, 1915-1916; Sophomore Hop Committee; Varsity Swimming Team, 1912.

MARGARET ELISE GERHART — SANTA ANA
Letters and Science.

MEMORY BOOK GLEANINGS

RONALD DOLZELL GIBBS   PASADENA
Agriculture Beta Theta Pi; Alpha Zeta, Big "C" Society, Winged Helmet, Freshman Football Team; Freshman Track Team; Varsity Football Team (3); Varsity Track Team (1), (2), (3)

DOLORES GIBSON   SANTA CLARA
Letters and Science—Alpha Xi Delta; Beta Kappa Alpha; Treble Clef (1), (2); Ukulele Club (2).

RUTH BEATRICE GIBSON   WILLIAMS
Letters and Science.

BERRY GILCREASE   LEMOORE
Commerce Tilicum; Cadet Lieutenant.

RAYNOR EUGENE GIMBAL   OAKLAND
Letters and Science—Kappa Sigma, Beta Beta, Freshman Baseball Team, (1); Basketball Team (3); Junior Curtain Raiser Cast, Varsity Baseball Squad (3), (4); Students Welfare Committee (4); Senior Men's Banquet Committee; Senior Peace Committee.

ANNE GLOVER   OAKLAND
Letters and Science.

WALLACE A. GODARD   DAYTON, WASH.
Pharmacy.

FRED BOTTAN GODBOLT   RED BLUFF
Dentistry.

GLADYS IRMA GOEGGEL   SAN FRANCISCO
Letters and Science—Alpha Omicron Pi; Treble Clef

NOAH NATHAN GOLDSTEIN   SAN FRANCISCO
Mechanics.

RUTH EMMA GOODSELL   BERKELEY
Letters and Science—Nu Sigma Psi; Parthenein Cast (3)

GILLETTE EDDY GORDON   RIVERSIDE
Agriculture

JAMES MARCO GORMAN   GLENDIVE, MONTANA
Civil Engineering

HARRIET SHEAFE GOULD   BERKELEY
Letters and Science.

IRENE MAE GRADY   MERCED
Letters and Science.

JOHN ROBERT GRAFF   BERKELEY
Agriculture

WILLIAM ALEXANDER GRAHAM   ALHAMBRA
Agriculture Abracadabra; Alpha Zeta.

JOHN WAINO GRANBERG   ASTORIA, OREGON
Commerce Sequoyah; Commerce Club; Oregon Club; Varsity Soccer Squad (3); Honorable Mention Bryce Historical Essay (4); Senior Reunion Committee

FANNIE ETOILE GRANGER   SAN JOSE
Letters and Science—Norroena Club; Le Cercle Francais, Das Deutscher Kranzchen, Secretary; President (2).

ROBERT FLOYD GRAY   ALAMEDA
Letters and Science.

HERMAN CHARLES GREENWOOD   BERKELEY
Mechanics—A. S. M. E.; Sigma Xi.

ALICE AUGUSTA GRIFFIN   LONOAK
Letters and Science—Newman Club; Newman Club Vice-President (3), Circulo Hispanero (3); Permanent Organization Fund Committee (4).

BYRON FLOYD GRIMMER   FRESNO
Mechanics—A. E. and M. E.; Mandolin Club.

ERNEST C. GRINER   LAKEPORT
Medical—Phi Alpha Gamma, Hahnemann Glee Club, Captain Basketball Team (1), (2).

ROBERT LEROY GROVES   MARYSVILLE
Letters and Science Bachelordon; U. N. X.

ERWIN GUSTAV GUDDE   BERKELEY
Letters and Science - Deutscher Verein, President (4).

LENA GUIDERY   BEN LOMOND
Letters and Science

NORMAN CLYDE GUINN   PORTERVILLE
Pharmacy—Phi Delta Chi.

EDWARD ROWE GUNDELFINGER   FRESNO
Commerce

IRENE MARGUERITE GUNN   BRECKENRIDGE, MINN.
Letters and Science—Alpha Gamma Delta; Fencing Class Team

RUBY MAE GUNN   BERKELEY
Letters and Science.

SAILENDRA NATHAN GUPTA   CALCUTTA, INDIA
Pharmacy.

ELMER LEONARD GUSTAFSON   SELMA
Pharmacy—Phi Delta Chi

BERNARD ANDREWS GUY   BERKELEY
Letters and Science.

BEST WISHES, K. C.   CONGRATS, JIMMIE

CHARLES DUDLEY GWINN — San Francisco
Dentistry; Xi Psi Phi; Epsilon Alpha; President Student Body 1917.

FRANK KELSEY HAIGHT — Fortuna
Letters and Science; Acacia Fraternity; Phi Chi Medical Fraternity.

JANE CAROLINE HALBERT — Oakland
Letters and Science; Delta Gamma; Sports and Prytanean Society (4); Swimming Manager (4); Water Polo Manager (4); Senior Advisor (4).

ANSEL FRANKLIN HALL — Oakland
Agriculture; Alpha Zeta; U. C. Forestry Club, President (2), (3).

REXFORD LUTHER HALL — El Cajon
Commerce; Member Students Welfare Committee; Chairman Board of Governors of Senate Hall for second Semester.

VERNA L. HALL — Nevada City
Letters and Science.

CARL J. HALLFORD — Porterville
Pharmacy.

JOSEPH MERRILL HAMBLIN — Missouri
Medical Transfer U. M. C. Cincinnati; Epsilon Pi (2); Habermann Sergeant-at-arms (3), (4); Entertainment Committee (3), (4).

IDA MAY HAMMERS — Newman
Pharmacy; Class Secretary (3), (4); Secretary Associated Students (4).

EDWARD HAMMILL — El Monte
Mechanics.

CAPTAIN KIDD

JOSEPH BELL HAMMON — San Jose
Agriculture; Sigma Pi.

KESSLER GILBERT HAMMOND — Fresno
Agriculture; Theta Delta Chi; Alpha Zeta.

WILLIAM HENRY HAMPTON — Live Oak
Chemistry; Alpha Chi Sigma; Phi Lambda Upsilon; Sigma Xi; Class Crew (4).

ADELLA ABBIE HANNA — Berkeley
Letters and Science; President Art History Circle (3); A. W. S. Executive Committee (3); Conse-ann Women's Rowing Crew (3).

HARVEY LESLIE HANSEN — San Francisco
Letters and Science; Dahlonega; President Scandinavian Club (3); Secretary Forestry Club (3), (4); Senate (2); Hamlet in "Tego" (4); Conrad in "Much Ado About Nothing" (2); Clermont in "Richelieu" (2); Theodore in Junior Curtain Raiser (3).

REINHOLT BERNHARD HANSEN — San Francisco
Civil Engineering.

JAMES EDWARD HARBISON — Sacramento
Letters and Science.

HUBERT EDWARD HARDING — Melbourne, Australia
Agriculture; Varsity Soccer Team (2), (3), Captain (4).

LOIS ELLEN HARDING — Berkeley
Letters and Science; Alpha Delta Pi; Ukulele Club.

ARTHUR COBB HARDY — Berkeley
Letters and Science; Sigma Xi.

JOHN EDWARD HARE — Redding
Letters and Science; Sigma Pi; 1915, 145-pound Basketball Team (2).

ISADORE FRANKLIN HARRIS — San Francisco
Letters and Science (Medical).

HARD-WORKING FARMER BOYS

MOSES IN THE BULRUSHES

GEORGIA HELEN HARRISON LOGANSPORT, IND.
Letters and Science.

GREGORY ALEXANDER HARRISON
  SAN FRANCISCO
Letters and Science—Phi Kappa Sigma; Phi Beta Kappa.

MABEL RUTH HARRISON BERKELEY
Letters and Science.

CLIFFORD CLAYDE HARTER MERRILL, OREGON
Letters and Science.

JOHN STEPHENSON HARTLEY REEDLEY
Letters and Science.

PAUL JAMES HARTLEY SAN DIEGO
Agriculture—Tilicum; Alpha Zeta.

WILLIAM POLLARD HARTLEY REEDLEY
Letters and Science.

JAMES BENTON HARVEY SACRAMENTO
Letters and Science—Delta Chi; Golden Bear; Daily Californian (1), (2), (3).

LAURENCE EMERSON HASELTINE BERKELEY
Agriculture—Alpha Zeta.

IRMA IMOGENE HASKELL BERKELEY
Letters and Science—Transfer (3).

BERTHA HASKETT WILLITS
Letters and Science—Member of the 1917 Women's Class Hockey Team (3), (4); Ukulele Club.

WENDELL M. HAUCH ALAMEDA
Letters and Science.

CLIFFORD FRANK HAWKINS BERKELEY
Pharmacy—Kappa Psi.

MARGARET CALDER HAYES ABERDEEN, WASH.
Letters and Science—Kappa Alpha Theta; Women's "C" Society (1), (2); Women's Varsity Tennis Team (1), (2); Secretary Sports and Pastimes (2); Transferred to Barnard College (3); Returned to U. of C. (4).

OLIVE GENEVIEVE HAYES OAKLAND
Letters and Science—Alpha Delta Pi.

ROBERT HENRY HEDGESPETH CORNING
Agriculture.

HOWARD WALDEN HEINTZ LOS ANGELES
Commerce—Theta Delta Chi.

ANNA ANGELINE HEIS GARDNERVILLE, NEVADA
Letters and Science.

HENRY THEODORE HELGESSON PORTLAND, ORE.
Mining—Phi Lambda Upsilon; Secretary of Mining Association.

ELISE HENDERSON LAKEPORT
Letters and Science—Alpha Delta Pi; Junior Farce; Finance Committee; Senior Adviser.

RODNEY WILLIAM HENRY NAPA
Civil Engineering.

GEORGE CARL HENSEL SAN FRANCISCO
Letters and Science.

HAROLD LUSH HERDEG RIVERSIDE
Agriculture.

EMERSON BROWN HERRICK SAN FRANCISCO
Agriculture—Pi Kappa Alpha; Junior Prom Decoration Committee; Pilgrimage Committee 1917; Freshman Track Team; Varsity Track Team 1915.

HAROLD LEWIS HERRICK SALT LAKE, UTAH
Letters and Science—Senate; Rifle Club; President, University Labor Club.

HUGH NATHAN HERRICK CONCORD
Mechanics—Alpha Sigma Phi; Tau Beta Pi; Eta Kappa Nu; Glee Club (1), (2), (3), (4); Senior Bench Committee 1917; A. S. U. C. Election Committee, 1915.

MELVILLE HAROLD HERSPRING
  SAN FRANCISCO
Agriculture.

PRINY SHOWS VISITORS AROUND

EDWARD HERVEY   Los Angeles
  Letters and Science—Psi Upsilon; Phi Delta Phi;
  Senior Pilgrimage Committee.

ERNESTINE HERZ   Alameda
  Letters and Science.

EDWIN HAROLD HESSELBERG   Winters
  Civil Engineering.

EDWARD F. HEUE   Woodland
  Pharmacy.

RUTH MARIAN HEYNEMANN   Healdsburg
  Letters and Science—Prytanean; Women's Big "C"
  Society; Y. W. C. A. Cabinet (3), (4); Chairman
  A.W.S. Mass Meetings (4); Chairman Senior Women's
  Banquet; Varsity Crew (2); All-California Swimming
  Team (4); Senior Adviser (4); Cast Junior Farce.

HERBERT HAROLD HIESTAND   Berkeley
  Mining—Chi Phi.

ALBERT EDWARD HILL   Oakland
  Agriculture.

FRANK LEROY HILL   Berkeley
  Mechanics—Alpha Sigma Phi; Tau Beta Pi; A. S. M. E.

PHOEBE HEARST HILL   Los Angeles
  Letters and Science.

AVERY SCOTT HILLS   Sacramento
  Letters and Science (Dental)—Theta Delta Chi; Delta
  Sigma Delta.

VERA HINCH   Eureka
  Letters and Science—Junior Prom Committee.

WILLIAM DODSON HINEY   Berkeley
  Civil Engineering—Acacia.

ERWIN HERBERT HIRSCHFELDER   San Francisco
  Commerce—Sequoyah; Senate; Commerce Club; Rally
  Committee (4); Freshman Track Team; Freshman
  Basketball Team; Varsity Track Team (3), (4); Assistant Basketball Manager (4), (4); Varsity Cross
  Country Team (4); Senior Informal Committee; Class
  Yell Leader (3), (4); Winter 1916 Prize Bleacher Yell;
  Senior Week Printing Committee; Cast of Senior
  Extravaganza.

VINCENT CECIL HOBBS   Walla Walla, Wash.
  Commerce—Sequoyah; Commerce Club; Senior Advisory Committee.

KEEP IT OFF THE TIN ROOF

LET'S ALL GET SICK

VERNE W. HOFFMAN   Corona
  Agriculture—Sigma Phi Sigma; Alpha Zeta; Agriculture Club (1), (2), (3); President (4); First Lieutenant Cadet Corps; Secretary Senior Men's Banquet
  Committee.

HENRY RAYMOND HOGABOOM   Los Angeles
  Mechanics—Pi Kappa Alpha; Golden Bear; Winged
  Helmet; Big "C" Society; A. S. M. E.; Class Yell
  Leader (1), (2); Assistant Yell Leader (3); Yell Leader
  (4); Freshman Crew (1); Varsity Crew (3); Captain
  Cadet Band (4).

ELANORE MARIAN HOLLAND   Berkeley
  Letters and Science.

RUFUS BURN HOLLAND   Hemet
  Agriculture.

RUTH WANELL HOLLAND   Berkeley
  Letters and Science.

HAZEL HELEN HOLLINGSWORTH   San Francisco
  Letters and Science—Prytanean; Treble Clef; Cast of
  "Much Ado About Nothing" (2); "Prunella" (3);
  Junior Farce (3); Partheneia (2), (3); Opera "What
  Next" (4); Treble Clef Treasurer (3); A. S. U. C.
  Finance Committee (2); Sophomore Informal (2);
  Junior Prom Reception (3); Y. W. C. A. Decoration
  Chairman (4); Senior Advisory Committee (4); A. W. S.
  Mass Meeting Committee (4); Ambulance Committee
  (4); Secretary Senior Singing (4); Women's Day Dance
  Stunt Chairman (4); Big "C" Sirkus Stunt Committee
  (4); Senior Women's Banquet Committee (4); Cast of
  Extravaganza (4).

MARC HOLZER   Los Angeles
  Electrical Engineering—Acacia; A. I. E. E. (3); Chairman (4) A. E. and M. E.; Mathematics Club (3),
  President (4); Circle "C" Society.

AILA BERNICE HOLM   Berkeley
  Letters and Science—Deutscher Verein.

ALBERT EARL HOLMES   Esparto
  Agriculture.

CAUGHT BY THE CAMERA

DOROTHY MARIA HOOPER BERKELEY
Letters and Science.

HELENE ESTHER HOOPER YREKA
Letters and Science.

LUCILE HOOPER PASADENA
Letters and Science—Delta Gamma; Senior Adviser.

RUTH FRANCES HOREL ARCATA
Letters and Science—Alpha Delta Pi; Dyalys; Cast of Parthenia (2); Ukulele Club (2), President (3); A. W. S. Point System Committee (3), Chairman (4); Senior Advisory Committee Captain; Senior Reunion Committee; Josh Department 1917 Blue and Gold; Parliamentary Society, Vice-President (2); Economics Club, Vice-President (2), President (3).

PAULINE INNES HORNE BERKELEY
Letters and Science (Pre Legal).

SHIRLEY CLEMENTS HORSLEY BRIGHAM, UTAH
Letters and Science. Transfer B. Y. U. Utah (3); Glee Club (4).

GEORGE HENRY HOTALING SAN FRANCISCO
Letters and Science—Psi Upsilon; Phi Delta Phi; Sphinx.

KENNETH WARD HOUSTON TEMPE, ARIZONA
Mechanics—Alpha Kappa Lambda; Tau Beta Pi; Eta Kappa Nu; H. K. N.; A. I. E. E.

LUVELLE DOWNEN HOWARD LAKEPORT
Letters and Science—Alpha Kappa Lambda; Congress; Y. M. C. A. Cabinet (3); Varsity Cross-Country Team (8), (4), (5); Captain Varsity Track Team; Captain Junior Track Team; Freshman Track Team; Circle "C" Society.

HUBBARD SPENCER HOYT PACIFIC GROVE
Letters and Science (Medicine). Beta Kappa Alpha; Y. M. C. A. Cabinet (4).

MARY CELESTIA HOYT PACIFIC GROVE
Letters and Science—Transfer from Occidental College (3).

MARTHA EDWINA HUFFAKER OAKLAND
Letters and Science.

DOROTHEA HARRIET HUGGINS BERKELEY
Letters and Science—Chi Omega; Parthenia (1), (2), (3), (4); Cast of Junior Curtain Raiser (3); Chorus Junior Farce (3); Junior Prom Reception Committee (3); Senior Permanent Organization Committee; Senior Ball Decoration Committee.

THOMAS EDGAR HUGHES ALAMEDA
Dentistry.

IRENE HUND ROSS
Letters and Science—Deutscher Verein; Ukulele Club.

FAITH IMOGENE HUNT BERKELEY
Letters and Science.

GERTRUDE ELIZABETH HUNT BERKELEY
Letters and Science.

IRENE MILDRED HUNT BERKELEY
Letters and Science.

WILLIAM GARBETT HUNT OAKLAND
Letters and Science.

HUGH ALLEN HUNTER BLOOMFIELD, INDIANA
Letters and Science—Gymnasium Club; Transfer from Indiana University (3).

EMILY HARRIET HUNTINGTON SAN FRANCISCO
Letters and Science.

IRENE ESTELLE HURLEY OAKLAND
Letters and Science—Class Crew (3); All Star Crew (3).

HAROLD ANTHONY HYDE WATSONVILLE
Letters and Science—Alpha Sigma Phi; Phi Beta Kappa; Golden Bear; Pharotriocton; Sphinx; Senate; Sophomore Debate; Senate Debate (2); Intercollegiate Debate (4); A. S. U. C. Executive Committee (4); Chairman California Ambulance Corps Committee; Senior Week Committee; Chairman Reunion Committee; Commencement Speaker.

GEORGE SHIGEKI IKI BERKELEY
Medicine—Beta Kappa Alpha; Varsity Wrestling Team (1), (2), (3), Captain (2); Member Circle "C" Society.

RICHARD NORMAN INCH SONOMA
Letters and Science.

A GOOD UNDERSTANDING

WILLIAM ELLIOTT INMAN — Norwalk
  Mining Secretary, Mining Alumni Association.

WILLIAM McCALLA IRVINE — Salinas
  Commerce.

LESLIE ALPHONSE ISAACSON — Marshfield, Ore.
  Letters and Science (Jurisprudence).

MASAO ITANO — Mill Valley
  Agriculture.

GEORGE BAGER IVERSON — Union
  Agriculture—Abracadabra; Freshman Track Team; Varsity Track Team (2).

EVANS CHICK JACOBSON — Onawa, Iowa
  Letters and Science.

HAROLD SAMUEL JACOBY — Oakland
  Letters and Science.

JOHN THOMAS JAMES — San Francisco
  Letters and Science—Boeotier Club; Greek Club; La Raporte Society; Y. M. C. A.

BRUSE JAMEYSON — La Junta, Colorado
  Civil Engineering—Tilicum.

FREDERIC FULLER JANNEY — Santa Barbara
  Agriculture—Delta Upsilon; Skull and Key; Beta Beta; Glee Club (2), (3); Sophomore Hop Committee.

JOHN JEROME JANSEN — Roseville
  Dentistry—Psi Omega.

HAMILTON MOORE JEFFERS — Pasadena
  Letters and Science.

DEMETRIO EUGENE JEFFRY — Healdsburg
  Letters and Science—Sigma Pi; Nu Sigma Nu.

ANDREW MARTIN JENSEN — Fresno
  Civil Engineering—Acacia; Sigma Iota Phi; Tau Beta Pi; Sigma Xi; President Civil Engineering Association Spring 1917.

LOUISE GRETCHEN JENSEN — Berkeley
  Letters and Science.

MARTHA JENSEN — Arlington, Wash.
  Letters and Science.

WARD CHARLES JENSEN — Racine, Wis.
  Agriculture.

MILDRED JESSUP — Berkeley
  Letters and Science—Alpha Nu; Y. W. C. A. Cabinet (3), (4); Senior Advisory Committee (4); Transfer from Whittier College (3).

OH GAWD! WHAT A SQUAD!

WHEN THEY GET AWAY

HELEN RANKIN JETER — Los Angeles
  Letters and Science—Sigma Kappa; Labor Day Committee (3); Senior Advisory Committee (4); Senior Women's Banquet Committee (4).

HILDEGARDE JOHANNE JOHE — San Rafael
  Letters and Science—Deutscher Verein; Treble Clef Quartette (3), (4); "Red Mill" 1914; "What Next" 1916; Treble Clef Executive Committee 1916.

MILTON VERNON JOHNS — Pacific Grove
  Letters and Science—Alpha Kappa Lambda; Phi Delta Kappa; Assembly Debating Society; Education Club; Freshman Track Team; Varsity Track Team (2), (3).

RALPH LESLIE JOHNS — Lodi
  Letters and Science—Delta Theta Chi (Sociology Honor); Congress (1), (2); Liberation Club (3), (4); Sociology Club (4); Congregation Club (3), (4); President Lodi Club (2), (3), (4); Editor Student Opinion (3); Vice-President Intercollegiate Press Association (4).

CHARLES EUGENE JOHNSON — Hollister
  Dentistry—Delta Sigma Delta.

ETHELBERT JOHNSON — Berkeley
  Agriculture—President Deutscher Zirkel (4); Agriculture Club (3), (4); Qualified for Rhodes Scholarship (4).

EVELYN GOLDIE JOHNSON — Santa Rosa
  Letters and Science.

GEORGE W. JOHNSON — Alameda
  Pharmacy.

WALTER HAROLD JOHNSON — Pomona
  Agriculture—Theta Xi; Big "C" Society; Varsity Football Team (4); Transfer Pomona College (2).

HOWARD MILNE JOHNSTON — Watsonville
  Dentistry—Xi Psi Phi; Epsilon Alpha; Class President (4).

A FAIR HOUSE

KATHRYN JOHNSTON OAKLAND
Letters and Science.

MASON ALLEN JOHNSTON YERINGTON, NEVADA
Letters and Science. Aegis; Phi Delta Kappa; Spanish Club; Junior Farce Cast (3).

FELIX JACOB JONAS LOS ANGELES
Letters and Science. Orchestra (1), (2), (3), President (3); Secretary California Menorah Society (3).

CHARLES WEST JONES BERKELEY
Civil Engineering.

FRANCES CAREY JONES BERKELEY
Letters and Science.

LEONA MILLS JONES VISALIA
Letters and Science. Bolivia; President Economics Club (4); Second Semester Secretary-Treasurer of Art History Circle.

LOUIS WILLIAM JONGENEEL PITTSBURG
Agriculture. Alpha Zeta.

LILLIAN M JORDAN RAWLINS, WYO
Letters and Science.

FLOURNOY ALBERT JUCH SAN DIEGO
Letters and Science (Jurisprudence).

RAY CAROL KAPLAN BERKELEY
Letters and Science.

ALVIN MATHIAS KARSTENSEN SAN FRANCISCO
Letters and Science (Architecture). Sigma Phi Epsilon; Architectural Association; Freshman Track Team (1); Soccer Team (2), (3), (4).

HAZEL ARDELLA KATZENSTEIN SACRAMENTO
Letters and Science—Die Plauderhrasche, Treasurer (2), Secretary (3), President (4); Women's Class Crew (2), (3); All California Crew (3); Manager Senior Women's Crew (4).

EARLE FRANCIS KAUFMAN BERKELEY
Letters and Science (Architecture). Stage Manager of 1916 Extravaganza; President of Architectural Association.

JACK KAUFMAN LOS ANGELES
Chemistry.

MELVILLE KAUFMANN SAN FRANCISCO
Letters and Science.

LETITIA REID KEAN BERKELEY
Letters and Science.

CORA FLOYD KEELER BERKELEY
Letters and Science—Gamma Phi Beta.

LOUISE EGERTON KEEN SAN DIEGO
Letters and Science—Alpha Chi Omega; Prytanean; Y.W.C.A. Cabinet (3); Managerial Staff of the 1917 Blue and Gold; Ukulele Club (3); Treasurer Y.W.C.A. (4); Senior Advisor Captain (4); Treasurer of the Prytanean (4); Senior Assembly Committee (4).

M'LOUISE KEENEY LOS ANGELES
Letters and Science.

ELIZABETH ERMINIE KEITH RIVERSIDE
Letters and Science—Alpha Gamma Delta; Senior Assembly Committee; Senior Endowment Committee.

MILDRED DOROTHY KELLOGG INGOMAR
Letters and Science. Delta Gamma.

ALDA BELLE KELSEY BERKELEY
Letters and Science.

ARTHUR HENRY KEMP BERKELEY
Agriculture.

WARREN RUNYON KEMPER SAN LUIS OBISPO
Mechanics—Alpha Delta Phi; Eta Kappa Nu; Associated Electrical and Mechanical Engineers; American Institute of Electrical Engineers; Senior Crew (4); Freshie Glee (1); Senior Ball Committee (4).

WILLIAM AVERY KENT POWAY
Agriculture.

CYRIL PHILIP KENVILLE OAKLAND
Mechanics.

PARRISH AND HYATT

FRANKLIN E. KERR   GRAND RAPIDS, OHIO
Medical — Hahnemann Basketball Team (3), (4); Captain II Volley-Ball Team (3), (4); Dance Committee (3), (4).

MARIE IRENE KESSELER   OAKLAND
Letters and Science.

LUCY KIELDSEN   BOISE, IDAHO
Letters and Science — Zeta Tau Alpha; Phi Beta Kappa.

GRACE ELEANOR KIMBLE   LOS ANGELES
Letters and Science — Freshman Club; Parliamentary Society; Senior Women's Hall Committee.

ESTHER LAURILLA KING   HAYWARD
Letters and Science — Delta Gamma; Prytanean; Torch and Shield; La Raposte; Women's Track Manager (3); Member of the Varsity Fencing Team (4); Women's Big "C" Society.

STANLEY CONRADT KING   WALLA WALLA, WASH
Civil Engineering.

ALICE MARIE KINGMAN   CHENAN, WASH
Letters and Science — The Pleiades (4); President (4); Chairman A.W.S. Boarding House Committee (4); Senior Advisory Committee (4), Women's Undergraduate Students Affairs Committee (4).

MARGUERITE KIRK   BOZEMAN, MONTANA
Letters and Science — Social Service Secretary of Library Work Y.W.C.A. (4); Cast, "Julius Caesar" (3).

THE MUMPS

ESTHER KITTREDGE   BERKELEY
Letters and Science — Alpha Chi Omega; Iota Sigma Pi; Parliamentary Club (2); Reporter on *Daily Californian* (2); Junior Women's Editor on *Daily Californian* (3); California Day Committee (3); Labor Day Committee (3); A.S.U.C. Elections Committee (3); Senior Advisor (4).

MATSUMURA KIYOSHI   OAKLAND
Pharmacy.

MARY LOUISE KLEINECKE   SONORA
Letters and Science — Secretary of Women's "C" Society; Class Crew (2); Stroke of All California Crew (3); Manager of Women's Rowing (4); President of Southern Club (3); Senior Advisor (4); Chairman Decoration Committee for La Fiesta (4); Member of Prytanean Fete Finance Committee.

LAWRENCE FREDERICK KNAUER   SACRAMENTO
Commerce — Delta Upsilon; Beta Beta; Senior Assembly Committee; Senior Peace Committee; Class Football (2), (3); Floor Manager Freshie Glee.

GLEN ORVAL KNIGHT   CHICO
Letters and Science (Architecture) — Sigma Phi Epsilon; Architectural Association; Business Staff *Occident* (4); Assistant Manager *Pelican* (4); Manager Architectural Year Book (4); Rally Committee.

CHARLES RICHARDSON KNOX   LOS ANGELES
Letters and Science — Zeta Psi; Theta Tau; Beta Beta; De Koven Club; Glee Club; Carnival Senior Committee; Chairman of the Decoration Committee, Senior Ball; Assistant Manager of the Extravaganza; Arrangements Manager of Big "C" Sirkus; Extravaganza Cast.

EARL JOHN KNUDSON   BINGHAM CITY, UTAH
Commerce.

HERLUF ALBERT KNUDSON   OAKLAND
Mechanics.

GEORGE MARTIN KOOPMAN   DUBLIN
Agriculture.

ISIDORE BENJAMIN KORNBLUM   LOS ANGELES
Letters and Science (Jurisprudence) — Music to 1915 Prize Song "Fight"; Music to Treble Clef Opera "What Next"; Manager "What Next," Glee Club.

THETA'S ONLY HOPE

GLADYS MAY KREAMER San Francisco
Letters and Science Phi Beta Kappa.

ADOLPH C. KROEGER Oakland
Mining Treasurer Mining Association (3); Tennis Squad (4).

FRIEDA L. KRUSE San Francisco
Medical Sigma Alpha Beta; II. Class Vice-President (1), (2); II. Student Body Secretary (2); Class Librarian (3), (4); H. Orchestra.

LE ROY FARNHAM KRUSI Alameda
Civil Engineering Beta Theta Pi; Golden Bear; Winged Helmet, Sigma Iota Phi, Tau Beta Pi; Editor Blue and Gold (3); Associate Editor Daily Californian (2); Secretary Civil Engineering Association (4).

TOYOKICHI KURAHASHI Riverside
Letters and Science (Architecture)—Japanese Student Club.

CHARLES DAVID LANE Angels
Letters and Science Beta Theta Pi; Winged Helmet, Skull and Key; U. N. X., Beta Beta; Blue and Gold Staff (4); Senior Peace Committee; Senior Ball Committee; Varsity Football Squad (2), (3), (4).

EUGENE THOMAS LANGENOUR Woodland
Agriculture—Theta Xi; Alpha Zeta.

PERRY EUGENE LANTZ Sunnyside, Wash.
Agriculture—Tilicum; Alpha Zeta.

ARTHUR THORNTON LAPRADE Winston, Ariz.
Letters and Science (Jurisprudence)—Delta Chi; Board of Governors, Senior Hall.

EWALD AXEL LARSON Kingsburg
Letters and Science.

ANITA DUNCAN LATON Sebastopol
Letters and Science Al Khalail; Phi Beta Kappa.

HARLEY LATSON Whittier
Civil Engineering Oread; Tau Beta Pi Sigma Xi; Librarian of Civil Engineering Association (4).

CARL LAUSEN Galveston, Texas
Letters and Science.

MORRIS LAVINE Los Angeles
Letters and Science—General Committee Senior Week; Chairman Publicity Committee Senior Week; Chairman Publicity of Students Union Committee; Committee for Belgian Relief (3); Congress; Congress-Senate Debate.

JOHN WATKIN LAWTON Los Angeles
Agriculture—Captain U. C. Cadets.

JACK ELTON LEARNER Oakland
Commerce—Freshman Track Team; Varsity Track Team (2).

PAUL GERHARD LEDIG Alta Loma
Chemistry.

JOSEPH SEUNG MUN LEE Canton, China
Medical—Vice-President II Student Body (2).

RUSSEL VAN ARSDALE LEE San Francisco
Letters and Science.

ARMISTEAD C. LEIGH, Jr. Los Angeles
Letters and Science Kappa Alpha, Beta Kappa Alpha

HANS LEMCKE Alameda
Agriculture Sigma Nu

EILEEN M. LEONARD San Francisco
Letters and Science—Class Basketball Team (1), (2); Student Opinion Staff (2), (3); Daily Californian Staff (3).

ARCHER LYNN LERCH Oakland
Letters and Science.

RUTH CORRINNE LESLEY Goldfield, Nevada
Letters and Science.

LOUIS LESS San Francisco
Letters and Science.

THE WILD WAVES SHOULD BE CROKED
BY THIS TIME

FREDERICK PHILIP LENE OAKLAND
Commerce

ESCHSCHOLTZIA LICHTHARDT SACRAMENTO
Letters and Science. Al Khalail, Beta Kappa Alpha (4); Senior Advisory Committee; Senior Pilgrimage Committee

JESSIE HOLLINGSWORTH LIESER VANCOUVER, WASH.
Letters and Science.

EDYTHE LILLIE BISBEE
Letters and Science Aldebaran, Senior Women's Banquet Committee (4).

CHESTER CHARLES LINCOLN CALISTOGA
Letters and Science.

HAZEL FREDERICKA CHARLOTTE LINDH OAKLAND
Letters and Science.

GEORGE MOORE LINDSAY SAN FRANCISCO
Letters and Science. Sigma Nu, Beta Beta; Freshman Glee Committee; Sophomore Hop Committee; Junior Prom Committee; Senior Ball Committee, Big "C" Committee; Varsity Swimming Team (1), (2), (3), (4); Manager Swimming Team (4); Captain Swimming Team (3).

RALPH WALDO LINGLE FRESNO
Mechanics—Eta Kappa Nu; Vice-President Associated Electrical and Mechanical Engineers 1916.

CHARLES S. LIPP RICHMOND
Dentistry Psi Omega; Epsilon Alpha.

STELLA MARGUERITE LISS SACRAMENTO
Letters and Science—Alpha Xi Delta.

JAMES KENNETH LOCHEAD FRESNO
Commerce —Dwight Club; Beta Gamma Sigma; Commerce Club.

ELBERT WILSON LOCKWOOD LOS ANGELES
Letters and Science (Jurisprudence) Abracadabra; Students Welfare Committee Chairman (3); Arrangements Committee, Senior Ball (1); Governor Senior Hall (4).

WALTER ROBERT LOCKWOOD PUENTA
Letters and Science. Enlisted in September, 1915; Sequoyah, Circle "C" Society; Varsity Soccer Team (2).

BENJAMIN BOONE LOGAN SACRAMENTO
Letters and Science (Jurisprudence).

EDITH HARRIET LOGAN LOS ANGELES
Letters and Science La Rapiere Fencing Society; Women's Varsity Fencing Team (2) Captain (3); Manager (4); Chairman Refreshment Committee, La Fiesta, 4; Senior Advisory Committee (4); Senior Week Pilgrimage Committee (4); Member Sports and Pastimes Women's Athletic Committee (4).

NESTOR MAXIMILLIAN LONN GOTHENBURG, SWEDEN
Dentistry.

CHARLES WHITNEY LORAINE LOS ANGELES
Letters and Science (Medical) Sequoyah, Phi Chi.

FRANCES CAROLINE LOWELL OAKLAND
Letters and Science Alpha Xi Delta; Sigma Kappa Alpha, President (4).

WALTER H. LOWELL OAKLAND
Dentistry Psi Omega.

KATHRYN MILDRED LUDDEN GLENDALE, ARIZ.
Letters and Science —Transfer from Nebraska University (4).

GENEVIEVE DALTON LUFF PETALUMA
Letters and Science Delta Zeta.

CARROLL THEODORE LUND SAN RAFAEL
Agriculture Theta Nu, Alpha Zeta.

GRACE JANE LYNCH STOCKTON
Letters and Science.

LOIS VALENTINE LYON SAN FRANCISCO
Letters and Science Zeta Tau Alpha.

THREE JACKS

SQUAW-MAN GIMBAL

NORMAN LYON   CINCINNATI, OHIO
Agriculture—Transfer from University of Cincinnati; Oread; Circle "C" Society; Secretary-Treasurer (4); Manager Varsity Swimming Team (4); Senior Adviser; Senior Emblement Committee; Senior Ball Decoration Committee.

ANNA HARDING McCABE   CRAWFORDSVILLE, IND.
Letters and Science

COE ELIZABETH McCABE   BERKELEY
Letters and Science—Alpha Chi Omega; Iota Sigma Pi; Torch and Shield; Prytanean; Reception Committee Freshie Glee; Junior Prom; Senior Ball; Cast Junior Curtain Raiser (3); Cast Senior Extravaganza (4); Senior Vice-President (4); A. W. S. Secretary (4); Arrangements Committee Sophomore Informal (2); Refreshments Committee Coördination Day (3); Labor Day Committee (3); Junior Informal Committee (3); Permanent Organization Committee (4); Parliamentary Society (1) (2); Senior Advisory Committee (3) (4).

ELVA AMES McCABILL   BERKELEY
Letters and Science (Jurisprudence); Le Cercle Francais (1), (2), (3); Parliamentary (4); Parthenia (1), (3).

ROY DRUMMOND McCALLUM   ST. PAUL, MINN
Agriculture—Alpha Zeta.

MILLARD EARL McCOLLAM   BERKELEY
Agriculture—Alpha Zeta.

ROSS McCOLLUM   LOS ANGELES
Chemistry—Alpha Chi Sigma; Freshman Track Team (1).

WILLIAM ARTHUR McCOLLUM   SAN FRANCISCO
Chemistry—Alpha Chi Sigma.

LOLA ELIZABETH McCORMICK   MODESTO
Letters and Science

FRANK DALE McCULLOCH   UPLAND
Commerce—Mecanoclubea; Big "C" Society; Varsity Football Team (4)

LESTER Le ROY McCUMBER   SAN FRANCISCO
Pharmacy

WILLIAM ALFRED McCUTCHAN   HEALDSBURG
Agriculture—Sigma Pi; Alpha Zeta.

GEORGE ERVINE McCUTCHEN   BERKELEY
Letters and Science

MARGARET ANNE McDERMED   OAKLAND
Letters and Science—Sigma Psi; Y. W. C. A. (4).

DORIS ELIZABETH McENTYRE   BERKELEY
Letters and Science—Alpha Chi Omega; Phi Beta Kappa; Prytanean; A. W. S. Standing Social Committee (1), (2); Cast, "Countess Cathleen" (1); Cast, "Shakuntala" (2); Cast "Julius Caesar" (3); Cast Parthenia (3); Senior Advisory Captain (3), (4); Senior Extravaganza Committee (4); Students Welfare Committee (4); Cast Senior Extravaganza (4); Commencement Speaker.

ELSIE JEANNETTE McFARLAND   BERKELEY
Letters and Science—Phi Beta Kappa; Cast of Junior Farce; Vice-President, Mathematics Club (4).

WILLIAM ROSS McKAY   LEMOORE
Letters and Science (Jurisprudence)—League of the Republic; Editorial Staff Brass Tacks; Congress; Class Secretary (4); Students Advisory Committee (4); General Committee Senior Week.

NORAH McKENZIE   CONCORD
Letters and Science—Alpha Xi Delta; Alpha Nu; Senior Advisory Committee.

PRETTY FACES

FLOYD THEALL McKUNE — Long Beach
Civil Engineering; Sigma Phi Epsilon; Sigma Iota Phi; Officers Club; Civil Engineering Association; Treasurer (3); University Orchestra (1, 2); Chairman Military Ball Reception Committee (4); Class Permanent Organization Committee; Cadet Captain and Quartermaster.

RICHARD ASHE McLAREN — San Francisco
Letters and Science; Psi Upsilon; Skull and Key; Kappa Beta Phi; U. N. X.; Assistant Manager of "Trap," "Countess Cathleen" (3); Assistant Manager of "Much Ado About Nothing" and "Helen" (4); Manager of Junior Farce (3); Manager of "You Never Can Tell" (4); Labor Day Entertainment Committee (3); Junior Banquet Committee; General Arrangements Committee Senior Week (4).

ALBERTA McNULLY — Sacramento
Letters and Science; Copa de Oro; Prytanean Society; Women's Big "C" Society; Nu Sigma Psi; Basketball (1, 2), Captain (4); All Californian (2, 3, 4); Hockey Captain (4); All Californian (4); Tennis (4); Crew Captain (2); Track (3, 4); (3, 4) Vice-President Class (2); Athletic Manager; President of Sports and Pastimes (4); Partheneia (3); Managerial Staff Blue and Gold (3); A. W. S. Finance Committee (2); Prom Arrangements Committee; Senior Endowment Committee; Pilgrimage Committee; Refreshment and Finance Committee; Women's Day Dance (4); Senior Advisor (4); Secretary of Sports and Pastimes (3).

JULIAN AENEAS McPHEE — San Francisco
Agriculture

CONNELL CHISHOLM McDAY — Berkeley
Mechanics

WHERE IS HARVEY?

JOHN IGNATIUS McVEY — San Diego
Letters and Science; Alpha Tau Omega; Tau Beta Pi

ERNEST GRIGG MAAS — Smith River
Agriculture

PHILIP JAMES MAAS — San Francisco
Civil Engineering

FLORENCE MARY MACAULAY — Oakland
Letters and Science; Gamma Phi Beta; Sigma Kappa Alpha

IVANDER MacIVER — El Paso, Texas
Letters and Science; Phi Beta Kappa.

UNA MACKE — San Diego
Letters and Science; Transfer from Ohio State University 1916.

HUGH FRASER MacKENZIE — San Francisco
Letters and Science

MARSHALL PIERCE MADISON — San Francisco
Letters and Science (Jurisprudence); Psi Upsilon; Phi Delta Phi; Big "C" Society; Circle "C" Society; Skull and Key; U. N. X.; Kappa Beta Phi

ALFRED LEO MAGUIRE — Los Angeles
Letters and Science; Delta Kappa Epsilon; Theta Nu Epsilon; Omicron Delta; U. N. X.; R. B. Winged Helmet; Varsity Boxing Team (2); Captain (3, 4); Junior Prom Committee; Senior Ball Committee; Football Squad (1, 2), (3, 4).

MARGARET MARCHANT — Ione
Letters and Science; Prytanean; Treble Clef; Senior Advisory Committee (4); Class Vice-President (4); Y. W. C. A. Cabinet (3, 4); Students Welfare Committee; General Committee Senior Week

MADELINE M. MARLOW — San Diego
Letters and Science; Sigma Kappa; Torch and Shield; Issue Officer; Junior Editor on Women's staff of Daily Californian (3); Editorial Y. W. C. A. Record (3); Y. W. C. A. Cabinet Member (4); Senior Advisor (4); Labor Day Committee (3); Prytanean Fete Committee (4); Decoration Committee Senior Ball (4)

EVA ESTHER MARTIN — Santa Ana
Letters and Science—Transfer from U. S. C. (4); Mekatina

PAUL S. MARRIN — Twin Falls, Idaho
Letters and Science—Dwight Club; Senate; Bonnheim Essay Prize, 1915 and 1916.

JAMES ANCRUM MARSHALL — Berkeley
Agriculture—Associate Manager Journal of Agriculture (4).

LEWIN WETHERED MARTINEZ — Berkeley
Civil Engineering; Beta Theta Pi; Glee Club.

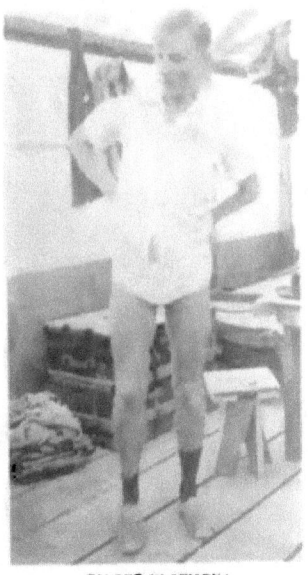

CAUGHT UNAWARES

THEY'RE ONLY STARES

EDWIN MARSHALL MASLIN WATSONVILLE
Letters and Science — Phi Delta Theta; Golden Bear; Winged Helmet; English Club; Sphinx; Press Club; Editor of Pelican (4); Daily Californian (1), (2), (3); Co-Author, Senior Extravaganza, "Youth Comes Up"; Winner of Irving Prize for Humor, 1915, 1916.

BENJAMIN FRANK MASTEN OAKLAND
Civil Engineering.

CALLA MATHISON LOS ANGELES
Letters and Science (Jurisprudence).

KIYOSHI MATSUMURA OAKLAND
Pharmacy.

SOTARO MATSUSHITA LOS ANGELES
Letters and Science.

GEORGE LAWRENCE MAXWELL, Jr. WOODLAND
Letters and Science — Alpha Kappa Lambda; Phi Beta Kappa; Phi Delta Kappa; Y. M. C. A. Cabinet (2), (3), President (4); Congress, Students Union Committee (4); Associate Editor Pelican (3); Cadet Lieutenant.

ARTHUR RAYMOND MAY SANTA MARIA
Mining — Tau Beta Pi; Theta Tau; Senior Adviser (4).

MAUD MAYENBAUM OAKLAND
Letters and Science.

ALMY COFRAN MAYNARD BERKELEY
Mechanics — Lambda Chi Alpha; Secretary U. C. Branch American Institute of Electrical Engineers.

ROBERT STONEY MAYOCK GILROY
Letters and Science (Jurisprudence).

WELBURN FRANKLIN MAYOCK GILROY
Letters and Science.

MAUDE MARION MEAGHER SAN FRANCISCO
Letters and Science — English Club; Prytanean; Lead in English Club Play (3); Lead in Parthenia (2); Author of Parthenian (3); Parthenia Committee (3); Junior Farce Committee (3); Senior Extravaganza Committee (4).

HAZEL KIRKE MEDDAUGH STOCKTON
Letters and Science.

CLARA AGNES MEEKS PETALUMA
Letters and Science.

BRADFORD MORSE MELVIN SAN FRANCISCO
Letters and Science — Transfer from Stanford University (3); Phi Delta Theta; Phi Delta Phi; Glee Club; Ye Koyal Club; Senior Men's Banquet Committee; Cast Skull and Key Show (4).

HUGO LUCIA MENKE SAN FRANCISCO
Pharmacy — Kappa Psi.

DAVID ROBERT MERRILL BERKELEY
Letters and Science — Alpha Chi Sigma; Sigma Xi; Phi Beta Kappa; Phi Lambda Upsilon.

GRACE EVELYN MERRILL ASHLAND, OREGON
Letters and Science — Die Deutsche Zirkel; Oregon Club; Extravaganza.

RUTH EARL MERRILL LOS ANGELES
Letters and Science — Varsity Fencing Team (3); Senior Fencing Team (4), Captain (4); La Espere (2), (3) (4); Senior Hall Proctor Committee (4); Senior Pilgrimage Committee (4).

MARGUERITE MERIOTT OAKLAND
Letters and Science.

MARGARET IRENE MERSEREAU OAKLAND
Letters and Science — Alpha Xi Delta; Speechverband (2); Parthenea (3); Y. W. C. A. Social Committees (1), (2); Meetings Committee (3); Die Deutsche Zirkel (3); Senior Advisory Committee.

THE STAIRS

ROLLIN EUGENE MEYER — OAKLAND
Mechanics

AIMEE JULIET MICHELBACHER — RIVERSIDE
Letters and Science — Spectroventiloomi.

MARTEL IRVIN MICKEY — BERKELEY
Civil Engineering — Track Squad (2), (3).

DOROTHY MILES — SAN FRANCISCO
Letters and Science

GRACE MILLAR — OAKLAND
Letters and Science

CAREY DUNLAP MILLER — BOISE, IDAHO
Letters and Science — Zeta Tau Alpha, Iota Sigma Pi, Alpha Nu.

DOROTHY DORRIS MILLER — ALTURAS
Letters and Science

JAMES ALEXANDER MILLER — PIEDMONT
Agriculture.

VERA DOUGLAS MILLER — OAKLAND
Letters and Science

JAMES McVICAR MILLS, Jr. — HAMILTON CITY
Agriculture — Theta Delta Chi, Alpha Zeta.

VERNE VICTOR MILLS — ASHLAND, ORE.
Civil Engineering — Delta Tau Delta.

EDWIN VAN HORN MINEAH — PROSSER, WASH.
Commerce.

JOHN FRANCIS MINIHAN — SAN FRANCISCO
Civil Engineering.

HENRY MISHKIND — SAN FRANCISCO
Pharmacy.

ARTHUR WILLIAM MOHR — SAN FRANCISCO
Chemistry — Sigma Pi; Alpha Chi Sigma; First Lieutenant.

EMORY JULIUS MOLTZEN — FRESNO
Pharmacy — Kappa Psi

DOROTHY MOMSON — FRESNO
Fine Arts — Delta Kappa Delta; President Dramatics and Art Club 1916; Member Ukulele Club.

TAKING IT EASY

CONGRATULATIONS SET

CLAUDE EZRA MONIEX — BERKELEY
Commerce; Armean; Big "C" Society; Golden Bear; Freshman Football Team, Varsity Football Team (2), Freshman Track Team, Varsity Track Team (1), (2), (3).

MARGARET MARY MONTGOMERY — SAN FRANCISCO
Letters and Science

WILLIS ROBERT MONTGOMERY — BERKELEY
Letters and Science — Phi Gamma Delta; Golden Bear; Winged Helmet; Skull and Keys; Omicron Delta; U. N. X.; H. B.; Big "C" Society; Freshman Baseball Team, Freshman Football Team, Varsity Football Team (1), (2), (3), Captain (3).

DOUGLAS E. C. MOORE — LOS ANGELES
Letters and Science — Kappa Alpha, U. N. X.

MARGARET ELIZABETH MOORE — LOS ANGELES
Letters and Science.

RAYMOND RICHIE MORGAN — SONOMA
Letters and Science — Pi Kappa Alpha

ADRIAN LEWIS MORIN — SAN FRANCISCO
Dentistry — Delta Sigma Delta; Epsilon Alpha.

ETHEL ANNE MOHONEY — SAN FRANCISCO
Letters and Science — Alpha Omicron Pi.

GLENN KENDALL MORRISON — ELLENDALE, N. D.
Mechanics — Tau Beta Pi; Eta Kappa Nu; A. I. E. E.; Cast of Senior Extravaganza.

ARMENA LOUISE MORSE — BERKELEY
Letters and Science

HAROLD A. MORSE — OAKLAND
Letters and Science.

BEATRICE JESSIE MORSMAN — OAKLAND
Letters and Science.

IRENE MOSBACHER — BERKELEY
Letters and Science.

DONNA MOSES — LOS ANGELES
Letters and Science — Kappa Kappa Gamma; Prytanean; Economics Club.

EDITH LENA MOSSMAN — NAMPA, IDAHO
Letters and Science.

GENEVIEVE GLASIER MOTT — PETALUMA
Letters and Science.

PROMINENT FEAT-URES

FERRIS SYLVANUS MOULTON RIVERSIDE
Commerce—Theta Delta Chi; Beta Gamma Sigma; Sphinx, Press Club; Daily Californian Managerial Staff (1), (2), (3); Business Manager (4); 1917 Blue and Gold, Managerial Staff (3); Junior Prom Committee (3); Labor Day Committee (3); Chairman Finance Committee Senior Week (4); Endowment Committee (4); Publicity Committee Senior Week (4); General Committee Senior Week (4).

LOUIS HENRY MOELLER SAN FRANCISCO
Letters and Science—Wrestling Team (2); Boxing Team (3), (4).

CARLOS SAMSON MUNDT ALAMEDA
Letters and Science—Le Cercle Francais (3); Mathematics Club (4); Radio Club (3), Chairman (4).

GEORGE F. MURPHY YOUNTVILLE
Pharmacy.

LUCILLE ALICE MURPHY LOS ANGELES
Letters and Science—Rediviva; Senior Women's Banquet Committee (4); Senior Endowment Committee (4).

WALTER JOHN MURPHY PETALUMA
Pharmacy; Kappa Psi; President Student Body College of Pharmacy.

J. R. MURRAY, JR. CHICO
Letters and Science—Sigma Alpha Epsilon; Theta Nu Epsilon; U. N. X.; Kappa Beta Phi; Skull and Key.

WILLIAM WALLACE MURRAY NEW YORK, N. Y.
Letters and Science (Pre-Legal).

GARABED HAGOP NAJARIAN FOWLER
Agriculture; Cosmopolitan Club; Agriculturist Club.

REGINALD HOWARD NANSCAWEN SAN ANDREAS
Letters and Science (Pre-Arch.)

ADOLPH NEUBERG NATHAN SAN RAFAEL
Agriculture.

ARTHUR EMIL NELSON TURLOCK
Agriculture; Theta Chi; Senior Football Team.

MABEL NELSON VACAVILLE
Letters and Science.

JOHN CURTIS NEWTON SANTA BARBARA
Letters and Science—Delta Chi; Sophomore Hop Committee; Junior Prom Committee; Senior Assembly Committee; Senior Endowment Committee; Rally Committee (4); Advertising Manager Daily Californian (4); Associate Manager Blue and Gold (3).

LUTHER ALLEN NICHOLS POMONA
Letters and Science—Sigma Phi; Winged Helmet; Golden Bear; Beta Beta; Skull and Key; Big "C" Society; Varsity Track Team (1), (2), (3), Captain (4); Students Affairs Committee (4).

RUTH PAULINE NICHOLS SAN PEDRO
Letters and Science; Philhellenon Retains; Class Basketball Team, Manager (3); Class Hockey Team (4).

ALICE CARLENA NOBLE BERKELEY
Letters and Science—Phi Mu; Treble Clef (1), (2), (3), (4); Cast "Keeping It Dark" (3); Y. W. C. A.; Spanish Club; Arrangements Committee Junior Prom; Senior Assembly Committee; Senior Assessment Committee; Prytanean Finance Committee (3), (4).

ERMYN NORTON BERKELEY
Letters and Science—Phi Mu; Class Permanent Organization Committee (4).

OF PROMINENT PEOPLE

WARREN DEXTER NORTON — Berkeley
Agriculture—Alpha Kappa Lambda; Alpha Zeta; Phi Delta Kappa; Golden Bear; Winged Helmet; Big "C" Society; Captain Freshman Baseball Team; Varsity Basketball Team (2), Captain (3); Students Welfare Committee (3), (4); President Agriculture Club (4); Y. M. C. A. Cabinet (3), (4).

THOMAS LINDSAY NUDD — Dixon
Mechanics—Theta Chi; A. I. E. E. Treasurer (3); A. E. and M. E., Vice-President (4); Freshman Crew; Freshman Football; Varsity Football Squad (1), (2) (3), (4); Hop Committee.

HILMER OEHLMANN — Alameda
Commerce—Dahlonega; Beta Gamma Sigma.

FRANK MACDONALD OGDEN — Oakland
Letters and Science (Jurisprudence)—Delta Upsilon; Phi Alpha Delta, Cadet Captain.

ROSALINDA AMELIA OGUSE — Honolulu
Letters and Science—Alpha Omicron Pi; Promoters Club; Emergency Fund Chairman; Executive Committee, Newman Club; Secretary Senior Women's Singing; Senior Adviser, Senior Week Committee.

SAMUEL JAMES OGHAVE — Berkeley
Mining—Chi Psi; Tau Beta Pi; Theta Tau, Staff Photographer Blue and Gold (2); Associate Editor Blue and Gold (3); Blue and Gold Staff (4).

HERMAN GRAYDON OLIVER — Sacramento
Mechanics—Kappa Alpha; A. S. M. E., President (4), and M. E. (4), Treasurer A. S. M. E. (4); Convention Senior Hall (4); Permanent Organization Committee (4); Pajamarino Stunt Committee (4); General Senior Week Committee (4); Chairman Senior Pilgrimage Committee (4).

ELWOOD RICHARD OLSEN — San Francisco
Medicine—Phi Chi.

FLOYD LISLE ONNETT — Palermo
Letters and Science.

MILDRED ORR — Pomona
Letters and Science.

WILLIAM H. OVERSHINER — Santa Ana
Civil Engineering—Dahlonega.

ROUGH ENGINEERS

FEEDING A CHICK

JOSEPH NASH OWEN — Carlsbad, New Mexico
Letters and Science—Delta Chi; Band; Senate (2); Glee Club (2); A. S. U. C. Store Committee (3); A. S. U. C. Executive Committee (4); Decoration Committee Senior Ball; Chairman Senior Assemblies.

IAN ANDREW OZOLIN — Lavonia (Baltic Province of Russia)
Letters and Science (Phil.); The Slavic Club of U. C.; Editor of The Prometheus (British Literary Magazine).

WILLIAM GUY PADEN — Alameda
Letters and Science—Phi Delta Kappa.

VIOLET AGNES PALMER — Tuolumne
Letters and Science.

ROSCOE A. PARCEL — Berkeley
Letters and Science.

KATHERINE MARY PARKER — San Francisco
Letters and Science.

WEBSTER LOCKE PARKER — Eureka
Agriculture.

LEON BURSON PARKER — San Francisco
Letters and Science.

CLIFFORD ALDACE PARKER — Lindsay
Pharmacy.

JOHN LEROI PARKS — Richmond
Pharmacy.

WALDO HAYS PATE — Paso Robles
Pharmacy—Phi Delta Chi; President Senior Class 1916 and 1917.

REMOVING THE DEAD

GILBERT LANSING PATTERSON Stockton
Letters and Science.

ANITA B. PATTERSON Boston
Letters and Science.

PERRY JASPER PATTON Gonzales
Letters and Science.

CARLYLE GILL PATTON Riverside
Civil Engineering.

JOHN A. PATTON Boulder, Colorado
Letters and Science. Beta Theta Pi.

LAURENCE MATTOR PAUL China
Mechanics.

PAUL WEAVER PENLAND Oxnard
Architecture—Theta Chi, Freshman Track Team, Varsity Track Team (2); Varsity Football Squad (3), (4); Senior Ball Decoration Committee.

LOUIS HUBBARD PENNEY Colville, Mass.
Letters and Science—Theta Chi, Big "C" Society; Winged Helmet; Golden Bear, Captain, Freshman Crew; Varsity Crew (2), (3), Captain (4); Class President (2); Junior Prom Committee; Interclass Football Team (4); Cadet Captain.

DONALD D. PENNY Los Gatos
Agriculture—Sequoyah.

MYRTLE EVELYN PETCH Berkeley
Letters and Science—Women's Big "C" Society, Vice-President (4); Parliamentary Club (2); Women's Class Basketball Team (1), (2), Captain (3); Women's Class Tennis Team (3), (4), Manager (4); Women's Class Track Team (2), Manager (3); Class Hockey Team (3); Manager (4); Sports and Pastime Committee (4); All Star Basketball Team (3); All Star Hockey Team (4); Senior Advisory Committee (4).

WILLIAM SIMON PETERSON Anaconda, Mont.
Mechanics—Tau Beta Pi; Eta Kappa Nu; Cadet Lieutenant (4).

ROSE MARIA PFUND Oakland
Letters and Science—Phi Beta Kappa; Deutscher Verein; Treasurer Women's Big "C" Society; Women's Fencing, Captain, Manager (2), (3); All Californian Fencing Team (3); La Raquete Society.

SOUTHALL ROZELLE PFUND Sacramento
Letters and Science (Jurisprudence); Phi Kappa Psi; Phi Delta Phi, Freshman Glee Committee; Junior Prom Committee; Junior Farce; "Lamentations," Big "C" Committee; Cadet Captain.

EDWARD PORTER PFINGST Watsonville
Letters and Science. Phi Delta Theta.

JOSEPHINE PHILLIPS Berkeley
Letters and Science.

EMMETT PHILLIPS, Jr. Sacramento
Letters and Science—Bachelordon.

OSCAR WESLEY PHILLIPS Berkeley
Agriculture.

MELVILLE F. PHILLIPS San Francisco
Letters and Science—Le Cercle Francais (2), (3), Vice-President (4); Camera Club (2), (3); Senior Paymaster Stunt Committee.

WARREN LEE PIERSON Los Angeles
Letters and Science—Phi Delta Theta.

IRENE PIIAT Santa Barbara
Letters and Science.

LEOLA MAY PINGER Berkeley
Letters and Science.

NARCISA PIODA Salinas
Letters and Science—Alpha Chi Omega, Y. W. C. A.; Parlement (1); Senior Adviser (3), (4); Senior Assembly Committee; Senior Ball Arrangements Committee.

BERTHA PISKE San Francisco
Letters and Science.

HELEN VIRGINIA PLATT Los Angeles
Letters and Science—Delta Gamma.

JOHN CHARALAMPUS POLOS Boston, Mass.
Agriculture.

WILLIAM KENNETH POTTS Novikoff
Mechanics—Theta Xi; Associated Electrical and Mechanical Engineers, President (4); Student Branch of American Society of Mechanical Engineers (4); Foreman Labor Day 1916.

MARIE PORTER Topeka, Kansas
Letters and Science—Kappa Alpha Theta.

BIG MILITARY MEN?

KENNETH CARL PORTER — HERMOSA BEACH
Dentistry

ELISE POSEN — OAKLAND
Letters and Science

CORINNE ELISE POWELL — SACRAMENTO
Letters and Science

NOBLE ALLEN POWELL — STOCKTON
Dentistry Psi Omega

ROBERT ALLAN POWERS — OROVILLE
Medical Phi Alpha Gamma, Beta Epsilon Sigma, B, Glee Club, Art Staff Pelican (3), (4); Circumnet Club; Assistant Editor Anteater; Literary Club

THOMPSON PRICE — DENVER, COLORADO
Mechanics Theta Nu Eta Kappa Nu

EUGENE MITCHELL PRINCE — TUOLUMNE
Letters and Science Jurisprudence; Phi Kappa Psi; Phi Beta Kappa, Phi Delta Phi, Pinafetenean Forum

HARRIET EMELINE PROCTOR — OAKLAND
Letters and Science

E. C. PREUSS — PASO ROBLES
Pharmacy

KATHARINE FRANCES QUINN — LOS ANGELES
Letters and Science Alpha Chi Omega, Receiving Society, Newman Club (3); Sword Chairman (4); Senior Adviser, Emergency Fund Committee, Tag Committee for Senior Stunt, Senior Stunt Committee for Pajamarino Rally

BERT FRANKLIN RABINOWITZ — SAN FRANCISCO
Letters and Science

WILBUR RAISNER — CORNING
Letters and Science Circle "C" Society; Cross-Country Team (2), (3), (4); Assembly Debating Society, Treasurer (3); Assembly Debating Team (3); Captain of Letters and Science Track Team (4)

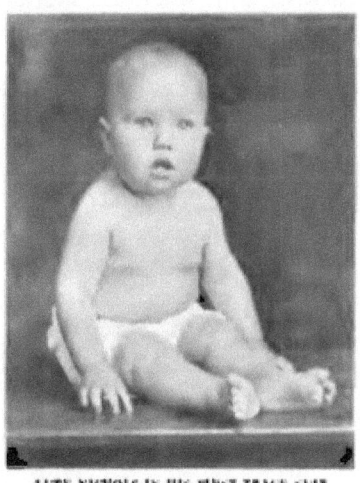

LUTE NICHOLS IN HIS FIRST TRACK SUIT

WHICH IS WHICH?

VANGALA SIVA RAM — ADILAI, INDIA
Letters and Science Nalanda Club; Cast of "Julius Caesar" (3) Student Opinion (2), (3); Composition Club; Staff of Daily Californian (3); Asiatic Student Alliance (3), Assembly Debating Society (1), (2); Forum Team (3)

MATTIE RAMELLI — VENTURA
Letters and Science

BETH M. RANTON — LONG BEACH
Letters and Science

LESTER DAVID RANTZ — LAKEPORT
Dentistry

GENEVIEVE HARRIET READ — OAKLAND
Letters and Science

HENRY LEO REICH — MANILA, P. I.
Mechanics Circle "C" Society, Sword (3), (4); Mathematics Club

EDWARD ALEXANDER REINKE — SAN DIEGO
Civil Engineering Tricamp; Circle "C" Society, Officer's Club, Secretary-Treasurer (4); Decoration Committee Military Ball (4); Cadet Captain; Senior Men's Banquet Committee

CHARLES REIS — SAN FRANCISCO
Pharmacy

PROSPER REITER, JR. — SAN FRANCISCO
Commerce Delta Tau Delta, Beta Gamma Sigma; Commerce Club, President (4); Glee Club; Military Band (2)

MILTON JOSEPH REINHART — ELKO, NEVADA
Letters and Science

CARL ALBERT RENZ — MILL VALLEY
Chemistry Sigma Nu

RUTH MARIE REPATH — LOS ANGELES
Letters and Science

GLADYS ISABEL RESTON SAN FRANCISCO
Letters and Science—Women's "C" Society; Class Crew (1), (2), (3); Varsity Crew (2); Parthenia (2); Southern Club (1), (2), (3); President (4); Senior Advisory Committee, Chairman Sophomore Goddle Mignta Committee; Senior Women's Treasurer (First Semester) A. S. U. C. Finance Committee (2), (3); Senior Pilgrimage Committee

FRED H. REYNOLDS LOS ANGELES
Agriculture—Theta Xi

CHARLES ELROY RHEIN ALAMEDA
Chemistry—Del Rey Club, Alpha Chi Sigma; Newman Club, Treasurer (4); Senior Endowment Committee (4); Class Secretary (4)

FLORENCE MAY RHODCHAMEL OAKLAND
Letters and Science

RUTH ANN RIED SAN FRANCISCO
Letters and Science

IOLA GLADYS RIESS SAN FRANCISCO
Letters and Science—Mekatena Club, Senior Week Program Committee

AINSLEY MEREDITH RING FERNDALE
Pharmacy—Phi Delta Chi

MARY ELIZABETH ROBERTS RICHMOND, IND.
Letters and Science

ESTHER MARIE RODKEY LOS ANGELES
Commerce—Nortonian

CHARLES F. B. ROETH OAKLAND
Letters and Science—Phi Sigma Kappa

SEEING THINGS

EMERY HERMAN ROGERS SANTA MONICA
Letters and Science—Beta Sigma Pi; Golden Bear; Beta Beta, U. N. X. Big "C" Society (2), (3); Treasurer (4); Freshman Tennis Team, Varsity Tennis Team (2), (3); Captain (4); Executive Committee Big "C" Circus, Rally Committee (3); Managerial Staff Blue and Gold; Senior Ball Arrangements Committee.

HAROLD LEROY ROGERS MODESTO
Pharmacy—Kappa Psi

ROMAYNE R. ROHLFING PLACERVILLE
Letters and Science—Phi Sigma Kappa, Senior Banquet Committee; Senior Endowment Committee

LEWIS SAMUEL ROSENBAUM SAN FRANCISCO
Letters and Science

HELEN EMMA ROSENBERG OAKLAND
Letters and Science—Nu Sigma Upsilon; Class Hockey Team, Captain (4); All California Hockey Team (4); Class Tennis Team (3), (4); Baseball Manager (4)

SAMSON HELLER ROSENBLATT SAN FRANCISCO
Mechanics (Electrical)—Eta Kappa Nu; A. I. E. E. (3), (4); A. E. and M. E. (3), (4); Executive Committee (3); Senior Men's Banquet Committee (4)

MURREY LEVERING ROYAR LOS ANGELES
Letters and Science—Achaean; Students Welfare Committee (4); Senior Endowment Committee (4); Senior Ball Committee

WILLIAM WHEELER RUCKER OAKLAND
Letters and Science

JAY LEON RUDDICK BERKELEY
Letters and Science—University Band; University Orchestra. Transferred from Bethany College, Lindsborg, Kansas (3)

PETER RUEGG SANTA CLARA
Letters and Science

HENRY AUGUSTO RUFFO LOS ANGELES

ELIZABETH MARY RUGGLES — San Francisco
Letters and Science. Gamma Phi Beta. Prytanean, Secretary (4); Chairman Senior Advisory Committee, Senior Ball Committee, Junior Prom Committee, Freshie Glee Committee, Parthneon Property Committee (3), Junior Labor Day (Chairman)

WALTER RUPPEL — San Francisco
Civil Engineering. Tau Beta Pi, Sigma Xi

MABEL MORRIS RUSHMORE — Ware, Mass.
Letters and Science

WILLIAM ALEXANDER RUSSELL — San Jose
Letters and Science. Sigma Phi. Winged Helmet, Golden Bear, Football (1), (2), (3), (4), Sophomore Hop Committee, Senior Ball Committee

JOHN R. RUSSELL — Santa Rosa
Pharmacy

HUGH E. RUTHERFORD — San Rafael
Pharmacy

ROBERT LAURENCE RYAN — Santa Barbara
Civil Engineering. Phi Gamma Delta. Sigma Iota Phi, Civil Engineering Association, President and Vice-President Civil Engineering Association (4); Students Welfare Committee, Varsity Track Team (2), (3), (4)

SARAH DAVIS SABIN — Portland, Oregon
Letters and Science

ETHEL MARTHA SAID — Bakersfield
Letters and Science

OLIVER SAGEN GEORGE — Princeton
Letters and Science. Spueaverland. Mathematics Club; Scandinavian Club; Soccer (3), (4), Circle "C" Society

ERMINIE URSULA SALA — Stockton
Letters and Science. Capa de Oro

ADELE LOUISE SALSBURY — San Francisco
Letters and Science. Coxswain Class Crew (1), (2)

DONALD WOLFRUM SALTER — Trout Creek, Mont.
Mining

MARY JANE SANDERSON — Berkeley
Letters and Science. Prytanean. Economics Club; Labor Day Committee (3), Captain, Senior Advisor (4); Senior Engineering Committee (4); Decoration Committee Senior Ball (4); Parthneon Properties (3), (4); Ticket Sales Chairman Prytanean Fete (4); Emergency Fund Committee (3), (4)

BURNETT SANFORD — Palo Alto
Agriculture

AUGUSTUS VICTOR SAPH — Berkeley
Civil Engineering. Sigma Xi, Tau Beta Pi, Sigma Iota Phi

ERIC HAROLD SARGEANT — Riverside
Letters and Science. Sigma Phi Sigma. U. C. Rifle Team (2), (4); Captain 1st U. C. Rifle Team Gold Medal (3), Sergeant (3); Mandolin Club

HARRY SARGENT — Riverside
Agriculture

HARRY HALL SCHEELINE — Reno, Nevada
Letters and Science. Zeta Psi. Skull and Key; Quarter Delta, U. N. X., Beta Beta; Glee Club, De Koven Club; European Glee Club Tour (2); Transfer from University of Nevada (1)

RAY JOHN SCHEELINE — Kingsburg
Letters and Science. Sequoyah Club

GERTRUDE AGNES SCHIECK — Berkeley
Letters and Science. Alpha Omicron Pi

KARL HOWARD SCHILLING — Berkeley
Letters and Science. Delta Epsilon, Theta Tau; Cadet Lieutenant

ALICE ELEANOR SCHLOTS — Elmwood, Ill.
Letters and Science. Iota Sigma Pi; Senior Advisory Committee

ANNA M. M. SCHNELLE — Hamburg, Germany
Letters and Science

NO WONDER VANDENBERGH COULDN'T STUDY

JUST LIKE A REGULAR POLITICIAN

MARGUERITE JULIA SCHOLL Los Angeles
Letters and Science — Transfer from Mills College, August, 1916.

HANS EMIL AUGUST SCHROEDER San Francisco
Letters and Science.

LEO WILLIAM SCHUCHARD Medford, Oregon
Dentistry.

CURT NICOLAUS SCHUETTE San Francisco
Mining.

NICHOLAS JAMES SCORSUR San Jose
Commerce — Sigma Phi Epsilon; Beta Gamma Sigma; Senior Pilgrimage Committee; Secretary Permanent Senior Endowment Fund.

KENYON JUDSON SCUDDER Seattle, Wash.
Letters and Science — Orchestra (2), (3), (4).

NELLIE MAUDE SECARA Madera
Letters and Science — Alpha Gamma Delta; Iota Sigma Pi; Class Basketball Team (1), (2).

EDWARD E. SEID San Francisco
Pharmacy.

ERNEST MARTIN SETZER Lodi
Dentistry — Xi Psi Phi.

HONG KIM SEENG Oakland
Mechanics — A. E. M. E.; A. I. M. E.; Vice-President of Chinese Student Club (4).

HARRY BOYD SEYMOUR Sacramento
Letters and Science — Chi Phi; Phi Beta Kappa; Golden Bear; Winged Helmet; Skull and Key; U N X; English Club; Press Club; Sphinx; *Daily Californian* (1), (2), (3), Editor (4).

JOHN LAURENCE SEYMOUR Santa Monica
Letters and Science — Alpha Kappa Lambda; Phi Beta Kappa; President Music Society (3); Vice-President Philhellenic Debate; Contributor of Music to 1916 Extravaganza; President Music Society (3); Vice-President Music Society, Contributor of Music to the 1917 Extravaganza.

DOROTHY ASHTON SHADE Pasadena
Letters and Science — Delta Delta Delta.

JAY RANDOLPH SHARPSTEIN Alameda
Letters and Science — Phi Chi; Secretary-Treasurer Associated Pre-Medical Students (1), (2), (3).

DAVID STODDART SHATTUCK Los Angeles
Letters and Science — Delta Tau Delta.

EDWARD BYER SHAW Olney, Illinois
Letters and Science — Nu Sigma Nu; Glee Club Executive Committee (3), Vice-President (4); Cast "Keeping it Dark" (3); Transfer from the University of Illinois (3).

RAYMOND LEE SHEARMAN Berkeley
Letters and Science — Phi Kappa Sigma; Freshman Track Team; Varsity Cross-Country Track Team (3), (4); Varsity Track Team (3), (4); Captain Cross-Country Team (4); Secretary-Treasurer, Circle "C" Society (3); President Circle "C" Society (4); Labor Day Commissary Committee.

HELEN ELIZA SHEEDY Bakersfield
Letters and Science.

HAZEL JULIA SHEPHERD Stockton
Letters and Science.

RUTH SHERMAN Berkeley
Letters and Science — Kappa Kappa Gamma; Phi Beta Kappa; Prytanean; Y. W. C. A. Cabinet (2), (3); Students Welfare Committee (4); Senior Advisory Committee (4); Treble Clef (1), (2), (3).

HUGH SHIPPEY Long Beach
Jurisprudence — Chi Psi; Phi Delta Phi; Beta Beta; Chairman of Committee for the Organization of Class Finance System (4); Secretary Associated Students Store Committee (4); Junior Prom Committee; Member Finance and Arrangements Committee for Senior Week.

NATIONAL ASSETS

H. R D SHOEMAKER   Santa Barbara
Medical Transfer Pomona College 1912. Transfer U C 1913. Phi Alpha Gamma; Sigma Alpha Beta. U Orchestra (4); U Glee Club; Dance Committee (1), (2), (3), (4).

AL. HENRY SIEMER   San Francisco
Civil Engineering Tau Beta Pi; Sigma Xi; Inter-Class Football (4).

PAUL FOSTER SINCLAIR   Berkeley
Letters and Science Phi Sigma Kappa; Transfer from Brown University.

HOWARD VAN ARSDALE SLATER   Los Angeles
Chemistry Alpha Chi Sigma.

THOMAS WILLIAM SLAVEN   Sacramento
Jurisprudence Bachelordon; President Senior Class (4); Chairman Arrangements Committee Senior Ball; Rally Committee (3); At General Senior Week Committee; 1917 Blue and Gold Editorial Staff (3); Freshman Track Squad.

MARY RUTH SMART   Los Angeles
Letters and Science President California Club (3); Brigands Relief Committee (4).

ROBERT LELAND SMIRLE   San Francisco
Commerce

AMRAH DINWIDDIE SMITH   Berkeley
Letters and Science

BERNICE DUNLAP SMITH   Honolulu, T. H.
Letters and Science

FRANK CAROL SMITH   Santa Barbara
Letters and Science.

HARVEY ALBERT SMITH   Sacramento
Civil Engineering.

JOSEPH THOMAS SMITH   Livermore
Letters and Science Bachelordon; Cadet Lieutenant

A PERFECT LADY!

JOHN WALTER SMITH   Piedmont
Agriculture

LILLIAN DUBOIS SMITH   Oakland
Letters and Science.

WILL HOWARD SMITH   Oakland
Civil Engineering.

ROBERT LACY SMYTH   Berkeley
Letters and Science - Alpha Delta Phi; Phi Beta Kappa, Phrontisterion.

SIDNEY HUGH SMYTH   Portland, Ore.
Mechanics.

MYRTLE MAY SNIDER   Denair
Letters and Science.

ELIZABETH SNYDER   Hollywood
Letters and Science - Pi Beta Phi; Senior Adviser (4); Transfer from Mills College (3).

ROBERT WADE SNYDER   Colusa
Letters and Science.

MILTON ALEXANDER SODERBERG   Kerman
Agriculture.

ANTOINETTE SOO-HOO   San Rafael
Letters and Science.

PETER LAURITZEN SPANNE   Lompoc
Civil Engineering.

ELDRIDGE TED SPENCER   Berkeley
Letters and Science (Pre-Agriculture.)

THOMAS SPENCER   Providence, R. I.
Mechanics Theta Xi.

NELSON EDWIN SPICKLEMIRE   Tulare
Civil Engineering Dahlonega.

WILLIAM WALLACE SPRAGUE   Menlo Park
Mining.

NELSON RUDGE SPRINKLE   Glendale
Agriculture.

ANGIE TIBBETTS STACEY   San Francisco
Letters and Science.

TO THINK WE ALL HAD AN EVEN START

VULGAR

RAUB MERRILL STAFFORD MARYSVILLE
Agriculture—Theta Xi; Alpha Zeta; Junior Prom Committee; Senior Assembly Committee.

STARR WALKER STANYAN WEST MEDFORD, MASS.
Letters and Science.

ROY STARBIRD SAN FRANCISCO
Mining—Chi Phi; Theta Tau; Tau Beta Pi; Big "C" Society; Sigma Xi; Freshman Baseball Team (1); Varsity Baseball Team (3), (4).

EDITH GEORGIE STARK MARTINEZ
Letters and Science.

NEAL STAUNTON LOS ANGELES
Letters and Science (Jurisprudence)—Alpha Tau Omega; Phi Delta Phi.

LOUISE HOLMES STEEL-BROOKE
FOXCROFT, MAINE
Medical—Graduate of Foxcroft Academy; Assistant Editor Pelicope (3); Dance Committee (1), (2), (3) (4); H. Class Librarian (3), (4).

J. FRED STEELE PERRY, IOWA
Medical—Phi Alpha Gamma; Hahnemann Class President (1), (2); H. Tennis Team; H. Basketball Team Captain (3), (4).

SARAH ELIZABETH STEELE PORTLAND, ORE.
Letters and Science.

PERCY ANSLEY STEEVES SAN JOSE
Dentistry—President of Epsilon Alpha (3), (4); Chairman of Honor Committee (2); President of Junior Class (3); Treasurer of Student Body (4); Chairman of Students' Affairs Committee (3); Member of Athletic Committee (3)

MARGARET ABBIE STEIGER VACAVILLE
Letters and Science; Treble Clef; Senior Advisory Committee (4); A. W. S. Finance Committee (2); "What Next"; Parliament (2)

FRITZ STEIN WANNE, GERMANY
Medical—Phi Alpha Gamma; H Student Body Treasurer (2)

ELFRIEDA STEINDORFF NEW YORK, N. Y.
Letters and Science; Phi Mu; A. W. S. Lost and Found Bureau (1), (2); Sophomore Rabble Committee (2); Labor Day Committee (3); Treble Clef Executive Committee (1), (2); Vice-President (3); President (4)

LILLIAN THEKLA STEPHANY BERLIN, GERMANY
Letters and Science—Kappa Alpha Theta; Dyslyt Club; Deutscher Verein; Greek Club; Social Committee Y. W. C. A.

GORDON FITZHUGH STEPHENS HOLLYWOOD
Letters and Science (Jurisprudence)—Alpha Delta Phi; Phi Delta Phi; Sphinx; Greek Club President (First Semester) (4); Captain Military (4); Chairman Military Ball Decoration Committee (4); Blue and Gold (3); Senior Assembly Committee (4).

WAITE HENRY STEPHENSON OAKLAND
Letters and Science (Jurisprudence)—Delta Chi; Senate; Assistant Manager "Prunella" (3); Secretary General Committee Senior Week; Senior Ball Committee

PHILIP CUSHING STETSON SAN RAFAEL
Letters and Science

NORMAN BENJAMIN STERN BERKELEY
Letters and Science—Psi Upsilon; Press Club; Sphinx; Chairman, Senior Extravaganza Committee; Associate Editor Occident (3), (4); Associate Editor Pelican (3), (4).

OLIVE LEE STEVENSON RIVERSIDE
Letters and Science; Mekatina

NANA STEVICK STANFORD UNIVERSITY
Letters and Science

BELLE RITCHIE STEWART BERKELEY
Letters and Science.

FLOYD WAYNE STEWART SAN JOSE
Letters and Science—Sigma Phi; Winged Helmet; Golden Bear; Skull and Key; Beta Beta; Manager 1917 Blue and Gold; Blue and Gold Advisory Committee (3), (4); Director A. S. U. C. Store (4); Undergraduate Chairman Students Affairs Committee; Chairman Honor System Committee; 1917 Re-union Committee; General Committee Senior Week; Senior Assemblies Committee; Class Football Team (4); President Associated Students (4).

WILLIAM JOSEPH STICH SACRAMENTO
Mechanics.

GEORGE WALTON STICKNEY UPLAND
Agriculture

VACCINATED

LAOMETTE HOLMES STINSON Associate
Pharmacy; Phi Delta Chi; Turtle Club; Captain Jinxing Basebal Team (4); Member Phi Committee (3); Member Graduate Staff (4); Sergeant-at-arms Student Body (4).

CLARENCE ALDEN STOCK Virginia City, Nev.
Dentistry; Xi Psi Phi; Vice-President Senior Class (4); Baseball (2).

MARY EDNA STONEBROOK South Pasadena
Letters and Science; Alpha Delta Pi; Freshie Glee Reception Committee; Partheneia Pi (2); Junior Prom Reception Committee; Ekonk's Club (4); Labor Day Committee (3); Senior Advisory Committee (4).

EVELYN ROWENA STONESIFER Berkeley
Letters and Science.

RAYMOND EARL STORIE Highvale
Agriculture; Agriculture Club; Senior Advisory Committee; Editorial Staff U. C. Journal of Agriculture (4).

EDNA WILLIAMS STRONG Oakland
Letters and Science.

CALMER JOHN STRIEBLE San Diego
Letters and Science; Alternate Sophomore Debating Team (2); Winner Bonnheim Essay Prize (2), (3), (4).

RUTH GRAY STUBBS Berkeley
Letters and Science.

ETHEL MARIE STYLES Willmar, Minnesota
Letters and Science; Zeta Tau Alpha; Transfer from Carleton College, Minnesota.

MARIAN SHAW STYNER Salt Lake City, Utah
Letters and Science; Chi Omega; Phi Beta Kappa.

CHARLES EDWARD SULLIVAN San Bernardino
Agriculture; Del Rey; Varsity Track Team (3), (4); Class Track Captain (4); Cross-Country Team (4); Treasurer Newman Club (4).

ELADIO SUSAETA Victoria, Spain
Agriculture; Transfer from the Chilean University, Santiago de Chile.

HOMER I. G. SUSSDORFF San Francisco
Letters and Science (Medicine).

BERNADINE SUTKAMP Berkeley
Letters and Science.

JACKSON AT HOME

GEORGE T. SWAIM Unadilla, Nevada
Agriculture; Tribunal; Big "C" Society; Track Team (1), (2), (3).

GLENN VERNELL SWAN Grinnell, Ia.
Letters and Science.

ARTHUR JACKSON SWANK Colusa
Mechanics.

DOROTHY MAY SWANK Colusa
Letters and Science.

KATHRYN L. SWEETSER Santa Barbara
Letters and Science; Zeta Tau Alpha.

FRANCES COMBA SWEEZEY Oakland
Letters and Science.

HELEN JETT SWORTFIGUER Berkeley
Letters and Science; Alpha Xi Delta; Ukulele Club (2), (4); Senior Advisory Committee (4); Managerial Staff 1917 Blue and Gold; Y. W. C. A. Membership Committee (4).

FRANCIS KAAHA SYLVA Honolulu, T. H.
Dentistry.

TAI LOUIS TADA Oakland
Mechanics.

HELEN WILLIAMS TALBERT Berkeley
Letters and Science.

JOSEPH RAEGEN TALBOT Santa Rosa
Letters and Science (Jurisprudence.)

KATHERINE ISABEL TAPSCOTT Yreka
Letters and Science.

ACHILLES ALFRED TAVERNETTI Salinas
Agriculture; Sigma Phi Sigma.

CENSORING THE RASPBERRY

OUR

FRED HENRY TAYLOR Susanville
Agriculture.

GEORGE FRANCIS TAYLOR Nevada City
Commerce—Dwight Club; Beta Gamma Sigma; Commerce Club, Le Cercle Francais, Secretary (3); Cast "What's Next" (4); Cast "Canterbury Pilgrims" (4).

JOHN C. W. TAYLOR Fountaintown, Ind.
Medical—Phi Alpha Gamma; II. Class President (1); II. Orchestra; Varsity Hockey Team (4); Civic "C" Society.

MARGARET POWERS TAYLOR Salt Lake City, Utah
Letters and Science—Delta Zeta; Parthenia Properties Committee (3), Captain (4).

GLADYS ANITA TEAGUE Berkeley
Letters and Science.

T. ARTIN TERZIAN Armenia
Medical—Student Interne Hahnemann Hospital (2), (3), (4); H. 8 tavant as-arms (1), (2), (3), (4).

MORTON THACHER El Cajon
Agriculture—Tilicum.

MILDRED FRANCES THOMAS San Francisco
Letters and Science.

CLAUDE VERNER THOMPSON Orland
Letters and Science (Medical)—Alpha Sigma Phi; Phi Chi.

HARRY OMER SCOTT THOMPSON Esparto
Agriculture.

MILDRED BENTLEY THOMPSON Oakland
Letters and Science.

RUBY CORNELIA THOMPSON Berkeley
Letters and Science.

JAMES HERBERT TIETZEN Berkeley
Letters and Science.

FRANK GILE TIFFANY Hollister
Agriculture—Alpha Zeta.

WILLIAM JOHN TOCHER Oakland
Agriculture—Tilicum.

JESSIE FLORENCE TODHUNTER Vancouver, B. C.
Letters and Science—Delta Delta Delta.

HOMER CLINTON TOLLEFSON Tacoma, Wash.
Dentistry—Xi Psi Phi; Epsilon Alpha.

AVERY TOMPKINS Berkeley
Letters and Science—Phi Delta Theta; Phi Beta Kappa.

CHESTER BENSON TONKIN San Jose
Commerce—Sigma Phi; Skull and Key; Beta Beta.

HOMER HAROLD TOOLEY New Hampton, Ia.
Commerce.

TANAKA TOSHII San Francisco
Dentistry.

HOPE EDITH TOWNSEND Oakland
Letters and Science.

MARGARET ADELINE TOYE Alameda
Letters and Science.

ELWOOD ELLSWORTH TRASK Los Angeles
Agriculture—Sigma Pi; Senior Men's Banquet Committee.

ELMER HOUSTON TUCKER Long Beach
Commerce—Beta Gamma Sigma; Phi Beta Kappa; Commerce Club, President (4); Senior Advisory Committee.

HAROLD SUMNER TURNER Santa Cruz
Letters and Science.

RUTH ALLISON TURNER San Francisco
Letters and Science.

HERALDA PALMA TYNG San Francisco
Medical—Hahnemann Student Body Secretary (4).

LAURA HARRIET ULRICH Janesville, Minn.
Letters and Science.

MANAGER

LESLIE UNDERHILL SAN FRANCISCO
Letters and Science. Gamma Phi Beta; President;
Y.W.C.A Cabinet (3), (4); Senior Adviser A.W.S.
Mass Meeting Committee (3), (4); Labor Day Committee (3); Junior Informal Committee 1915; Junior
Curtain Raiser 1916; Senior Ball Arrangements Committee.

FLORENCE EMMA UNDERWOOD BERKELEY
Letters and Science.

LESTER ALLEN UPHAM RIO VISTA
Pharmacy. Kappa Psi.

TOMAS STANLEY VANASEK ALHAMBRA
Letters and Science. Gymnasium Club, President (4);
Manager (4); Mathematics Club (3); Secretary-Treasurer (4); Rifle Club (4).

ROLLAND A. VANDEGRIFT STOCKTON CITY
Letters and Science. Acacia; Treasurer Assembly
Debating Society (3).

A RARE ONE

ALPHA DELT HASH

JOHN JAMES VANDENBURGH LOS ANGELES
Civil Engineering. Phi Kappa Sigma; Golden Bear;
Winged Helmet; Sigma Iota Phi; Captain and Regimental Adjutant.

BESSIE MAY VANDERBURGH MADERA
Letters and Science.

DOUGLAS VAN DYKE LOS ANGELES
Letters and Science. Psi Upsilon; Phi Delta Phi;
Varsity Track Team (4).

GEORGE McGILL VOGT OAKLAND
Letters and Science.

SYLVIA MARIA VOLLMER LAS VEGAS, N. M.
Letters and Science. Konversationsklub Secretary 1916;
President 1917; Membership Committee of Newman Club.

HAROLD JOSEPH VON DETTEN STOCKTON
Letters and Science. Sigma Chi.

MARIETTA VOORHEES BERKELEY
Letters and Science. Hockey Team (3).

ERNEST EDWARD VOSPER SAN FRANCISCO
Letters and Science. Sigma Chi.

DEAN QUIGLEY WADDELL LOS ANGELES
Letters and Science. Phi Kappa Sigma; Phi Chi; Arrangements Committee Easter and Front Mart; Arrangements Committee Senior Ball.

NADA B. WAGNER SAN DIEGO
Letters and Science.

JOHN M. WAKEFIELD IOWA
Dentistry. Psi Omega; Epsilon Alpha; Baseball (3);
Chairman College Dance Committee (3); Secretary and Treasurer (3); Vice-President College of Dentistry Student Body.

LAURA AMY WALDEN ALAMEDA
Letters and Science. Delta Gamma; Treble Clef.

ESTELLA EVANGELINE WALKER OAKLAND
Letters and Science.

D. F. MUSICIANS

THEN WORK WHILE YOU SLEEP

PIERRE JAQUA WALKER HOLLYWOOD
Letters and Science (Pre-Medical); Alpha Sigma Phi; Phi Chi; Beta Kappa Alpha; Senate; Bonnheim Essay Prize (1); Class Debating Team (2); Senate Debating Team (3).

JEAN E. WALKER VISALIA
Letters and Science.

RALPH MERVIN WALKER SELMA
Agriculture; Alpha Kappa Lambda; Alpha Zeta; Fencing Team (2), (4); Y. M. C. A. Cabinet Secretary (3), (4); Agriculture Club.

ETHEL CAROLYN WALL BERKELEY
Letters and Science — Vice-President Class (2); A. W. S. Finance Committee (1), (2), (3); Sophomore Hop Reception Committee (2); Parthon in Cast (1), (2); Parthon in Costume Committee (2), (3), (4); Chairman Finance Committee Sophomore Banquet (2); Chairman Finance Committee A. W. S. Jinx (3), (4); A. W. S. Rooms Committee (3); Junior Prom Decoration Committee (3); Senior Advisor (3), (4); Chairman Senior Women's Hall (4); Curtain Raiser Cast (3); Pilgrimage Committee; Senior Week Finance Committee (3); Senior Assembly Finance Committee (4); Labor Day Committee (3); Class Tag Sale (3); Women's Day Stunt Committee (4); Crew (2), (3), (4); Varsity (2); All Californian (3); Captain (3); *Daily Californian* Staff (2), (3); Treasurer Sports and Pastimes (3), (4); *Blue and Gold* Staff (3); Prytanean Finance Committee (2), (3); Extravaganza Costuming Committee (3); Women's Day *Occident* Staff (2); Emergency Fund Committee (1), (2), (3).

ISN'T THIS CUTE?

DORACE GLENN WALLACE LOS GATOS
Dentistry.

ROSSELET WALLACE BERKELEY
Letters and Science — Alpha Phi.

OVERTON LINCOLN WALSH LOS ANGELES
Mining — Delta Kappa Epsilon.

ETHEL PEARL WALTHER ELK GROVE
Letters and Science; California Home Club; Beta Kappa Alpha; Biological Society; Phi Beta Kappa.

IMRA MARGARET WANN BERKELEY
Letters and Science — Gamma Phi Beta; Prytanean; Symposium; Kappa Beta Pi; Informal Committee (2), (3), (4); Junior Farce Committee (3); Cast, Curtain Raiser (3); Labor Day Committee (3); Y. W. C. A. Social Service (3); Women's Undergraduate Student Affairs Committee (Spring) (3), (4); Class President (4); Senior Adviser (3); President Y. W. C. A. (4); Christian Women's Students' Union Committee (4); General Committee Senior Week (4); Finance Committee Senior Week (4); Class Reunion Committee (4); General Committee Ambulance Fund (4).

WELL, SNIP!

ARTHUR LAFAYETTE WARREN BERKELEY
Letters and Science — Alpha Kappa Kappa; Beta Kappa Alpha; Military; Captain; Class Secretary (1); Class Treasurer (2); Gymnasium Club (3); Secretary-Treasurer (4); Class Auditing Committee (1); Guard 130-Pounds Basketball Team (2); Military Ball Committee (3).

MURRELL CHARLES WARREN BERKELEY
Agriculture.

ROY EVERET WARREN BERKELEY
Letters and Science.

WILLIAM GLENN WATERHOUSE PASADENA
Agriculture.

ROY NORTON WATERS SAN FRANCISCO
Agriculture.

CLARKE ELMER WAYLAND BERKELEY
Mechanics; Member Student Branch American Society of Mechanical Engineers; Associated Electrical and Mechanical Engineers, Secretary (3); University Orchestra (1); University of California Cadet Band (1), (2), (3); Lieutenant (4).

HOWARD EDWARD WEBBER Ross
Letters and Science—Beta Gamma Sigma.

HENRY REGINALD WEBER Berkeley
Commerce—Acacia, Cadet Captain.

MARTHA AUGUSTA WEBER Berkeley
Letters and Science—Deutsche Circle, Vice-President (4); Wonder Angel, Assistant Manager and Secretary; Senior Women's Treasurer (4), Parthenia (3), (2).

DOROTHEA WEBSTER San Diego
Letters and Science—Deutscher Verein.

JACKSON LEMUEL WEBSTER Berkeley
Letters and Science—Boozhe Club, Varsity Soccer Team (2), (3), (4).

RUPERT GOLDING WEDEMEYER Homer
Civil Engineering.

JOHN STEWART WEEKS Oakland
Mining.

LEONA ELLEN WEEKS Oakland
Letters and Science.

WINIFRED M. WEEKS Hot Springs, Arkansas
Letters and Science.

MILTON BRAY WEIDENTHAL San Francisco
Agriculture.

LINDA FRYER WEILL Santa Barbara
Letters and Science.

FRANCES MAUDE WELCH Berkeley
Letters and Science.

LUCILE WELCH Woodland
Letters and Science—Alpha Xi Delta.

RALPH ERIE WEST Martinez
Letters and Science—Dwight Club; Senate Debating Society.

WHAT D'YOU SEE, FAY?

DOROTHY ELIZABETH WETMORE Berkeley
Letters and Science—Pi Beta Phi, Prytanean; Mask and Dagger, Torch and Shield, Parthenia Manager (3); A. W. S. Executive Committee (4); Senior Ball Arrangements Committee (4); Senior Advisory Committee (3); Parthenia Costume Committee (3); Cast "The Bear," "Androcles and the Lion," Extravaganza, "Pygmalion," Junior Curtain Raiser, Parthenia (1), (2).

ANNE RADFORD WHARTON Los Angeles
Letters and Science—Kappa Kappa Gamma, Prytanean, Torch and Shield; Joyce, Daylyn, Editorial Staff Daily Californian (3); Editorial Staff 1917 Blue and Gold; Parthenia Publicity Committee (3), Chairman (4).

HERBERT HARVEY WHEELER Santa Barbara
Chemistry—Alpha Chi Sigma, Graduate in December, 1917.

MARY RUTH WHEELER Oxnard
Letters and Science.

NORMA WHEELER Los Angeles
Letters and Science—Transfer from Mills College, August, 1916.

GEORGE LEONARD WHITE Berkeley
Letters and Science—Delta Chi.

FRED VINCENT WHITLEY Red Bluff
Pharmacy.

LOWERING THE COLORS

JOLLY SKINNY

GERTRUDE NANCY WHITTON — BERKELEY
Letters and Science — Alpha Nu; Chairman Senior Women's Social Committee (4), 1916; Chairman Senior Women's Schedule Committee (4), 1917; Senior Election Committee (4); Senior Advisory Committee (4)

FRANK HOWARD WILCOX — ONTARIO
Letters and Science — Phi Beta Kappa; English Club; Sphinx; Associate Editor *Occident* (4)

VIC IN HIS ELEMENT

WALTER SCOTT WILKINSON, JR. — BLYTHE
Agriculture — Sigma Pi; Freshman Crew (1); Sophomore Hop Committee; Captain Sophomore Interclass Crew (2)

THOMAS LAWRENCE WILLIAMS — SEATTLE, WASH.
Letters and Science — Sigma Nu

GIFFORD GUSTAV WILLS — SAN FRANCISCO
Civil Engineering

FLORA MARGARET WILSON — SANTA CRUZ
Letters and Science — McKinley Club; Newman Club; Permanent Organization Fund Committee

MARGARET CELIA WILSON — TWIN FALLS, IDAHO
Letters and Science

WARREN SCOTT WILSON — SAN FRANCISCO
Letters and Science

BILL!

ELIZABETH WITTER — BERKELEY
Letters and Science — Kappa Kappa Gamma; Treble Clef; Torch and Shield; Parliamentary Society (3); Dansk Club (4); Chorus "Red Mill" and "Keeping It Dark"; Parthenea (4); Students Welfare Committee (4); Senior Extravaganza (4); Decoration Committee Senior Ball (3); Arrangements Committee "Big C" Sirkus (4).

ESTHER LOUISE WITTER — OAKLAND
Letters and Science — Senior Advisory Committee (4), (4); Editorial Staff 1917 *Blue and Gold*; Senior Women's Entertainment Committee; Senior Assembly Committee; "California Day" Committee; Labor Day Committee; Y. W. C. A. Cabinet (3); Y. W. C. A. Friendship Luncheon Committee (4)

WILLIS GUY WITTER — BERKELEY
Letters and Science — Zeta Psi; Golden Bear; Skull and Key; Beta Beta; U. N. X.; Phi Delta Phi; Varsity Track Team (2), (3); General Chairman Senior Ball; Vice-President A. S. U. C.; Reunion Committee; Permanent Organization Committee; Secretary Law Association

TINY BIG!

CHARLES DORMAN WOEHR REDLANDS
Letters and Science Dahlonega.

BING CHIN WONG BERKELEY
Letters and Science.

T. L. WONG HONOLULU, T. H.
Medical—Editor Pereneope 1917; Treasurer Hahnemann Student Body (4).

ARTHUR WOOD TULARE
Agriculture—Orund, Track Team.

FRANK WOOD TULARE
Agriculture Alpha Zeta.

MILO NELSON WOOD STEVENS POINT, WIS.
Agriculture.

ROY WOODHAMS REDWOOD CITY
Medical-Civil Engineering—Winner R. F. Tomlinson Surgery Prize, 1917, President Student Body of Hahnemann College (4).

BASIL KIRKMAN WOODS ST. LOUIS, MO.
Letters and Science—Pi Kappa Alpha.

LEONARD WOODS BERKELEY
Letters and Science—Dahlonega.

HAROLD EVANS WOODWORTH BERKELEY
Agriculture—Sigma Pi; Alpha Zeta.

CAROL WILLARD WRIGHT EUREKA
Agriculture—Sigma Pi; Alpha Zeta, Agriculture Track Captain (3); Freshman Track Team; Varsity Track Team (1), (2), (3), (4); Labor Day Committee.

ELWOOD WELLMAN WRIGHT BERKELEY
Agriculture—Delta Upsilon; Freshman Track Team; Class Secretary (4); Class Football Team (1); Senior Endowment Committee (4); Cast Senior Extravaganza (3); Class Constitution Committee (4).

MILTON ABOLIEN WRIGHT ST. HELENA
Commerce—Orund; Cadet Lieutenant.

WHITNEY BRAYMER WRIGHT CAMDEN, N. J.
Mining—Chi Psi; Theta Tau, Glee Club; Sophomore Boxing Committee (2); Labor Day Committee (3); Senior Informal Committee (4).

EMORY LEWIS WYCKOFF NAPA
Pharmacy—Phi Delta Chi, Turtle Club, Vice-President of Junior Class; Vice-President of Student Body of the College of Pharmacy 1915 and 1916.

EMORY Z. WYCKOFF NAPA
Pharmacy.

MERLE ELIZABETH YOUNG NEWHALL
Letters and Science Alpha Gamma Delta.

WILLIAM JEROME YOUNG SAN FRANCISCO
Letters and Science—Delta Chi.

FLORENCE ZANDER BERKELEY
Letters and Science Alpha Xi Delta; Vice-President Women's Class Crew (2), (3), (4); Senior Advisory Committee.

FRANCIS VACLAV ZLATNIK PRAGUE, BOHEMIA
Commerce.

OLIN THE THIRD

JUNIOR CLASS

GRANT HUNT

RUTH WALKER

OFFICERS

First Semester:
President, Grant James Hunt
Vice-President, Ruth Benjamin Walker
Secretary, John Robert Edwards
Treasurer, Raymond Rainier Brown
Sergeant-at-arms, Harry Bluett Liversedge
Yell-Leader, Leslie Scott Nelson

Second Semester:
President, Ruth Benjamin Walker
Vice-President, Donald Cline Bull
Secretary, Fuller Clarkson
Treasurer, Raymond Rainier Brown
Sergeant-at-arms, Thomas Carroll Winstead
Yell-Leader, Leslie Scott Nelson

Donald Abercrombie
Ralph Allise
Yuguro Amagata
Elveda Antonovich
James Armstrong
Juliette Atwater

Donald Ahlare
George Alpn
Agnes Ambrose
Harry Appelgarth
Alta Arnold
Marion Avery

Herbert Adler
Emmet Allen
Brita Anderson
Jean Applegate
Catherine Ashley
Frances Ayer

Roy Akagi
Robert Allen
Zula Andrews
Helen Arata
Edward Atchison
Addie Babb

Laura Akin
Milton Almquist
Alexander Angelou
Ida Arbuckle
Caroline Atherton
Willard Babcock

Paul Batcheller
Marjorie Baker
Irving Banker
Will Barrow
Phyllis Bates
Stella Baumunk

Ralph Bagley
Portia Baker
Hal Barker
Enohe Basye
Stanley Bates
Frank Baxter

Ellis Bailey
Howard Baldwin
Clyde Baroom
Gladys Basye
Walter Batterman
James Baxter

John Baird
Virginia Baldwin
Cedric Baroudis
Phyllis Bateman
Alice Baucom
Laurence Bayley

Mabel Baird
John Ball
Dorothy Baroudis
Edward Bates
Ina Baughman
Gladys Beats

Annie Beck
Frances Bell
Eleanor Benedek
Doris Hepler
Hortense Berry
Earl Blair

Alvin Becker
Hazel Bell
Howard Bennett
Helen Berglund
Vera Bhend
Laurence Blanchard

Leila Beckley
Mary Bell
Jesse Bennett
Reyna Berka
Vera Bicknell
Lazar Blochman

Sophie Beekhuis
Russell Bell
Thomas Benson
Rita Berka
Alicia Birch
Jay Blayney

Gladys Beeman
William Bender
Avery Bent
Robert Bernstein
Hollis Black
Edward Bleeker

John Booth Jr.
Benjamin Borchardt
Blanche Bostetler
Donetta Brainard
Edna Breen
Everett Brise

Clarence Behnhoff
Gertrude Borchardt
Nicholas Boyd
Anne Brake
Gus Brehm
Helen Brooke

Antoinette Boes
Rebecca Borradale
Arthur Bradford
Robert Brant
Pearl Brier
Fred Brooks

Gladys Bonner
Marcia Bowe
Alice Bradley
Jolene Bray
Laura Briggs
Bradley Brown

Fred Boyle
Mildred Boyne
Harold Bradley
Irene Bruselton
Marcella Brinkmeyer
Clifton Brown

Edwin Browne
Leslie Brown
Fred Brownlee
Vera Hofwinkel
Melvin Buster
Ward Cadwallader

Florence Brown
Marian Brown
Henry Bru
Marion Buzzell
Burton Butler
Louise Cahoon

Helen Brown
Raymond Brown
Porter Bruck
Lucille Burke
Winifred Butler
Joseph Cain

Quincy Brown Jr.
Robert Brown
Donald Bull
Eleanor Burnham
William Butler
Robert Caine

Lavinia Brown
May Brown
Margaret Mullen
Ruth Burnham
Anne Byrne
Orville Caldwell

Mary Calloway
Marston Campbell Jr.
Gustav Carlson
Isabel Carroll
Irene Catland
Ray Chambers

Florence Campbell
May Campbell
Vivian Carlson
William Carroll
Arline Cavins
Calvin Chapman

Gladys Campbell
Muriel Cameron
Edith Carlton
George Carson
Bud Champlin
Gordon Chapman

Jane Campbell
Alice Cannan
James Carpenter
Lilias Carter
Louise Chandler
Arthur Chrim

Laura Campbell
Grover Carlson
Emily Carter
Breckenridge Carter
Marian Chandler
Edith Chichester

Ah Chow
Karl Clark
Thomas Clements
Howard Cole
Thomas Connelly
Olleraye Cortelyou

Vera Christie
Marjorie Clark
Herbert Clifford
Martha Cole
Estelle Cook
Virginia Cory

John Cipress
Morris Clark
Forrest Cobb, Jr
Mario Coldanno
Jack Conley
Stanley Cosby

George Clark
Fuller Clarkson
Frances Cochrane
Donald Collins
Dorothy Cooper
John Coulston

Gertrude Clark
Leslie Cleaty
Edith Cody
Francis Collins
Homer Cornick
Blanche Coulter

John Coulter
Katherine Cox
Ella Crawford
George Cunningham
Helen Daley
Sisak Darlinian

Joseph Covington
Sara Craddock
Vern Croson
Floyd Cutler
Peter Daley
Corena Daugherty

Freddie Cowan
Ethel Craig
Francisco Crove
Curtis Cutter
Marie Dumanakos
Anna Davis

Valance Cowan
Jefferson Cralle
Leon Curnan
Lara Dahl
Helen Dana
Earl Davis

Dorothy Cox
Frank Crane
Grant Cunningham
Rudolph Dasger
Alice Daniels
Helen Davis

Reginald Davis
Paul de Fremery
John Desmond
Carrie Dingley
Robert Donald
Hal Draper

Margaret Dawson
Lillian Demarest
Matthew Desmond
Amy Dinkelspiel
Marion Doolan
Ione Dresden

John Day
Lester De Mund
Walter Dresauer
Addison Dike
James Doolittle
Evan Draper

Russell Deane
Lois Denman
Abee de Wit
Grace Dixon
Lenora Doran
Eileen Drobish

Joseph Deane
Vera Denton
Harold Dimock
Van Duyn Dodge
Mary Downie
Muriel Drury

Daniel Duncan
Alice Eastwood
John Edwards
Ray Ellis
Walter Kederich
Evelyn Farrar

Carroll Dunabee
Elmo Eby
Caroline Effinger
Elmer Ellsworth
Mary Estill
Jennie Fayant

Elinor Darbrow
William Edmands
Lilian Eggleston
John Elmore
Leila Evans
Winifred Ferro

Fletcher Dutton
Abby Edwards
William Elkins
Philip Embury
Edgania Everton
Martha Fibush

Leonard Dykes
Alta Edwards
Bernard Ellis
Mae Irwin
Margaret Farman
Pauline Finnell

Ruth Fisk
George Foster
John Frank
Aversigo Frediani
Thomas Galstert
Mirian Garland

Isabelle Fiedlgrund
Mira Foster
Mason Franklin
Charles Frost
Mary Games
Wymond Garthwaite

Henry Flock
Ruth Foster
Ruth Franklin
Kenzo Fujinami
Ruth Games
Mae Gatlin

Fred Flatberg
Esther Fowler
Georgia Frasert
Zelna Fults
Victor Galvin
Daphne Gerry

Dorothy Flynn
Melvyn Frendy
Mona Frasert
Victor Furth
Ruth Gardner
Beatrice Gerlwrding

Fred Gibbons
Berenice Gilligan
Helen Glase
Dorothy Goodwin
Charles Grant
Ingo Hackh

Ruth Gibbons
Dorothy Gilson
Jean Goff
Ailene Gordon
Phil Grant
Dorothy Hahn

Falba Gibson
William Girton
Orel Goldaracena
Walter Gordon
Everett Gray
Esther Hahn

Thomas Gilson
Carlton Gildersleeve
George Goodall
Sophus Goth
Virginia Green
Helen Hahn

Louise Gilks
William Glaser
Sheldon Goodman
Hervey Graham
Harwood Griffith
John Halbert

Thomas Hall
Marie Hanlon
Laura Harding
Edith Hartman
Elsa Hawkins
Leonard Henry

Nina Hallock
Herman Hanna
Harvey Hardison
Edith Harshbarger
Kenneth Hawkins
Lucille Henry

Alvin Hambly
Chester Hansen
Frederick Hare
Joe Hart
Glen Hayden
Zoe Hermie

Laurentine Hamilton
Julius Hansen
Franklin Harper
Stanley Harvey
Montgomery Hawks
George Herrington

Mary Hamilton
Kenneth Hanson
Luren Harris
Allan Hauser
Myrtle Hennei
Lester Hesse

George Hicks Lawrence Higgins Walter Hildebrand Bruce Hill Dorothy Hillman
Louie Hinck Philip Hodgkin Margaret Hoefer Will Hohenthal Josephine Holden
Hugo Holm Earl Holman Frank Holman Aubrey Holmes Paul Holsinger
John Holt Pormelia Holt William Holt Everett Honeycutt Margaret Honeywell
Ralph Hooper George Hosford Claude House Margaret Howe Anie Howard
Norene Howe Cletus Howell Merriam Howells Josephine Hoyt Bernice Hubbard

Martin Huberty	Martha Huffaker	Ruth Hulbert	Walter Hulting	Grant Hunt
Alan Hurd	Marjorie Huxley	Eugene Hyatt	Joe Hyman	Carl Iddings
Florence Ingram	Esther Ireland	Florence Isaacs	Chester Isaacson	Junzaburo Ishii
Letha Ison	Bernerdine Jackson	Eleanor Jackson	John Jackson III	Mildred Jackson
Edward Jaffa	Marin Jameson	Eleanor Jennings	Edna Jensen	Gretta Jensen
Alice Johnson	Juliet Johnson	Marguerite Johnson	Olive Johnson	Robert Johnson

Claire Johnston, Mark Kandarian, Katherine Kellogg, Mary Kenyan, Donald Keefer, Ruth Kimball

Effie Johnston, Margaret Kase, Herbert Kendall, Louise Kern, William Kessner, Carl King

Laura Joy, Katsujiro Katsuyama, Edwin Kengla, Anna Kessler, Harvey Kilburn, Clinton King

Fanny Juda, Louise Keats, Jennie Kennedy, Arthur Kidder, Howard Killam, Charlotte Knapp

Mabel Keiber, Asla Keiser, Karl Kennedy, Harold Indwell, Genevieve Kilpatrick, Thurston Knudson

Ralph Koehler
Ruth Krol
Marjorie La Grave
Harry Langford
Richard Lauwen Jr.
Helen Leete

Louise Koenig
Janey Kronenberg
Frank Lamb
Malin Langstruth
Theodore Lawson
Charles Leggett

Tokutaro Kogure
William Kyle
Charles Lambert
Myrtle Larsen
Donald Lawton
Marie Leonard

Carlos Kolder
Margaret La Barre
Ruth Lange
Harriet Latta
Edith Lee
Hester Lester

Toyoji Konno
George Lacoste
Herbert Langhorne
Louise Lauritzen
Mary Lee
Alice Levy

Melville Levy
Mary Lipman
William Lopes
Fondalite Lowry
Charles Lyman
Gladys McCray

Cyril Lewenus
Dorothy Lippett
Jack Loutzenheiser
Eugene Lloyd
George Mass
Everett McCullough

Winifred Lillie
Harry Liveredge
Dorothy Love
Gottlieb Luippold
Mervyn McCabe
Gaylor McCullough

Allan Lindsay
Viola Lockhart
Alice Lovejoy
Gladys Lukes
Frank McCorkle
Alice Macdonald

Albert Linn
Marian Lockwood
Minerva Lovell
Ruth Lundell
Horace McCoy
Dorothy Macdonald

Ernest MacDonald
Charlotte MacGregor
Jack McKinley
James Mallock
Ramona Marks
Katherine Mason

John MacDonald
Dorothy Mackay
Arthur McLean
Julius Mantley
Edward Martin
Paul Masters

Russell MacDonald
Henry Marsouler
Joseph McMorrow
Beatrice Mark
Leah Martin
John Mathews

Penelope McIntyre
Fraser Macpherson
Gaynor Maddox
Stephen Mark
Mabel Martin
Philip Mathews

Elizabeth Maetie
Ritchie McKee
Mildred Madison
Charles Marquis
Stephen Martinelli
Phyllis Mathews

William Mathews
Barbara Mensing
Edith Meyer
Charles Miller
Laurence Mitchell
Edith Monroe

Karl Mee
Gunford Meredith
Harry Meyer
Edward Miller
Vera Mitchell
Alberto Montijo

Edwin Meyer Jr
Nathan Merenbach
Wilson Meyer
Hobart Miller
Dorothy Monson
Leo Moody

Eleanor McLean
Grace Merrill
Anna Meyers
Leffler Miller
Flora Monahan
Ruth Mossley

Lester Mekler
Manfred Nelson
Way Middough
Evan Mills
Blythe Monroe
Mary Moore

Edward Morgan
Ellis Morris
Madeline Muldoon
Clydice Nevan
Alvin Nielsen
Helen Nutting

John Morgan
Alice Morrison
Ida Muller
Welles Neustaedt
Walter Nelson
John Oakley

Josephine Moriarty
William Morrison
Margaret Murdock
Leta Nicholas
Clarence Nohrmann
John Oaks

Toshaki Moriya
Earle Morton
Marguerite Neely
Elmer Nichols
Andy Noell
Milton Oender

Jane Morrill
Amelia Muar
Leslie Nelson
Knox Nicholson
Lucius Norris
Helen Olmsted

Bernice Olney
Grace Palmer
Nelson Partridge Jr
Marshall Paxton
Alberta Perkins
Edgar Persell

Jack O'Melveny
Earl Paltenghi
Doris Patchett
Marion Pease
Ernon Perkins
Martha Persons

Butler Osborne
Lucile Parr
George Patterson
Harry Peet
George Perkins
Leota Peter

Erin Ownesby
George Parrish
Irven Paul
Frank Pellissier
Lena Person
Laurence Phelps

Donald Packer
Gail Partridge
Leslie Paul
Edna Penfield
Dorothy Perry
Josephine Phillips

Walter Phillips
Perry Poage
Philipp Prell
Edward Proebsting
Claude Quackenbush
Irene Ray

Edson Pillsbury
James Center Pogue
Kenneth Premo
Verling Proberto
Haven Halgren
Abraham Reading

William Pillsbury
Edna Port
Eva Pressley
Law-Ying Pon
Ruth Randall
Elizabeth Reed

Dohrmann Pischel
Margaret Potter
Harold Prestel
Camille Purdy
Frank Ransom
Freeman Reed

Virginia Platt
Marie Pratt
Chalmers Price
Janet Pushie
Charles Ray
Harold Reed

Helen Reed
Jack Reth
Fred Richardson
Elmore Roberts
George Rohrbacher
Teo Rosenberg

Nellie Reese
Samuel Reaser
Harro Ridgway
Archbold Robinson
Claude Rohner
Martin Rosenblatt

Marie Reese
Anthony Reynders
Paul Ritter
James Robinson
Ray Rohwer
Emanuel Rosenthal

George Restel
Lester Rich
Agnes Riddi
Ronald Robinson
Homer Root
Helen Ross

Helen Reubaus
Darrel Richardson
Bertha Roberts
Rollin Rudolph
Esther Rosen
Theodore Rothman

Flora Roufeau
Annie Sanderson
Louise Scammell
Leslie Schlingheyde
Harold Schwalenberg
Donald Searles

Reginald Rule
Lemuel Sanderson
Esmond Schapiro
Abe Schmakowitz
Ernest Schulte
Mary Sebastian

Gladys Nair
Marion Sanderson
Earl Schlauss
Paula Schoenholz
Herbert Schulz
Clyde Seibert

Elmer Saimans
Virginia Sanderson
Eberhardt Schlapp
Richard Schofield
Blanche Scott
Edward Sewell

John Sampson
Miriam Kaplan
Henry Schlapp
Bernice Schorer
Myrtle Scovill
Frederick Shanks

Albert Shaw Gwendolyn Shaw Margo Sleppa Frances Sheppard Ada Slowman
Bernard Shimonowsky Cyril Shutterhamer Paul Shuey Lillian Sidey Douglas Sides
Esther Siemens Morris Silverberg Cyril Simard Marguerite Sims Esther Sinclair
Elsie Sinnock Minnie Sisson Emma Skaale Edson Slater Eva Slater
Myrtle Sloan Brodie Smith Carroll Smith Ernest Smith Mary Smith
Sydney Smith Francis Smyth Helen Smyth Lorenas Snee Preston Snook

Melvan Solomon
Henry Spohn Jr
Amy Stannard
Helen Steen
Wayne Stephenson
Frances Stranahan

Alta Soule
Eldon Spofford
Cedric Stannard
Lillian Steinhoff
George Stewart
Frank Strehy

Albion Spear
Searle Sprigg
Raphaniel Starbuck
Lillian Stephany
Walter Stokes
Sarah Strother

Arlo Sperry
Eugene Spunn
Mary Starkweather
Jackson Stephens
Dorothy Stoner
Marjorie Stuart

Nellie Spiegelman
Henry Stafford
Edwyn Steen
Earnest Stephenson
Esther Stout
Edna Stut

Charles Suits
Chester Tallbott
Margaret Taylor
William Teach
Ira Thompson
Charles Tilden Jr.

Maureen Sullivan
Elizabeth Talbot
Myrtle Taylor
Elsie Thomas
Max Thornburg
Verna Tinker

Cloyd Hedges
Jo Tapscott
George Teale
William Thomas
Miltona Thwing
Dart Tinkham

Genevieve Taggard
Emmett Taylor
Marguerite Templeton
Asia Thompson
Penelope Thwing
Winslow Tinning

Luis Taceoda
Laurence Taylor
Samuel Terry
Elmer Thompson
Marion Tiffany
Ellsworth Tippett

Lloyd Toole
George Trowell
Charles Tuttle
Ray Vandervoort
Ford Vernon
Florence Waldo

Abro Tuole
Ethel Trumbly
Edith Ueland
Ethel Van Haren
Amber Vestal
George Wale Jr.

Leonard Tanner
Marjorie Tuft
Marion Underwood
Kendrick Vaughan
Edward von Adelung
Irene Walker

Rose Tracie
Arthur Turck
Sarah Una
Lucille Vasello
Henry Wagner
Kathryn Walker

Elda Trout
Howard Turner
Mildred Valerga
Morrell Veeks
Karl Wagner
Pierre Walker

Ruth Walker
Winnifred Walsh
Sarah Washington
Laura Watson
Olin Wellborn III
Essie White

Bertha Walkmeister
Frances Walton
Dorothy Waterhouse
Fred. Westenmuller
Earl Wells
Florence Whittell

Earle Wall
Stafford Warren
Selby Waters
Adelaide Weihe
Donald Wheaton
Katharine Whitton

Annie Wallingford
Noble Warrum
Harry Watkins
Raymond Westrud
Howard Wheeler
Loyal Whitton

Edward Walsh Jr.
Marie Wasem
Allan Watson
Joseph Weuse
Roy Wheeler
Harry Whitthorne

Adrian Wilcox
Jack Wilson
Onie Wilson
Helen Wirt
Frank Wisongmeyers
Jean Wright

Richard Wiley
Pearl Wilson
Beatrice Winder
Carolyn Withington
Beulah Woods
Gladys Wright

Edna Williams
Arthur Wilson
Gladys Windham
Charles Wormser
Paul Woods
Quincy Wright

Lesley Williams
Eva Wilson
Louis Windmuller
Milton Wolfe
Catherine Woolsey
Rose Wright

Ethel Wilson
Loretta Wilson
Carroll Winstead
Irma Wollenberg
Pierce Works
William Wurster

Irene Wyllie   Teno Yahands   Tamotsu Yutaka   Edward Yoreo   George Young
Madeline Young   Henry Zimmerman   Hilier Zobel   Dave Zobit
Francyl Zumbro   Hazel Zumbro   Edgar Zumwalt

THE CAMPANILE PLAZA

SOPHOMORE CLASS

GEORGE PETERSON

EARL DAVIS

OFFICERS

First Semester:
President, George Steeley Peterson
Vice-President, Elizabeth Burnham
Secretary, Ogle Charles Merwin
Treasurer, Earl Stanley Ward
Sergeant-at-arms, Kenneth George Uhl
Yell-Leader, Walter Stewart McManus

Second Semester:
President, Earl Adams Davis
Vice-President, Helen Maclise
Secretary, Ogle Charles Merwin
Treasurer, Marc Templeton Morrissey
Sergeant-at-arms, Jack Frederick White
Yell-Leader, Walter Stewart McManus

FRESHMAN CLASS

GORDON KEITH

PAUL FOLLETT

OFFICERS

First Semester:
President, Gordon Lyons Keith
Vice-President, Madeline Becker
Secretary, Walter Ungermann Fredericks
Treasurer, Kenneth James Reid
Sergeant-at-arms, Charles Greene De Coudres
Yell-Leader, James Edward Drew

Second Semester:
President, Paul Beach Follett
Vice-President, Madeline Becker
Secretary, Walter Ungermann Fredericks
Treasurer, Kenneth James Reid
Sergeant-at-arms, Charles Greene De Coudres
Yell-Leader, James Edward Drew

FRATERNITIES

Bridge Across Strawberry Creek Near the Football Statue

FRATERNITIES

Bridge Across Stillwater Creek Near the Football Statue

FRATERNITIES

Fraternity Statistics

The following statistics concerning the national fraternal organizations have been compiled from the *World Almanac* for 1917, and Baird's Manual of American College Fraternities, eighth edition. The dates of the establishment of the local chapters, as well as the number of active members, have been taken from the lists which were submitted to the BLUE AND GOLD staff by the respective organizations. Any cases of doubt or conflict in dates were referred to the local chapters for verification:

Fraternities

	FRATERNITY	WHERE FOUNDED	Date	Chapter Estab.	Active Members	No. Active Chapters	Total Membership
1	Acacia	University of Michigan	1904	1905	25	25	3,436
2	Alpha Delta Phi	Hamilton University	1832	1908	31	25	8,800
3	Alpha Kappa Lambda	University of California	1914	1914	42	1	
4	Alpha Sigma Phi	Yale University	1845	1913	38	17	1,656
5	Alpha Tau Omega	Virginia Military Institute	1865	1900	45	68	12,000
6	Beta Theta Pi	Miami University	1839	1879	40	78	21,689
7	Chi Phi	Princeton University	1824	1875	27	21	6,500
8	Chi Psi	Union College	1841	1895	35	18	5,638
9	Delta Chi	Cornell College	1890	1910	14	23	14,087
10	Delta Kappa Epsilon	Yale University	1844	1876	19	43	13,089
11	Delta Sigma Phi	College of City of New York	1899	1915	36	11	1,728
12	Delta Tau Delta	Bethany College	1859	1898	42	52	10,464
13	Delta Upsilon	Williams College	1834	1896	46	43	10,500
14	Kappa Alpha (South)	Washington and Lee	1865	1895	34	49	11,000
15	Kappa Sigma	University of Virginia	1869	1901	39	84	14,549
16	Lambda Chi Alpha	Boston University	1909	1913	40	27	1,540
17	Phi Delta Theta	Miami University	1848	1880	41	79	20,594
18	Phi Gamma Delta	Washington and Jefferson	1848	1886	32	58	16,134
19	Phi Kappa Psi	Washington and Jefferson	1852	1899	39	46	14,044
20	Phi Kappa Sigma	University of Pennsylvania	1850	1903	55	29	6,000
21	Phi Sigma Kappa	Mass. Agricultural College	1873	1909	33	28	43,000
22	Pi Kappa Alpha	University of Virginia	1868	1912	38	41	6,500
23	Pi Kappa Phi	College of Charleston	1904	1909	32	12	7,000
24	Psi Upsilon	Union College	1833	1902	27	25	13,200
25	Sigma Alpha Epsilon	University of Alabama	1856	1894	25	80	18,101
26	Sigma Chi	Miami University	1855	1886	35	68	15,000
27	Sigma Nu	Virginia Military Institute	1869	1892	35	73	13,000
28	Sigma Phi	Union College	1827	1912	22	10	3,083
29	Sigma Phi Epsilon	Richmond College	1901	1910	32	40	4,000
30	Sigma Phi Sigma	University of Pennsylvania	1908	1910	44	3	325
31	Sigma Pi	Vincennes University	1897	1913	41	10	13,000
32	Theta Chi	Norwich University	1856	1915	29	19	1,800
33	Theta Delta Chi	Union College	1848	1904	31	29	6,000
34	Theta Xi	Rensselaer Polytechnic	1864	1910	39	20	2,421
35	Zeta Psi	College of City of New York	1847	1870	37	24	8,177

Sororities

1	Alpha Chi Omega	Depauw University	1885	1909	48	23	3,200
2	Alpha Delta Pi	Wesleyan F. College	1851	1913	44	26	4,000
3	Alpha Gamma Delta	Syracuse University	1904	1915	34	14	1,300
4	Alpha Omicron Pi	Barnard College	1897	1907	40	8	1,646
5	Alpha Phi	Syracuse	1872	1901	43	20	3,099
6	Alpha Xi Delta	Lombard College	1898	1909	41	19	1,414
7	Chi Omega	University of Arkansas	1895	1902	36	34	2,152
8	Delta Delta Delta	Boston University	1888	1900	48	58	5,500
9	Delta Gamma	University of Mississippi	1872	1907	44	28	5,100
10	Delta Zeta	Miami University	1902	1915	35	11	526
11	Gamma Phi Beta	University of Syracuse	1874	1884	40	20	4,600
12	Kappa Alpha Theta	Depauw University	1870	1890	48	39	7,200
13	Kappa Kappa Gamma	Monmouth College	1870	1897	45	40	7,000
14	Phi Mu	Wesleyan College	1852	1916	37	24	3,000
15	Pi Beta Phi	Monmouth College	1867	1900	46	51	9,000
16	Sigma Kappa	Colby College	1874	1910	39	13	1,200
17	Zeta Tau Alpha	Virginia State Normal	1898	1915	36	16	1,188

Professional Fraternities

	FRATERNITY	WHERE FOUNDED	Date	Chapter Estab.	Active Members	No. Active Chapters	Total Membership
1	Alpha Chi Sigma	University of Wisconsin	1902	1913	58	24	1,485
2	Alpha Kappa Kappa	Dartmouth College	1888	1898	16	44	4,000
3	Delta Sigma Delta	University of Michigan	1884	1881	26	25	4,865
4	Kappa Psi	Cheshire Military Academy	1879	1910	27	33	5,000
5	Nu Sigma Nu	University of Michigan	1882	1881	43	32	5,700
6	Omega Upsilon Phi	Buffalo University	1896	1914	10	12	1,500
7	Phi Alpha Delta	Chicago Law School	1897	1911	26	34	2,045
8	Phi Alpha Gamma	New York Homeo. Med. College	1885	1906	17	7	1,500
9	Phi Chi	University of Vermont	1888	1909	12	47	7,175
10	Phi Beta Chi	University of Michigan	1884	1882	27	15	5,000
11	Phi Delta Phi (California)	University of Michigan	1869	1913	34	46	12,500
	Hastings			1884	13		
12	Psi Omega	Baltimore College of D. S.	1892	1903	51	48	8,281
13	Xi Psi Phi	University of Michigan	1889	1895	38	25	4,858

Local Organizations

	MEN'S HOUSE CLUBS	Date Founded	Active Members		WOMEN'S HOUSE CLUBS	Date Founded	Active Members
1	Abracadabra	1895	46	1	Alchemae	1889	42
2	Acheron	1912	44	2	Al Khalud	1914	16
3	Bachelordom	1884	34	3	Cuge de Oro	1885	32
4	Dahlonega	1901	28	4	Mekatina	1914	26
5	Del Rey	1881	34	5	Nostroum	1915	26
6	Dwight	1900	33	6	Reshuva	1908	27
7	Japanese Club	1913	48				
8	Otrond	1910	44				
9	Sequoyah	1914	45				
10	Tiberato	1911	48				

Scholarship Report

ORGANIZATION	Jan.-May 1916	Rank	Aug.-Dec 1916	Rank	Four-Year Average Ending May, 1916	Rank	ORGANIZATION	Jan.-May 1916	Rank	Aug.-Dec 1916	Rank	Four-Year Average Ending May, 1916	Rank
Abracadabra	2.517	16	2.3876	15	2.541	11	Lambda Chi Alpha	2.360	18	2.4018	46	2.2707	4
Acacia	2.411	22	2.6898	49	2.1429	26	Phi Delta Theta	2.302	19	2.3742	12	2.379	16
Acheron	2.340	14	2.4747	22	2.465	8	Phi Gamma Delta	2.530	15	2.3871	11	2.30007	18
Alpha Delta Phi	2.160	5	2.2425	2	2.290	7	Phi Kappa Psi	2.451	30	2.1290	7	2.127	25
Alpha Kappa Lambda	2.1866	12	2.1766	1	2.185	1	Phi Kappa Sigma	2.205	10	2.4022	5	2.2533	5
Alpha Sigma Phi	2.418	25	2.5268	20	2.3545	13	Phi Sigma Kappa	2.359	40	2.6892	48	2.481	31
Alpha Tau Omega	2.571	40	2.4530	11	2.3606	33	Pi Kappa Alpha	2.132	4	2.3530	10	2.2130	3
Bachelordom	2.703	42	2.5444	30	2.088	10	Pi Kappa Phi	2.567	20	2.5099	44	2.430	27
Beta Theta Pi	2.182	8	2.2870	4	2.278	6	Psi Upsilon	2.172	6	2.4985	25	2.362	15
Caesar	2.375	21	2.4553	32	2.416		Sequoyah	2.504	36	2.5274	29	2.567	**
Cha Phi	2.431	24	2.4543	23	2.156	40	Sigma Alpha Epsilon	2.637	**	2.7318	41	2.404	40
Chi Psi	2.354	17	2.4188	5	2.345	12	Sigma Chi	2.483	31	2.5645	33	2.413	37
Dahlonega	2.208	11	2.4125	18	2.243	10	Sigma Nu	2.402	12	2.4698	13	2.455	29
Del Rey	2.365	30	2.6282	37	2.0883	52	Sigma Phi	2.204	9	2.6417	35	2.3548	14
Delta Chi	2.420	23	2.5408	27	2.4590	24	Sigma Phi Epsilon	2.667	31	2.4496	20	2.452	28
Delta Kappa Epsilon	2.1853	41	2.7659	42	2.705	43	Sigma Pi	2.659		2.3893	16	2.201	2
Delta Sigma Phi	2.506	36	2.6531	39	2.383	18	Theta Chi	2.843	32	2.4881	32	2.626	38
Delta Tau Delta	2.3530	14	2.4200	19	2.108	21	Theta Delta Chi	2.413	28	2.4043	17	2.414	22
Delta Upsilon	2.442	27	2.5586	31	2.416	23	Theta Xi	2.478	**	2.4771	23	2.387	19
Dwight	2.416	20	2.5158	34	2.381	17	Tiberato	2.129	3	2.2384	3	2.203	**
Kappa Alpha	2.539	37	2.4601	9	2.551	34	Zeta Psi	2.501	35	2.5412	26	2.50061	35
Kappa Sigma	2.179	7	2.3129	6	2.2981	20							

*Established as chapter of Sigma Phi Sigma, December, 1916.
**Not ranked with the other undergraduate organizations but put on the Supplementary List because of the lack of at least one representative in each of the four undergraduate classes for this period or some part of it.

Zeta Psi

Founded at College of the City of New York, June 1, 1847.
Iota Chapter—Established in 1870.

FACULTY

George Cunningham Edwards
Joseph Nisbet LeConte
Orrin Kip McMurray
Carl Copping Plehn
Joseph Cummings Rowell
Wallace Irving Terry

GRADUATE

Loui Charles Beauman

SENIORS

Ben Alexander
**George Washoe Baker
Alva Putnam Conklin
Theodore Randolph Finley, Jr.
Benjamin Blackwood Foster
Charles Richardson Knox
Henry Augusto Ruffo
Harry Hall Scheeline
James Herbert Tietzen
Willis Guy Witter

JUNIORS

Paul Fuller Bachellor
George E. Carson
John O'Neil Ciprico
Fletcher Holland Dutton
Orel Andrew Goldarncena
William Knox Holt
Malin Thomas Langstroth
Richard Lauxen, Jr.
Homer Boice Root
Albion Whitney Spear

SOPHOMORES

*Josiah Knowles Adams
Robert Allen Guthrie, Jr.
I. J. Harvey, Jr.
James Edward Holbrook
Orra Crosby Hyde
Edwyn J. Jolly
Randolph R. Nickerson
George James O'Brien
William Rennie, Jr.
Walter Schilling

FRESHMEN

William Brinkley Alverson
John Herman Duhring
John Sweeney Gifford
George Brownlow Metcalfe
Hurford Clarence Sharon
Lewis Emerson Spear

Henry Ernest Walrond

---

*Absent on leave.
**Graduated December 1916.

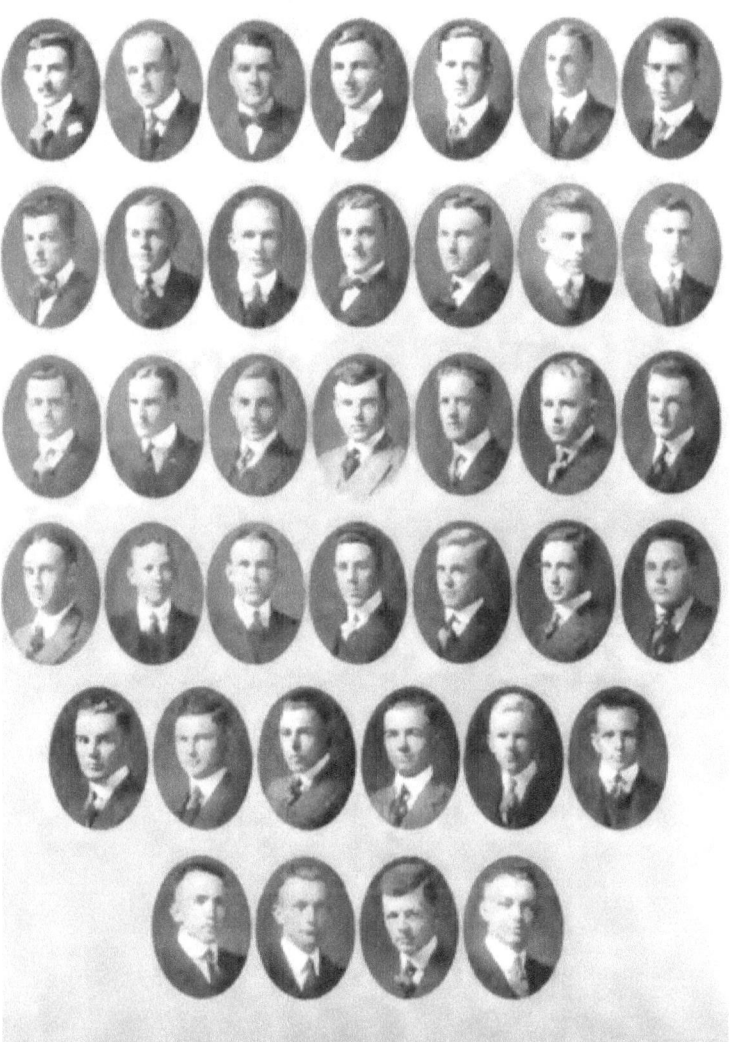

Louis Beaman B. Alexander Geo. Baker Alva Conklin T. Finley, Jr. R. Foster Chas. Knox
Henry Ruffa H. Schwine H. Tietzen Guy Witter P. Hachwilse Geo. Carson John Ciprico
P. Dutton O. Gobluraevus Wm. Holt M. Langstroth R. Lauzen, Jr. Homer Hoot Albson Spear
Josiah Adams H. Guthrie, Jr. I. J. Harvey, Jr. J. Holbrook Otto Hyde Edwyn Jolly H. Nickerson
Geo. O'Brien W. Renner, Jr. W. Schilling W. Alverson John Duhring John Gifford
G. Metcalfe H. Sharon E. Spear H. Walrond

Chi Phi

Founded at Princeton University, 1824.
Lambda Chapter—Established, February 11, 1875.

GRADUATE
James Townsend Barstow

SENIORS

Walter Herman Barthel
**Douglas Bray Cohen
Wright Ethelbert D'Evelyn
**Edwin Lowell Garthwaite
Herbert Harold Hiestand
Harry Boyd Seymour
John Stewart Weeks

JUNIORS

Nicholas Kettle Boyd
John Quincy Brown, Jr.
Wymond Bradbury Garthwaite
Russell Flavius Macdonald
*Darwin Jackson Smith
George Washington Young, Jr.

SOPHOMORES

*Gordon McCausland Boyes
Benjamin Stiles Hayne, Jr.
George Henry Sanderson

FRESHMEN

Harold Frederick Behneman
Thomas Coulter, Jr.
Frederick Malcolm Hook
Albert Joshua Houston
Morris Chester Lawyer
Kenneth Ransom Lynch
Archibald Sylvester Macdonald
John Stuart Morehead
Reginald C. Parker
Donald Lewis Tupper

*Absent on leave.
**At Davis.

James Barstow Walter Barthel Douglas Cohen Wright D'Evelyn Edwin Garthwaite
Herbert Hostand Harry Seymour Stewart Weeks Nicholas Boyd Quincy Brown, Jr.
Wymond Garthwaite Russell Macdonald Darwin Smith George Young, Jr. Gordon Hayes
Benjamin Hayne, Jr. George Sanderson Harold Behrmann Thos. Coulter, Jr. Albert Houston
Reginald Parker Kenneth Lynch Archibald Macdonald John Morehead Donald Tupper

Delta Kappa Epsilon

Founded at Yale University, June 22, 1844.
Theta Zeta Chapter—Established December 8, 1876.

FACULTY

Carlos Bransby
Joseph Dupuy Hodgen
Ralph Smith Minor
Charles Gilman Hyde
William Angustus Merrill

GRADUATES

Guy Webb Adriance
Blair Sterrett Shuman
Chandler Parks Barton

SENIORS

**Franklin Otis Booth
George Winthrop Fish
Overton Lincoln Walsh
Alfred Leo Maguire
J. Brayton Philbrook

JUNIORS

Thomas Mardenbro Benson
Charles Lee Tilden, Jr.
*Leo Joseph Maguire

SOPHOMORES

Albion P. Jordan
Phillip Ford Maddox
Conlin Clough Smith
Harry Young Stebbins
Guy Le Roy Stevick, Jr.
William Paul Thomas

FRESHMEN

Walter Harrison Pillsbury
*Frederick Lyman Tyler

*Absent on leave.
**At Davis, January-May, 1917.

Guy Admaner   Chandler Barton   Blair Shuman   Otis Bouth   George Fish
Alfred Maguire   Brayton Phalbach   Overton Walsh   Thomas Benson   Lew Maguire
Charles Tilden, Jr.   Allison Jordan   Phillip Maddot   Colm Smith   Harry Sieblum
   Guy Stevick, Jr.   William Thomas   Walter Pillsbury   Frederick Tyler

Beta Theta Pi

Founded at Miami University, August 8, 1839.
Omega Chapter—Established March 8, 1879.

REGENTS OF THE UNIVERSITY

Guy Chaffee Earl Charles Adolph Ramm Charles Stetson Wheeler

FACULTY

William Dallam Armes
Louis deFontenay Bartlett
Leon Milchaine Davis
James K. Fisk

Henry Rand Hatfield
Herbert Charles Moffitt
H. T. Summersgill
George Malcolm Stratton

GRADUATES

Herbert Edwin Hall
***John Cary Howard

*Albert Carnahan Simonds
Nicholas Lloyd Taliaferro

SENIORS

Raymond Kavanghan Boutz
**John Michael Coffeen
Austin Robert Eimer
**Ronald Dotzell Gibbs
Emery Herman Rogers

LeRoy Farnham Krusi
Charles David Lane
Travis Pollard Lane
Lewin Wethered Martinez

JUNIORS

John Louis Cooley
George William Davis
John Russell Deane
George Herbert Dunlap

**Grant James Hunt
*Thomas Joseph Lennon
John Bradburne McKinlay
William Adam Magee, Jr.

SOPHOMORES

Gardner Black
Paul William deFremery
Alexander Blake Hill, Jr.
Jerry Dayton Phinney

Bruce Howard
*William Moller
Andrew Lloyd Muir

FRESHMEN

Henry Jocelyn Bates
Guy Cecil Calden, Jr.
Harold Dexter
Robert Minor Eschen
Harold Warren Forsey
Lewis Gregory Harrier

Calvin Tracy Littleton
Hale Harper Luff
Clinton Rice Madison
George Earl Martin
William Chase Paulton
Britton Rey

*Absent on leave.
**At Davis, January-May, 1917
***Graduated December, 1916.

Herbert Hall   John Howard   Albert Simonds   Raymond Bonta   John Coffeen   Austin Einer
Ronald Gibbs   LeRoy Krusi   Charles Lane   Lemin Martines   Emery Rogers   John Coodry
George Davis   George Dunlap Grant Hunt   Thomas Lennon   John McKinlay   Claribee Bleck
Paul de Fremery Blake Hill, Jr. Bruce Howard   William Moller   Andrew Muir   Jerry Phinney
Henry Bates   Guy Caldes, Jr. Harold Dexter   Robert Eschen   Harold Forsey   Lewis Harner
Calvin Littleton Hale Luff   Clinton Madison   George Martin   William Paulton Button Rey

Sigma Chi

Founded at Miami University, June 28, 1855.
Alpha Beta Chapter—Established June 12, 1866.

FACULTY

Elmer Edgar Hall
George Rupert MacMinn
Charles Albert Noble
James Lyman Whitney
William Hammond Wright

GRADUATES

Howard Elmer Chambers
David Wells Conrey

SENIORS

Alois Hubert Felchlin
***Gillette Eddy Gordon
Gilbert Lansing Patterson
Donald Shumway Rockwell
Harold Joseph von Detten
**Ernest Edward Vosper
Donald Clark Williams
Lawrence Ariel Woodworth

JUNIORS

Hollis Mansfield Black
Robert Tasker Donald
George Washington Foster
Frank Lamb
Arthur Lawrence McLean
Harold Gordon Prestel
Frank Combs Ransom
Frank Scribner
Noble Warrum, Jr.
William Wilson Wurster

SOPHOMORES

Rudolph Block, Jr.
Arthur Blair Cantwell
*Leon Hoyt Chamberlain
Ralph Harrison Countryman
William Norton Keeler
Ralph Yorke MacIntyre
Gilbert James Shea

FRESHMEN

Carrol Kendall Barker
Paul Peterson Browne
William Conrad Hughes
George Campbell Latham
James Lyman Muir
Ralph Walter Nicholson
Marcus Carl Petersen
Eric Andrew Ruthledge

*Absent on leave.
**Graduated December, 1916.
***At Davis.

Howard Chambers David Conrey Alois Felchlin Eddy Gordon Gilbert Patterson Harold von Detten
Donald Williams L. Woodworth Hollis Black Robert Donald George Foster Frank Lamb
Arthur McLean Harold Prestel Frank Ransom Noble Warrum, Jr. William Wurster Rudolph Block, Jr.
Blair Cantwell Leon Chamberlain Ralph Countryman William Kesler Ralph MacIntyre Carrol Barker
Paul Browne William Hughes George Latham R. Nicholson James Muir
Andrew Rutledge Marcus Petersen

Phi Gamma Delta

Founded at Jefferson College, April 22, 1848.
Delta Xi Chapter—Established October 23, 1886.

FACULTY
Charles Derleth, Jr.   ****George Holmes Howison
Woodbridge Metcalf

GRADUATE
Merritt Barton Curtis

SENIORS
Edward Duerdin Bronson
John Bradford Crow
*Frederick Edward Delger
Edwin Madison Elam
Frank Thomas Elliott
**Lyman Dunlap Heacock
Willis Robert Montgomery
Robert Laurence Ryan

JUNIORS
***John Floyd Cutler
Carlos Chester Kohler
Donald Carroll Lawton
John L. Reith
***Cloyd Jonathan Sweigert

SOPHOMORES
Sheldon Braly Crow
Richard Curtis Enderly
Myron Edward Etienne
Horace Houx Hayes
Gerald Reid Johnson
Howard Harry McCreary
Oscar James McMillin
Clay Haulin Sorrick
George Jacob Tschumy
John Frederick White

FRESHMEN
Erskine Phelps Clark
Charles Crossen Dexter
*William Kendall Hathorn
Norman Charles Heinz
Albert Sheridan Hubbard
Ramon Hill Landsberger
Ernest Jesse Phillips
Ernest Sevier

*Absent on leave.
**Graduated December, 1916.
***At Davis, January-May, 1917.
****Deceased, December 31, 1916.

Edward Bronson Bradford Crow Frederick Deiger Edwin Elam Thomas Elliott Lyman Heacock
Willis Montgomery Robert Ryan Floyd Cutler Carlos Kohler Donald Lawton John Beath
Cloyd Sweigert Sheldon Crow Richard Enderly Myron Etienne Horace Hayes Gerald Johnson
Howard McCreary Oscar McMillin Clay Sotruck George Twohany John White Erskine Clark
Charles Dexter Kendall Hathorn Norman Heinz S Hubbard R. Landsberger
Ernest Sexier Ernest Phillips

Phi Delta Theta

Founded at Miami University, December 26, 1848.
California Alpha—Established December 7, 1873.
Re-established December, 1886.

REGENT OF THE UNIVERSITY
Clement Calhoun Young

FACULTY

Edward Booth
W. W. Cort
William Carey Jones

Victor H. Henderson
Joel Henry Hildebrand
Olly Jasper Kern

GRADUATES

Thomas Waterman Huntington
Curtis Dion O'Sullivan
Carroll Marshall Wagner

SENIORS

*Emerson McMillan Butterworth
James Somers Candee
Douglas Mackay Longyear
Edwin Marshall Maslin

Edward Porter Pfingst
Warren Lee Pierson
Avery Tompkins
Edgar Forbes Wilson

JUNIORS

Morris Richard Clark
John Thomas Coulston
Guillaume Daniel Delprat
Evan Cook Dresser
Montgomery Waddell Hawks

Covington Henry Littleton, Jr.
Stephen Gaspar Martinelli
**Lucius Grinnell Norris
**Darrel Hardin Richardson
Henry Francis Wagner

SOPHOMORES

Robert Moulthrop Boag
Richard Holmes Kessler, Jr.
Haswell Thomas Lensk

Lawrence Kendall Requa
Wellington Treat Switzer
William Ewing Waste

Harry Burton Wilcox

FRESHMEN

David Boucher
Edwin McLaren Busser
Franklin Bergson Doyle
Loren Languunde Hiffman
Thomas Ralph Miller
Yates Owsley

Salem Camillo Pohlmann
Archibald Giles Quinn
Gerald Barlow Schuyler
Robert Cochran Stoops
Donald Lohse Thomas
Julian Redman Wagy

Leslie Rudolf Wieslander

---

*Graduated December, 1916.
**At Davis, January-May, 1917.

T. Huntington   C. O'Sullivan   E. Butterworth   Jas Cassler   D. Longyear   F. M. Maslin   E. Phugel
W. L. Pierson   A. Tompkins   E. F. Wilson   M. R. Clark   John Coulston   Evan Dresser   M. W. Hawks
S. G. Martinelli   L. G. Nottis   D. Richardson   H. F. Wagner   Robt. Boag   R. Kessler, Jr.   H. T. Leask
E. S. Briggs   H. B. Wilcox   Wm. Waste   D. Hoseiber   E. Bussey   F. B. Doyle   L. E. Hellman
Thos. Miller   Yates Oswley   N. C. Pohlmann   A. G. Quinn   G. B. Schuyler   Robt. Stoops
D. J. Thomas   J. R. Wogy   L. R. Weelander

Sigma Nu

Founded at Virginia Military Institute, January 1, 1869.
Beta Psi Chapter—Established March 21, 1892.

SENIORS

Frank Conver Bell
George James Carr
Vernon George Garrett
**Albert Edward Hill
**Bruce Campbell Hill

Hans Lemcke
George Moore Lindsay
Carl Albert Renz
*William Sayer Snook
Otis Mitchell Tupper, Jr.

Thomas Lawrence Willms

JUNIORS

Jacob Harry Barker
*Charles Franklin Harper

Marshall William Paxton
Preston Edward Snook

Benjamin Kendrick Vaughan

SOPHOMORES

Henry Philip Anewalt
Donald Salisbury Bartlett
Loys Melville Blakeley
Arthur Merrill Brown
John Clauss, Jr.
Russell Guerne deLappe

Samuel Teel De Remer
Kenneth Keith Little
Lorens Foard Logan
Harry Edison Lloyd
Howard Francis McCandless
Merton Melville Maze

Ronald Bowman Stewart

FRESHMEN

David Farragut Ashe
Robert Francis Baker
Wallace William Hewitt

Joseph Minton Meherin
Herbert Bonner Pawson
Henry Westbrook, Jr.

*Absent on leave.
**At Davis, January-May, 1917.

Frank Bell George Carr Vernon Garrett Edward Hill Bruce Hill Hans Lemcke
George Lindsay Carl Rons Sayer Snook Otis Tupper, Jr. Thomas Williams Harry Barker
Franklin Harper Marshall Paxton Preston Snook Kendrick Vaughan Philip Atenwalt Donald Bartlett
Melville Blakeley Merrill Brown John Clauss, Jr. Russell deLappe Samuel de Remer Kenneth Little
Lorena Logan Harry Lloyd H. McCandless Merton Maag Ronald Stewart David Ashe
Robert Baker Walker Hewitt Joseph Melicrin Herbert Paxson H. Westbrook, Jr.

Sigma Alpha Epsilon

Founded at University of Alabama, March 9, 1856.
California Beta Chapter—Established May 4, 1894.

FACULTY

John Peterson Buwalda
Roy Elwood Clausen
Stuart Daggett

GRADUATE

Charles Henry West

SENIORS

Ernest Camper
John Marshall Denbo
Robert Dean Easton
Donald Surface Jarvis
J. R. Murray, Jr.
Elmer Ellsworth Stone
Robert Judson Stull
John Bardini Winston

JUNIORS

James R. Carpenter
John Lewton Freeman
Percy Cortelyou Smith

SOPHOMORES

John James O'Connor, Jr.
George Steely Peterson
Ralph Winfield Scott
Alfred Adolph Siebert
Leland Warren Sweeney
Warren Mortimer Turner

FRESHMEN

Forrest Leeper Campbell
George William Davis
Herbert Lee Jones
Joseph Hirshfelder Maddux
John Paul Rohrer
John Godfrey Schaffer
Walter Porter Shaw

Charles West Ernest Canger John Denlo Robert Easton Donald Jarvis
Elmer Stone Robert Stull John Winston James Carpenter John Freeman
Percy Smith George Peterson Ralph Scott Alfred Siebert Leland Sweeney
Warren Turner Forrest Campbell George Davis Herbert Jones Joseph Masklus
  John Rohrer John Schaffer Walter Shaw

Chi Psi

Founded at Union College in 1841.
Alpha Delta Delta—Established November 30, 1895

FACULTY

Frederick Clinton Lewitt
David Townsend Mason

SENIORS

Samuel Adair
John Robert Bruce
Daniel Parsons Foster
**Benjamin Willy Gally
Samuel James Ogilvie
*Russell Dick Pennycook
Hugh Fenimore Shippey
***Ernest Smith
Roy Starbird
Whitney Braymer Wright

JUNIORS

Joseph Nightingale Caine
Robert Warwick Caine
Francis Kenyon Carey
William Breckinridge Carter
Walter Budd Champlin
Herbert George Clifford
Thomas Arthur Gabbert
*Livingston Gibson Irving
Edgar Clinton Persell
Cyril Thomas Simard
*Franklyn Vincent Smith

SOPHOMORES

Franklin Cummings
Willard Cronise Griffin
Orlin Clyde Harter
Raymond Henry Muenter
Ernest Ransome Percy
James Hodnett Pitts
*William Franklin Pitts
Lester Michael Tynan
Percy Robert Welch

FRESHMEN

Donald Armstrong
Mark Carter Elworthy
Fergus Ferguson
Norman Waterlow Ford
Howard Smith McKay

*Absent on leave.
**At Davis, January-May, 1917.
***Affiliated Colleges.

Samuel Adair	John Brorr	Daniel Foster	Benjamin Gally	Samuel Ogilvie	Russell Pennycook
Hugh Slippey	Ernest Smith	Roy Starbird	Whitney Wright	Joseph Caine	Robert Caine
Francis Carey	Breck'ridge Center	Rudd Champlin	Herbert Clifford	Thomas Gobbert	Livingston Irving
Edgar Frewell	Cyril Simard	Franklyn Smith	Frank'n Cummins	Willard Griffin	Orlin Harter
Ray'd Muenter	Ernest Percy	James Pitts	Lester Tynan	Perry Welch	Donald Armstrong
	Mark Elsworthy	Fergus Ferguson	Norman Ford	Howard McKay	

Kappa Alpha

Founded at Washington and Lee University, December 26, 1865.
Alpha Xi Chapter— Established May 6, 1895.

FACULTY
George Arnold Smithson

GRADUATES
Aloysius Ignatius Diepenbrock Leo David Hermle
***Hans von Geldern

SENIORS
**Warner Sabin Chadbourne *Frederick Sidney Jones
Neil Francis Dougherty Armstead Leigh, Jr.
John Herman Fenton Douglas Edwin Cochran Moore
Graydon Herman Oliver

JUNIORS
Grover Cleveland Carlson Ivan Walter Lilley
Thomas Gerald Hall Leavitt Mead McQuesten
Harold Rentsch Rivers

SOPHOMORES
Frederick Aicher, Jr. Ernest Frederick Marquardsen
*Albert Botzum Ernest Charles Milliken
Maurice Loyal Huggins Orlof Rush
Joseph Benjamin McFarland Glenn Maurice Still
Lloyd Haughton McPherson Raymond Louis Suppes

FRESHMEN
Norman Angell John Wayne Higson
Sullivan Burgess Harry Loveless Jenkins
Raymond Winter Cortelyou Stanton Knowlton Livingston
Charles Greene DeCoudres Karl Lester Sneath
Samuel Alvin Thomas, Jr.

*Absent on leave.
**At Davis.
***At Affiliated Colleges.

A. J. Diepenbrock   Leo D. Hermle   Hans von Geldern   W. S. Chadbourne   Neil Dougherty   John Fenton
Frederick Jones   A. Leigh, Jr.   Douglas Moore   H. G. Oliver   G. C. Carlson   Thos. G. Hall
Ivan W. Lilley   L. McQuesten   H. R. Rivers   F. Archer, Jr.   Albert Betsum   M. L. Huggins
Jos. McFarland   E. Marquessen   F. C. Milliken   Glenn Still   M. L. Suppes   Norman Angell
Sullivan Burgess   H. W. Cortelyou   Chas. DeCoudres   John Higson   H. L. Jenkins
S. K. Livingston   Karl Sneath   S. A. Thomas, Jr.

Delta Upsilon

Founded at Williams College, November 4, 1834.
California Chapter- Established March 13, 1896.

FACULTY

Thomas S. Elston
Alexis Frederick Lange
George Rapall Noyes
Carleton Hubbell Parker
Herbert N. Witt
Arthur Upham Pope
Merritt Berry Pratt
Lawrence Marsden Price
Joseph B. Umpleby

GRADUATES

Leslie Hollis Brigham
Elmer Granville Burland
Robert Clarence Ogden
**Hugh Gallaher
Richard Peter Minor

SENIORS

Charles Josef Carey
**Frederic Fuller Janney
Lawrence Frederick Knauer
Elwood Wellman Wright
Frank Macdonald Ogden
Karl Howard Schilling
**William Glenn Waterhouse

JUNIORS

Russell White Bell
*George Mateo Hicks
**Eugene Pooler Hyatt
Ronald Squire Robinson
Carroll Hutchinson Smith
Pierce Works

SOPHOMORES

John George Atcheson
Edgar Dickinson Boal
George Rayner Geisendorfer
Moreland Leithold
Russell Gent Meekfessel
Eugene Harold Pratt
John Shirley Ward
Robertson C. Ward

FRESHMEN

Elmer Jensen Beck
Archie Ballard Davidson
William Henry Grul
Harold Robert Johnson
Walter Stuart Lewis
Lawrence Campbell Merriam
William Thomas Nilon
*Harold Marion Rodgers
Franklin Joseph Simons
Edward Albert Williams, Jr.

*Absent on leave.
**At Davis, January-May, 1917.

Elmer Burland	Richard Minor	Robert Ogden	Josef Carey	Frederic Janney	Lawrence Knauer
Frank Ogden	Karl Schilling	Elwood Wright	Russell Bell	George Hicks	Eugene Hyatt
Ronald Robinson	Carroll Smith	Pieren Works	George Atchenon	Edgar Beal	Rayner Geisendorfer
Moreland Leithold	Russell Merkfessel	Eugene Pratt	John Ward	Robertson Ward	Elmer Beck
Archie Davidson	William Grul	Robert Johnson	Walter Lewis	Lawrer Merriam	William Nilon
Marion Rodgers	Franklin Simons	E. Williams, Jr.

Delta Tau Delta

Founded at Bethany College, February, 1859.
Beta Omega Chapter Established February 4, 1898.

FACULTY

Frances Seeley Foote
Elijah S. Haynes
Charles Edward Rugh
Armin Otto Leuschner
Warren Charles Perry

GRADUATES

Harry Vaughn Adams
**Alfred Poyneer Briggs
Rudolph Leonard Gianelli
**Charles Edward Locke

SENIORS

*George Weller Atherton
Edward C. N. Brett
Clifford Bert Cole
David Stoddard Shattuck
Charles Stanley Dimm
Verni Victor Mills
Prosper Reiter, Jr.

JUNIORS

Fred Warren Boole, Jr.
Fred Gray Gibbons
Walter John Hulting
William Huggins Lyons
Merwyn Louis McCabe
Welles Hollister Newlands
***George Parrish
Wayne B. Stephenson

SOPHOMORES

Raymond Evan Gardner
Albert Leo McGinness
Fred Percival Williams
Walter Stewart McManus
Charles Wilson Whitmore

FRESHMEN

John Harrold Dorn
George Spencer Huschke
Leslie William Irving
Sherwood L. Kingsley
*Louis Pirtle Price
Harold Weston Sayre
Rollin Wood Tenney
Raymond Perry Tracy

*Absent on leave
**At Affiliated Colleges.
***At Davis, January-May, 1917.

Harry Adams	Alfred Briggs	Rudolph Gianelli	Charles Locke	George Atherton	Edward Brett	
Clifford Cole	Stanley Dinum	Verne Mills	Prosper Reiter, Jr.	David Shattuck	Fred Rode, Jr.	
Fred Gibbons	Walter Hulting	Mervyn McCabe	Welles Newlands	George Parrish	Wayne Stephenson	
Raym'd Gardner	A. McGuinness	Walter McManus	John Dorn	George Hinsdale	Leslie Irving	
	S. Kingsley	Harold Sayre	Rollin Tenney	Raymond Tracy		

Phi Kappa Psi

Founded at Washington and Jefferson College, February 19, 1852.
California Gamma Chapter—Established April 15, 1899.

FACULTY
George Washington Corner George Whiting Hendry
John Albert Marshall

GRADUATES
****John Oliver Armistead John Carey Dement

SENIORS
Albert Laurence Dunn Southall Rozelle Pfund
Warren Emmet Hardison Eugene Mitchell Prince
Andrew McDonald Hazzard **Emerson Upton Slyfield
***Clifford McElrath Frederick Q. Tredway

JUNIORS
Everett Raymond Brite Miles Way Middough
George Morton Gowen Harold Blackmer Reed
John Bentley Halbert Theodore Charles Rethers
Herman Julius Hanna Raymond Jessup Starbuck
Stanley Bevan Harvey ****Millard Joseph Streeter
Paul Wilbur Masters Morrell Emerie Veeki

SOPHOMORES
*Ray M. Alford Arthur L. Drummond
Henry Elling Arey Harold John Fitz Gerald
Frank Morin

FRESHMEN
Edison Deuel Bills Warren Dean Loose, Jr.
Charles Robert Boyd, Jr. Sumner Mering
Wilson Cummings Cecil Loveland Morrow
John Freeborn Florida George Palmer
Ernest Domingo Hardison Laurence Boyden Updike
Robert Sydney Hopkins Russell Ringo Yates

*Absent on leave, January-May, 1917.
**Graduated December, 1916.
***At Davis, January-May, 1917.
****At Affiliated Colleges.

four hundred and sixteen

John Armistead   John Dement   Laurence Dunn   Warren Hardison   Andrew Hazzard   Southall Pfund
Eugene Pruce   F. Q. Tredway   Everett Boto   George Gowen   John Hulbert   Herman Hanna
Stanley Harvey   Paul Masters   Way Mahhough   Harold Reed   T. C. Rothers   R. J. Starbuck
Millard Streeter   Maxwell Verki   Ray M. Alford   Henry Arey   D. Fitz Gerald   Frank Moran
Edison Bills   Chas. Boyd, Jr.   John Florida   Ernest Hardison   Warren Lowe, Jr.   Cecil Morton
    George Palmer   Laurence Updike   Russell Yates

Alpha Tau Omega

Founded at the Virginia Military Institute, Richmond, Va., September 11, 1865.
California Gamma Iota Chapter—Established April 10, 1900.

FACULTY

Exum Percival Lewis Oliver Miles Washburn

GRADUATES

William Stephen Webster Kew Dan Edwin Root
William Sears Rainey Gustav Henry Wendt

SENIORS

John Knox Ballentine John Robert Graff
*Frank Adelbert Easton John Ignatius McVey
Lloyd William Goeppert ***Frederick George Maggs
Neal Staunton

JUNIORS

**Harold Edgar Bradley Philip Wood Janney
Stanley Wallace Cosby Herbert Devall Langhorne
John Brigg Day *Nathan Herbert Mull
Joseph Tenison Deane Leslie Scott Nelson
Donald Hardy Packer

SOPHOMORES

*Edwin David Cooke Carroll Henry Johnson
*Kenneth Robert Cormack Edwin Joseph Mejia
Alan Mercy Denison William Story Nash
George Haldane Scovel

FRESHMEN

Roy Herbert Gerard Hugh Cromer Minter
Karl Theodore Goeppert Paul Stark Packard
Henry William Grady Raybourne Wycoff Rinehart
Gerald Fisher MacMullen Howard Louis Seaton

*Absent on leave
**At Davis
***Graduated December, 1916.

William Rainey   Dan Root   John Ballentine   Lloyd Goeppert   John McVey   Frederick Maass
Neal Staunton   Harold Bradley   Stanley Cosby   John Day   Joseph Deane   Philip Janney
Herb't Langhorne   Nathan Mull   Leslie Nelson   Donald Parker   Edwin Cooke   K. Cormack
Alan Denison   Carroll Johnson   Edwin Mejia   William Nash   Haldane Scovel   Roy Gerard
Karl Goeppert   Henry Grady   G. MacMullen   Hugh Minter   Paul Packard
R. Rinehart   Howard Sexton

Theta Delta Chi

Founded at Union College, October 31, 1847.
Delta Deuteron Chapter Established April 18, 1900.

FACULTY
Herbert Eugene Bolton David Naffziger Morgan
Chester Linwood Roadhouse

GRADUATE
Dexter Rankin Ball

SENIORS
Corbin Corbin ***Avery Scott Hills
**Kessler Gilbert Hammond **James McVicar Mills
Howard Walden Heintz Ferris S. Moulton

JUNIORS
John Dryer Ball Phillip Hodgkin
Arthur Robert Bradford John Putnam Jackson III
Marston Campbell, Jr. *Fred Lewis Shanks
Opal Selby Waters

SOPHOMORES
*Arthur Donald Alvord Jules Verne Hilton
Clarence John Borgeson Tilton Somerville Powell
Percy Osborne Brewer Benjamin Franklin Sisson
William Rude Davis, Jr. John Dorsey Wheeler

FRESHMEN
Edwin Carnall Balaam Arthur Ambrose McNamara
Richard Henry Butcher Richard Thomas Phillips
Fay Irvin Christie Thomas Gano Richards
Robert Emmett Connolly Eben Knight Smart
Frederick Eugene Starr

*Absent on leave
**At Davis
***At Affiliated Colleges

Dexter Ball   Corbin Corbin   Kessler Hammond   Howard Heintz   Avery Hills   James Mills
Ferris Moulton   John Ball   Arthur Bradford   M. Campbell, Jr.   Phillip Hodgkin   John Jackson III
Fred Shanks   Selby Waters   Donald Alvord   Clarence Bergeson   Perry Brewer   Wm Davis, Jr.
Jules Hilton   Tilton Powell   Benjamin Sweet   John Wheeler   Edwin Balaam   Richard Butcher
Fay Christie   Robert Connolly   A. McNamara   Richard Phillips   Thomas Richards
Frederick Starr   Elten Smart

Kappa Sigma

Founded at University of Virginia, December 10, 1869.
Beta Xi Chapter—Established August 17, 1901.

FACULTY

James Gordon Cummings Clifford Franklin Elwood
Stanley Sawyer Rogers

GRADUATES

****Edwin Louis Bruck ****Charles Behbe Fowler
Thomas Gassner Chamberlain William Dan Sink
***Charles Edward Street

SENIORS

Harold Alfred Black Thomas Calvert Judkins
Raynor Eugene Gimbal William Wallace Murray
**Alfred Braley Parsons

JUNIORS

Donald Laughlin Abshire John Joyce Lontzenheiser
George Magee Cunningham Albert Dunnedin Shaw
Kenneth Charles Leggett *Samuel Walker Terry
Edward Marion Walsh, Jr.

SOPHOMORES

Whenton Hale Brewer Leroy Monroe Gimbal
Matthew Maxwell Conley *Paul Johnston McCoy
Lindsay Alexander Crawford James Bandy Merritt
Charles L. Detoy Raymond Worth Sayre
Harold Pearson Etter *Henry Norris Shindler
Harry Havelock Etter Harold Bertram Synes

FRESHMEN

Amasa Morse Bowles William Crutcher Huntley
William Augustus Brewer, Jr. *Arthur Craig Huston
John Elliott Cook Elliott McAllister, Jr.
Henry Myers Hale William Arthur Martin
Lowell Carey Hall John Okell
Andrew Carl Rowe

*Absent on leave. ***At Hastings College of Law.
**At Davis, January-May, 1917. ****At Affiliated Colleges.

Edwin Bruck   T Chamberlain   Chas. Foster   William Senk   Chas Street   Harold Black   Raymor Gimbal
Thomas Judkins Wm Murray   Alfred Parsons D Aloluire   G Cunningham   K Leggett   J Leutzenheiser
Albert Shaw   Samuel Terry   W Brewer   M Conley   L Crawford   Chas Detoy   Harry Etter
Harold Etter   Leroy Gimbal   James Merritt   H Sayre   Henry Shindler   Harold Symes   Attess Bowles
W. Brewer, Jr. John Cook   Henry Hale   Lowell Hall   Wm Huntley   Arthur Huston E. McAlister, Jr.
                               Wm Marion   John Okell   Andrew Rose

Psi Upsilon

Founded at Union College, November 24, 1833.
Epsilon Chapter—Established August 18, 1902.

FACULTY

Albert Edward Chandler
Edward Bull Clapp
Bernard Alfred Etcheverry
Martin Charles Flaherty
Charles Mills Gayley
Roswell Grey Ham
Richard Warren Harvey
Howard Christian Naffziger
Leonard Outhwaite
Leon Josiah Richardson
Seldon Rose
Rudolph Shevill
Keith Vosberg
Chauncey Wetmore Wells
Edward James Wickson

GRADUATE

Eugene Alston Hawkins

SENIORS

Charles Haughton Bayly
Edward Hervey
George Henry Hotaling
Marshall Pierce Madison
Richard Ashe McLaren
**Kenneth Monteagle
Norman Benjamin Stern
Douglas Van Dyke

JUNIORS

*George Hugh Bruning
*Lawrence Cleveland Blanchard
***Robert Alston Brant
Edward Porter Brnek
Benjamin Howell Burton, Jr.
*Charles Hyde Lewis
John O'Melveny

SOPHOMORES

Cesar Jordan Berthenu
*Austin William Clark
Fridtjof Carl Erickson
Harris Crozer Kirk
Harold Ernst McGowan
William Hall Moreland

FRESHMEN

Edwin Harris Carrigan
George Perry Griffith, Jr.
Emery Lovett
John Wigmore
Arthur Wallace Wilde

*Absent on leave.
**Graduated December, 1916.
***At Davis, January–May, 1917.

Eugene Hawkins Charles Bayly Edward Hervey George Heisling Marshall Madison
Richard McLaren Kenneth Monteagle Norman Stern Douglas Van Dyke Lawrence Blanchard
Robert Brant Porter Brock Benjamin Burton Jr. Hyde Lewis John O'Melveny
Cesar Bertheau Fridtjof Erickson Harris Kirk Harold McGowan Hall Moreland
Edwin Carrigan George Griffith, Jr Emery Lovett John Wigmore Arthur Webb

Phi Kappa Sigma

Founded at the University of Pennsylvania, October 19, 1850.
Alpha Lambda Chapter—Established March 23, 1903.

FACULTY

Albert Lloyd Barrows
David Prescott Barrows
Thomas Buck
John Uberto Calkins, Jr.
George Davis Louderback
Maurice Edward Harrison
Walter Morris Hart
Tracy R. Kelly
Ivan Mortimer Linforth

SENIORS

Stephen Sears Barrows
John Herbert Brown
Sherman Kennedy Burke
Robert Campbell Clark
Gregory Alexander Harrison
Raymond Lee Shearman
John James Vandenburgh
Dean Quigley Waddell

JUNIORS

Robert Lee Brown
Philip Albert Embury
Merriam Joseph Howells
Herbert Raymond Kendall
Max Weston Thornburg
Harvey Maher Kilburn
Wilson Meyer
Edwyn French Steen
Heber Spencer Steen

SOPHOMORES

Maurice Embry Gibson
Clifton Rogers Gordon
*Donald Munson Gregory
John Milton Hample
Donald Leigh Leavitt
John Campbell Moses

FRESHMEN

*Thomas Anderson Campbell
William Walter Davison
Hamilton Richmond Howells
Harold James Hunter
George LeRoy Klingaman
Sanford Vincent Larkey
James Francis McCone
Gerville Mott
Winslow Haskell Randall
Fenwick Leonard Smith
**Edward Tyson Woodruff
Robb Roy Young

*Absent on leave.
**At Affiliated Colleges.

Stephen Stammons   Herbert Brown   Sherman Burke   Robert Clark   Gregory Harrison   Ray'd Shoreman
J. Vandenburgh   Dean Waddell   Robert Brown   Philip Embury   Merriam Howells   Herbert Kendall
Harvey Kilburn   Wilson Meyer   Edwyn Steen   Helmt Steen   Max Thornburg   Maurice Gilson
Clifton Gordon   Donald Gregory   John Hample   Donald Leavitt   John Moses   Thomas Campbell
William Davison   Hamilton Howelle   Geo. Klinganson   Sanford Lackey   James McCone   Gerville Mott
            Winslow Randall   Fenwick Smith   Robb Young

Acacia

Founded at University of Michigan, April 21, 1904.
California Chapter—Established April 15, 1905.

REGENT OF THE UNIVERSITY
Edward Augustus Dickson

FACULTY

Richard Gause Boone
Frederick Warren Cozens
Russell Tracy Crawford
John C. Fryer
Karl Clayton Leebrick
**Arnold Valentine Stubenrauch

Wilson Joseph Wythe

GRADUATES

Ralph Graham Houston
William Donald McDonald
Merton Jay Minkler
Strother Perry Walton

SENIORS

Charles Robert Bell
***Leland Morrison Bell
Frank Kelsey Haught
William Dodson Hiney
Marc Hollzer
Andrew Martin Jensen
Mason Allen Johnston
Claude Ezra Moulux
*William James Quinville
Rolland A. Vandegrift

Henry Reginald Weber

JUNIORS

Chalmers G. Price
Richard Schofield

Halley Earnest Stephenson

SOPHOMORES

Neil Cook Ferguson
Howard Scott Killian
Jesse Andrew Rasor
Ralph Arthur Reynolds

FRESHMEN

Leo Harrison Burton
Follett Fox Morris

Charles Leslie Swanton

*Absent on leave.
**Deceased, February 12, 1917.
***At Davis, January-May, 1917.

Ralph Houston
Leland Bell
Mason Johnston
Chalmers Price
Jesse Ruser

William McDonald
Frank Haight
Claude Montua
Richard Schofield
Ralph Reynolds

Merton Minkler
William Hiney
William Quinville
Earnest Stephenson
Leo Barton

Strother Walton
Marc Hellier
Rolland Vandergift
Neil Ferguson
Foliet Morris

Charles Bell
Andrew Jensen
Henry Weber
Howard Kilian
Charles Swanton

Alpha Delta Phi

Founded at Hamilton College, January 1, 1832.
California Chapter—Established August 15, 1908.

FACULTY

Leonard Bacon
Frank Stanley Baxter
Herbert McLean Evans
Malcolm Goddard
Thomas Harper Goodspeed
*Charles Samuel Harold Howard
Frank Louis Kleeberger
Hans Lisser
Ralph Palmer Merritt
William Francis Rubke
Payson Jackson Treat
Benjamin Ide Wheeler
Frederick James E. Woodbridge

GRADUATES

Henry Temple Howard
John Boardman Whitton

SENIORS

Samuel Earl Breck
Warren Runyon Kemper
Richard George Martens
Robert Lacy Smyth
Gordon Fitzhugh Stephens

JUNIORS

Fred Thomas Brooks
Fred Parke Brownlee
Donald Clue Bull
Curtis Harold Cutter
John Ruskin Holt
Dohrmann Kaspar Pischel
William Hill Thomas
Charles Whitcomb Tuttle
Olin Wellborn III

SOPHOMORES

John Thomas Donnellan
Carroll Gillis Grunsky
Lee Borden Milbank
Richard Gill Montgomery
Harold Dohrmann Pischel
Harry Allan Sproul
Kenneth George Uhl
Weston Fay Vollberg

FRESHMEN

Everard Carlton Allsopp
Peter Cook, Jr.
Charles Francis Honeywell
Thatcher John Kemp
Chay Killian
Andrew MacKenzie Moore
Gordon Alpheus Wight

*Deceased.

Henry Howard   John Whitton   Samuel Breck   Warren Kemper   Richard Martins
Robert Smyth   Gordon Stephens   Fred Bemka   Fred Brownlee   Donald Bull
Curtis Cutter   Dohrmann Pischel   William Thomas   Charles Tuttle   Olin Wellborn III
John Donnellan   Carroll Grunsky   Lee Millbank   Richard Montgomery   Harold Poehel
Allan Sproul   Kenneth Uhl   Weston Volberg   Everard Allsopp   Peter Cook, Jr.
Charles Honeywell   Thatcher Kemp   Clay Killian   MacKenzie Moser   Gordon Wight

Phi Sigma Kappa

Founded at Massachusetts Agricultural College, March 15, 1873.
Omega Chapter—Established February 12, 1909.

FACULTY

Herbert Ellsworth Cory Farnum Pond Griffiths
Alfred Smith

GRADUATES

John Howard Becker Forrest Arthur Cobb
A. Howard Hankey

SENIORS

*Fred William Brown ***Robert Edward Graff, Jr.
Lewis Ryan Byington Charles F. B. Roeth
Hugh Frederick Dormody Romayne R. Rohlfing
Henry Kirk White

JUNIORS

Charles Lawrence Frost Fraser Lapp Macpherson
John Ritchie McKee Edward Borland von Adelung
Stephen Norman Wilson

SOPHOMORES

Clifford Ten Eyck Dodds Richard Joel Russell
Louis Jay Fredley Edward Vernon Tenny
Andrew Thomas Hass Fred Turner
Miller Roe Huston Edwin Howard Uhl
James Alexander Wasson

FRESHMEN

Louis Charles Barrette William Hathaway McClain
Carlton Carswell Chesley Frank Buckley McGiurna
Donald Blake Crystal Victor Waldemar Nielson
Ernest Merville Frellson *Harold Andrew Roberts
**Arthur John Sknale

*Absent on leave.
**At Affiliated Colleges.
***Graduated December, 1916.

Forrest Cobb   Howard Hankey   Fred Brown   Lewis Byington   Hugh Dormody   Robert Graff, Jr.
Charles Roeth   H. Bohling   Charles Frost Hutchie McKee   F. Macpherson   Ed. von Adelung
Stephen Wilson Clifford Dodds   Louis Fredley Andrew Hass   Miller Huston   Richard Russell
Edward Tenny   Fred Turner   Edwin Uhl   James Wasson   Carlton Chesley Donald Crystal
                Ernest Frolicon   William McClain Frank McGiurrin Harold Roberts

Pi Kappa Phi

Founded at Charleston College, December 10, 1904.
California Gamma Chapter—Established December 8, 1909.

GRADUATE
Orrin S. Cook

SENIORS

Henry Spencer Brink, Jr.
Charles Clarence Merrell
William Irving Morgan

Ronald Lowe Ring
*Carl Gordon Shafor
Rupert Golding Weidemeyer

JUNIORS

Francis Hobart Miller
Laurence William Phelps
Fred Ruben Richardson
Donald Wilber Searles

***Jesse De Witt Stockton
Jo Joslin Tapscott
Karl Michael Wagner
**Frederick Ernest Weidenmuller

Rey B. Wheeler

SOPHOMORES

Joseph Hamilton Conkling
Leroy A. Fowler
James Stanley Hook
Charles Ernest Magnus

Arthur Elwood Mead
William Dean Oliver
Sheldon Thomas Paull
Earle Abram Sanborn

Alonzo Earl Washburn

FRESHMEN

Alfred Clement
Harold Kelso Hirst
Fred Dewey Kent
Louis Douglas Null

Stanley Persons
Petrie Ludger Robert
Arthur Herbert Simock
Wallace Ferlys Thomas

*Absent on leave.
**At Davis.
***At Hastings College of Law.

Henry Brink, Jr. Charles Merrell William Morgan Ronald Ring Carl Shafor R. Wedemeyer
Hobart Miller Laurence Phelps Fred Richardson Donald Searles Jesse Stockton Justin Tapscott
Karl Wagner F. Weidenmuller Roy Wheeler Joseph Conkling James Hook Charles Magnus
Arthur Mead William Oliver Sheldon Paull Earle Sanborn Earl Washburn Alfred Clement
Kelso Hurst Fred Kent Douglas Null Stanley Persons Petrie Robert
Arthur Sinnock Wallace Thomas

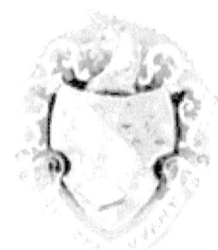

Theta Xi

Founded at Rensselaer Polytechnic Institute, April 29, 1864.
Nu Chapter—Established March 22, 1910.

FACULTY

Adolphus James Eddy
Thomas Forsyth Hunt
William James Raymond
Edwin Coblentz Voorhies
Harold A. Wadsworth

GRADUATES

**Paul Carle
Milton William Vedder

SENIORS

Robert James Archibald
Walter Harold Johnson
**Eugene Thomas Langenour
**Carroll Theodore Lund
William Kenneth Potts
Thompson Price
Fred H. Reynolds
Herbert Kuno Schulz
Thomas Spencer
Raub Merrill Stafford

JUNIORS

Claude Williams House
**Claus William Johnson, Jr.
**Donald Linn Kieffer
Horace Knight McCoy
Freeman Albert Reed
Ray Rohwer

SOPHOMORES

Richard Berry Adams
Hendrik Jan Ankersmit
Frank Rattan Beede
Truman Everett Boudinot
Frank Brewster Bowker
Harry Boquist Bowker
Norman Standart Hamilton
George Logan Henderson, Jr.
Clarence Taylor Jackson
Milton Gates Odenheimer
Harold Charles Silent
Gifford Gray Todd

FRESHMEN

Curtis Herbert Cleaver
Herndon Hural Cobb
*Frank Jennings Cowan
Alvin Kmucar House
Otto Herman Jemm
George Frederick Korn
John Franklin Osborn
Dean Goodwin Searles
*Kenneth Eugene Tipton

*Absent on leave.
**At Davis, January-May, 1917.

Milton Vedder	H Archibald	W Johnson	E Longemore	Carrol Land	Wm Potts	T Price
Fred Reynolds	Herbert Schulz	Thos Spencer	Hugh Stafford	Claude House	C Johnson Jr	Donald Kueffer
Horace McCoy	Freeman Boyd	Ray Holmes	R Adams	H Ankcorn	Frank Beede	Frank Bowker
Harry Bowker	T Boudinot	N Hamilton	G Henderson, Jr	C Jackson	M Oblenheimer	Harold Silent
Gifford Todd	Curtis Cleaver	Herman Cobb	Frank Cowan	Alvan House	George Koen	John Osborn
		Dean Searles	K Tipton	Otto Jemm		

Sigma Phi Epsilon

Founded at Richmond College, November 10, 1901.
California Alpha Chapter—Established November 10, 1910.

FACULTY
Robert Grant Aitken

GRADUATE
Carl Louis Thiele

SENIORS

Wayne Kraemer Ball
John William Benton
C. Coleman Berwick
Joyce Canfield Haun
Arnold Watlington Howe

Alvin Mathias Karstensen
Glen Orral Knight
**Maurice Herbert Knowles
Floyd Theall McKune
Nicholas James Scorsur

JUNIORS

Gus Adolf Brelin
Orville Robert Caldwell
Walter John Escherich

John Walter Oakley
John Henry Spohn
Quincy Lorenzo Wright

SOPHOMORES

Hiram Rufus Baker
George Winn Boyd
Harry Lester Hopkins
George Garrison Mitchell

John Kenneth Moody
Harold Gladstone Snodgrass
Richard August Stumm
William Harry Wraith

FRESHMEN

Douglas Carryl Aitken
Harold Kelsey Beresford
*Raymond Campbell Elliot

Robert Hazelhurst Evans
Charles Hall Fishburn
Spencer Shepard Kapp

Laurence Everett Wraith

*Absent on leave.
**Graduated December, 1916.

Carl Thiele John Benton Coleman Berwick Arnold Howe Alvin Karstensen Glen Knight
Maurice Knowles Floyd McKune Nicholas Seosour Gus Brehn Orville Caldwell Walter Escherich
John Oakley John Spohn Quincy Wright Hiram Baker George Boyd Harry Hopkins
George Mitchell Kenneth Moody Harold Snodgrass Richard Stunem Harry Wraith Douglas Aitken
Harold Beresford Robert Evans Charles Fishburn Spencer Kapp Laurence Wraith

Delta Chi

Founded at Cornell University, October 13, 1890.
California Chapter—Established November 22, 1910.

FACULTY

J. Roy Douglas *Thomas H. Reed

GRADUATES

Richard Henry Chamberlain
George Lukens Collins
Robert Rosborough Gardiner
Frederick William Kant
Joseph Leo Knowles
Donovan Otto Peters

SENIORS

Bradford Walsworth Bosley
Walter George Buell
James Benton Harvey
Arthur Thornton LaPrade
*James Eldon McFarland
John Curtis Newton
Joseph Nash Owen
George Clement Perkins
Frank Carol Smith
Waite Henry Stephenson
George Leonard White
Thornton Wilson

William Jerome Young

JUNIORS

*Alvin Sargent Hambly
William Frederick Kiessig
George John Lacoste
Anthony Laurence Mitchell
William Griffiths Pillsbury
Claude Rohwer
Van Hartwell Steel
Thomas Jackson Stephens

Arthur William Turck

SOPHOMORES

Robert McKee Adams
Thomas Reese Bowen Ashby
Robert Prince Casey
George Presly Coyne
Kenneth Sanborn Craft
Perry Ralph McCutchen
*George Yates Peters
Victor Llewellyn Wells, Jr.

*Clair Emanuel Woland

FRESHMEN

Ernest C. Anderson
George Russel Ellison
John Myron Jameson
Thomas Wills Nelson
Baldwin Peter Quintero
*Paul Stephens

Leon Laselle Thornburg

*Absent on leave.

R. Chamberlain	R. Gardiner	Frederick Kant	Jos. Knowles	Donovan Peters	R. Bodey	Walter Buell
Benton Harvey	A. LaPrade	John Newton	Joseph Owen	Geo. Perkins	Frank Smith	W. Stephenson
George White	T. Wilson	Wm. Young	Alvin Hambly	Wm. Kieoon	Geo. Lacoste	Larry Mitchell
Wm. Pillsbury	C. Rohwer	Van Steel	Jack Stephens	Arthur Turck	Robt. Adams	Thos. Ashby
Robt. Casey	Kenneth Craft	George Coyne	P. McCutcheon	George Peters	Y. Wells, Jr.	Clair Woloud
E. Anderson	Geo. Ellison	John Jameson	Thos. Nelson	R. Quintero	Paul Stephens	L. Thornburg

Pi Kappa Alpha

Founded at University of Virginia, March 1, 1868.
Alpha Sigma Chapter—Established on April 16, 1912.

FACULTY

William Leslie · Roy Everet Warren

GRADUATES

Philip Howard Arnot · Lloyd Nelson Hamilton
Robert Carson Martin

SENIORS

Bruce Cartwright Basford · Henry Raymond Hogaboom
Owen Robertson Blois · **Howard Alexander Houston
***Frederick Carrington Corey · Leslie Alphonse Isaacson
Thomas Wilford Dahlquist · Lester Frederick Kohle
***Emerson Brown Herrick · *Lester Ray Ogden
Carl George Hjelte · James Rolla Thomas
Basil Kirkman Woods

JUNIORS

William Lee Bender · Chester LeRoy Isaacson
George Williams Clark · *David Porter Miles
Mason Emory Franklin · Raymond Ritchie Morgan
Everett Johnson Gray · James William Center Pogue
Rodney Searle Sprigg

SOPHOMORES

Ralph Wesley Arnot · LeRoy Jesse Miller
*James Anthony Callan · *Russell Sidney Thompson

FRESHMEN

Leland Chester Adams · Elwynn Herman Mannhart
Edmund Frank deFreitas · Frank Albert Morgan, Jr.
Russell Hamilton Green · Herbert John Orchison
Carlton Dewey Hulin · Marshall Gill Stone
Albert Eugene West

*Absent on leave.
**Graduated, December, 1916.
***At Davis, January-May, 1917.

Philip Arnot	Robert Martin	Owen Bleis	Frederick Corey	Thomas Dahlquist	Emerson Herrick
George Hjelte	H. Hogaboom	Howard Houston	Leslie Isaacson	Lester Kohle	Lester Ogden
James Thomas	Basil Woods	William Bender	George Clark	Mason Franklin	Everett Gray
Chester Isaacson	Raymond Morgan	James Pogue	Searle Spring	Ralph Arnot	Anthony Callan
LeRoy Miller	Russell Thompson	Edm'd deFreitas	Russell Green	Carlton Hulin	Elwynn Mannhart
	Frank Morgan, Jr.	Herbert Orchison	Marshall Stone	Albert West	

Sigma Phi

Founded at Union College, March 4, 1827.
Alpha of California—Established September 12, 1912.

FACULTY

William Vere Cruess
Harold Lewis Leupp
Robert Seldon Rose
Guy Robertson Stewart

GRADUATE

Roe Emerson Shaub

SENIORS

Luther Allen Nichols
William Alexander Russell
*Frank Milton Sizer
Floyd Wayne Stewart
Chester Benson Tonkin

JUNIORS

Aubrey Foster Holmes
Carl King
**Guifford Fuller Meredith
**Nelson Howard Partridge, Jr.
Edwin Sprague Pillsbury

SOPHOMORES

Edward Bell Kennedy
James Stewart Kinnear
Richard Davidson Perry
***Charles Aldrich Sweet
James Sherrill Taylor

FRESHMEN

Albert Charles Buttolph, Jr.
Milnor Peck Paret, Jr.
Edwin Hugo Richards
Charles Edwin Stephens
Irving Francis Toomey
Harry Haws Trefts

*Absent on leave.
**At Davis, January-May, 1917.
***At Affiliated Colleges.

Luther Nichols   William Russell   Milton Sizer   Floyd Stewart   Chester Tonkin
Aubrey Holmes   Carl King   Guilford Meredith   Nelson Partridge, Jr.   Edwin Pillsbury
Edward Kennedy   James Kinnear   Richard Perry   Charles Sweet   Sherrill Taylor
Albert Buttolph, Jr. Milton Pacvi, Jr. Edwin Richards   Charles Stephens
Irving Toomey   Harry Trefts

Alpha Sigma Phi

Founded at Yale University, December 1, 1845.
Nu Chapter—Established February 3, 1913.

FACULTY

E. J. Best
John William Gregg
E. J. Hauser
Donald E. Martin
Benedict Frederick Raber
J. Maurice Scammell
Alfred Solomon

GRADUATES

Orville Reddick Emerson
Paul Longstreth Fussell
Waldron Ashley Gregory

SENIORS

James McNeil Crawford
*Earl Wilder Edson
Hugh Nathan Herrick
Frank Leroy Hill
Harold Anthony Hyde
Clifford Verne Mason
Claude Verner Thompson
*Frederick Eric Wesson

JUNIORS

Howard Edwin Bennett
Cletus Ignatius Howell
Harry Bluett Liversedge
Philip Strong Mathews
Charles Lortz Miller
Leffler Bequette Miller
Albert Brodie Smith
Pierre Jaqua Walker

SOPHOMORES

John Harvey Fellows
Francis Dale Hamilton
Frank Foli Hargear
Ronald Walter Hunt
Perry Kittredge
Leland Harris Nielson
Elwin Leo O'Hara
Charles Edward Parslow
Bryson Shillington
George Eliott Smith
Robert Henry Young

FRESHMEN

James Edward Drew
Donald Benjamin Fowler
Harold Eugene Fraser
Norman Sterne Gallison
Harlan Hilton Howard
Melvin Jessup McClean
Malcolm Durham McKenzie
George Edward Wightman

*Absent on leave.

Orville Emerson	Paul Fussell	Waldron Gregory	McNeil Crawford	Hugh Herrick	Frank Hill
Harold Hyde	Clifford Mason	Claude Thompson	Frederick Wesson	Howard Bennett	Cletus Howell
Harry Liveresdge	Philip Mathews	Charles Miller	LeRler Miller	Brodie Smith	Pierre Walker
John Fellows	Francis Hamilton	Frank Harwear	Ronald Hunt	Perry Kittredge	Leland Nielsen
Edwin O'Hara	Charles Pardoe	B. Shillington	George Smith	Robert Young	Edward Drew
Donald Fowler	Harold Fraser	Norman Gallison	Harlan Howard	Melvin McClean	George Wightman

Sigma Pi

Founded at Vincennes University, May 10, 1897,
Iota Chapter - Established May 5, 1913.

FACULTY

Samuel H. Beckett   William G. Hummel

SENIORS

Cecil Amos Ditty   Arthur William Mohr
Joseph Bell Hammon   Elwood Ellsworth Trask
John Edward Hare   **Walter Scott Wilkinson, Jr.
Demetrio Eugene Jeffry   Harold Evans Woodworth
William Alfred McCutchan   Carol Willard Wright

JUNIORS

Harold Edwin Dimock   Eugene Clair Lloyd
**Carroll Francis Danshee   Allen Raymond Watson

SOPHOMORES

John Daniel Bullock   Charles William Day
Warren Nicholas Craddock   Cecil Arthur Lathrop
Chester Seymour Crittenden **Franklin Blades Lewis
Earl Adams Davis   Dixwell Lloyd Pierce
          Olof Eugene Snyder

FRESHMEN

Ensley Miles Bent   Herbert Sanford Howard, Jr.
Southard Tolchard Flynn   Julius Gordon Hussey
Henson Mason Garrett   Ottiwell Wood Jones, Jr.
Walter Allen Green   *Richard Palmer Mills

*Absent on leave.
**At Davis, January-May, 1917.

Cecil Ditty Joseph Hammon John Hare Demetrio Jeffry Wm McCutchan Arthur Mohr
Elwood Track W. Wilkinson, Jr. H. Woodworth Carol Wright Harold Dimock Carroll Dunsbee
Eugene Lloyd Allen Watson John Bullock Warren Craddock C. Crittenden Earl Davis
Charles Day Cecil Lathrop Franklin Lucas Russell Payne Olof Snyder Lesley Bent
Southard Flynn Hewson Garrett Walter Green H. Howard, Jr. Ottiwell Jones, Jr.
Richard Mills Julius Hussey

Theta Chi

Founded at Norwich University, April 10, 1856.
Mu Chapter - Established November 7, 1913.

GRADUATES

Elbert Willard Davis
Logan Combs Edwards
Samuel Frederick Hollins

SENIORS

William Earl Bowen
Paul Duncan Edwards
**Arthur Emil Nelson
Thomas Lindsay Nudd
Paul Weaver Penland
Louis Hubbard Penney
Manley William Sahlberg
Roy Dill Sifford

JUNIORS

Edward Spann Bleecker
***Charles Westley Craig
Harold Edwin Fielder
George Edwin Goodall
Charles Edward Marquis
Erwin Fontaine Perkins
*Clive Arden Walker

SOPHOMORES

*Albert Jeffries Hodges
Albert Howard Jacobs
Richard Caldwell Kerr
Dudley Whitney Steeves
LeRoy Emery Williams

FRESHMEN

Rees Thompson Dudley
Frederick Didier Heegler
Edward Ray Horton
Donald Monroe Hummel
Alvin Davison Hyman
Harold Lockhart Norris

*Absent on leave.
**At Davis, January-May, 1917.
***At Affiliated Colleges.

Elbert Davie   Logan Edwards   Samuel Hollins   William Bowen   Paul Edwards   Arthur Nelson
Thomas Nield   Paul Penland   Louis Penney   Manley Sahlberg   Roy Sifford   Edward Bleecker
Charles Crane   Harold Fiedler   George Goodall   Charles Marquis   Erwin Perkins   Albert Hodges
Albert Jacobs   Richard Kerr   Dudley Steeves   LeRoy Williams   Frederick Hessler   Edward Horton
Donald Hummel   Alvin Hyman   Harold Norris

Lambda Chi Alpha

Founded at Boston, November 2, 1909.
Mu Zeta Chapter Established December 15, 1913.

FACULTY

Charles Burrows Bennett
Ira Brown Cross
Felix H. Burni
Charles Atwood Kofoid
Robert Orton Moody

GRADUATES

**Arthur Elmer Belt
**Lloyd Elliott Hardgrave
**J. Grey McQuarrie
**Oscar Kempher Mohs
Stanley Vernon Wilson
**Elmo Russell Zumwalt

SENIORS

Almy Cofran Maynard
*Kenneth McCausland Metcalf
Leroy Bassett Sharp
Thomas Russel Simpson
Harvey Albert Smith
*William David West

JUNIORS

Hubert Rogers Arnold
***Elba Norse Bailey
Grant Cunningham
Frederick William Flodberg
Thomas Essington Gibson
Axel Berg Graven
William Dalton Hohenthal
Douglas Richards Sides
Walter Tyrrell Stokes
Charles Herman Woessner
Milton E. Wolfe

SOPHOMORES

Gwin Belshaw
William Adelbert Cowell
Donald Sidney Deskey
Elliot Glen Hart
Edward Howard LeBreton
Oliver Clarence Stem
John Archer Stewart

FRESHMEN

Henry Michael Buckley
Arthur Romo Clay
Ralph McIntyre Darling
John Harvey Danshee
Marcus Mohler
Percy Nelson
*Hubert Blase Quinn
James Tyrrell Rutherford
Paul Winning Sharp
Alfred Brunson Willoughby

*Absent on leave.
**At Affiliated Colleges.
***At Davis, January-May, 1917.

Lloyd Hardgrave Oscar Mohs   Stanley Wilson   Kenneth Metcalf Leroy Sharp   Thomas Simpson
William West   Hubert Arnold   Elba Bailey   G. Cunningham   Fred. Fledberg   Thomas Gibson
Axel Geseron   Wm. Hohenthal   Douglas Soles   Walter Stokes   Chas Worsaner   Milton Wolfe
Gwin Belshaw   William Cowell   Donald Deskey   Elliot Hart   Edward Lefferton Oliver Stem
John Stewart   Henry Buckley   Arthur Clay   Ralph Darling   John Danchew   Marcus Molder
       Percy Nelson   Hubert Quinn   Jas. Rutherford   Paul Sharp   A. Willoughby

Alpha Kappa Lambda

Founded at the University of California, April 22, 1914
California Chapter

FACULTY

James Turney Allen
Henry Chalmers Biddle
Robert Thomas Legge
William Brodbeck Herms
Ruliff Stephen Holway

GRADUATES

**Robert Ingersoll Daley
***Knowles Augustus Ryerson

SENIORS

Elmon Frank Coe
Ray Orren Diether
***Harry Everett Drobish
Bryant Hall
George Mitchell Hill
Kenneth Ward Houston
Euvelle Downan Howard
Milton Vernon Johns
George Lawrence Maxwell
*William Clarence Morrison
Warren Dexter Norton
Laurence Seymour
Fred Henry Taylor
Ralph Mervin Walker

JUNIORS

Alvin Gustav Becker
***Melvin Wright Buster
John Wesley Coulter
John Peter Daley
Chester O. Hansen
George Newton Hosford
Theodore Carey Lawson
Earl Willson Wells
***Jack Sloan Willson
***Edward Shaler Yocco

SOPHOMORES

John Lewis Barter
Elbridge Houghton Blanchard
William Ray Dennes
Roland Archibald Way
Edwin Stanley Leonard
Ralph Prestidge
Charles Ray

FRESHMEN

John Britton Matthew
Theodore Matthew
Charles Alexander Moore
Harold Willard Poulson
Bruce Zimmerman
Herbert Wesley Riemenschneider
Allison Edmond Schofield
Milton Maxin Smith
James Roy White

*Absent on leave.
**Graduated December, 1916.
***At Davis, January-May, 1917.

Hubert Daley   N. Ryerson   Elmon Coe   Ray Diether   Harry Dredish   Bryant Hall   George Hill
N. Houston   F. Howard   Milton Johns   L. Maxwell   Wm. Morrison   Warren Norton   L. Seymour
Fred Taylor   Ralph Walker   Alvin Becker   Melvin Buster   John Coulter   Peter Daley   C. Hansen
Geo. Hosford   T. Lawson   Karl Wells   Jack Wilson   Edward Yereo   John Barter   F. Blanchard
Edwin Leonard   R. Prestolge   Charles Ray   Roland Way   John Matthes   T. Matthes   Charles Miner
                H. Riemenschneider Allison Schofield Milton Smith James White Bruce Zimmerman

Delta Sigma Phi

Founded at the College of the City of New York, February 23, 1899.
Hilgard Chapter Established November 28, 1915.

FACULTY
Edward Oyyo Amundsen

GRADUATE
John Wesley Cook

SENIORS

**Walter Victor Atkinson
***Robert Ellis Berng
John Gilbert Boardman
Leonard Avon Coburn

****Clinton George Davis
Clarence Gatchell Dow
George Adair Fleming
**Warren Harvey Parker

Carlyle Gill Patton

JUNIORS

Ralph Albee
John Newton Baird
*Lester Darrell De Mond
Leonard Roland Dykes
Henry Stephen Flock
Paul Harold Holsinger

Thurston Pendroy Knudson
Albert Howard Linn
Killis Chess Reese
***Charles William Suits
William Carl Tesche
Frank Ignatius Wolongiewicz

*Orrin Burns Zoline

SOPHOMORES

Victor Norman Christopher
Vincent Edward Duffey
***John Frederick FitzPatrick
Harry Anthony Godde

Aaron Francis Hatfield
Donald MacPherson MacKenzie
Ogle Charles Merwin
Clarence Whitman Wagner

FRESHMEN

*Albern Baltzley Jones
John Thaddeus Knudson

*Newell Linton Moore
*Philip Smith Postell

Byron Jenning Showers

*Absent on leave.
**Graduated December, 1916.
***At Davis, January-May, 1917.
****At Affiliated Colleges.

John Cook   Walter Atkinson   Robert Bering   John Boardman   Leonard Coburn   Clarence Dox
George Fleming   Warren Parker   Carlyle Patton   Ralph Silvey   John Baird   Lester De Mund
Leonard Dykes   Henry Fleck   Paul Holsinger   T. Knudson   Albert Linn   Killis Brose
Charles Suits   William Towle   F. Wolcott   Byron Zeiser   V. Christopher   Vincent Duffey
John FitzPatrick   Harry Goldie   Francis Hatfield   Donald MacKenzie   Ogle Sherwin   Clarence Wagner
    Albert Jones   John Knudson   Newell Monte   Philip Postell   Byron Shomers

Sigma Phi Sigma

Founded at University of Pennsylvania, April 13, 1908.
Epsilon Chapter—Established December 14, 1916.

FACULTY

Thomas Clay Mayhew
Albert F. Swain
Thomas Frederick Tavernetti
Reuben S. Tour

GRADUATES

****Frederick Panciano Feliz
***Mervyn Francis Frandy
***Charles Clarke Hall
***Cavino Deter Hart
Oscar Charles Parkinson

SENIORS

Oliver H. Cory
Chester Rudolph F. Cramer
William Dinsmore
Verne W. Hoffman
**George Martin Koopman
Hugh Fraser MacKenzie
**Robert Charles Maris
*David Germain Sala
Eric Harold Sargeant
**Achille Alfred Tavernetti
***Willard Snenton Westwood

JUNIORS

Eugene Burton Butler
*William Lancelot Butler
**Earl Daniel Davis
Melvyn Lloyd Frandy
Gailor Sayle McCullough
**John Quincy McDonald
*Edgar Joseph Mayo
George Henri Rohrbacher
*Robert Wade Snyder
Eldon Battles Spofford
Herbert M. Woodruff

SOPHOMORES

Walter Carl Hoffman
Milton Ladd Kingsbury
*Douglas May
Howard Elmo Miller
Oscar Clarence Olsen
Arnold Poppie, Jr.
*Rupert Edison Starr

FRESHMEN

Edward Christian Anderson
Samuel John Binsacca
Ralph Wesley Bird
Beverly Burgess Castle
*Lester Edward Gnekow
Reuben John Irvin
*John Joseph Lucas
Hubert Leonard Pascoe
Frank Zea Pirkey

*Absent on leave.
**At Davis.
***At Affiliated Colleges.
****Hastings College of the Law.

Frederick Felix	Charles Hall	Cavins Hart	O. Parkinson	Wm. Dinsmore	Chester Cramer	Verne Hoffman
Geo. Koopman	H. MacKenzie	Robert Maris	David Sain	Eric Sargeant	A. Tavernetti	W. Westwood
Wm. Butler	Norton Butler	Earl Davis	M. Frendy	G. McCullough	John McDonald	G. Rohrbacher
Robt. Snyder	E. Spafford	H. Woodruff	W. Hoffman	M. Kingsbury	Douglas May	Howard Miller
Oscar Olson	A. Poppie, Jr.	Rupert Starr	E. Anderson	S. Binsacca	Ralph Bird	B. Castle
	Lester Ginskow	Reuben Irvin	John Lucas	Hubert Pacece	Frank Pirkey	

PROFESSIONAL FRATERNITIES

Phi Delta Phi
[Legal]

Founded at University of Michigan, November 22, 1869.
Pomeroy Chapter — Established at Hastings College of the Law in 1883.

FACULTY

George Lewis Bell
Goblen Woolfolk Bell

Richard Calhoun Harrison
Robert Waite Harrison

Edward Robeson Taylor

SENIOR

Harry M. Creech

MIDDLE YEAR

Lawrence Mitchell Bliss
John Dorrance Hoyt

Garton Donald Keyston
Herbert George Lyttle

Mountford W. Wilson

JUNIORS

Aubrey Donald Duncan
Wendell Speer Kuhn

Eugene Shattuck Selvage
Edwin Newton Snitjer

Charles Edward Street, Jr.

Phi Delta Phi
[Legal]

Founded at the University of Michigan, November 22, 1869.
Jones Chapter – Established at the University of California in 1914.

FACULTY

John Uberto Calkins, Jr.
William Edward Colby
Maurice Edward Harrison
William Carey Jones

Alexander Marsden Kidd
Matthew Christopher Lynch
Orrin Kep McMurray
Arthur Gould Tasheira

Austin Tappan Wright

SENIORS

Elmer Granville Burland
Thomas Gwynne Chamberlain
Forrest Arthur Cobb
Aloysius Ignatius Diepenbrock
Jacob Goldberg

Leo David Hermle
Samuel Frederick Hollins
Ralph Edwin Hoyt
Richard Morris Lyman, Jr.
William Ashley Sutton

Matt Wahrhaftig

JUNIORS

James Townsend Barstow
James Clifford Nichols

John Boardman Whitton
Theodore Lyster Withers

FRESHMEN

Harold Alfred Black
Sherman Kennedy Burke
Lewis Ryan Byington
Charles Josef Carey
George Washington Cohen
Edwin Madison Elam
Gregory Alexander Harrison
Edward Hervey
George Henry Hotaling

Leslie Alphonse Isaacson
Marshall Pierre Madison
Curtis Dion O'Sullivan
Southall Hazelle Pfund
Eugene Mitchell Prince
Hugh Shippey
Neal Staunton
Gordon Fitzhugh Stephens
Douglas Van Dyke

Willis Guy Witter

Delta Sigma Delta
[Dental]

Founded at University of Michigan, March 5, 1882.
Zeta Chapter—Established October 31, 1891.

FACULTY

Malcolm Goddard
Herbert Turbitt Moore
Arnold L. Morse
Homer Lash Sams

James Graham Sharp
William Fuller Sharp
Homer I. Spare
Allen Holman Suggett

Frederick Wolfsohn

SENIORS

John Oliver Armistead
Lloyd Crocket Austin
Eddy Tallman Boyd
Charles Dustan Bradley

Carl Nichols Dorman
Avery Scott Hills
Charles Eugene Johnson
Adrian Lewis Morin

JUNIORS

Robert Bell
James Steward Craig
William Howard Haskins
Ernest Rosekrans Ker
Theodore Hardiman Pohlmann

John Lloyd Rickley
John Franklin Robertson
Millard Joseph Streeter
Thomas Edwin Tilden
Leo Luke Vorwerk

FRESHMEN

Lester Elmer Breese
Claude Tony Cochrane
Clinton Ashby Fowler
Roy Albert Green

Lyman Dunlap Hencock
Ernest Leroy Johnson
Samuel Ripley Olswang
Alvin William Pruett

Herbert Moore	John Armistead	Lloyd Austin	Eddy Boyd	Charles Bradley
Carl Dorman	Avery Hails	Charles Johnson	Adrian Morin	Robert Bell
James Craig	William Haskins	Ernest Key	Theodore Poldmann	John Hackley
John Robertson	Millard Strewing	Thomas Tilden	Leo Vorwerk	Lester Brewer
Claude Cochrane	Clinton Fowler	Roy Green	Ernest Johnson	
Samuel Olessing	Alven Pruett			

Xi Psi Phi

[Dental]

Founded at the University of Michigan, February 8, 1889.
Iota Chapter—Established in 1895.

FACULTY

George L. Bean
Frank C. Bettencourt
Harold J. Bruhns
Thorton Craig
Harry H. Heitman

Joseph D. Hogden
Harold C. Kausen
Guy S. Millberry
Charles B. Musante
Melvin Rhodes

Otto Roller

SENIORS

Ralph Peary Chessall
Fred Bolton Godbolt
Charles Dudley Gwinn
Havard Milne Johnston

Nestor Maximillian Lonn
Lester Bevard Ranta
Ernest Martin Setzer
Clarence Alden Stock

Herne Clinton Tollefson

JUNIORS

Elmer Holmes Berryman
Clyde Holmes Carmean
Charles Westley Craig
Paul Ehorn
George Almon Goff
Frederick Hugill Hare
Vernon Edward James

Chester William Johnson
Carl Eugene King
Philip Thomas Lynch
Leon Wesley Marshall
Samuel Josiah Roberts
Chalmers Ephriam West
Sylvan Edmond West

John LuRell Wood

FRESHMEN

William Jennings Banker
Charles Edward Boyd, Jr.
Robert Carmel Frates
Pearce Glasson
Winfred Leo Golden
George H. Grover
Walter Joyce Hawkins

Rollin Edgar Hurd
Jesse Alvin Lingenfelter
John Edgar Russell
John Reed Sink
Lester Lauren Smith
Cecil Caspar Steiner
Willard Smeaton Westwood

Ralph Chesnut   Fred Gulledt   Dudley Gwinn   Havard Johnston   Nestor Lenn   Lester Hantz
Ernest Setzer   Clarence Stock Clinton Tolleson Elmer Berryman   Clyde Carmean   Charles Craig
Paul Ehren   George Goff   Frederick Hare   Vernon James   Chester Johnson Carl King
Philip Lynch   Leon Marshall   Samuel Roberts   Chalmers West   Sylvan West   John Wood
William Banker Charles Boyd, Jr. Robert Frates   Pearce Glasson   George Grover   Walter Hawkins
Rollin Hurd   Jesse Langenfelter John Russell   Lester South   Cecil Steiner   Willard Westwood

Alpha Kappa Kappa

[Medical]

Founded at Dartmouth College, September 28, 1888.
Sigma Chapter—Established in 1899.

FACULTY

Roy C. Abbott
Walter C. Alvarez
Walter Isaac Baldwin
Eldridge J. Best
C. R. Brown
Lloyd Bryan
Joseph H. Catton
Jean Valjean Cooke
Arnold A. D'Ancona
George Elliot Ebright
Ludwig A. Emge
Ernest H. Falconer

John Nicison Force
Clain F. Gelston
Carl Leslie Hoag
Eugene Sterling Kilmore
Howard Markel
Robert Orton Moody
Howard Morrow
Saxton Temple Pope
Howard Edwin Ruggles
Wilbur Augustus Sawyer
Milton Schutz
Charles L. Tranter

Alanson Weeks

INTERNES

Joseph Allen Owen

Henry Hunt Searls

SENIORS

Orrin S. Cook
Hiram Edgar Miller

Vinton A. Muller
William Wallace Washburn

JUNIORS

Sidney Olsen

Laurence Taussig

Fletcher Brandon Taylor

SOPHOMORES

Thomas Ayres

*Cletus Henry Graves

FRESHMEN

C. Coleman Berwick
John Clement Dement

Darrell Bertrand Hawley
*Hans Frank Schluter

Arthur Lafayette Warren

*Absent on leave.

Orrin Cook   Hiram Miller   Vinton Muller   William Washburn
Sidney Olsen   Laurence Taussig   Fletcher Taylor   Cletus Graves
Coleman Bernick   John Dement   Darrell Hawley
Hans Schluter   Arthur Warren

Nu Sigma Nu
(Medical)

Founded at University of Michigan, March 2, 1882.
Phi Chapter—Established in 1900.

FACULTY

Edgar W. Alexander	Lovell Langstroth	Harry Partridge
Herbert W. Allen	Robert T. Legge	V. H. Podstatta
Fayette W. Bartch	Milton B. Lennon	Jesu P. Pratt
Leroy H. Briggs	John V. Leonard	John M. Rehfisch
Theodore C. Burnett	Frederick C. Lewitt	Robert L. Richards
Herbert M. Evans	William B. Lewitt	Glanville G. Rusk
Harry E. Foster	William P. Lucas	Wallace I. Terry
Frederick P. Gay	Frank W. Lynch	Herbert S. Thomson
Richard W. Harvey	Albert W. Meads	Edward Topham
Thomas P. Huntington	William G. Moore	Charles A. von Hoffman
William W. Kerr	Howard C. Naffziger	John H. Woolsey

INTERNES

Paul E. Cook	Harold P. Hare	L. Montney Morris
Dunnlough Corey	Warren D. Hosmer	Frank W. Pinger
Brython Davis	Maurice Joses	John C. Ruddock
Thomas B. M. Dunn	Frederick G. Lude	William B. Thompson
	Marshall G. Williams	

SENIORS

Frank Phillip Brendel	Leonard W. Buck	Howard Webster Fleming
	James Ernest Harvey	Daniel Warren Sooy

JUNIORS

Robert Wilson Binkley	Frederick Carl Cordes	Henry Chipman Dodge
	Harold Homer Hitchcock	William Dan Sink

SOPHOMORES

Philip Howard Arnot	Charles Beebe Fowler	Charles Edward Locke, Jr.
Alfred Poyneer Briggs	Lloyd Elliot Hartgrave	Frederick George Muggs
Edwin Lewis Bruck	Thomas Waterman Huntington	Robert Carson Martin
	Oscar Kempfer Mohs	

FRESHMEN

Dexter Rankin Ball	Daniel Parsons Foster	Kenneth McCausland Metcalf
William Henry Bingaman	Hal Rexford Hoobler	Gilbert Lansing Patterson
Hugh Frederick Dormody	Demetrio Eugene Jeffry	Henry Albert Sawyer
	Edward Byer Shaw	

Robert Binkley   Frederick Cowles   Chapman Dodge   Harold Hitchcock   Dan Sack
Philip Arnot   Alfred Briggs   Edson Brack   Charles Fowler   Lloyd Hardgrave
Thomas Huntington   Charles Locke, Jr.   Frederick Maggs   Robert Martin   Oscar Mohs
Dexter Hall   William Bangaman   Hugh Dornush   Daniel Foster   Hal Hoosier
Demetrio Jeffry   Kenneth Metcalf   Gilbert Patterson   Edward Shaw

Phi Delta Chi

[Pharmacy]

Founded at Ann Arbor, Michigan, in 1883
Zeta Chapter—Established March 2, 1902.

FACULTY AND HONORARY MEMBERS

Gaston E. Bacon
Henry Benjamin Carey
Franklin Theodore Green
Frederick William Nish

Albert Schneider
William M. Searby
Haydn Mozart Simmons
Isaac Tobriner

Harley Rupert Wiley

SENIORS

Homer Lucian Asselin
Richard Roy Bravin
Harry E. Chaubes
Norman Clyde Guinn
Elmer L. Gustafson

Carl J. Hallford
Waldo Hays Pate
Ainsley Meredith Ring
LaMotte Holmes Stimson
Ival Vincent Whatley

Emory Lewis Wyckoff

JUNIORS

George Albert Austin
Edwin Ralph Clark
Alva Mason Deacon
Mark Douglas
Oscar LeRoy Garhelds
Charles Gibson
Nelson Miles Leoni
Willey M. Moody

Roy Myers
Clifford Aldace Parker
Otto Warren Reynolds
Foster Richardson Roper
George Robert Schuh
Hugh Rush Selvy
Fred Nathaniel Spickerman
Fred T. Stevin

Homer Asschn	Richard Bravin	Harry Charles	Norman Gunn	Carl Halford
Waldo Pate	Ainsley Bing	LaMotte Stinson	Irad Whitey	Emory Wyckoff
George Austin	Edwin Clark	Alva Deacon	Mark Douglas	Oscar Garlo he
Charles Gibson	Nelson Levns	Wiley Moody	Roy Myers	Clifford Parker
	Otto Reynolds	Foster Roper	George Schuh	Hugh Selvy
		Fred Spockerman	Fred Toster-n	

Psi Omega
(Dental)

Founded at Baltimore College of Dental Surgery in 1892.
Beta Delta Chapter—Established in 1903.

FACULTY

Henry B. Carey
Jean V. Cooke
Stanley L. Dod
Henry O. Eggers
Clark R. Giles
John E. Gurley
William H. Hanford
Carl E. Hoag
George E. Hubbell

Robert E. Keys
Benjamin F. Lowell
Earl L. McGlashan
Harry J. Mathen
Edwin H. Mauk
F. Vance Simonton
George Simonton
Jacob B. Steffan
Clifford W. Welcome

Sherman A. White

SENIORS

William Gordon Bornoite
Ernest Henning Colvin
*James Raymond Griffiths
Jerome John Jansen

Charles Schiller Lipp
Walter Hazelwood Lowell
Noble Allen Powell
Frank Oleese Stoakes

John Myron Wakefield

JUNIORS

Cedric Cyril Baronidis
Ward Glenn Cadwallader
Leon George Cuenin
Louis Robert Huck
Otto Richard Jungermann

Carl Paul Rapp
Leslie Huntington Reardan
Harris E. Ridenour
Carlton Wise Shepherd
Ernest Leroy Smith

*Irvin R. Warren

FRESHMEN

Clements William Brown
Hazen Glenn Burnett
*Claud Leland Busick
Eugene Allison LaBarre
Paul Emmett Marmotte

Webster Hasbrouck Martin
Joseph Edward Mathewson
J. Vance Matteson
Clarence Wilson Neff
Clayton Westhay

Warner Frederick Wildanger

*Absent on leave.

William Barnum Ernest Colvin James Griffith Jerome Jaxsen Charles Lipp Walter Lowell
Allen Powell Frank Stenken John Wakefield Cedric Butonolis Ward Cadwallader Leon Curnin
Louis Hinrk Otto Jungermann Carl Paul Rapp Leslie Beasdan Harris Robinson Carleton Shepherd
Ernest Smith Clemenza Brown Hazen Burnett Claud Busick Eugene LaBarre Paul Mamoine
Webster Marsin Vance Matteson Clayton Westlay Warner Wablanger

Phi Alpha Gamma
(Medical)

Founded at New York, March 25, 1894.
Mu Chapter—Established March 25, 1906.

FACULTY

N. P. Barbour
Joseph S. Brooks
E. H. Coleman
C. M. Fleissner
Edgar H. Howell
J. T. Kergan
Hubert E. Law

Guy E. Manning
J. H. D. Roger
Lee S. Seward
J. J. Smith
Joseph Visali
James W. Ward
H. J. Wright

INTERNES

Lester E. Tretheway

Charles L. Trout

SENIORS

Sharon Marion Atkins
Royal Rohan Baronidis
Marius André Francoz
Ernest Clarence Griner

Robert A. Powers
Doulton Ronald Shoemaker
John Fred Steele
Fritz Stein

John W. Taylor

JUNIORS

Vernon George Alderson
Dean Alfred Crew
H. G. Griffith

John Kiernan
Joseph Andrew Polla
Monroe Sutter

Sharon Atkins   Royal Baronidis   Marius Francois   Ernest Gruner
Robert Powers   Houlton Shoemaker   John Steele   Fritz Stren
John Taylor   Vernon Alderson   Dean Crow   H. Griffith
                       John Kirkman   Joseph Polits

Phi Chi
[Medical]

Founded at University of Vermont, March 1, 1886.
Phi Delta Phi Chapter—Established December 31, 1908.

FACULTY

Rene Bine
George Washington Corner
Louis Philippe Howe
Phillip Edward Smith
Felix Henri Hurni
George H. Martin
James Craig Neel

INTERNES

Charles P. Mathe
Robert Stanton Sherman

FELLOWS
Hooper Foundation for Medical Research.

Arthur Elmer Belt
Charles C. Hall
Harry Pratt Smith

SENIORS

Pini Joseph Calvi
Charles Alfred Craig
William Christenson Frey
George Stevenson Holeman
Elmo Russell Zumwalt
Merrill Windsor Hollingsworth
Hugh Elmer Penland
Lewis L. Seligman
John Chilton Williams

JUNIORS

Thomas Floyd Bell
Cavius Deter Hart
William Patrick Joseph Lynch
William Otto Saloman

SOPHOMORES

Dwight Elmer Farrington
John M. Keefe
Rolland Louis Thompson
James McGeough Sullivan
Bert Stanford Thomas

FRESHMEN

Marmion Hugo Childress
Granville Sinclair Delamere
Frank Kelsey Haight
Charles Whitney Loraine
George Anderson Williams
Irvine McQuarrie
Elwood Richard Olsen
Randolph Sharpstein
Claude Verner Thompson

Felix Harni	Arthur Belt	Charles Hall	Harry Smith	Pete Calvo	Charles Craig
William Frey	George Holeman	M. Hollingsworth	Hugh Fenland	Lewis Seligman	John Williams
Elmo Zumwalt	Thomas Bell	Cavins Hart	William Lynch	William Soloman	D. Farrington
James Sullivan	Bert Thomas	Roland Thompson	Matnson Childress	Granville Delamere	Frank Haight
	Irvine McQuarrie	Elwood Olsen	R. Sharpstein	Claude Thompson	

Kappa Psi
[Pharmacy]

Founded at Richmond College in 1879
Beta Gamma Chapter—Established, 1910

FACULTY
J. N. Patterson

GRADUATE
George F. Murphy

SENIORS

Ellsworth Myrl Cipperly
James Paul Doyle
Clifford Frank Hawkins
Edward F. Henle
Hugo L. Menke
Emory Julius Moltzen
Walter John Murphy
Ernest C. Pruess
Harold LeRoy Rogers
John Ray Russell

Lester Allen Upham

JUNIORS

Vernon Douglas Bagley
Orlo George Bailey
Harold Tartan Bush
Everett C. Cox
Kenneth Fredrick Farnsworth
David Roosevelt Hutchinson
Rudolphus Clay Knowlton
Francis Culbertson Moody
Charles Wesley Phelps
Joseph Augostino Piuma
Harold Colvin Turner
Oliver Roy Tuttle
Cairns Howard Vogelman
James Herbert Walker

George Versell Williams

George Murphy   E. Cipperly   Clifford Haskins   Edward Hente   Hugo Menke   Emory Moltzen
Walter Murphy   Ernest Pruess   Harold Rogers   John Russell   Lester Upham   Vernon Bagley
Orlo Bailey   Harold Bush   Everett Cox   K. Farnsworth   D. Hutchinson   H. Knowlton
Francis Moody   Charles Pledge   Joseph Pruess   Harold Turner   Oliver Tuttle
Carus Vogelman   James Walker   George Williams

Phi Alpha Delta
[Legal]

Founded at Chicago Law School in 1897.
Jackson Temple Chapter—Established in 1911.

HONORARY

Frank M. Angellotti John E. Richards
Andrew Y. Wood

FACULTY
James Arthur A. Ballentine

THIRD YEAR

Thomas Churchill Nelson Charles Verne Taylor
Oscar Charles Parkinson Charles Tryer
Robert Merrill Tapscott Strother Perry Walton

SECOND YEAR

Loui Charles Beauman Herbert Edwin Hall
Carter Corson Camp Lloyd Nelson Hamilton
Merritt Barton Curtis Eugene Alston Hawkins
Elbert Willard Davis Reginald Heber Linforth
Frederick Ponciano Feliz, Jr. Robert Clarence Ogden
Paul Langstreth Fussell Henry Roscoe Schultheis
Gerald Hanna Hagar Milton William Vedder

FIRST YEAR

Eliot Frost Landon Frank McDonald Ogden
John Emmett McNamara Stanford Geary Smith
Howard Fitzroy Magee Jesse DeWitt Stockton

Oscar Parkinson   Charles Taylor   Strother Walton   Leon Beaumont
Carter Camp   Elbert Davis   Paul Fuwell   Herbert Hall
Eugene Hawkins   Robert Ogden   Milton Vedder
Jesse Muckluh   Frank Ogden

Alpha Chi Sigma

(Chemistry)

Founded at University of Wisconsin, December 11, 1902.
Sigma Chapter—Established January 16, 1913.

FACULTY

Henry Chalmers Biddle
Walter Charles Blasdale
William Vere Cruess
Franklin Theodore Green

Joel Henry Hildebrand
Gilbert Newton Lewis
Edmond O'Neill
Merle Randall

GRADUATES

**Jesse Wright Barnes
Charles Stewart Bisson
Parry Borgstrom
Thomas Bow Brighton
Arthur William Christie
Ermon Dwight Eastman
William Grenville Horsch

Donald Babcock Keyes
Roy Frederick Newton
Axel Ragnar Olson
Worth Huff Rodebush
Charles Caesar Sedious
Melvin Henry Schlesinger
Ewing Carruth Scott

SENIORS

Clarence Walter Beebe
Robert Nelson Donaldson
William Frederick Fosling
Angier Hobbs Foster
William Henry Hampton
Joyce Catfield Haun

Ross McCollum
David Robert Merrill
Arthur William Mohr
Carl Albert Ranz
Charles Elroy Rhein
Howard Van A. Slater

Herbert Harvey Wheeler

JUNIORS

Willard Gail Babcock
John Stephen Desmond
Julius Theodore Hansen
Carl Iddings

William Arthur McCollum
*David Porter Miles
William Douglas Ramage
Reginald Bryant Rule

SOPHOMORES

Dwight Cooley Bardwell

Leland Harris Nielsen

Lewis August Penn

---

*Absent on leave.
**Graduated December, 1916.

Jesse Barnes	Parry Burgesson	Thomas Brighton	Arthur Christie	William Hotsch	Roy Newton
Axel Olson	Charles Scaloue	M. Schlesinger	Ewing Scott	Clarence Bevie	R. Donaldson
William Foshag	Hobbs Foster	William Hampton	Ross McCollum	David Metcalf	Arthur Mohr
Carl Reus	Charles Risen	Howard Slater	Herbert Wheeler	Willard Babcock	John Desmond
	Julius Hansen	Carl Iddings	Wm. McCullum	William Ramage	Reginald Rule
		Dwight Bardwell	Lewis Penn		

Phi Delta Kappa
[Educational]
Founded at the University of Indiana in 1910.
Lambda Chapter—Established in 1913.

HONORARY MEMBERS

Philander P. Claxton
David Prescott Barrows
Alexis Frederick Lange

FACULTY MEMBERS

John Siegfried Bolin
Richard Ganse Boone
Ruliff S. Holway
Ira Woods Howerth
William Grandville Hummel
William Webb Kemp
Frank L. Kleeberger
Charles Edward Rugh
Winfield Scott Thomas
Baldwin M. Woods

GRADUATES

George Leslie Albright
William John Cooper
Frederick Warren Cozens
Harold Hammond Cozens
Paul Stout Crafton
Leroy Lowry Doig
Albert Howard Hankey
Robert Williard Hodgson
Einar William Jacobsen
Milton Vernon Johns
Earl Alexander McDermont
Lloyd Meeham
Guy Evan Needham
William Henry Poytress
William Gerry Rector
Knowles Augustus Ryerson
Clarence Nevil Smith
Herman Adolph Spindt
Carl Louis Thiele
Leo Ainslie Wadsworth
Arthur Pryor Watts

SENIORS

William Campbell Binkley
Ray Orten Diether
Carl George Hjelte
Mason Allen Johnston
George Lawrence Maxwell
Warren Dexter Norton
L. Ray Ogden
William Guy Paden
Roy Everet Warren

William Cooper   Harold Cearns   Paul Crafton   Leroy Deep   Howard Hankey   Robert Hodgson
Einar Jacobsen   Milton Johns   Earl McDermont   Lloyd Merkam   Guy Needham   William Poviews
William Hector   Knowles Byerson   Herman Spindt   Carl Theile   Leo Wadsworth   Arthur Watts
    William Binkley   Ray Doerber   George Hpelte   Mason Johnston   Lawrence Maxwell
            Warren Norton   Ray Ogden   William Paden

Omega Upsilon Phi
Founded at the University of Buffalo, November 15, 1894.
Omega Chapter—Established in 1914.

FACULTY
William Ford Blake

JUNIOR
Charles Louis Freytag

SOPHOMORES
Chester Arthur DeLaney Heinz George Hummel
Hans von Gehlern

FRESHMAN
Clarence Griffith Potter

PRE-MEDICAL
Thomas Gerald Hall Morrell Emeric Vecki
Albert Howard Linn Allan Raymond Watson
Frank Ignatius Wolongiewicz

Charles Freytag Chester DeLancy Hans von Geldern
Clarence Potter Thomas Hall Albert Linn
Morrell Veeks Allan Watson Frank Wislongowics

SORORITIES

Kappa Alpha Theta

Founded at De Pauw University January 3, 1870.
Omega Chapter--Established April 12, 1890

FACULTY
Maude Cleveland

GRADUATES
Jane Birdsall Bangs **Helen Crawford
Ruth Mary Edinger

SENIORS
Pauline Adams
**Gertrude Van Dyke Bangs
Katherine Van Dyke Bangs
Elise Carolyn Berthem
Barbara Burke
Marian Elizabeth Christensen
Pauline Dillman
Olivetta Faulkner
**Marion Eccelston Fitzhugh
Margaret Calder Hayes
*Katherine Kirkpatrick
**Jessie Mildred Lewis
Anna Harding McCabe
**Sepha Dohrman Pischel
*Marie Porter

JUNIORS
Eleanor Burnham
Helen Crenshaw
Abby White Edwards
Margaret Eddy House
*Ruth Evelyn Kroll
Hanna Rahtjen
Helen Barton Smyth
Lillian Thekla Stephany
Winifred Tinning

SOPHOMORES
Mary Ware Allen
Marion Merideth Bogle
Elizabeth Burnham
Catherine Holton Fletcher
Helen J. Geary
Margaret Louise Geary
Mary Elizabeth Harrison
Merodine Keeler
Erida Louise Leuschner
Agnes Ricker Polsdorfer
Augusta Payne Rathbone
Ruth Vincent

FRESHMEN
Margaret Lois Carr
Helen Holman
Selena Pope Ingram
*Lucretia McNear
Elizabeth Thacher
Katherine Amelia Towle
Mary Hoadley West
Pauline Patten Whittlesey
Pauline Wilkinson

*Absent on leave
**Graduated December, 1916.

Jane Bangs	H. Crawford	Pauline Adams	Gert'de Bangs	Kath'ne Bangs	E. Bertheau	Barbara Burke
M. Christensen	P. Dillman	O. Faulkner	M. Fitzhugh	Marg't Hayes	K. Kirkpatrick	Jessie Lewis
Anna McCabe	Sophia Paekel	Marie Porter	E. Burnham	H. Crenshaw	Abby Edwards	Margaret Howe
Ruth Krull	H. Rahtjen	Helen Smyth	L. Stephany	W. Tinning	Mary Allen	Marion Bogle
E. Burnham	C. Fletcher	Helen Geary	Marg't Geary	M. Harmon	M. Keeler	E. Leuerbner
A. Poindorfer	A. Rathbone	Ruth Vincent	Marg't Carr	Helen Hidman	Selena Ingram	E. Thacher
	Kath'ne Towle	Mary West	P. Whittbery	Pauline Wilkinson		

Gamma Phi Beta

Founded at the University of Syracuse, November 11, 1874.
Eta Chapter—Established November 4, 1894.

GRADUATES

Phyllis Ackerman
Sarah Paine Daniels
Jeannette Ralph Dyer

SENIORS

Margaret Louise Boveroux
Barbara Bridge
**Elizabeth Hoyt
Frances Carey Jones
Cora Floyd Kesler
Florence Mary Macaulay
*Elizabeth Whitney Putnam

Elizabeth Mary Ruggles
Sarah Davis Sabin
*Annie Hardin Sherman
Frances Coulon Sweezey
Leslie Underhill
Inita Margaret Wann
*Ellender Wills

JUNIORS

Alice Bradley
Muriel Margaret Cameron
*Elsie Keeney Jones
Lesley Edith Williams

Irene Ray
Esther Sarah Sinclair
Beatrice Washburn

SOPHOMORES

Ruth Anderson
Eunice Marie Barstow
Carolyn Jane Bolles
*Dorothy Ward Clarke
*Isabel Bonnar Faye
Jennie Laura Fiske

Florence Amelia Hofer
*Helen Grieve McLean
Olive Mills
Jessie Ingram Roberts
*Genevieve E. Tully
Ruth Ethel Wetmore

FRESHMEN

Helen Brehm
Elizabeth Ross Buffington
Ida Persis Edwards
Helena Kemp Fairbanks
Eleanor Ruth Gardner
Dorothy Ellis Hannah
Katherine Martha Lahann

Dorothy Dalrymple Meredith
Marie Lydia Park
Ellen Mary Power
Annette Emilie Ruggles
Pearly Saul
Helen Earle Sutherland
*Frances Von Barneveld

*Absent on leave.
**Graduated December, 1916.

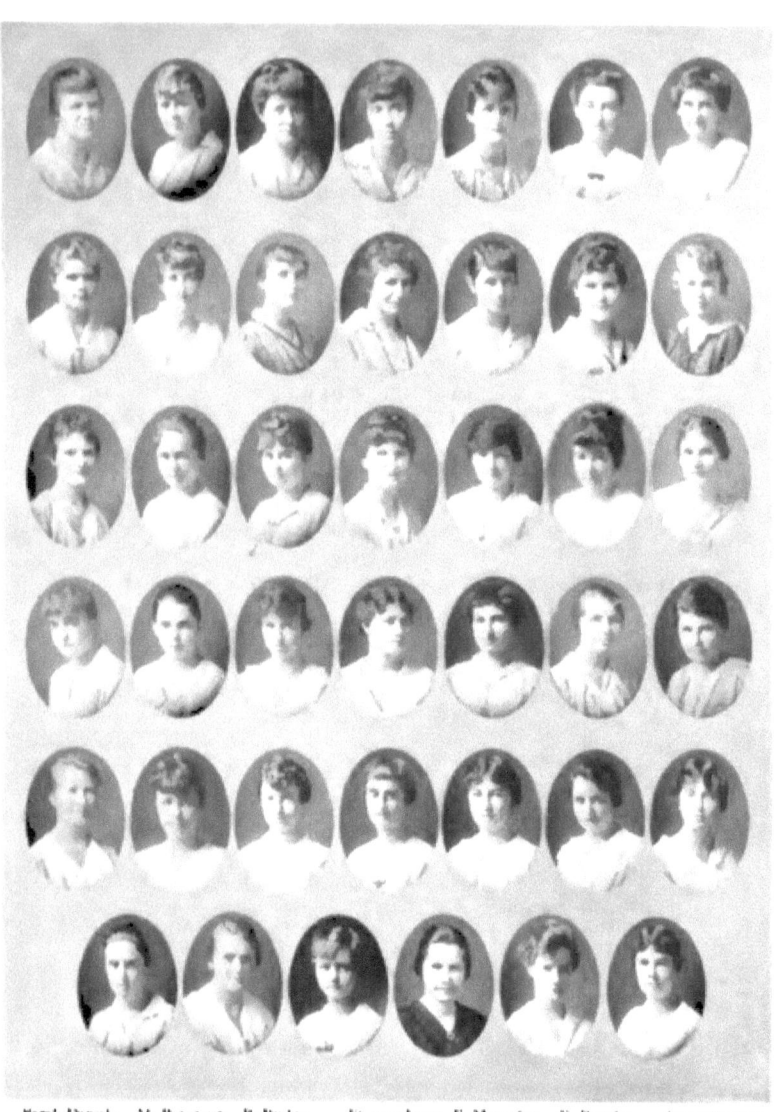

Sarah Daniels   M. Bevereau   B. Budge   Frances Jones   F. Macaulay   E. Ruggles   Annie Sherman
F. Sweeney   L. Underhill   Imra Wann   Alice Bradley   M. Cameron   Elsie Jones   Irene Ray
Esther Sinclair   L. Williams   Ruth Anderson   E. Burstow   C. Holler   Dorothy Clark   Isabel Faye
Jenne Fiske   Florence Holet   Helen McLean   Olive Mills   Jessie Roberts   Ruth Westmore   Helen Brehm
E. Buffington   Ida Edwards   H. Fairbanks   F. Gardner   D. Hannah   K. Lobaan   D. Meredith
        Marie Park   Ellen Power   A. Ruggles   Pearly Saul   H. Sutherland   F. Van Barneveld

Kappa Kappa Gamma

Founded at Monmouth College, October 13, 1870.
Pi Chapter—Established May 22, 1880; Re-established August 5, 1897.

FACULTY

Marjorie John Armour Mrs. Mary Blossom Davidson

GRADUATE

Dulce de la Cuesta

SENIORS

Leila Baldwin Berry
Margarette Dermont
Emily Harriet Huntington
Donna Moses
Elise Posey

Ruth Almede Smith
Nana Stevick
Ruth Allison Turner
Anne Radford Wharton
Elizabeth Louise Witter

Esther Louise Witter

JUNIORS

Vera Lillian Christie
Estelle Eliza Cook
Clarascott Goodloe

Myrtle Ramon Henrici
Florence Isaacs
Ruth Sherman

Dorothy Stoner

SOPHOMORES

Madeline Mary Benedict
Bernice Charlme Carr
Helene Cowell
Sara d'Ancona
Dorothy Park Davis

Henrietta Katharina Johnson
Margaret Elizabeth Monroe
Constance Rogers
Dorothy Virginia Schulze
Edith Cain Stirman

Marjorie Waldron

FRESHMEN

Mary Knowles Adams
Delight Brown
Jean Budge
Narcissa Mary Cerini
Florence Crellin
Mildred Fleming
Helen Virginia Gohn

Mignon Keith Henrici
Virginia Lane
Elizabeth Amelia Merrill
Dorothy Palmer
Mildred Spencer Ponting
Marietta Reed
Mildred Alexander Salmons

Susan Talmadge

Leila Berry	M. Dermont	F. Huntington	Donna Moses	Elsie Posey	Ruth Turner	Anne Wharton
E. Witter	Esther Witter	Vera Christie	Estelle Cook	C. Goodloe	Myrtle Heuter	Florence Isaacs
Ruth Sherman	D. Stoner	M. Benechet	Bernice Cutt	Helene Cowell	Sara d'Ancona	Dorothy Davis
H. Johnson	M. Monroe	C. Rogers	D. Schulte	M. Waldron	Mary Adams	Delight Brown
Jean Budge	N. Crosa	Florence Crellin	M. Fleming	Virginia Godin	M. Henrici	Virginia Lane
	E. Merrall	D. Palmer	M. Ponting	Marietta Reed	M. Salmons	Susan Talmadge

Delta Delta Delta

Founded at Boston University, November 29, 1888.
Pi Chapter—Established April 14, 1900.

GRADUATES

*Marion Clark
Edith Frisbie
Virginia Mills
Alice Spaulding Watson

SENIORS

Lois Brulyn Benton
Beatrice Louise Bonner
Miriam Eckart
Alice Bunnell Elliot
Elizabeth Van Everen Ferguson
Myrtle Viola Fitschen
Valerie Ailene Foveaux
Ruth Seymour
Dorothy Ashton Shade
Jessie Florence Todhunter

JUNIORS

Catherine Margaret Ashley
Marion Avery
**Louise Cahoon
Blanche G. Coulter
Valance Scott Cowan
Anna Margarette Davis
Muriel Drury
Virginia Marsden
Edith Louise Monroe
*Ellis Ellis Morris
Alice Rebecca Morrison
Bernice Lorraine Olney
*Helen Mary Roeth
Lucille Rother Vazeille

SOPHOMORES

Margaret Carter
Elinor Clark
Hilda Noble Cowan
Vera Helen Gardiner
Gladys Minnie Gotham
Anita Howard
Ruth Lowe
**Bessie Rae Markheim
Helen Rebecca Montgomery
Dorothy Cornelia Rudy
*Wilma Wilson Sill
*Ada Smith
Carolyn Steel

FRESHMEN

Emma Madeline Becker
Placie Margaret Howard
Emma Elizabeth Jarvis
Margaret Alicia Wood
*Margaret Elizabeth Leach
Carmelita Parma
Elizabeth Seymour

*Absent on leave.
**At Affiliated Colleges.

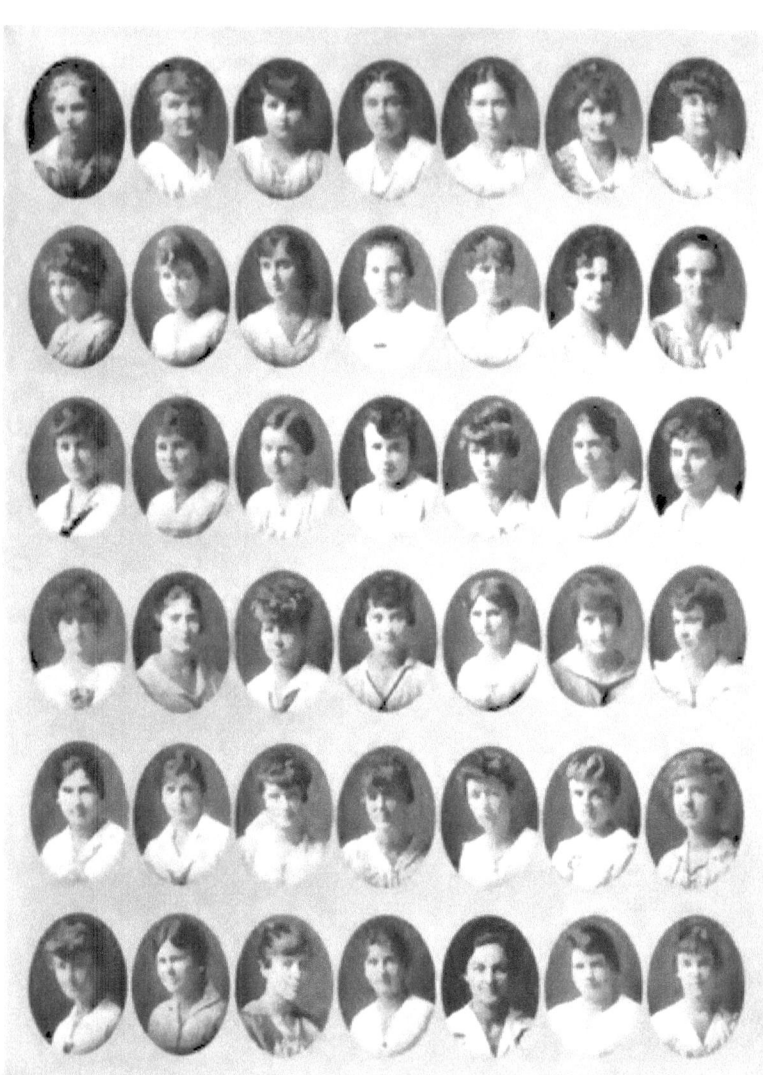

Lois Benton	L. Bonner	Miriam Eckart	Alice Elliot	E. Ferguson	M. Finchen	V. Foreman
Hugh Seymour	Dorothy Steele	J. Trollinger	C. Ashley	Marion Avery	Louise Calhoun	B. Coglier
V. Cowan	Anna Davis	Mabel Drury	N. Marsden	Edith Monroe	Elsie Morris	A. Morrison
Bernice Osley	Helen Roesh	L. Angelle	M. Carter	Elinor Clark	Hoda Cowan	Vera Gardiner
Gladys Graham	Anita Howard	D. Markham	H. Montgomery	D. Reely	Wilma Silt	Carolyn Steel
Madeline Becker	Phene Howard	Emma Jarvis	M. Leach	C. Parton	E. Seymour	Margaret Wood

Pi Beta Phi

Founded at Monmouth College, April 28, 1867.
California Beta Chapter—Established August 27, 1900.

GRADUATES

**Adah Roberts Holmes
Mirabel Minnie Stewart
Olive Payn Taylor
Katherine Helen Westbrook

SENIORS

Rosamond Jordan Bradbury
Pauline Chamberlain
Marion Clarice Downey
Octavia Downie
Elizabeth Mabelle Snyder
Dorothy Elizabeth Wetmore

JUNIORS

Alice Dorothy Daniels
Mary Carmichael Downie
Pauline Finnell
Marie Naomi Gravin
Marjorie Ethel Hendricks
Madeline Marritt Sanford
Catherine Helene Woolsey

SOPHOMORES

Frances Latham Bolton
Kathryn Coe
Marguerite Ella Eastwood
Irene Howard
Gladys Amelia Hulting
Eva McClatchy
Martha Kathryn Magaw
Doris Sabra Moulton
Margaret Rolph
Genevieve Spader
Lillian Suydam
Janet Thompson
Muriel Loftus Tottenham
Ruth Isabel Ware

FRESHMEN

*Dorothea Blair
*Henriette Brousseau
*Harriet Carter
Edith Bertha Corde
Harriet Gregory Crabtree
*Louise Gimbal
Helen Carey Hayes
Mary Nelson Johnson
Agnes Land
*Ruth Lucas
Mildred Metzner
Marion Josephine Mills
Elizabeth Jane Rutherford
Pauline Isabel Turner
Grace Walker

---

*Absent on leave.
**At Affiliated Colleges.

Alpha Phi

Founded at Syracuse University, October 20, 1872.
Lambda Chapter—Established May 9, 1901.

GRADUATES
Belle Tuttle Radcliff

SENIORS

Anna Frances Barrows
Katherine Chaney
Gladys Gray Hobron

Louise Keeney
Ruth Kinkead
Rosselet A. Wallace

JUNIORS

Hortense Louise Berry
Margaret Wilson Honeywell
Ramona Marks
Jane Marie Morrill
Margaret Elliot Murdock

Helen Matlack Olmsted
*Julia Dart Tinkham
Katherine Whitton
E. Pauline Wood
Jean Wright

SOPHOMORES

Ella Cole Barrows
Geraldine Markham Hall
*Christine Howells
Esther Margaret Langley
M. Ethel Langley
*Helen McGee
Helen Morlise

Laurinne Easter Mattern
Helen Hall Moreland
*Josephine Ella Park
Katharine Pratt
*Dorothy Sanford
*Edith Louise Shearman
Frances Geraldine Shurtleff

FRESHMEN

Eleanor Barnard
Frances Edward Beveridge
Katherine De Celle
*Helena Howells
*Marion Anita Kergan
Margaret McLaughlin

Mary Griffith Nichols
Helen Mumford Playter
*Jane Charlotte Richardson
Catherine Barclay Russell
Marjorie Scott
*Leontine Wallace

*Absent on leave

B. Radcliff	A. Burrows	K. Claney	G. Hebron	L. Kersey	R. Kinkead	R. Wagner	
H. Berry	M. Honeywell	R. Marks	J. Morrill	M. Murdock	H. Olmstead	D. Tinkham	
K. Whitton	P. Wood	J. Wright	E. Burrows	G. Hall	C. Howells	E. Langley	
Ethel Langley	H. McGee	H. Maclow	L. Matter	H. Moreland	J. Park	K. Pratt	
D. Sanford	F. Shearman	F. Shurtleff	E. Barnard	F. Beveridge	K. De Celle	M. McLaughlin	
M. Kergan	M. Nichols	H. Playter	J. Richardson	C. Russell	M. Scott	L. Walker	

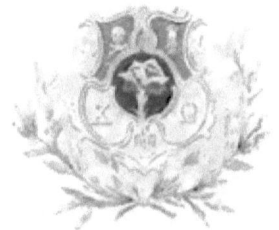

Chi Omega

Founded at University of Arkansas, April 5, 1895.
Mu Chapter—Established August 13, 1902.

GRADUATES

Loretta Bernice Ross
Mabel Wyllie
Hazel Odette Thompson

SENIORS

Zelma Alice Carroll
Dorothy Harriet Huggins
Marian Shaw Stayner
Meta Nelson
Joycelyn Elaine Reynolds

JUNIORS

Laura Lillian Akin
Helen Virginia Davis
Beatrice Gerberding
Marie Maps Hanlon
Kathryn Irene Wyllie
Norene Howe
Ruth Helen Kimball
Elizabeth Anne Muefie
Genevieve Taggard

SOPHOMORES

Maurine Elise Gilliam
Clara Bailey Gregory
Virginia Holmes
Ethel Howell
Pauline Du Bratz Justice
Lulu Grace Wells
Mildred Teresa Kenworthy
*Dorothy Wade Lowell
Ruby Elizabeth McLellan
Dorotea Alicia Newell
*Nellie Laura Walker

FRESHMEN

Marion Bushnell Ayer
Margaret Berkeley Beatie
Elizabeth Wood Carnahan
Hilma Davis
Julia Thomas Hamilton
Louise Emma Pfister
Ruth Robinson
Grace Nicholl Willson

*Absent on leave.

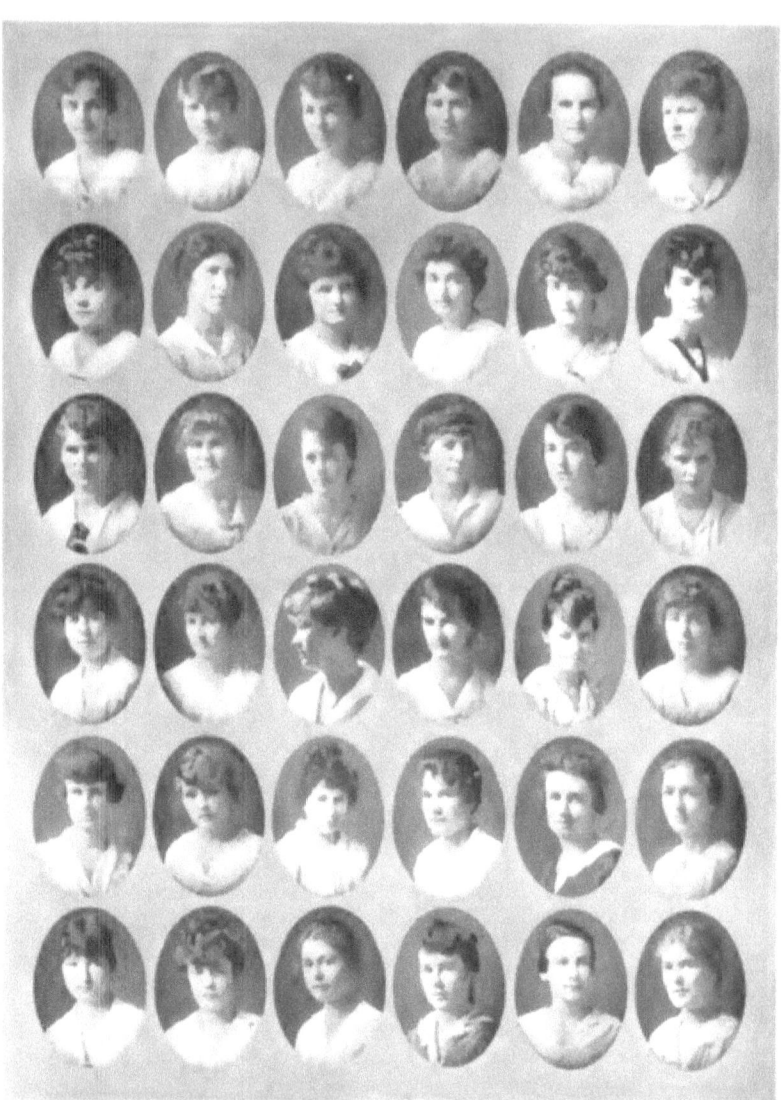

Loretta Ross / Joycelyn Reynolds / Norene Howe / Clara Gregory / Ruby McLellan / E. Carnahan
Hazel Thompson / Marian Stayner / Ruth Kimball / Virginia Holmes / Dorotea Newell / Hilma Davis
Mabel Wyllie / Laura Akin / Elizabeth Macfie / Ethel Howell / Nellie Walker / Julia Hamilton
Zelma Carrol / Helen Davis / Genevieve Taggard / Pauline Justice / Lulu Wells / Lenore Phater
Dorothy Huggins / B. Gerhardbing / Irene Wyllie / M. Kenworthy / Marion Ayer / Ruth Robinson
Meta Nelson / Marie Hanlon / Maxine Gilliam / Dorothy Lowell / Margaret Beane / Grace Wilson

Alpha Omicron Pi

Founded at Barnard College, Columbia University January 2, 1897
Sigma Chapter—Established February 8, 1907.

GRADUATE
Edna May Taber

SENIORS

Marion Bachman
Helen Wheeler Clowes
Alice Beulah Cranston
Elizabeth Frances Elliott
Gladys Irma Goeggel
*Kathryn Hubbard
Ethel Anna Moroney
Rosalinda Amelia Olcese
Gertrude Agnes Schieck

JUNIORS

*Winifred Marie Butler
Ella Genevieve Crawford
*Bernice Hubbard
Marguerite Eugenie Neely

SOPHOMORES

Marjorie Armstrong
Miriam Anna Beal
Gertrude Briggs Day
Thelma Evelyn Donovan
*M. Aileen Evans
Margaret Forsyth
Lucile Graham
Margaret Rosemary McVey
Helen Louise Schieck
Dorothy Weeks
Mary Roberta Wight

FRESHMEN

Marion Alice Black
Nancy Esther Cardwell
Virginia Cook
Catharine Virginia Cox
Laura de Veuve
Nadine Guerne Donovan
Anna Gay Doolittle
Hattie Marie Heller
Mildred Mallon
Marian Hilliard Matthew
Katherine Virginia Pride
Gertrude Edwina Robie
Marjorie Inez Selwood
Beatrice May St. John
Amelia Newbury Williams

*Absent on leave

Edna Taber — Marion Bachman — Helen Clowes — Alice Cranston — E. Elliott — Gladys Goerged
Ethel Moloney — Gertrude Schoek — Marie Butler — Ella Crawford — Bernice Holdstadt — Marguerite Neely
M. Armstrong — Miriam Beal — Gertrude Day — Thelma Donovan — Margaret Forsyth — Lucile Graham
Margaret McVey — Helen Schoek — Dorothy Weeks — Mary Wight — Marion Black — Nancy Cardwell
Virginia Cook — Catharine Cox — Nadine Donovan — Anna Gay Doolittle — Hattie Heller — Mildred Mallon
Marion Matthew — Katherine Prole — Edwina Rolor — Marjorie Selwood — Laura de Veuve

Delta Gamma

Founded at the University of Mississippi, January 2, 1872.
Gamma Chapter—Established April 12, 1907.

GRADUATES

Doris Marianne Hutchins
Mabel Harrison Longley

SENIORS

Euphemia Marguerite Allen
Maud Carol Eberts
*Vivien Ellerbeck
Dorothy Epping
Jane Caroline Halbert
Lucile Hooper
Mildred Dorothy Kellogg
Esther Laurilla King
Margaret Elizabeth Moore
Helen Virginia Platt
*Ernst Denny Taggart
**Ruth Elizabeth Thornburg

Laura Amy Walden

JUNIORS

Virginia Armstrong Baldwin
Lavinia Brown
Leslie Brown
Marian Brown
Margaret Denton Cornwall
Lucia Byrne Fox
Helen Katherine Kellogg
Helen Bailey Leete
Mary Edith Lipman
Dorothy Hills Perry

SOPHOMORES

Helen May Allan
Helen Baker
Kathryn Cook
Angus Barbara Cowan
*Marie Consuelo Dieckmann
Ruth Wedgwood Doggett
Margaret Carter Gridlin
Clara Gertrude Huffman
Helen Leuthold
Eleanor Lowell
Louise Ratcliffe
*Margaret Jane Welch

FRESHMEN

Ada Maie Applegate
Lenore Barclay
Margaret Alice Breedlove
Margaret Eberts
Dorothy Speare
Dorothy Helen Williams

Evelyn Butler Witherspoon

*Absent on leave.
**Graduated, December, 1916.

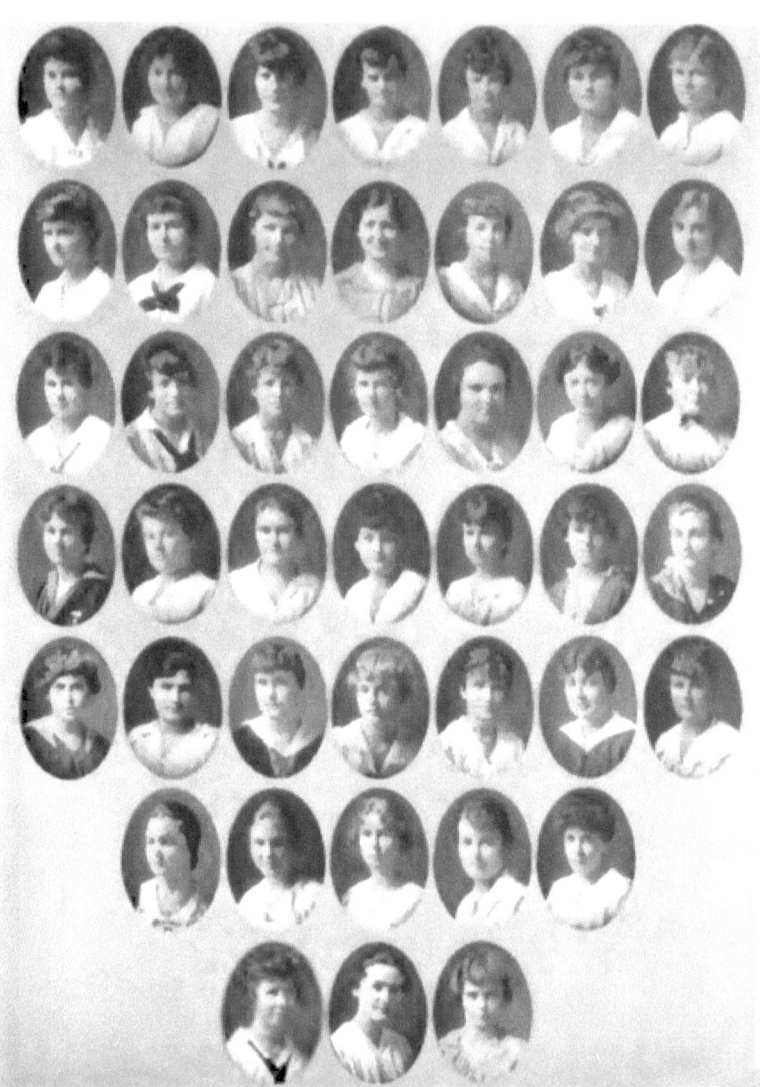

Alpha Xi Delta

Founded at Lombard College April 17, 1893.
Omicron Chapter—Established May 9, 1907.

FACULTY
Ruth C. Risdon

GRADUATES
Ruth Ransom Calden
Alice Gertrude Plummer

SENIORS
Freda Cadell Bayley
Marion Evans
Dolores Gibson
Stella Marguerite Liss
Frances Caroline Lowell
Norah McKenzie
Margaret Irene Mersereau
Helen Jett Swortfiguer
Lucile Welch
Florence Zauder

JUNIORS
Phyllis Marian Bateman
Donetta Channing Brainard
Vera Bullwinkle
Grace Lucille Dixon
Evelyn Farrar
Dorothy Johanna Hillman
Eileen Rose Kengla
Marjorie Isabel Stuart
Margaret Jane Taylor
Marguerite Templeton
Florence Grace Waldo
Beatrice Vesta Winder

Madeleine Grant Young

SOPHOMORES
Ruth Dewing Barry
Ruth Margaret Carmichael
Carolyn Ramona Gray
Eugenie Phyllis Hawkins
Helene Hickman
Katherine Holmes
Almira Ada McLaughlin
Margaret Elizabeth Martin
Doris Margaret Sherman
Dorothy Shrodes

Florence Welch

FRESHMEN
Mary Kathleen Cooper
Ruth Estelle Cooper
Melba De Witt
Beatrice Ellen Dorn
Mervil Hiscox
Katherine Dorenda Maltby

Adrienne Williams

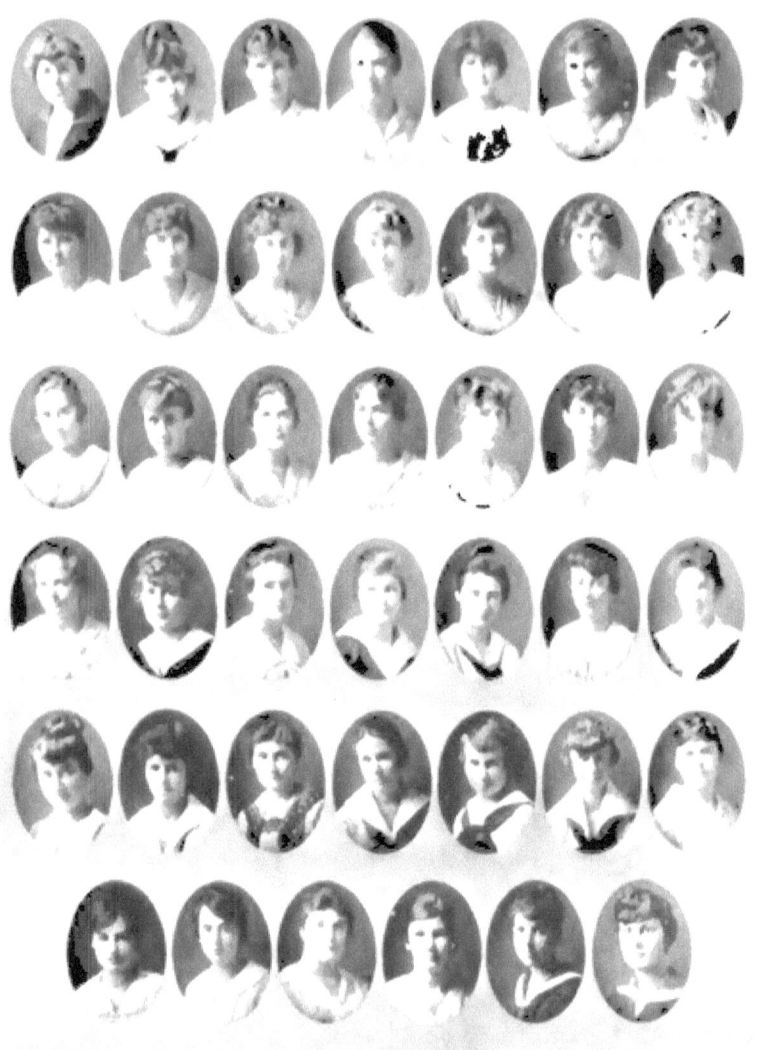

Alpha Chi Omega

Founded at De Pauw University, October 15, 1885.
Pi Chapter—Established May 7, 1900.

GRADUATES

Katherine Crossley
Blanche Mabel Marshall
Frances Lodema Shurtleff

SENIORS

Bertha Mabel Galloway
Louise Egerton Keen
Esther Kittredge
Coe Elizabeth McCabe
Doris Elizabeth McEntyre
Narcisa Poola
Katharine Frances Quinn
**Ruth Robbins Swasey

JUNIORS

Leila Antoinette Beckley
Corena Emogene Daugherty
Mary Daviess Gaines
Ruth Virginia Gaines
Lucille Henry
Pernelia Catharine Holt
Ruth Raymond Lange
Mary Roselia Lee
Penelope R. McEntyre
*Katharine Rose Mason
Edith Catharine Meyer
Gayle Elizabeth Partridge
Virginia Somes Sanderson
Elsie Mae Simmock
Gladys Mary Windham

SOPHOMORES

Margaret McMillan Allen
Alma Caroline Berude
Florence Leone Champlin
Vera Mae Chatfield
Lyllis Aileen Daugherty
Edith Caroline Horstman
Madeline Farrington Keith
Louise Esther Lackland
*Miriam Dinn Marks
Gertrude Elsie Marshall
*Kathleen Shores
Ethelwynne Beth Sites

FRESHMEN

Ruth Brown Chatfield
Mildred Wynta Estabrook
Rose Sedgwick Keith
Madelyn Gertrude Lenahan
Mignon Beth Merrick
Irma Claire Pfitzer
Frances Alice Porter
Helen May Searls
Aline Verne
Margaret Bethany Westenberg

*Absent on leave
**Graduated December, 1916.

hundred and ten

Sigma Kappa

Founded at Colby College, November 20, 1874.
Lambda Chapter—Established April 25, 1910.

GRADUATES

Grace Van Dyke Bird
*Pearl Cessna
Marguerite Cordell
Helen Hopkins
Rosamond Parvin
Ruth Irene Preston
Claire Althea Tucker

SENIORS

Helen Lucille Brayton
Algeline May Marlow
**Emilie Roberta Poppe
Helen Teter
Gertrude Lucy Young

JUNIORS

Helen Elizabeth Brown
Alice Ida Eastwood
Nina Marie Hallock
Marjorie Clothilde LaGrave
Myrtle Aileen Larson

SOPHOMORES

Camille Albee
Irma Leone Bennett
*Edith Jane Lawrence
Margaret Lucile Smith
Alma Thornburg
Leona Ellen Weeks
May Palmer Wright

FRESHMEN

Margaret Dorothy Alburtus
Frances Gertrude Baron
Marjorie Mae Bonner
Nellie Susan Campbell
Alice Ray Dickson
Alberta Elms
Marguerite Mae Fellows
*Hughena Gordon
Ruth Elaine McGarry
Bertha Marie Owen
Frances Caroline Preston
Ruth Jennette Rogers
Lucille Mae Slade
Arline Gertrude Weeks
Ruby Kusan West

*Absent on leave.
**Graduated December, 1916.

Pearl Crouse	Helen Hopkins	Claire Tucker	Helen Brayton	A. Marlow	Emilie Poppe
Helen Jeter	Gertrude Young	Helen Brown	Alice Eastwood	Nina Hallock	Marjorie LaGrave
Myrtle Larson	Camille Altee	Irma Bennett	F. Lawrence	Marg't Smith	Alma Thornburg
Leona Weeks	May Wright	M. Albertus	Frances Bacon	M. Bonner	Nellie Campbell
Alice Dickson	Alberta Elms	M. Fellows	H. Gordon	Ruth McGarry	Bertha Owen
Frances Preston	Ruth Rogers	Lucile Slade	Arline Weeks	Ruby West	

Alpha Delta Pi

Founded at Wesleyan College, May 15, 1851.
Psi Chapter—Established December 6, 1913.

GRADUATES

Enid Maude Childs
Constance Gray Edmunds
Emma Mary Freeman
Rose Verl Gardner
Helen DeHaven Haynes
Olive Kuntz
Effie Maude Wilton

SENIORS

Ruth Lillian Barnes
Angenetta Idell Beasley
Mary Dorcas Batman
**Edna May Harding
Lois Ellen Harding
Olive Genevieve Hayes
Elise Henderson
Ruth Frances Hotel
Mary Edna Stonebrook

JUNIORS

Evelyn Chamberlin Adriance
Addie Viola Babb
Vera Lorraine Bicknell
May Elma Campbell
Vera Emily Crispin
Letha Belle Isom
Docia Isabel Patchett
Marion L. Underwood
Ruth Benjamin Walker
Dorothy Jean Waterhouse
Edna Margaret Williams

SOPHOMORES

Alpha June Bonney
Maud Virginia Braffett
Rosalie Davis
Eva Janet Dresser
Gladys Irene Garner
Eugenie Irene Haynes
Margaret Emily Lawton
Edith Marion McLenegan
Thelma Rothwell
*Carrie Henrietta Tessin

FRESHMEN

Helen William Bicknell
Marian Louise Blankinship
Marion Haviland
Lillian Isom
Myrtle Jeanette Morrison
Marian Powell Peterson
Alice Muirhead Wilson

*Absent on leave.
**Graduated December, 1916.

Enid Childs C. Edmunds Emma Freeman Rose Gardner Helen Haynes Olive Kuntz Effie Wilson
Ruth Barnes A. Beasley Mary Butman Edna Harding Lou Harding Olive Hayes E. Henderson
Ruth Horel M. Stonebrook E. Adanger Addie Babb Vera Bicknell May Campbell Vera Crogan
Letha Ison D. Patchett M. Underwood Ruth Walker D. Waterhouse Edna Williams Alpha Beasley
Maud Braffett Rosalie Davis Eva Dresser Gladys Garner E. Haynes Mary Lawton E. McLenegan
T. Rothwell Carrie Temin Helen Bicknell M. Blankinship M. Haviland Lillian Ison
M. Morrison M. Peterson Alice Wilson

Alpha Gamma Delta

Founded at Syracuse University, May 30, 1904.
Omicron Chapter Established March 12, 1915.

GRADUATES

Ilma Letta Badgley
**Irene Carmichael
Ruth Amy Munro

SENIORS

Marjorie Flynn
Elizabeth Erminie Keith
Violet Agnes Palmer
**Nellie Maude Secara
Jessie Elizabeth Thomas
**Merle Elizabeth Young

JUNIORS

Alta Evelyn Arnold
*Dorothea Bolster
Margaret Bullen
Lois Chilcote
Dorothy Flynn
*Virginia Fidelia Green
Irene Marguerite Breckenridge Gunn
Mary Eliza Moore

SOPHOMORES

Maud Nichols Klasgye
Mary Abigail McCleary
Dorothy Victoria Munro
Bernice Rankin
Francesca Alice Tetley
Helen Elizabeth Whiting
Elsie Mae Wocht

FRESHMEN

Roma Enola Connor
Mildred Gwin Corrick
Eleanor Gray Curtis
Harriet Anna Fink
Lois Josephine Lyons
Alice Elizabeth Mundorf
Georgia Uarda Smart
Martha Esther Smith
Lois Vivian Walker
Sarah Gertrude Wallace

*Absent on leave.
**Graduated December, 1916.

Zeta Tau Alpha

Founded at Virginia State Normal, October 29, 1898.
Upsilon Chapter—Established May 14, 1915.

GRADUATES

Anna McKenzie
Olive Smith
Carol Taber
Eva Ruth Young

SENIORS

Mary Margaret Chilson
Moxie Covington
Olga Winifred Foyle
Sadie Fredericks
Gertrude Frost
Lucy Kieldsen
Lois V. Lyon
Carey Dunlap Miller
Ethel Marie Styles
Katharyn Sweetser

Bessie Weixel

JUNIORS

Irene Baucom
Dorothy Lawrence Healy
Effie Truitt Johnston
Charlotte Favor MacGregor
Una Merryfield
Mildred Valerga
Frances Esther Walton
Pearl E. Wilson

SOPHOMORES

Alice Dixon
Marguerite Ellis
Sara June Johnston
Dorothea Langguth
Phoebe Matthews
Helen Ward Spencer
Grace Cowes Stearns
*Anna Sylvester

*Lillian Whitney

FRESHMEN

Helen Kieldsen
Helen MacGregor
Estelle Maschmeyer
Gladys Ethel Murphy

*Absent on leave.

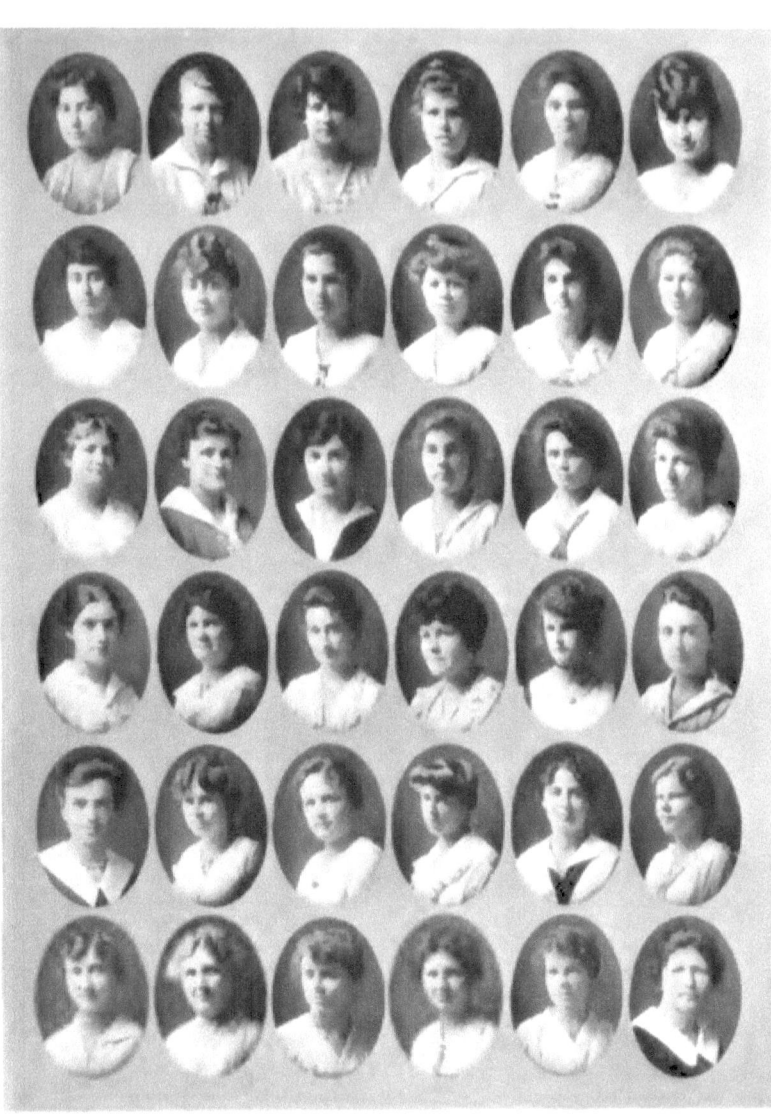

Delta Zeta

Founded at Miami University, October 24, 1902
Mu Chapter—Established August 15, 1915

GRADUATES

Augusta Ovida Caldwell
Leslie Louise Hayes

Dorothy Nell Porter
Caroline Louise Sheppa

SENIORS

Frances Leslie Brown
Winnifred Cummings
**Mildred Marie Goyette

Verna Maude Lane
Genevieve Dalton Luff
Margaret Powers Taylor

JUNIORS

Zelma Fults
Mary Esther Hamilton
Eleanor Kenyon Jennings

Helen Janet Nutting
Margo Sheppa
Edith Ueland

Gladys Dorothy Wright

SOPHOMORES

*Marian Louise Barber
Marie L. Bowes
Elinor Mary Boyle
Frances Mary Halliday
Helen Harris

Lillian Johanne Hegarty
Dora McKinlay
Mildred Violet Swanson
Carolyn May Tilley
Wilma Walton

FRESHMEN

Gladys Charity Barnum
Birdie Rosalind Fowler
Gladys Gerrish
Bernice A. Hutchison

Bessie Arvella Lepley
Gertrude Clara McGowan
Martha Helen Shea
Hulda Christine Siess

*Absent on leave.
**Graduated December, 1916.

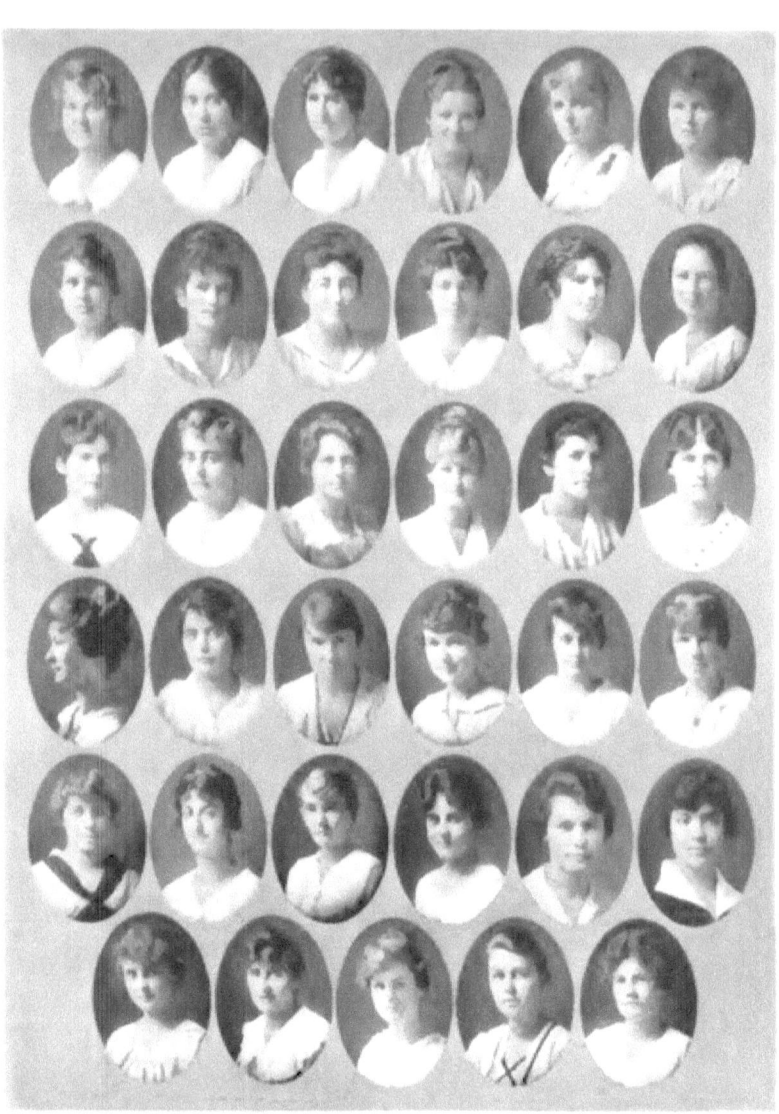

Augusta Caldwell	Leslie Hayes	Dorothy Porter	Louise Sheppe	Frances Bruno	W. Cummings
Mildred Goyette	Verna Lane	Genevieve Luff	Margaret Taylor	Zelma Fults	Mary Hamilton
Eleanor Jennings	Helen Nutting	Margo Sheppa	Edith Veland	Gladys Wright	Marsaa Barber
Marie Bowes	Elmer Boyle	Frances Halliday	Helen Harris	Lillian Hegarty	Dora McKinley
Mildred Swanson	Carolyn Tilley	Wilma Walton	Gladys Barnum	Birdie Fowler	Gladys Gerrish
	B. Hutchison	Bessie Lepley	G. McGowan	Hulda Siese	Heba Shea

Phi Mu

Founded at Wesleyan College, January 4, 1852.
Zeta Alpha Chapter—Established August 18, 1916.

GRADUATES

Helen Dorothy Dormody
**Caroline Neill

**Josephine Clara Squire
Jane Young

SENIORS

Stella Clara Andres
Ruby Catherine Campbell
Edna J. Filkin

Alice Carlena Noble
Ermyn Norton
Elfrieda Steindorff

JUNIORS

Rebecca Candelaria Borrodaile
Dorothy Dee Cooper
Leonora Margaret Doran
Louise Gretchen Jensen

Genevieve Kilpatrick
Amy Daphne Noell
*Esther English Richards
Lillian Steindorff

Alice Sheridan Towle

SOPHOMORES

Eloise Evelyn Bower
*Mable Clare Canavan
*Elsie Eva Geary
*Madeline Ethel Wadsworth

Agnes Dolores Ward
Frances Ward
Phoebe Hearst Westwood
Nellie Vance Wilson

FRESHMEN

Pauline Georgia Borrodaile
*Helen Elizabeth Bower
Caroline Matilda Brandt
Gladys Myrtle Brown
Lela Ewert

Marie Ruth Hardy
Doris Dorothea Holler
Ethel Vera Jack
Sophie Elizabeth Kohlmoos
Enid Aldweth Rogers

*Absent on leave.
**Graduated December, 1916.

Helen Donnely Josephine Squire Jane Young Stella Andrew Ruby Campbell Edna Filkin
Alice Noble Ernest Norton F. Steinhoff M. Botterdale Dorothy Cooper Leonora Doran
Louise Jensen G. Kilpatrick Amy Neill Esther Borlande Lillian Steinhoff Mary Toole
Elsne Bower Mable Canavan Elsie Geary M. Wadsworth Agnes Ward Frances Ward
Phoebe Westwood Nellie Wilson P. Botterdale Helen Bower Caroline Brandt Gladys Brown
Lela Ewert Marie Hardy Doris Holler Ethel Jack Sophie Robinson Enid Rogers

MEN'S HOUSE ▫ ▫ CLUBS ▫ ▫

Bachelordon
Organized January 3, 1894.

SENIORS

Bruce Burkis
William Henry Bingaman
Charles Lester Clark
Depue Falck
Waldemar A. Falck
Lester Albert Fowler
Robert Leroy Groves
James Edward Harbinson
George Curtis McFarland
Harold A. Morse
Floyd Erle Onyett
Emmett Phillips
Thomas William Slaven
Joseph Thomas Smith

Joseph Raegen Talbot

JUNIORS

Emmett Joseph Allen
**William Francis Carroll
Francis Eusebius Collins
Elmore William Roberts

Arthur Reihl Wilson

SOPHOMORES

Robert Ferdinand Hickey
*Vernon James
George Jackson Milburn
Kenneth Mead Morse
Abner Jean Norton
Milton Louis Roberts
Norman Irving Sangmaster
Carleton Gross Wells

FRESHMEN

Clinton Cecil Monroe
William Martin Webb

*At Affiliated Colleges.
**At Davis, January-May, 1917.

Bruce Barkus	William Bougsman	Charles Clark	Deyoe Falck	Waldemar Falck	Lester Fowler
Robert Graves	James Hathaway	George McFarland	Harold Morse	Floyd Onyett	Emmett Phillips
Thomas Slaven	Joseph Smith	Joseph Talbot	Kenneth Allen	William Carroll	Francis Collins
Elmore Roberts	Arthur Wilson	George Milbourn	Kenneth Morse	Abner Norton	Milton Roberts
	N. Sangmaster	Carleton Wells	Clinton Monroe	William Welsh	

Abracadabra

Organized, August, 1895.

FACULTY

Matthew Christopher Lynch
George H. Martin, Jr.
Leslie T. Sharp
Robert G. Sproul

GRADUATES

Fred Harold Allen
Walter Wadsworth Bradley
J. D. Mehl
Edgar Francis Sullivan
John Parker Van Zandt

SENIORS

Charles Thomas Brooks
Harold Putnam Detwiler
Evans Ronald Foster
*Ralph Evander Goodsell
**William Alexander Graham
George Hager Iverson
Elbert Wilson Lockwood
Frank Dole McCulloch
Frederick Stryker Overton
***Frank McCray Spurrier

JUNIORS

**Alvin John Nielsen
James Bestor Robinson
Henry Edwin Stafford

SOPHOMORES

Clarence Wesley Farmer
Clyde Francis Lamborn
Edward Charles Overton
Edwin LeRoy Westberg
Harold Cruver Whittlesey
Robert Francis Wright
Ross Jackson Wright

FRESHMEN

George Alfred Betts
Charles Merritt Cowell
Samuel Sterling Sherman
James Francis Shiells
*Robert Raymond Spencer
*Lee Ignacio Talbot
Gloyd Marlin Wiles

*Absent on leave.
**At Davis.
***Graduated December, 1916.

J. D. Mehl Charles Brooks Harold Detwiler Evans Foster Ralph Goodsell
William Graham George Iverson Elbert Lockwood Frank McCullowh Frederick Overton
Frank Spurrier Alvin Nielson James Robinson Henry Stafford Clarence Farmer
Clyde Lambson Edward Overton Edwin Westberg Harold Whittlesey Robert Wright
Ross Wright George Betts Charles Cosell James Shiells
Robert Spencer Lew Talbot

Dwight

Organized August, 1900.

FACULTY

Harold Child Bryant Irving Franklin Davis
Joseph Eggleson Johnston

GRADUATES

Rayford Young Barum Ames Peterson
Randall Mills Dorton Victor Eugene Simpson

SENIORS

Eugene Arthur Breyman Edwin Van Horn Mineah
Robert Earle Dorton *Benjamin Hill Ormand
James Kenneth Lochead George Francis Taylor
Paul Sylvester Marrin Ralph Eric West

JUNIORS

Randolph Arthur Christie *Elverton Chase Sutton
Harry Eldridge Peet George Francis Teale
Hubert William Sandner Edward Walter Webb

SOPHOMORES

*Gordon Williard Brayley Benjamin Stanley Parks
William Phillip Bryant Norman Cecil Raab
William Adam Fetterly Wallace Elwyn Simpson
Charles Kaiser Vergil Thomas Smith
Charles Dohn Nielson Maximillian Leo Topel
*Benjamin Franklin Ward

FRESHMEN

Lawrence William Frankle *William Austin Spridgen
George Leo Welsh

*Absent on leave.

Joseph Johnston Rayford Buram Randall Dutton Amos Peterson Eugene Breyman Robert Dutton
James Lockhead Paul Moran Edwin Muench Benjamin Ormand George Taylor Ralph West
R. Christie Harry Peet Hubert Sander Everton Sutton George Teale Edward Webb
Gordon Brayley William Bryant William Ferrerly Charles Nielsen Benjamin Parks Norman Raab
Wallace Simpson Vergil Smith Leo Topel Benjamin Ward Lawrence Frankle
George Welsh William Spridgen

Del Rey

Organized November 1, 1904.

FACULTY

****George L. Albright
William R. Ralston

GRADUATES

John Lloyd Mecham
Sidney Olsen
Herman Adolph Spindt
Leo Ainslie Wadsworth

SENIORS

William Bigelow
**Cletus Henry Graves
*Carl Paul Rapp
Charles Elroy Rhein
Hans Frank Schluter
Charles Edward Sullivan

JUNIORS

Vivian Everett Carlson
Fuller Clarkson
***Herbert Morey Coles
Carleton Carlyle Gildersleeve
Hervey King Graham
Harold Raymond Schwalenberg
Emmett Charles Taylor
Thomas Carroll Winstead

SOPHOMORES

Mervin Almon Grizzle
William Urquhart Hudson
Marc Templeton Morrissey
Lester Hall Nuland
T. Eric Reynolds
Frank Rawson Steele
Lloyd Richards Wilson
John Shelby Winstead

FRESHMEN

Lawrence Augustus Brown
Charles Hoyt Clough
William Marvin Coles
Frank Harold Graves
****Verne Frye Graves
Merrill Lee Hampton
Joe Edward Riley
Budd J. Smith
William Glenn White

*Affiliated Colleges.
**Graduated December, 1916.
***At Davis, January-May, 1917.
****Deceased.

Lloyd Meeham   Herman Spundt   Leo Wadsworth   William Barlow   Cletus Graves   Charles Rheen
Charles Sullivan   Hans Schluter   Vivian Carlson   Fuller Clarkson   Herbert Coles   C. Gildersleeve
Hervey Graham   H. Schmalenberg   Emmett Taylor   Carroll Winstead   Mervin Grazzle   William Hudson
Marc Morrowey   Lester Nuland   Eric Reynolds   Frank Steele   Lloyd Wilson   John Winstead
Lawrence Brown   Charles Clough   William Coles   Frank Graves   Verne Graves
Merrill Hampton   Joe Riley   William White

Dahlonega
Organized on August 8, 1909.

FACULTY
Baldwin Munger Woods

GRADUATES
Charles Morel Fryer Olin Harris McCord
James Wallace Spofford

SENIORS
David Frazer Bush Hilmer Oehlmann
Guy Harrison Gale William Humphreys Overshiner
Harvey Leslie Hansen Nelson Edwin Spicklemire
Will Carleton McKern Charles Dorman Woehr

JUNIORS
Donald LeRon Abercrombie Kenneth Foster Premo
Leslie Allen Cleary Earle Raymond Wall
Karl Eliot Kennedy Harry Sherman Whitthorne

SOPHOMORES
Carl St. John Bremner Eugene L. McGrane
Claude Moore Chaplin Joseph Secondo Mazildi
Martin Webster Jones Severus Lawrence Mini
Myron Alden Tobins

FRESHMEN
LeRoy Cogwin Bush Romeo Adolph Mini
Edgar Louis Buttner Glenn Allen Shepherd
Edward Irving White

Otto McCord	James Spofford	David Bush	Gus Gale	Harvey Hansen	Will McKeen
Hilmer Ochlmann	Wm. Greenlauer	N. Spocklemire	Charles Woehr	D. Abercrombie	Leslie Cleary
Karl Kennedy	Kenneth Premo	Earle Wall	Harry Whitehorne	Carl Bremner	Claude Chaplin
Martin Jones	Eugene McTirane	Joseph Manddi	Severus Mim	Myron Tobias	LeRoy Bush
	Edgar Buttner	Romeo Mim	Glenn Shepherd	Edward White	

Achaean

Organized August 12, 1912.

FACULTY

Robert Willard Hodgson — Carl Julius Williams

GRADUATE

Joseph Walton Dismukes

SENIORS

Russel Dolman Berst
George Butler Gleason
Lorin S. Hadley
Harry Sargent
Rufus Hurn Holland
**Robert Bruce Price
Murrey Levering Royar

JUNIORS

Raymond Rainier Brown
Thomas Hubbard Clements
James Harold Doolittle
*John Francis Fahey
Joe Hart
*Don M. Yost
Leo Roy Moody
**Clyde Martin Seibert
**Frank Henry Strieby
George Earl Troxell
George Wale, Jr.

SOPHOMORES

Ira Franklin Brown
Ralph Lincoln Hooper
George Randolph Miller
Merrill Lionel Warne
Lewis August Penn
Arnold Valentine Stubenrauch
Harold Perry Thompson

FRESHMEN

Leon Luther Bowen
Richard Nelson Donelson
Paul Willard Price
Frank James Moody
Walter Leland Moody

---

*On leave of absence January-May, 1917.
**At Davis, January-May, 1917.

Robert Hodgson Joseph Dismukes Loan Holley Robert Price Murrey Royat
Raymond Brown Thomas Clements James Doolittle John Fahey Joe Hart
Leo Moody Clyde Seibert Frank Strohy George Troxell George Wale, Jr.
Dan Yost Ira Brown Ralph Hopper George Miller Lewis Penn
Arnold Stalsenrauch Harold Thompson Merrill Wayne Leon Boxen Richard Donelson
 Frank Moody Walter Moody Paul Price

Sequoyah
Organized October 17, 1913.

GRADUATES

**William Patrick Joseph Lynch
Eugene Klotske Martin
**Lewis L. Seligman
**Bert Stanford Thomas

SENIORS

Edward William Berg
Fisher A. Buckingham
Hugh McCauley Cochran
Granville Sinclair Delamere
John Waino Granberg
Erwin Herbert Hirschfelder
Vincent Cecil Hobbs
Walter Robert Lockwood
Charles Whitney Loraine
Donald DeWitt Penny
Alexander John Robertson
Ray John Scheline

JUNIORS

Sophus Carl Goth
Ronald Louis Thompson

SOPHOMORES

Edward Henry Bolze, Jr.
*Herbert David Crall
Earl Bond Hansen
George Richard Magee
Charles V. Rugh
Otto Lee Schattenburg
Eugene Carl Ward

FRESHMEN

Edmond Kephart Albert
Lincoln Stevenson Batchelder
*Myn Braden Bell
Henry Proctor Buckingham
William Kendall Cates
John Ross Dunnigan
William Stokley Fortson
*Henry Hanson
H. Stanley Mentzer
Douglas Daniel Stafford

*Absent on leave.

William Lynch Eugene Martin Lewis Seligman Bert Thomas Edward Berg F. Buckingham
Hugh Cochran G. Delamere John Gaudeau E. Hirschfelder Vincent Hobbs Walter Lockwood
Donald Penny A. Robertson Ray Scholze Sophus Goth R. Thompson Edward Behr, Jr
Herbert Crail Earl Hansen George Moore O. Schattenburg Eugene Ward Edmund Albert
L. Batchelder A yn Bell H. Buckingham William Cates John Dunnigan William Fortson
Henry Hanson Stanley Mentzer Douglas Stafford

Tilicum
Organized December 14, 1913.

GRADUATES
*John Roland Calder
Ernest Raymond Sprague DeChenne
Harold Preston Darling

SENIORS
Baptiste Barthe
**Clifford Arthur Bly
Bert A. Bone
Sidney Harold Davidson
Carl Torrey Dixon
Berry Gilcrease
**Paul James Hartley
Richard Norman Inch
Bruce Jameyson
Flournoy Albert Juch
Perry Eugene Lantz
Alexander H. Munro
Edward Alexander Reinke
George Tupper Swaim
**Morton Thacher
William John Tocher

JUNIORS
Clifton S. Brown
Henry Wade Macomber
**Howard Wheeler
Leigh Emerson Martin
Butler Joseph Osborne

SOPHOMORES
Ralph Sheldon Armstrong
*Merle Swope Foreman
Dorris Dimmock Gurley
Thomas Moore Pierce

FRESHMEN
Sidney Alden Anderson
Innis Mansfield Bromley
Charles Hiram Carmichael
Robert Leavitt Fuller
Harold Everett Hedger
Stuart Marshall Maule
Archie Lothian Mock
Alfred John Nois
Norman Oliver Norsworthy
John Lyons Stevenson

*Absent on leave.
**At Davis, January-May, 1917.

John Calder   H. Darling   E. DeChenne   R Barthe   Clifford Bly   Bert Rose   S Davidson
Carl Dixon   B Gilcrease   Paul Hartley   Richard Inch   H Jameyson   Flournoy Juch   Perry Lantz
A Munro   E. Kronke   George Swaim   M Thacher   Wm. Tocher   C. Brown   H. Marcoulier
Leigh Martin   Butler Osborne H. Wheeler   R. Armstrong   Merle Foreman   Durris Gurley   Thomas Pierce
S. Anderson   Innis Bromley   C. Carmichael Robert Fuller   Harold Hedger   Stuart Maule
Archie Mock   Alfred Noa   N. Norsworthy   John Stevenson

1916

Orond

Organized October 9, 1916

SENIORS

George Donald Allin
Walter Nels Anderson
Harley Latson

Norman Moras Lyon
Arthur Wood
Milton Alcorn Wright

JUNIORS

Thomas Joseph Connelly
Howard Cone Ellis
Victor William Galvin
Harry Langford

William Gregory Lopez
*Leland James Medina
Elmer James Salmina
Adrian Clyde Wilcox

Dave Victor Zolot

SOPHOMORES

Harry Christie Aitkin
John Toute Binkley
Xenophon Peter Bouris
Roger Nugent Conant
Thomas Francis Corcoran
Alfred Augustus Gropp
Albert Valentine Haberfelde

Glen Lester Hancer
Leon Leonard Hooper
Arthur Alexander Johnson
Clarence McCormick
George Russel Mitchell
Robert Hull Munun
Robert James Ramsey

Newton Brice Wisecarver

FRESHMEN

Herbert Carroll Davis
John Floyd Long

Benjamin Aloysius Lopez
Eugene Baptist Morosoli

*At Davis, January-May, 1917.

George Allin Walter Anderson Harley Letson Norman Lyon Arthur Wood Milton Wright
Thomas Connelly Howard Ellis Victor Galvin Harry Langford William Lopez Elmer Salmon
Adrian Wilcox Dave Zebot Harry Aitkin John Binkley Xenophon Hoarts Roger Conant
Thomas Corcoran Alfred Gropp Albert Haberfelde Glen Hauser Leon Hooper Arthur Johnson
C. McCormick George Mitchell Robert Munon Robert Ramsey N. Wiswasser Herbert Davis
John Long Benjamin Lopez Eugene Moronoli

Japanese Student Club

Organized August 5, 1913.

GRADUATES

Kinuji Kobayashi
Shigeru Mitoma
Isamu Morimoto

Shinkichi Nagata
Satoaki Ozaki
Orikei Shinji

SENIORS

Koshiro Endo
Tokutaro Hayshi
Shigeki Iki
Masao Itano
Tai Jada
Yoshimichi Kitsuda

Kunisada Kiyasu
Toyokichi Kurahashi
Sotaro Matsushita
Goroichi Noda
Bintaro Tanaka
Joe Yoshida

JUNIORS

Hidemichi Akagi
Yajuro Amagata
Kengo Fujinori
Jinzaburo Ishii
Katsujiro Katsuyama
Tokutaro Kogure

Toyoji Konno
Taiji Moshihara
Kiyoshi Matsumura
Sakichi Toda
Teizo Yshauda
Tamotsu Yatabe

SOPHOMORES

Yoshisada Furuya
Masae Kitagawa
Shutaro Matsushita
Toshiki Moriya

Minekichi Okatoyo
Seijiro Okuno
Chiyokichi Tagashira
Kiyoshi Togasaki

FRESHMEN

Takaichi Fujii
Shokichi Kato
Shinobau Kawasaki
Seichi Nakahara
Teizo Shimazu

Kagato Shimoda
Saikichi Shirasawa
Yoshiji Sugiyama
Masamitsu Yamazaki
Tokiji Yokoyama

K. Kobayashi S. Matoma I. Morimoto S. Nagata S. Ogaki Oribei Shoji Kotaro Endo
T. Hayshi Shigeku Ike Masao Itano Y. Kuroda A. Koyama T. Koyabashi S. Matsushita
Gisuchi Noda B. Tanaka Joe Yoshida H. Akagi Y. Amagata K. Fujinoya J. Ishii
K. Katsuyama T. Kogure Toyoji Kono T. Mashahara K. Matsumura Tar Tada Tizzo Yahataka
T. Yatabe Y. Furuya M. Katogawa S. Matsushita T. Moriya M. Okamoto Saguro Okuno
C. Tagashira K. Togasaki T. Fuji B. Kawasaki S. Nakahara T. Shimazu K. Shimoda
S. Shirasawa Y. Sugiyama M. Yamazaki T. Yokoyama

WOMEN'S HOUSE CLUBS

Rediviva

Organized as Pioneer Club, 1874
Re-organized April 10, 1903

GRADUATES

Alice Helen Metcalf
Lucille Peyton

SENIORS

Vivien Gardner
Leona Jones
**Hazel Joy McCurdy
Lucille Alice Murphy

JUNIORS

Gertrude Borchardt
Minerva Bosse
*Mildred Little
Viola Lulu Lockhart
Edith Craig Owen
Mary Elizabeth Smith
Elizabeth Talbot
Verva Tinker

SOPHOMORES

Ethel Mae Allen
Eleanor Nydia Corcoran
*Alice Marie Fowler
Helga Marie Nielsen
*Marion Strobridge
Eleanor Caroline Thomas
Clara Josephine Van de Grift
Olive Eola Wadsworth

FRESHMEN

Lenora Charlotte Clark
Pearl Clara Gidney
Dorothy Louise Handy
Gwen Howe
Vern Elizabeth Lautenschlager

---

*Absent on leave.
**Graduated December, 1916.

Alice Metcalf　Lucille Peyton　Navien Gardner　Lavona Jones　Hazel McCurdy
Lucille Murphy　Gertrude Borchardt　Minerva Busse　Veola Lockhart　Edith Craig Owen
Mary Smith　Elizabeth Talbot　Verna Tucker　Ethel Allen　Nydia Corcoran
Alice Fowler　Helga Nielsen　Eleanor Thomas　Josephine Vande Grift　Olive Wadsworth
Lenora Clark　Pearl Gidney　Dorothy Handy　Gwen Howe　Vera Lautenschlager

Copa de Oro
Organized April 15, 1905.

GRADUATES

Edith Benn
Loveretta Dash
Ila Jean Meddaugh
Flora Hazel Slocum

SENIORS

Frances Norene Ahl
Zela B. Jarvis
Alberta McNeely
Corrinne Elise Powell
Emma Prestage
Erminie Ursula Sala

JUNIORS

Marjorie Mae Baker
Alice Cannan
Eva Emma Slater
Linda Werle
Helen Lucile Wirt

SOPHOMORES

*Dorothy Derrington Bond
Eleanor May Dexter
Agnes Belle DeYoung
Edith Helmer
Ruby Helmer
Margaret McCully
Ethel Marguerite Macpherson
*Pearl Lily Meeker
Esther Phillips
Mildred Lola Stegman
Alice Gertrude Stewart
Portia Faye Wagenet
Marian Ethel Wiley

FRESHMEN

Isabel May DeYoung
Winona Gladys Isaac
Velma Gladys Lyon
Florence Hilreth Sterling

*Absent on leave.

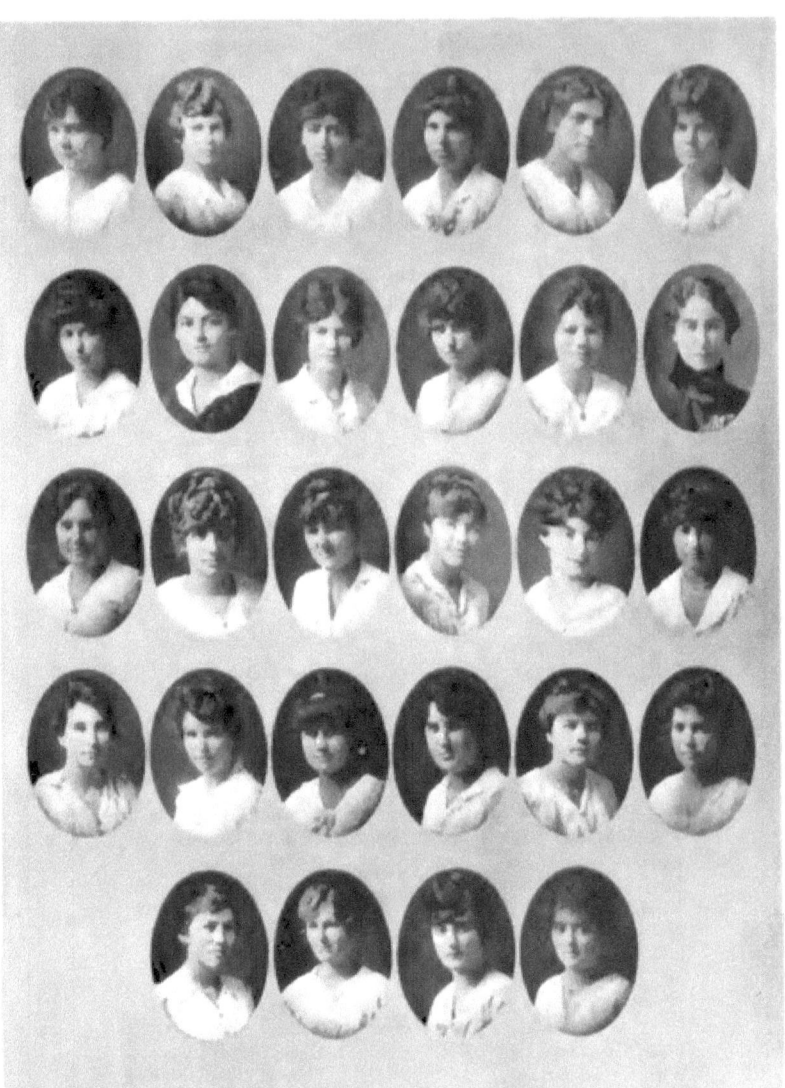

Edith Beam　　　Loveretta Dash　　Jean Meehlaugh　Flora Slocum　　Frances Ahl　　Alberta McNeely
Corinne Powell　Ernanne Sala　　Marjorie Baker　Alice Cauman　　Eva Slater　　Linda Welle
Helen Wert　　　Dorothy Bond　　Eleanor Dexter　Agnes DeYoung　Edith Helmer　Ruby Helmer
Margaret McCully　Ethel Macpherson　Mildred Stegman　Alice Stewart　Portia Wagener　Marian Wiley
　　　　　　　　Isabel DeYoung　Winona Isner　　Velma Lyon　　Florence Sterling

Aldebaran

Organized May 8, 1909, by the California Branch of the Associated Collegiate Alumnae.

HONORARY

Winifred Bangs
Mary Gordon Holway

GRADUATES

Elizabeth Janet Easton
Hattie Belle Paul
Hazel Tindell

SENIOR

Edythe Lillie

JUNIORS

Jean Margaret Applegate
Ella Francis Ayer
Florence May Campbell
Irene D. Catland
Alta Eugenia Edwards
Mae Agnes Erwin
Daphne Eska Gerry
Louise Lucinda Hesse
Ruth Faustina Hulbert
Margret Kane
Elizabeth May Nutting
*Marguerite Sims
Marjorie Ellen Tuft
Bertha Walkmeister
Adelaide Carrie Weihe

SOPHOMORES

*Josephine Isabelle Hornung
May Hulbert
Lilly Lang
Hazel Pearle Neely
Helen Janet Smith

FRESHMEN

Octavia Dell DeLap
Alma Edna Fendt
Hazel Pearl Fry
Lelah Mary Lewis
Frances Maria Loeber
Muriel Genevieve Noakes
Charlotte Delia Smith
Marie Louise Thoroman

*Absent on leave.

Elizabeth Easton   Hattie Paul   Edythe Liller   Jean Applegate   Ella Ayer   Irene Cathcard
Florence Campbell Alta Edwards Mae Erwin   Daphne Gerry   Louise Hesse Ruth Hulbert
Margaret Kane   Elizabeth Nutting Marguerite Sims Margaret Tait B. Walkinshaw Adelaide Weibe
J. Hornung   May Hulbert   Lilly Long   Hazel Neely   Helen Smith   Octavia DeLap
                   Alma Fendt   Hazel Fry   Leilah Lewis   Frances Lasher
                        Muriel Noakes   Charlotte Smith   Marie Thessman

Al Khalail
Organized April, 1900.
Reorganized December 4, 1913.

FACULTY
Lillian Mary Moore

GRADUATES
Anna Maude Barlow
Ruth Browning Compton

SENIORS
Anna Eldora Carlson
Anita Duncan Luton
Eschscholtzin Lichthardt
*Mary Elizabeth Roberts

JUNIORS
Ruth Elaine Gibbons
Louise Evelyn Gilks
Edith Rodgers Hershberger

SOPHOMORES
Marjorie Louise Davidson
Helen Gertrude Halliday
Mildred Matilda White
Nancy Yerkes

FRESHMEN
Laura Louisa Barlow
Emma Shone Fink

*Absent on leave.

Lillian Moore
Anita Laton
Louise Gilke
Mildred White

Anna Barlow
Eschscholzia Lichthardt
Edith Harshberger
Nancy Yerkes

Ruth Compton
Mary Roberts
Marjorie Davidson
Laura Harlow

Eleanor Carlson
Ruth Gibbons
Helen Halladay
Emma Fisk

1914

Mekatina
Organized May 6, 1913.

GRADUATES
Celma Regina Goethals
Marion Buffington Hosmer
Laura Lybrook Moore
Elizabeth Strasburg

SENIORS
Mary Lois Baker
Harriett Louise Bowman
Gladys Irene Lemon
Eva Esther Martin
Iola Gladys Riess
Olive Lee Stevenson
Flora Margaret Wilson

JUNIORS
Sophie Frederique Beekhuis
Blanche Bertha Bouteiller
Arline Blanche Cavins
Aileen Lois Drobish
Ruth Ada Gardner
Allene Lenore Gordon
Louise Emily Stickney

SOPHOMORES
Grace Houdijn Beekhuis
Miriam Young Bonner
*Virginia Gilbert
Clara Colette Sanford
Mabel Marguerite Squire
Rose Mary Thelen

FRESHMEN
Adriana Jongeneel
Violet Florence Rhein

*Absent on leave.

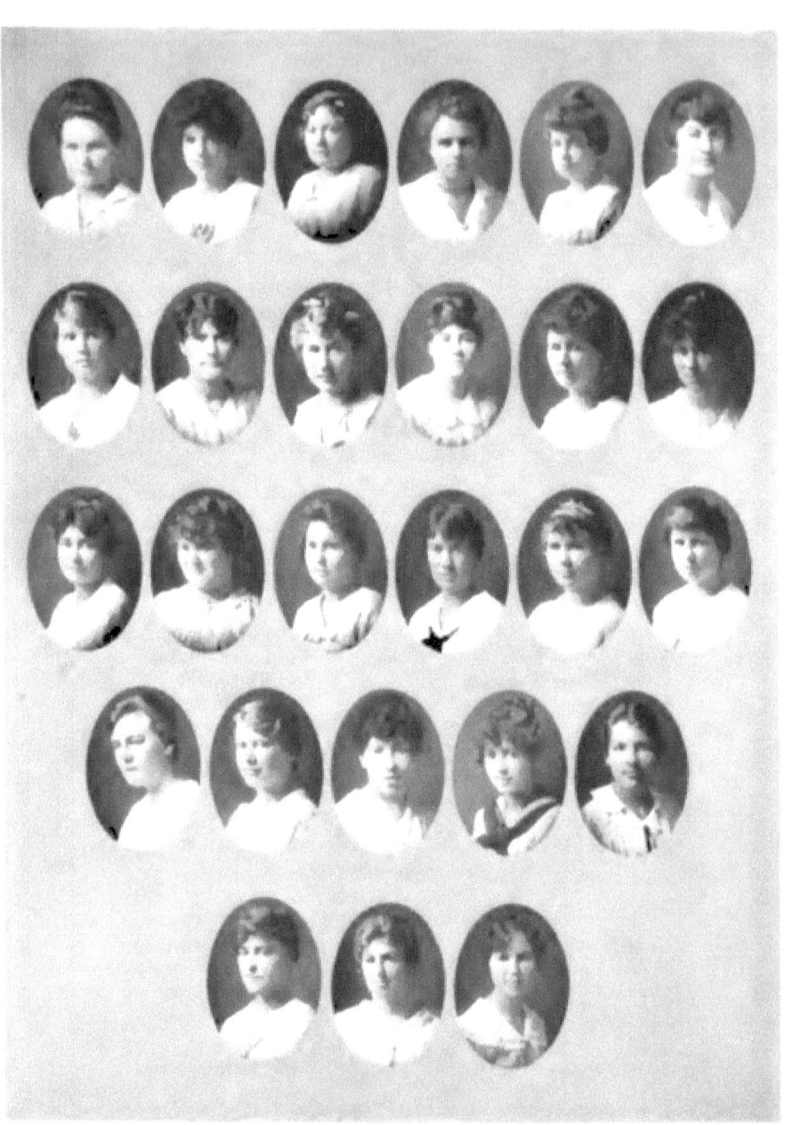

Celma Goethals   Marion Bonner   Laura Moore   F. Strasburg   Mary Baker   Harriett Bouman
Gladys Lemon   Eva Martin   Iola Hoss   Olive Stevenson   Flora Walcott   Sophie Beckhaus
Blanche Bouteiller   Aileen Diedrich   Arline Cavins   Ruth Gardner   Allene Gordon   Louise Stickney
   Grace Beckhaus   Miriam Bonner   Virginia Gilbert   Clara Sanford   Mabel Squire
      Rose Thelen   Adrianna Jongeneel   Violet Rhein

Norroena

Organized November 1, 1915.

GRADUATES

Sarah Evelyn Fairchilds   Louise Brewster Koehler

SENIORS

Flossie Banks   Fannie Etoile Granger
Louise Agnes Doran   Louise Allene Kern
Estha Marie Rodkey

JUNIORS

Marcella Brinkmeyer   Myrtle Molle
*Annette Girard   Clyffice Bernardine Nevin
Lenora Anna McLaughlin   Grace Evelyn Palmer
Barbara Martha Mensing   Frances Ann Stranahan
Anne Wallingford

SOPHOMORES

Viola Ruth Boyd   *Catherine Clement
Catherine Agnes Brennan   Maude Frances Hudson
Marie Maude Miller

FRESHMEN

Marie Emily Bowen   Geraldine Holden
Lenora Wilhelmina Crutchett   Edna Mae Hopkins
Edith Gwynne Robertson

*Absent on leave.

JOSHES

The night was dark
The sky was blue;
The sweet Young Thing
Found an inch of space
Next a pair of cords,
With a weed in its face.
The juice went off,
The lights went out —

What d'ye mean, Tommy Reed says its hard for even an honest man to keep his hands in his pockets?

"Is there an opening here for a bright, energetic young man?"
"Yes; an' close it as you go out."

BEING STUCK FOR THE DRINKS

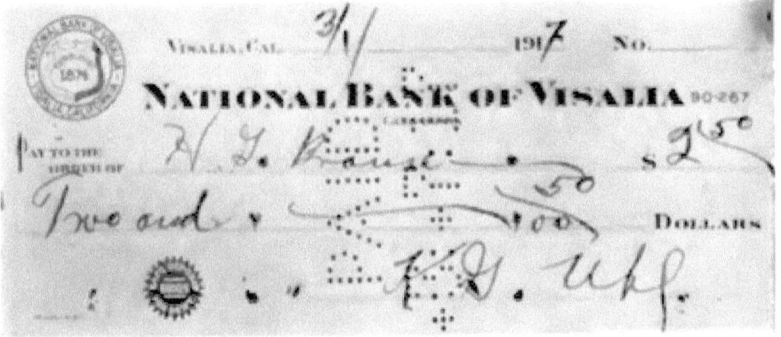

CANCELLED EVIDENCE.

EN ROUTE—VISALIA TO BERKELEY
UHL STOPS FOR REFRESHMENTS

Prof.—Why is it my boy, that you students are always wasting your time loafing around the bench?
Stude—Why-er- its merely a matter of form—you know.

IF PRICES KEEP ON SOARING

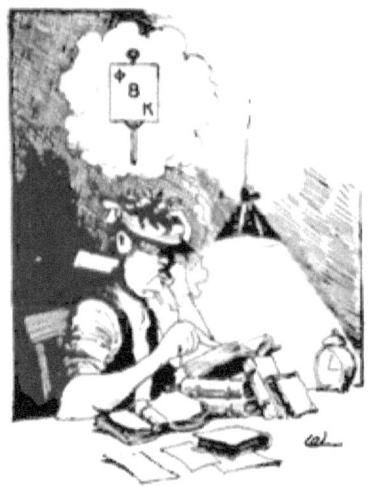

THE KEY ROUTE

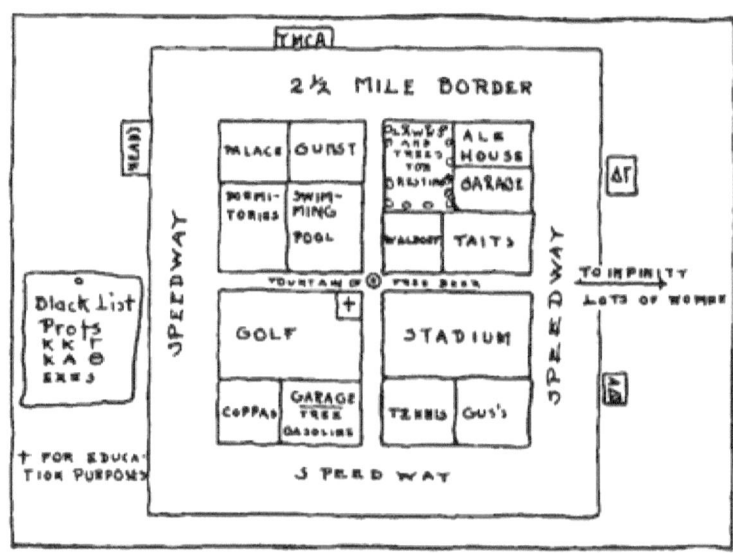

BAB CLARKSON'S IDEA OF AN IDEAL CAMPUS

A Shear's Prayer

After reading the little poem appearing in the Women's Issue of the Pelican, entitled "She's the Limit" by Art Wilson.

Dear God, forgive us for our sins,
For powder, paint and hump-back pins,
For colored hose and skittish air,
For cigarettes smoked anywhere—
        It's done for ART.

Be merciful when we do try,
The thrills that lurk in "Extra Dry,"
French classes teach us how to live,
And we to that attention give—
        For it is ART.

Forgive us for our high-heeled shoes,
For non-attendance, unpaid dues,
For gawdy skirts, unduly short,
Forgive us for we merely court,
        To ART.

Forgive us then for all these things,
Including bracelets and ear-rings,
You see it is not jest or play
But deadly earnest so we may,
One of us some happy day
        Be engaged to ART.

The Vanished Lottery

When we went wooing, ages since, we learned the lady's views
  Concerning churches, dances, books, or expurgated news;
We thrilled to hear her talk about the topics of the day,
  Like Dicken's newest novelette, or Browning's sweetest play.
'Twas joy enough for us to see the damsel of our choice,
  It didn't matter WHAT she said, we liked to hear her voice.
We took her inner views on faith, we wooed and won and wed,
  Before we had the vaguest glimpse of what was in her head.

It's different now —these modern girls discuss with pith and zest
  The things their grandmas didn't know —or kept inside the chest.
The fresh young voices prate of sin, the social evil vice,
  And divers other vital things which aren't considered "nice."
The swain who woos in days like these, no doubt can plague or vex—
  He knows his darling's inmost thoughts on every phase of sex.

Our ancient charmers—bless their hearts —did so devise their dress
  That of the things they wore beneath no manly man might guess.
They showed us hooped and flouncy frocks, which perfect forms revealed,
  The men were fooled, deceived, beguiled, by imperfections thus concealed.
We had to marry ere we knew what ladies really wore—
  At least no righteous male dared own he'd found it out before.

But nowadays, the modest maid rejoices to display,
  Her raiments' inner mysteries adown the broad highway.
Serene, unblushing, calm and cool, to passers-by she shows
  The ribbons of her brassiere, the texture of her hose.
Chemise and slip and knickers, too, the modern fashion bares—
  None save a blind man now need wed, unknowing what she wears.

We paid our court to maids whose forms escaped our avid gaze,
  Who cheated nature's lines and curves in many cunning ways.
If they wore freckles on their arms—as damsels often did—
  These sweet defects, like dearer charms, remained securely hid.
They showed their faces, bared their hands, revealed a furtive shoe.
  But bow-legged, knock-kneed, stout or slim,—we wed 'em ere we knew.

But days of yore no longer are; the present woman kind
  Displays most everything she has, each single curve and line.
No modern lover raves about his ladies lips or eyes,
  Why should he? He's a connoisseur of ankles, knees and thighs.
The mysteries we used to solve are cleared at tea or dance.
  THANK GOD! A MAN CAN MARRY NOW AND NEVER TAKE
    A CHANCE.

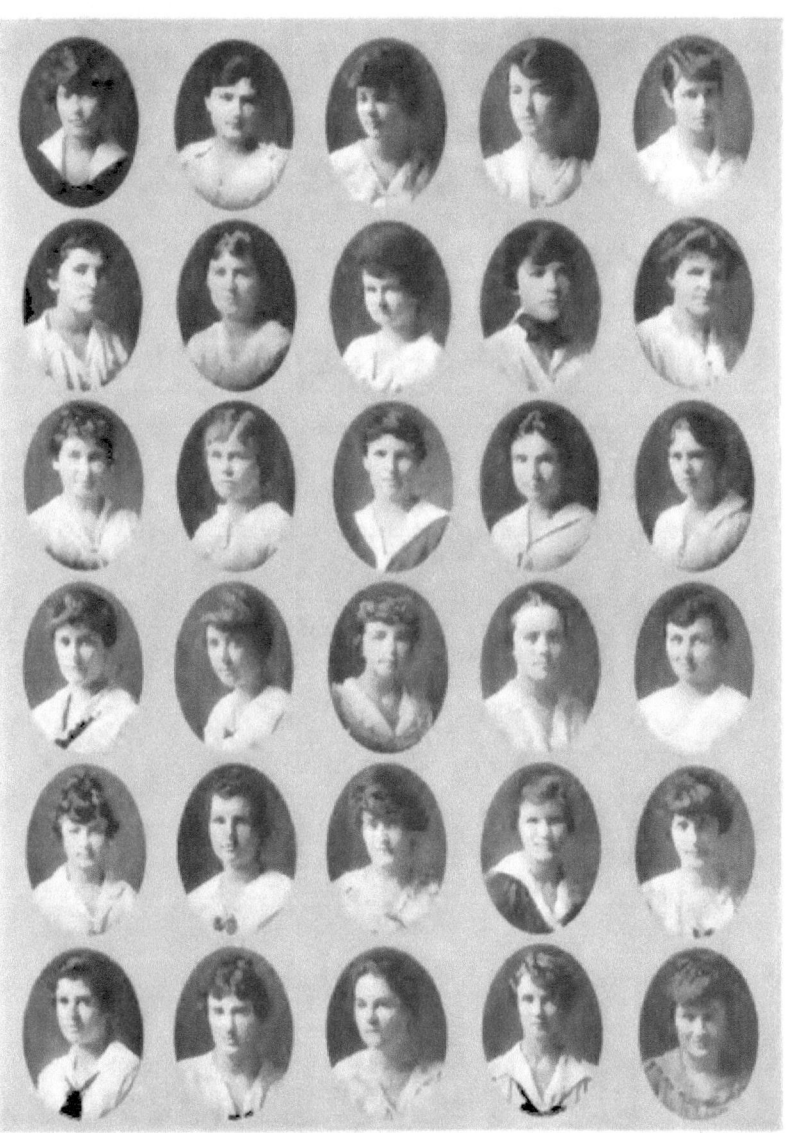

HBR CLUB

(See page five hundred and ninety-one.)

PROTECT YOUR FUTURE

Consider your SAVINGS ACCOUNT as you would your education. Saving is an education and from the study of it the best the world has to offer can be obtained. A good income in old age is often the result of dollars carefully saved in youth.

Start An Account Today In the Students Bank

TELEGRAPH AVE. BRANCH

Berkeley Bank *of* Savings and Trust Co.

Knox Hats *for* Berkeley

We are now the exclusive distributers of this famous Hat for Berkeley
A large variety of shapes and colorings to select from

Our Tailoring Department has been enlarged and we are now prepared to take care of your tailoring wants better than ever. A visit to our shop will convince you that your next Suit or Hat will be bought at

WOODWARD & SCHUESSLER
Tailors and Hatters
2221 SHATTUCK AVENUE, BERKELEY

There is nothing that looks as well on the Campus as a

MILDER MADE SAILOR SUIT or MIDDY BLOUSE

Send for free illustrated catalogue

1089 SUTTER STREET   Telephone Franklin 3930   SAN FRANCISCO, CAL.

CLEANING THE CITY

Half a Yard Upward

When the price of textile fabrics
Took to soaring toward the skys
Sweet Miss Flight—the crafty creature—
Said "I'll economize."
Hence the briefness of the dresses,
Hence the skirts cut apron-wise—
May save a strain on the pocket-book,
But just doubles the strain on the eyes.

Being Subtle

I love all the coeds,
  Their skirts are so short
And if I don't tell them
  They'll give me much sport.
So I'll tell them they're pretty,
  Not drive them away,
And their ankles I'll look at
  On each windy day.

Political Prattle

Come around, come around
  Any old man
Give us your ballots
  As fast as you can
If you'll vote for us
  We'll have you to tea
Never mind for what office
  Elect the A. Phi.

Kappa Alpha Theta runs thru the town
  Looking at pedigrees and coed's gown.
Turning up their noses at every one in sight
  Saying "Bow before me, I wear a kite."

April 13th — McKee says a fork-full in favor of himself for Senior representative.

The Student's Friend   On the Corner—on the Square

FARLEY'S
The Store of Service

Telegraph Avenue at Bancroft   Berkeley, California

Wholesale   Retail

Humboldt Fruit Co.
for Quality
Fruits, Vegetables & Produce

2175 Shattuck Avenue   Phones: Berkeley 7787   7788

The Ladies' Shop

S. H. Brake Company

Always something new in Waists, Neckwear, Gloves, Hosiery, Underwear, Ribbons, Handkerchiefs, Art Goods, Corsets, Brassieres, Household Linens, Wash Goods, Bedding, Etc. Absolutely correct in Style, Material and Price

Telegraph Avenue at Durant

Phone Berkeley 4308

Jarvis Hardware Co.
Athletic Goods

2311-2313 Telegraph Ave.   Berkeley, California

Under the Shade of the Old Apple Tree in Dixie

Sentimental Sam: Listen Gal, what makes dese trees sigh and moan so?

Lukewarm Liza: Huh, nigger, if yo' wuz just half as full o' green apples as dese trees is, you'd sigh and moan too.

Time Out

Bunch at Eata Bita Pie House: Yea Bo! some class to that suit.

Don Dresswell: Surething, I got it from "Bill" West and take it from me, "Big Bill" has the "hop on the ball" when it comes to building better clothes, with better style, at a better price. If you are wise, you'll look him up. He will hardly have time to drop around this way soon, on account of classes and football. Watch for his announcement in the "Cal."

"BILL WEST 20"

W. Leon West

"Builder of Individual Clothes"

Since 1910

G. L. SCHNEIDER
OPTOMETRIST

SHATTUCK HOTEL BLDG.
BERKELEY

Phone Berkeley 434

Ferry Drug Store
Edw. L. Baldwin Co.

DRUGS :: SUNDRIES :: PHOTO SUPPLIES
POST CARDS AND STATIONERY

The First Drug Store on Market Street   20 MARKET STREET   SAN FRANCISCO

VICKERY, ATKINS & TORREY
Fine Arts

556 SUTTER STREET   SAN FRANCISCO

Take the Bunch and follow the Bunch to

Sole Agency:
BURT & PACKARD "KORRECT SHAPE" SHOES

PETERS BROS.

Oakland: 482 TWELFTH STREET
Bet. Broadway and Washington

San Francisco: 766 MARKET STREET
Phelan Building

DEPENDABLE Upholstered Furniture Made to Order. General Furniture Repairing, Refinishing, Mattress Making and Renovating. : : : : : : : : :

F. G. Schulte

PHONE BERKELEY
7 2 3 8
2108 Allston Way
BERKELEY, CAL.

COLLEGE PRESS
PRINTING

2432 Bancroft Way   LEROY BOWMAN, Manager   Berkeley, California

---

Second Hand
University
Text Books

The Oxford Book Shop

E. W. PLUMMER, MANAGER
2208-10 ALLSTON WAY

HAIR DRESSING   FACIAL AND SCALP WORK   MANICURING

AIMEE La FARGE ANDERSON
SPECIALIST

Phone BERKELEY 4588   2009 SHATTUCK, BERKELEY

SKULL AND KEY RUNNING

Husband—Helen, dear, you had better take the baby. You know I have my best suit on.

GLEANED FROM THE BALLOT BOX

MEALS   ICE CREAM   CAKES
CANDIES   PUNCH

Winston
The Best Only

Telephone Berkeley 276   2148-52 CENTER STREET

LYNNE STANLEY

H^{ABERDASHE}ATTE R

Hatter

14th and Broadway   Oakland, California

SPECIAL TERMS TO FACULTY AND STUDENTS

CLIFT HOTEL
350 OUTSIDE ROOMS WITH BATH
DAILY RATES FROM $2.00 UPWARDS

Geary and Taylor Streets   San Francisco, California

WOMEN HATERS — NEVER WITH 'EM   FEMININE FOLLOWERS — ALWAYS WITH 'EM

STANFORD	AB	R	H	PO	A	E		CALIFORNIA	AB	R	H	PO	A	E
Cowan, ss	4	0	0	0	3	1		Smith, 3b	5	3	2	0	1	0
Stevens, lf	4	1	1	2	1	2		Adair, cf	4	2	2	2	0	0
Hayes, 1b	4	0	2	11	1	0		C. Rohrer, ss	3	4	1	0	0	0
Lilly, cf	4	1	1	2	0	1		R. Rohrer, lf	3	2	2	0	0	0
Braden, 2b	3	0	0	1	1	1		Works, rf	5	2	1	1	0	0
Dickey, lf	2	0	0	0	0	1		Starbird, 1b	4	2	2	13	1	0
Walkins, cf	4	0	0	2	0	1		Gandol, c	3	1	1	8	1	0
Campbell, c	2	0	0	2	0	0		Hudson, 2b	4	1	2	2	10	0
Mattei, p	1	0	0	0	2	0		Dunock, p	5	1	0	0	2	0
Draper, p	2	0	0	1	5	0		Edwards, c	0	0	0	1	1	0
Walcott, c	1	0	0	3	0	0								
Totals	30	2	4	24	14	7		Totals	38	16	11	27	16	0

SCORE BY INNINGS

Stanford   0 1 0 1 0 0 0 0 0 — 2
   Base Hits   0 1 0 2 0 0 0 1 — 4
California   2 3 0 2 1 3 1 4 * — 16
   Base Hits   1 3 1 2 2 0 1 4 * — 14

SUMMARY

Seven runs, 7 hits, 20 at bat off Mattei in 3 2-3 innings. Replaced by Draper in fourth inning, 2 out. Charge defeat to Mattei. Runs responsible for—Off Mattei, 4; Draper 4; off Dunock, 2. Home runs—Lilly, R. Rohrer. Three-base hit—Gandol. Two-base hits—Hayes, Hudson, Works. Sacrifice hits—C. Rohrer, Hudson. Sacrifice fly—C. Rohrer. Stolen bases—Smith 4, Adair, R. Rohrer, Works, Starbird. First base on balls—Off Dunock 4, Mattei 4, Draper 5. Struck out—By Dunock 9, Draper 3, Mattei 1. Left on bases—Stanford 2, California 6. Scorer—Cortelyou. Umpire—Hildebrand. Time of game—2 hrs. 12 min.

THIS IS STILL THE JOSH DEPARTMENT

Feb. 25th — Joe Carey asked to resign from Students Welfare Committee.

Back Numbers of BLUE AND GOLD
can be had at

Sadler's
2253 TELEGRAPH AVE.
BERKELEY, CALIFORNIA

Books
Periodicals
Stationery

School and College Text Books and
Supplies — Kodak Developing
and Printing

*"If we do not have what you need we will
get it for you."*

Mail Orders Specially Solicited

Always
Something
New

for
College
Men
and
Girls

The Walk-Over Boot Shop
764 MARKET STREET
SAN FRANCISCO

Brasfield's
"Tie Shoppe"

General
Haberdashery

Berkeley, U. S. A.

SWASEY'S

Framing
& Gilding

FINE IMPORTED
PRINTS

Masonic Building
2289 Shattuck Avenue
Phone Berkeley 4134

Oct. 20th—Bul Eppung and Vivien Liberbeck watch Skull & Key running from Campanile

War Orders:

Forward March! Double Time!
Squads Right! Watch that line!
Company Halt! At Rest!
You're at Gillick's Print Shop, the BEST.

James J. Gillick
QUALITY
Commercial Printing

First National Bank Building, Berkeley
"A Little Better Than You Expected"

D & ROLFWELL ADVERTISING SERVICE

Hotel Carlton
BERKELEY, CALIFORNIA

Noted for
Home Comforts
&
Excellent Meals
European and American Plans

College Banquets
Our
Specialty

S. M. ESTABROOK, Manager

HINK'S

EXCLUSIVE
DRY GOODS

Berkeley's Largest
Mercantile Establishment

"He profits most who serves best"

SHATTUCK AT KITTRIDGE

Campanile
Chocolates
THE FLAVOR COUNTS

"Pex"

PHONE BERKELEY 2603

Shattuck at Bancroft

BERKELEY   CALIFORNIA

SPIRO'S

1127 BROADWAY   OAKLAND, CAL.

Oakland's Only Exclusive
Sporting and Outing Goods Store

Everything for the Sportsman, Athlete, Traveler, Hiker, Autoist, Camper, and all Lovers of the Great Outdoors

---

Court House Grill
Home of the Famous "Peru"

Italian and French
DINNERS

E. JACOPETTI, Mgr.

625-629 Washington St., San Francisco

Phone Oakland 2654   We Aim To Please

Hogan & Evers
FLORISTS

FLORAL DESIGNS OUR SPECIALTY

1454 Broadway   Oakland, Cal.

Musical Instruments
OF ALL KINDS

FIRST CLASS
REPAIRING

H. C. Hanson   111 KEARNY ST., SAN FRANCISCO

Official Keys of
PHI BETA KAPPA
SIGMA XI
Class and Fraternity Emblems
Made to Order

A. A. Handle Co.
Gold and Silversmiths
Watchmakers and
Optometrists

2119 CENTER ST., BERKELEY, CAL.

S. P. R. R. Co. Watch Inspectors   PHONE BERKELEY 1148

Phone Oakland 8640

Louis Schuman

SOLE AGENT FOR THE
Par Fay and Lord Caesar
CIGARS

1312 Broadway   Oakland, Cal.

DRESS SUITS
rented and sold for all occasions

Latest Styles

L. SKOLL

305 Kearny St.   San Francisco

BASEBALL TERMS

Mar. 10th—Joe Carey edits Raspberry Sheet.

THE FIRST NATIONAL BANK
of SAN FRANCISCO

Capital and Surplus - - $4,500,000

An Account with This Bank Combines the
Maximum of Safety, Convenience and Service

First Federal Trust Company
(Affiliated with the First National Bank)

Capital - - - - - - $1,500,000

Pays Interest on Deposits. Transacts a General
Trust Business. An Account May Be Opened
With a Small or Large Deposit

POST AND MONTGOMERY STREETS, SAN FRANCISCO

L. F. SHEAN   J. L. TAYLOR

VARSITY CANDY SHOP
Call for Campus Chocolates   Frozen Desserts Furnished   For All Occasions

Fine Candies ❦ Frozen Delicacies

COR. TELEGRAPH AVENUE AND BANCROFT WAY

PHONE BERKELEY 967   BERKELEY, CALIFORNIA

A Compact Dissolving Balopticon in a Single Outfit

THIS wonderfully compact dissolving outfit includes two separate optical systems mounted in a single lantern, with a lamp house containing two Mazda Lamps. The outfit is nearly as small and portable as a single lantern. The gas-filled Mazda Lamps are automatic like the ordinary incandescent. While a slide is being projected one's own lamps burns, reducing the heat and resulting in lamp and current economy. The outfit attaches to any house socket. Its operation is simplicity itself. The change from one slide to another is made by slowly throwing the switch, which cuts off the current from one lamp and admits it to the other by degrees.

The only satisfactory substitute for the two lantern outfit—a system operating from Mazda Lamps produces the dissolving effect.

BAUSCH & LOMB OPTICAL COMPANY *of* **CALIFORNIA**
Write for illustrated circular   154 Sutter Street, San Francisco, Cal.

S. J. Sill Company

BERKELEY'S LEADING
Grocers

*Special Attention and Prices
to Student Organizations*

FRESH FRUITS AND VEGETABLES
HOME MADE CAKES AND PIES
KITCHEN UTENSILS

2145 UNIVERSITY AVENUE, BERKELEY
Phone Berkeley 5204

A LITTLE TRUTH

DELTA GAMMAS HAVE A MATRIMONIAL RACE

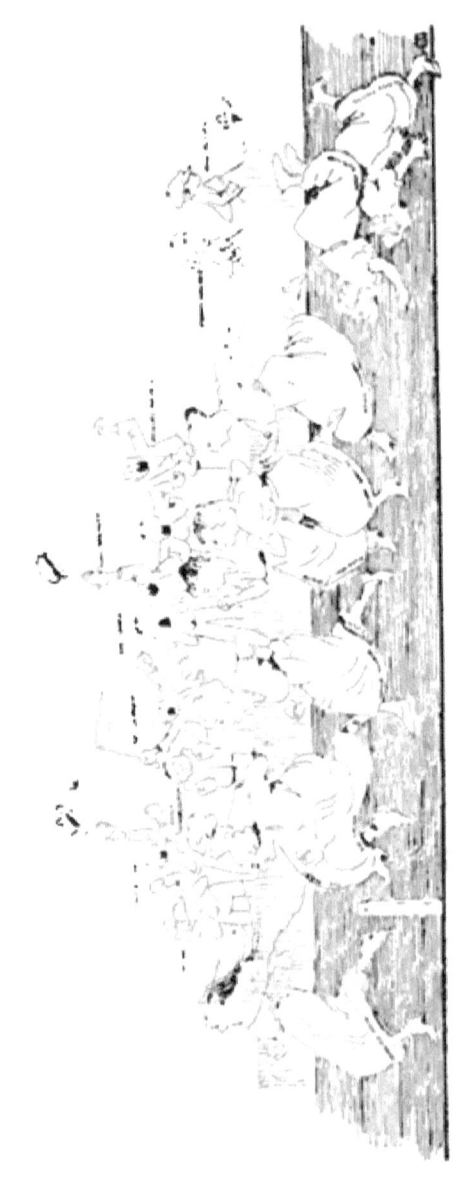

S true in *quality* as it is in *style*—

Florsheim-Schaefer Shoe Co.
12th STREET AT BROADWAY   OAKLAND, CALIFORNIA

Palace Hotel
San Francisco
Center of Collegiate Affairs, Fraternity Conventions, etc.

Dancing
Every Evening except Sunday

Concert
Every Sunday Evening beginning at 7:00 o'clock
Herman Heller, Director
Admission Free

Dinner
Table d'hote at $2.00 per cover
Also a la Carte

From Your Hat to Your Hose

—and all in between

Roos Bros.
INC.

"The House of Courtesy"

will clothe you best, and at least cost when you consider quality

Three Stores at Your Service

Washington at 13th   Market at Stockton   Shattuck at Center
Oakland   **San Francisco**   **Berkeley**

Phone Berkeley 6336   Call and Deliver

SATHER GATE CLEANING HOUSE

Ladies and Gents Tailoring
CLEANING, DYEING, PRESSING AND REPAIRING

2216 TELEGRAPH AVE.   Monthly Contracts

KODAKS *and* FILMS

Developing, Printing and Enlarging
By Modern Methods

We Make Picture Frames Too

MARTIN'S CAMERA SHOP
Phone Berkeley 366
2023 Shattuck Ave.   Berkeley, Cal.

If you are thinking about milk
Why not

Varsity Pasteurized

VARSITY CREAMERY CO.
2113 University Ave.
Phone Berkeley 65

Telephone Berkeley 4018

LACK BROS.
PRINTERS

2156 CENTER ST., BERKELEY

Madera Daily Mercury

MADERA, CALIFORNIA — TUESDAY, JAN. 3, 1917

NABBED TWICE AS SPEEDER IN THREE DAYS

Mar. 25th, 26th, 27th—Phi Gamma Delta holds annual banquet.

Everything in Music

STEINWAY PIANOS
Other Good Pianos from $250

PIANOLA PIANOS
Player Music Rolls

VICTOR VICTROLAS
Victor Records

HOLTON BAND INSTRUMENTS
String and Orchestra Instruments

UKULELES

SHEET MUSIC

CATALOGUE SENT UPON REQUEST
EASY TERMS

Sherman, Clay & Co.

Kearny and Sutter Streets, San Francisco
Fourteenth and Clay Streets, Oakland

Sacramento　　Stockton　　San Jose　　Santa Rosa　　Fresno

The Press of The COURIER

H. S. HOWARD

2055 ADDISON STREET
BERKELEY

Specialists in
the better kind of
Printing

Phone Berkeley 1028

OLDEST AND LARGEST BANK IN ALAMEDA COUNTY

Berkeley Branch

The Oakland Bank of Savings

SAVINGS — COMMERCIAL — TRUST

RESOURCES OVER
$32,000,000

L. L. HOTCHKISS, *Assistant Manager*   W. A. SHOCKLEY, *Manager*

Apr. 20th — D. U.'s assured of *Pelican* next year.

"Conflagration Proof"
Fire • Automobile • Baggage
Insurance

Queen Insurance Company
ROLLA V. WATT, *Manager*
Royal Insurance Building
San Francisco

We Insured the "Blue and Gold"

Now located in our New Home

2161
CENTER STREET
Right at the Center St. Gate
BERKELEY

Printing

LEDERER, STREET & ZEUS CO.
INCORPORATED
Phone Berkeley 630

The world's greatest vaudeville
all the year round

PANTAGES
THEATRE

12th AND BROADWAY
OAKLAND, CALIFORNIA

Matinee Daily

Two Shows Nightly
7:00 and 9:00 p. m.

Popular Prices

ALEXANDER PANTAGES
Proprietor and General Manager

CORDOVAN BALS
BUCK-TOP BALS

Now in our new store with a
great variety of Men's and
Women's High-Class Shoes

The Booterie
2233 SHATTUCK AVE., near Kittridge

Aug. 16th — A. T. O. Eating House holds its semi-annual button scramble

---

Phone Kearny 3660

Whittier Coburn Co.

MANUFACTURERS AND IMPORTERS
PAINTS :: OILS :: VARNISH

Whittier Quality Paints

HOWARD AND BEALE STREETS   SAN FRANCISCO, CALIFORNIA

LOYALTY

Throughout your undergraduate days there has been an ever-present suggestion of an active plea for loyalty to your country and your college. Thus do you set for yourself a standard which makes you strive for better things and to cultivate professional ideals.

If in the practice of your profession you do not seek and get **Quality** in every article of equipment and material you use, you are lowering that standard so essential to your success and you are violating that code of ethics which prescribes the duty you owe your patients.

We distribute only the products of the world's standard manufacturers, our guarantee to you of naught but the best.

THE JAMES W. EDWARDS CO.   The Pioneer Dental Supply House of the Pacific Coast   311 GEARY STREET   SAN FRANCISCO

Where are we going tonight?

Why to the

Maryland
Dance Pavilion

The Finest Place of
Its Kind in the West

A place where we can spend a pleasant evening at small expense and make good social acquaintances.

Hof Brau

FRED. SCHULTZ, Mgr.

Oakland's Leading Family Cafe

At Eleventh and Broadway

A Cafe

We solicit your patronage on the good quality of our food and the excellence of our service

DINNER DANSANTS

Are you a college man?

Then play the part, buy your clothes from **AMBROSE** and always have the "College Bred Look."

College Men's Goods Made in a College Man's Way.

Ambrose the Tailor Pantages Theatre Building
Phone Oakland 880

PREPAREDNESS!

Scientific care of the eyes *now* is the best way to prepare for future good vision. Consult your oculist, then call on us

CHINN-BERETTA
EYEGLASSES *and* SPECTACLES

120 Geary Street *and* 164 Powell Street, San Francisco, Cal.

WE SPECIALIZE IN GOOD FURNITURE AT LOW PRICES. LET US FIGURE WITH YOU.

We Will Absolutely Save You Money

Gilchrist Furniture Co.
1218-1220-1222 Clay St.   Oakland, California

HIS CLUB

(See page five hundred and sixty-seven)

Dec. 9th—Ed Garthwaite signifies intention of going to the farm—campus rejoices.

HOTEL CLAREMONT

BERKELEY

Located in the Berkeley Hills a short distance from the University of California, which is easily reached by a car line or walk :: Special Rates are made for those wishing to spend any length of time at the Hotel.

HOTEL CLAREMONT, BERKELEY
TELEPHONE BERKELEY 9300

Nov. 23rd—Frick Gibbs proves to be unknown woman's secret sorrow.

Recall the last hand-me-down suit?

How the haircloth came out of the lapel.

How it wrinkled back of the coat collar.

Royal Tailors

$20 and Up Suits and Overcoats
1113 BROADWAY, OAKLAND

Phone Berkeley 1851 / 1852

LESSER BROTHERS

Lincoln Market

Wholesalers and Retailers of
Meats, Provisions and Poultry
"Good Things to Eat"

University and Shattuck Avenue — Berkeley, California

"Your Hatter" **FRED AMMANN**

Has the { HATS and CAPS } You Want

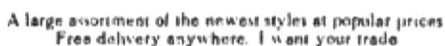

A large assortment of the newest styles at popular prices.
Free delivery anywhere. I want your trade.

72 MARKET STREET — OPPOSITE NEW S. P. BUILDING

R. C. ENDRISS

OPTICIAN AND OPTOMETRIST

509 FOURTEENTH STREET
OAKLAND, CAL.

Telephone Oakland 1428

April 3rd — Steve Barrows celebrates his 42nd birthday

BYRON MAUZY GOLD MEDAL PIANOS
PLAYER PIANOS

VICTROLAS • EDISON • COLUMBIA
MACHINES AND RECORDS

VIOLINS, VIOLAS, CELLOS, CORNETS
STRINGS FOR ALL INSTRUMENTS

GENUINE HAWAIIAN UKULELES

Byron Mauzy
ESTABLISHED 1884
GOLD MEDAL PIANOS
244-250 STOCKTON   ON UNION SQUARE
SAN FRANCISCO, CAL.

SMITH BROS.

Oakland's 30 Year Old Bookstore

Headquarters for
STUDENTS' SUPPLIES
Eastman Kodak Agency
Fine Writing Papers
Books of All Kinds

THIRTEENTH STREET
Between Broadway and Washington

Taft & Pennoyer Company

Suits
Dresses
Coats
For the College Woman
Seeking Style

EXCLUSIVENESS AT A
MODERATE PRICE
Ready-to-Wear Section   Second Floor

Clay at Fourteenth and Fifteenth Streets
Oakland, California

Young Men's Smart Clothes from Stein-Bloch Ready for Spring

HOUTS & RAMAGE

OAKLAND'S FOREMOST CLOTHIERS

1311-1317 WASHINGTON ST.　　　　　　　　OAKLAND, CALIFORNIA

Shoes Repaired in a Jiffy　　Quick Motorcycle Service　　Work Called for and Delivered

Good Shoe Service Company

Prices Right

1105 BROADWAY　　　　　OAKLAND　　　　　Phone ELMHURST 271

EVERYTHING FOR THE STUDENT

SURGICAL SUPPLIES, X-RAY COILS, ELASTIC HOSIERY AND BELTS

Special Discounts to Students

PERCY J. MEYER & CO., 359 Sutter Street, San Francisco

California Lunch Room

Ben Hollman, Prop.　　　　　　　　　　　　Open Until 12 p. m.

LOOK!

4 Hints *for* Your Vacation

1. An Eastman Kodak
   Prices $1.00 to $77.00
   Inquire about the autographic feature

2. A Fountain Pen
   Waterman or Conklin
   Prices $2.50 to $12.00

3. A Tennis Racket
   Wright & Ditson or Spalding
   Prices $1.00 to $12.00

4. Our Kodak Finishing Mail Service
   We pay return postage

The
Sather Gate Book Shop
2302 TELEGRAPH AVE.

Ed's
Barber Shop

Next to . . .
Carlton Hotel

Marx Bros.

Agents for Manila Cigars:
LA INSULAR *and* ISABELLA

Tampa Cigars:
HAVANA, UNION TRUST SPECIAL
and CERVANTES

Two Stores:
Bush and Montgomery Sts., 740 Market St.
SAN FRANCISCO, CAL.

A MINER) SPORT

CO-COED

Aug. 24th — Alpha O's break pledge with prospective sister —

FULL SACK JACK!
Our Coal Man Says

We specialize on supplying
Clubs, Fraternities, etc.
with Fuel

Rhodes-Jamieson & Co.
Consolidated with PACIFIC FUEL & BUILDING MATERIAL CO.
RETAIL DEPT. OF JAMES P. TAYLOR

OAKLAND: Broadway and Water St. ALAMEDA: Park and Blanding
Phone Oakland 770 Phone Alameda 440

Wells Fargo Nevada National Bank
OF SAN FRANCISCO

Capital and Surplus . $11,068,423.38
Total Assets 62,680,867.27

Accounts of Individuals, Professional, Salaried and
Business Men, Firms, Corporations and Banks Invited

Safe Deposit Boxes and Storage Space for Rent

ESTABLISHED 1852

Northeast Corner Market and Montgomery Sts., San Francisco

The Ellery Arms Company
563-85 MARKET ST
SAN FRANCISCO, CA
THE SIGN OF QUALITY

Authoritative
OUTING EQUIPMENT

The Poheim Tailored Man

Stands out in a crowd

JOE POHEIM
The Tailor
806 Market Street
San Francisco

Phone Berkeley 3128

EVELYN FISHER
DRESSMAKER

2314 Telegraph Avenue — Corner Bancroft Way

LOYALTY and SERVICE

These two words express our attitude toward the students of the University of California and our confidence in their recognition of it in the purchase of Men's Wear

Herbert Jones, Inc.   2308 TELEGRAPH   2201 SHATTUCK   Berkeley

---

Phone Berkeley 656 — Phone Berkeley 1327

Berkeley ICE Company

Dealers in
Distilled Water Ice

EMBROIDERIES
STAMPING

Studio Shoppe of MISS DAVIS
MRS. OLIVER

CARDS—
Original Designs
Embroidery Materials

2136 CENTER ST.
BERKELEY

Sept. 12th, 24th; Oct. 6th, 18th; Dec. 2nd, 8th; Feb. 5th, 9th, 21st; Mar. 1st, 14th;

Clean Traveling

Electric travel does away with the grime, soot and other disagreeable inconveniences that go with usual railway travel.

You are brought to your destination just as fresh as when you started.

Use the electric line between San Francisco, Oakland and Sacramento, Woodland, Oroville, Colusa and Chico.

OAKLAND, ANTIOCH & EASTERN RAILWAY

L. H. RODEBAUGH
Traffic Manager
Oakland, Cal.

Oakland's
Department Store
Beautiful

SIXTY DEPARTMENTS AND
A BARGAIN BASEMENT

QUALITY MERCHANDISE
AT LOWEST PRICES

J·F·NEWMAN
150 POST STREET
SAN FRANCISCO

New York   Chicago

JEWELER
TO THE
COLLEGE :: FRATERNITIES
CLUBS AND HONOR
SOCIETIES

The
Park Shoe Co.

Gives back five
cents for every
dollar you spend.

Save our profit-sharing
checks—it pays. We are
doing the largest shoe
business in Oakland

Park Shoe Co.
475 FOURTEENTH ST., OAKLAND
Opposite City Hall Park

John Reid & Son
Tailors

ARCHIBALD REID JOHN REID

SUITS FROM $35.00
OVERCOATS FROM $40.00

CLAUS SPRECKELS BUILDING
Third and Market Streets
SAN FRANCISCO

H. C. GOLCHER CO. 508 Market St. San Francisco, Calif.
TELEPHONE GARFIELD 828

Guns, Fishing Tackle
Camp Equipments
Outing Suits, Outing Boots and Shoes
Golf
Tennis, Base-Ball and Athletic Supplies
Angora Sweater Jackets and Coats
Indoor Golf — Instruction Given

Phone Berkeley 4943 Auto Delivery

Pacific Floral Co.
Floral Artists

2109 University Avenue Berkeley, California

—and when you return

carry your allowance in a savings account with "*The Bank of Superior Service*" More than thirty thousand savings account depositors enjoy our service

Central National Bank ( ) **Central Savings Bank**
14th STREET and BROADWAY, OAKLAND, CAL.

WALTER KING
Music De Luxe

PIPE SHOP

H. SUTLIFF

Frantz Premier

WE HAVE OVER EIGHT THOUSAND of these famous **Electric Vacuum Cleaners** in daily use in Oakland, Berkeley and Alameda giving perfect satisfaction each and every day. Distributors for **Frantz Premier**, Eureka and Royal Cleaners, Humphrey Automatic Gas Water Heaters, Detroit Gas Ranges and Apex Electric Washers.

Woods-Creighton Company
Formerly PACIFIC COAST SPECIALTIES COMPANY
531 Thirteenth St.   Phone Oakland 6183   Oakland, Cal.

ILLUSTRATED SONGS: "WHEN GROWN UP LADIES ACT LIKE BABIES"

There was a maid pretty and coy,
Her presence to all was a joy —
   Rushees were inspired
   By this maid who was hired
For she was a Theta decoy.

WHEN THE FIJI SOPHS ARE SENIORS

HUSTON SHOES ARE THE FOUNDATION OF GOOD DRESS

Avoid the loss and disappointment that follow an ill-chosen style.

Our shoes are not only of the highest quality, but represent the full range of styles authorized by good taste and fashion.

HUSTON BROS. *Two Stores* 2310 TELEGRAPH AVE. 2216 SHATTUCK AVE.

Hupmobile

Osen & Hunter Auto Company

C. L. Helfrich, Manager

Agents for
Hupmobile, Mitchell and
National Motor Cars
Kleiber Trucks

Garage and Shop Open
Day and Night

12th and JACKSON - 3080 to 3096 BROADWAY
OAKLAND

F. Ponsi & Son
2232 TELEGRAPH AVENUE
Opposite Bank

MEN'S Furnishings
The Best on the Market

SUITS MADE TO ORDER

The Bare Facts

A pretty cave girl with hair of gold
Looked at the cave man bold,
   Who had the sand
   To ask her hand,
As his love he hotly told.

"Suppose," she asked, and hung her head,
"That after we were wed
   We were lost in the forest wide—
   No cave, no fire, and cold your little bride!
What would you do?" she said.

That cave man's smile became a grin
As he eyed the prize he'd win
   "Hacha," he laughed,
   "D'ye think I'm daft?
I'd snuggle you close in your little bear skin!"

Hush Alpha Phis, upon the hill-top,
  If Nan should sneeze, the campus would rock.
If she should leave, the campus would fall
  And down would come Alpha Phi, Y. W. and all.

PI PHIS THE MORNING AFTER

Again you should not have to worry!

JUST phone Berkeley 2804 and give your order to the **B. W. PERKS COMPANY,** Berkeley Florists, then you know you will receive only fresh, choice flowers, artistically arranged for every occasion.

The College Tailor

LOUIS SCHEELINE

Largest and Most Exclusive Line
of Novelties West of Chicago

406 FOURTEENTH ST.   OAKLAND, CAL.

Jan. 29th. Dark horse violate craves permission on Executive Committee.

MEMBER OF FACULTY, SUMMER SESSION 1917

Men's Suits at $30.00 and Up
Ladies' Suits at $45.00 and Up
To Your Measure

DANIEL RYGEL, Tailor and Furrier

2710 College Ave. at Derby St.   Berkeley, California

STUTZ MOTOR CARS

C. W. Studebaker Co., Agents
Latham Davis & Co.

1111 Van Ness   San Francisco

AT THE SIGN OF THE BEAR—2307 Telegraph Ave.
THE BEAR—2015 Shattuck Ave.

CANDIES   LUNCHEON   FROZEN DESSERTS

Special Rates for Fraternities or Clubs

Telephone Berkeley 2888

Mrs. Nora O. Watkins
Modiste

Rooms 7-8 Blackenson Building   Berkeley, California

Southwick's
VARSITY BOOT SHOP

—Style
—Quality
—Service
—Economy

2111 CENTER STREET
BERKELEY, CAL.

BOWLING
At the
California Bowling Alley
2314 Telegraph Ave.

Alleys always in the Best Condition
BEST OF SERVICE

Monthly Contracts   Phone Berkeley 525

Anderson & Leggett
DRY CLEANERS
HATS CLEANED AND BLOCKED

2427 Bancroft Way   Berkeley, Cal.

Jan. 31st—Dark horse proves to be a night-mare.

Union Trust Co. of San Francisco
JUNCTION OF MARKET AND O'FARRELL STREETS AND GRANT AVENUE

STRONG ~ PROGRESSIVE ~ CONVENIENT

Capital, Surplus and Profits - $ 3,100,000.00
Deposits - - - - - - - - 29,000,000.00

Isaias W. Hellman, Chairman of the Board

Officers

I. W. Hellman, Jr., President
Charles J. Deering, Vice President
H. G. Lamb, Cashier
Charles du Parc, Assistant Cashier
W. C. Fite, Assistant Cashier
I. J. Gay, Assistant Cashier
L. E. Owen, Trust Officer
F. L. Brickwedel, Assistant Trust Officer

COMMERCIAL, TRUST AND SAVINGS DEPARTMENTS
The Largest and Most Modern Safe Deposit Vaults West of New York City

---

LET us help you in arranging the equipment, furnishings and decorations of your new offices, a service which we are rendering the profession without cost or obligation.

Our experience in this work will enable us to be of assistance to you in solving these problems, by drafting detailed plans and offering suggestions to fit your particular case.

"Fifty-five Modern Dental Office Plans" our book, explaining this service in detail, together with interesting catalogs of Columbia Dental Equipment, will be sent with our compliments upon receipt of request and dealer's name.

THE RITTER DENTAL MFG. CO.
Rochester, N. Y.

New York   Philadelphia   Chicago

Edition De Luxe

Blackstone down to date—Edited by William Carey Jones, Director of the School of Jurisprudence of the University of California— Contains many of the famous Hammond Notes, translation of all Latin maxims and of foreign terms and phrases, immediately following such terms in the text. Five other valuable features.

Students' Edition—2 Volumes—Buckram
Price, Delivered $9.00
Printed from the same plates as the De Luxe Edition

Bancroft-Whitney Co.
200 McAllister Street, San Francisco

KNABE, HAINES BROS. & OTHER PIANOS
AMPICO REPRODUCING PIANO
HAINES BROS. AUTO DE LUXE
PLAYER PIANOS

Omer N. Kruschke Company

2205 SHATTUCK AVENUE
BERKELEY, CALIFORNIA

Better { Service
Pianos
Prices
Terms

EDISON DIAMOND DISC PHONOGRAPHS
PATHE TALKING MACHINES

BEFORE AND BEHIND

Would-be Graduate (to the President) — Sir, what degree do I get? An A. B.?
President (after a moment's thought) — No, your degree will be an A. S. S.
Would-be Graduate (somewhat disappointed) — Well, that's something to fall back upon, anyway. — *Ex.*

THE WAY THEY LOOK TO THE BLUE AND GOLD STAFF

Charles E. Shaw

Official Photographer
1915 - 1916 - 1917 - 1918
Blue and Gold

2164 Oxford Street, Berkeley
Phone Berkeley 409

Charles E. Shaw

Reprints of any photograph in
this book made in any
size, style or finish
at special rates

2164 Oxford Street, Berkeley
Phone Berkeley 409

The Best

Steamships
Beaver Rose City
"The Columbia River Scenic Route"

Los Angeles   Portland   San Francisco

Through tickets sold to all points in the United
States, Canada and Mexico, in connection
with these luxuriant passenger steamers.
Write for low rates, sailings and full information

The San Francisco & Portland Steamship Co.
Ticket Office: 722 MARKET STREET, SAN FRANCISCO

Mar. 20th. Alpha Kappa Lambdas defeat Skee Burks for Y. M. C. A. secretary. Steamrolled!

Mining Engineers

You Can Depend Upon

HERCULES

POWDER

Hercules Dynamite
Hercules Extra L. F. Dynamite
Hercules Gelatin   Hercules Red H
Hercules Blasting Powder and Blasting Supplies

Hercules Powder Company

Chronicle Building   San Francisco

The Quality Product of the Philippines

Alhambra
"The Manila Cigars"

Made in Cuban Shapes
for American Smokers

M. A. GUNST BRANCH

Telephone Piedmont 865

The Drake Catering Co.

AUTO DELIVERY

Weddings, Dinners, Teas
Luncheons & Receptions

China, Silver, Linen, Tables and Chairs Rented — "The Ferns" for Weddings, Dances, Card Parties Etc.

TELEGRAPH AVE at 36th STREET
OAKLAND, CAL.

Mitchell Furniture Co.

Furniture
Carpets
Draperies
Stoves

Cash or Credit

In Our

EXCHANGE DEPARTMENT

You can trade off old goods for new

539-41 12th St., cor. Clay

PHONE OAKLAND 2036

A "stude" one bright winter day.

CROCKER SAFE DEPOSIT VAULTS

JOHN F. CUNNINGHAM, Manager

CROCKER BUILDING
Junction Post and Market Streets

SAN FRANCISCO

W. P. FULLER & CO.

SPECIALIZED PAINT AND VARNISH PRODUCTS FOR EVERY PURPOSE

Importers and Manufacturers of

PAINTS

OILS AND GLASS
Pioneer Lead and Varnishes

TENTH AND ALICE STREETS, OAKLAND, CALIFORNIA
Telephone Oakland 6486

Mt. Diablo Cement
Awarded Gold Medal P. P. I. E.

Used on the following buildings at the University:

    Benj. Ide Wheeler Hall
    Hilgard Hall
    Chemistry Building

Cowell Santa Cruz Lime
Always Used Where Quality Counts

All Building Material

HENRY COWELL LIME AND CEMENT CO.
2 MARKET STREET, SAN FRANCISCO, CAL.

BRANCHES: OAKLAND   SACRAMENTO   SANTA CRUZ   SAN JOSE
            PORTLAND, OREGON   TACOMA, WASHINGTON

Chas. C. Moore & Company

ENGINEERS

Complete Power Plant Equipment

HIGH GRADE MACHINERY
Power, Lighting, Mining, Pumping

Home Office: Sheldon Building, San Francisco

Information and Catalogues at Our Nearest Office

SAN FRANCISCO	Sheldon Building	TUCSON	Santa Rita Hotel
LOS ANGELES	I. H. Van Ness Building	SALT LAKE CITY	Kearns Building
SEATTLE	Mutual Life Building	NEW YORK CITY	Fulton Building

The German Savings and Loan Society

(The German Bank)

Savings — **Commercial**

526 CALIFORNIA STREET, SAN FRANCISCO

December 30, 1916

ASSETS

United States, State, Municipal and Other Bonds (market value $20,338,296.00), standing on books at	$18,750,166.74
Loans on Real Estate, secured by First Mortgages	41,077,918.24
Loans on Bonds and Stocks	780,173.92
Bank Buildings and Lots, Main and Branch Offices (value $1,000,000), standing on books at	1.00
Other Real Estate (value $105,000.00), standing on books at	1.00
Employees' Pension Fund, ($2,127,17.28), standing on books at	1.00
CASH	5,000,483.97
Total	**$69,644,745.94**

LIABILITIES

Due Depositors	$63,499,342.39
Capital Stock actually paid in	1,000,000.00
Reserve and Contingent Funds	2,144,403.55
Total	**$69,644,745.94**

For the six months ending December 30, 1916, a dividend to depositors of 4% per annum was declared.

six hundred and twenty

Stiegeler Bros.
Tailors

The House of
Quality :: Style
Moderate Prices

Dress Neatly—
It Costs No More

711 MARKET ST. SAN FRANCISCO

Insure in the
Fireman's Fund Insurance Company
Fire, Marine, Automobile Insurance
Capital $1,500,000
Assets of the Fireman's Fund
1917, $13,445,953.99
Are Larger Now
Than in Its History
Notwithstanding
Its Losses in the
San Francisco Conflagration
of Over
Eleven Million Dollars
Its Risks Are
Carefully Selected
And Properly Distributed
Agents Everywhere

Jan. 16th — Alpha Phis say Thetas flunked out four. Thetas, indignant, say they only flunked out two!

*Couple
Your
Education
With a
Heald
Training*

THERE are always positions of responsibility open for the educated provided they have a business training.

Heald's is the right place to get your business training — it is easy to start at Heald's day or night schools — there is no red tape — no lost motion — no time wasted — you will have practical teachers and fine equipment - the cost is not large — you can start any time.

If you want to make a success in life talk it over at Heald's on any business day or go to Heald's Monday, Wednesday or Friday evenings 7 to 9 — or telephone Prospect 1540 — Ask for Mr. Lesseman.

HEALD'S
VAN NESS AND POST, SAN FRANCISCO
16TH AND SAN PABLO, OAKLAND

Jan. 1st — Truck Lane loses his capacity.

CATALOG ENGRAVERS

COLOR PLATE MAKERS

AMERICAN ENGRAVING & COLOR PLATE CO.

The owners of this business are also its actual active superintendents — not by proxy, but in person. ❦ Being practical Photo Engravers, every detail of production in all departments is under their direct supervision. ❦ The plant is the most complete in the West, modern in every detail. ❦ Combined, the above conditions assure you a Reliable Service — plus Quality.

AMERICAN ENGRAVING
& COLOR PLATE CO.
109 New Montgomery Street
ENGRAVERS
ARTISTS

The 1918 Blue and Gold
IS A PRODUCT OF THIS PLANT

WITH THE BIGGEST BATTERY OF PRESSES IN THE ENTIRE WEST, AND A STAFF OF HIGHLY SKILLED MEN IN ITS MANY DEPARTMENTS, THE SUNSET PUBLISHING HOUSE OFFERS UNUSUAL ADVANTAGES IN THE DESIGNING, CREATING AND PRINTING OF BOOKS, PERIODICALS, CATALOGS, ADVERTISING BOOKLETS AND FOLDERS. :: :: :: :: :: :: :: :: ::

The Sunset Publishing House
Sunset Building, 448-460 Fourth Street
San Francisco

Apr. 14th - Don Bull was to have written these date liners, but was incapacitated.

Quality=Service
PRINTING :: BINDING

¶ In the conduct of our business, service consists of more than simply the prompt filling of orders. Quality-Service includes dependable quality of paper, the rapid, careful attention to orders and punctual delivery of same, immediate, courteous and intelligent treatment of customers and the charging of fair prices.

¶ We have always appreciated the fact that the general nature of business demands Quality-Service; through years of business experience we have developed an organization which is loyal to our standard of distinct, co-operative service.

¶ We would like an opportunity to demonstrate the value of Quality-Service to you, if you are not already enjoying it; telephone Douglas 351 for our representative to call or make us a personal visit.

John Kitchen Jr. Co.
BOOK BINDING
PRINTING LITHOGRAPHING RULING
LOOSE LEAF LEDGERS

67 FIRST STREET, SAN FRANCISCO

Binders of this Publication

An Appreciation

AS the presses are rumbling away on the last few pages of the 1918 BLUE AND GOLD and we can do no more, the editor and manager cannot help but let their minds wander over the past year, recalling its trials and tribulations along with its joys and pleasures. And as we review the past, we realize the utter impossibility of bringing the present volume to its completed form without the help of those who have labored without honor and unthanked, with an interest and sincerity which merits obligations. And we wish to take this means, meager as it may seem, of showing our appreciation.

To Pedro J. Lemos and Mr. and Mrs. Charles E. Shaw, do we wish to extend our deepest and heartfelt thanks. For without their sincere and untiring efforts the 1918 BLUE AND GOLD would be lacking in many of its finer details and attractive features. Their willingness to give their time and assistance at the sacrifice of their own interests has made an everlasting impression upon the members of the staff who have been in closer touch with the progress of the book.

And to the members of the staff, who have labored unceasingly in their efforts to comply with the persistent demands of the editor and manager, in an endeavor to make their burden lighter, we desire to express our appreciation.

We wish further to thank the Sunset Publishing House whose congenial staff of employees, by their co-operation and suggestions, have made the work a pleasure; the American Engraving and Color Plate Company, for the prompt and efficient manner in which the high-grade cuts were delivered; John Kitchen, Jr., whose interest and ever ready advice have made for a better volume; Blake, Moffitt & Towne, for the courteous treatment and straightforward business dealings; and the Independent Pressroom who have exceeded their obligations in the production of the color work.

Index

Abracadabra	528
Acacia	428
Achaean	526
Advertisements	568
A. E. and M. E.	152
Agricultural Club	152
Agricultural Trips	62
Aldebaran	552
Al Khalail	554
Alpha Chi Omega	510
Alpha Chi Sigma	152
Alpha Delta Phi	430
Alpha Delta Pi	514
Alpha Gamma Delta	516
Alpha Kappa Kappa	466
Alpha Kappa Lambda	458
Alpha Nu	540
Alpha Omicron Pi	504
Alpha Phi	500
Alpha Sigma Phi	446
Alpha Tau Omega	418
Alpha Xi Delta	508
Alpha Zeta	179
Alumni Association	144
Alumni Fortnightly, The	105
Architectural Association	152
American Society of Mechanical Engineers	157
Art History Circle	152
Art School College Year	58
Associated Pre-Medical Students	152
Associated Students	137
Associated Women Students	142
Athletic Organizations	143
Authors and Co-authors	134
Axe Rally	72

B

Bachelordon	526
Baseball	237
Basketball	279
Beta Beta	101
Beta Gamma Sigma	182
Beta Kappa Alpha	193
Beta Theta Pi	396
Big "C" Society (Officers)	143
Big "C" Society (Members)	283
Blue and Gold, The	97

C

Cadet Band	91
Cadet Officers	89
Campus Scenery	15
California Law Review	103
California-Stanford Debate	108
Carnot Debate	110
Charter Day	50
Chi Omega	502
Chi Phi	392
Chi Psi	408
Christian Science Society	148
Circle "C" Society (Members)	293
Circle "C" Society (Officers)	143

Civil Engineering Association	153
Classes, The	305
College of Dentistry, San Francisco	60
Commencement Week Program (1916)	39
Commencement Week Program (1917)	64
Commencement Week (1916)	40
Commerce Club	153
Congress Debating Society	150
Contents	11
Copa de Oro	550
Cosmopolitan Club	153
Crew	209
Cross Country	286

D

Dahlonega	534
Daily Californian, The	94
Dances	75
Debating	107
Debating Council	151
Debating Societies	150
Dedication	8
Del Rey	532
Delta Chi	440
Delta Delta Delta	496
Delta Epsilon	195
Delta Gamma	506
Delta Kappa Epsilon	394
Delta Sigma Delta	462
Delta Sigma Phi	456
Delta Tau Delta	414
Delta Upsilon	412
Delta Zeta	520
Departmental Organizations	152
Deutscher Kranzchen	153
Deutscher Verein	153
Deutscher Zarkel	154
Die Plaudertasche	154
Dramatics	113
"Absent on Leave"	42
"Androcles and the Lion"	115
Curtain Raiser, The	120
Football Show	124
"Helena's Husband"	127
Junior Farce, The	122
Junior Farces (Statistical)	113
Senior Extravaganza (Statistical)	113
"The Bear"	124
"The Canterbury Pilgrims"	128
"The Intener"	126
"The Maker of Dreams"	126
"What Next"	118
"Youth's Adventure"	131
"Youth Comes Up"	132
Dwight	530
Dwight	201

E

Economers Club	199
Education Club	154
Engineering Summer Camp	48
English Club	155

Epsilon Alpha	391
Eta Kappa Nu	198
Executive Committee	128

F

Farm College Year	54
Football	203
Forestry Club	154
Foreword	7
Forum Debating Society	151
Fraternities	387
Fraternity Statistics	388
Freshie Glee Committee	76
Freshman Class Officers	385
Freshman Debating Society	150
Freshman Rally	68
Freshman-Sophomore Contests	66
Freshman-Sophomore Debate	108

G

Gamma Phi Beta	492
Glee Club	161
Golden Bear	174
Gymnasium Club	143

H

Half-Day Drills	84
Honor Societies	173
Humboldt Club	154

I

Ice Hockey	294
Il Circolo Italiano	154
Informal Committees	81
In Memoriam	30
Intervarsity Debates	111
Iota Sigma Phi	184
Istye	200

J

Japanese Students Club	544
Junior Class Officers	354
Junior Class Photographs	352
Junior Prom Committee	78
Joshes	564
Journal of Agriculture, The	108

K

Kappa Alpha	410
Kappa Alpha Theta	490
Kappa Kappa Gamma	494
Kappa Psi	478
Kappa Sigma	422
Konversationsklub	154

L

Lambda Chi Alpha	452
Law Association	154
Le Circle Francais	154
Lesh Club	155

M

Mandolin Club	165
Mask and Dagger	186
Mekatan	556
Menorah Society	155

Military	83
Military Ball Committee	80
Military Department (Officers)	99
Mining Association	155
Minor Sports	285
Music	159

N

Newman Club	149
Nostrems	558
Nu Sigma Nu	468
Nu Sigma Psi	197

O

Occident, The	99
Officers Reserve Corps	87
Omega Upsilon Phi	486
Orchestra	163
Orund	452

P

Pajamarino Rally	70
Pelican, The	101
Phi Alpha Delta	480
Phi Alpha Gamma	474
Phi Beta Kappa	173
Phi Chi	476
Phi Delta Chi	470
Phi Delta Kappa	484
Phi Delta Phi (California)	460
Phi Delta Phi (Hastings)	464
Phi Delta Theta	402
Phi Gamma Delta	400
Phi Kappa Psi	416
Phi Kappa Sigma	428
Phi Lambda Upsilon	180
Phi Mu	522
Phi Sigma Kappa	432
Philheilenon Hetaera	155
Phrontisterion	169
Pi Beta Phi	498
Pi Kappa Alpha	442
Pi Kappa Phi	444
Pre-Legal Association	155
Press Club	187
Prytanean	180
Psi Omega	472
Psi Upsilon	424
Publications	93

R

Rallies	67
Regents	32
Reshven	518
Religious Organizations	146
Rifle Club (Officers)	143
Rifle Shooting	292

S

Salutatory	5
Scandinavian Club	154
Senate Debating Society	151
Senior Ball Committee (1916)	45
Senior Ball Committee (1917)	79
Senior Class Officers	305

Senior Extravaganza (1916)	43
Senior Extravaganza (1917)	132
Senior Records	308
Senior Class Undergraduate Reminiscences	300
Senior Week Program (1916)	39
Senior Week Program (1917)	64
Sequoyah	538
Sigma Alpha Epsilon	406
Sigma Chi	498
Sigma Iota Phi	201
Sigma Kappa	512
Sigma Kappa Alpha	196
Sigma Nu	404
Sigma Phi	444
Sigma Phi Epsilon	438
Sigma Phi Sigma	458
Sigma Pi	448
Siskiyou Club	156
Skull and Key	177
Skull and Key Running	52
Slavic Society	156
Soccer	287
Sophomore Class Officers	384
Sophomore Labor Day	63
Sophomore Hop Committee	77
Southern Club	156
Southern Mines Club	156
Spanish Club	156
Sphinx	188
Sprechverband	156
Staff	12
St. Mark's Club	149
Student Body Organizations	137
Student Committees	139
Summer Military Training Camps	85
Swimming	288

T

Tau Beta Pi	178
Tennis	277
Theta Chi	450
Theta Delta Chi	420
Theta Tau	181
Theta Xi	436
Thorpe, Lieut. Truman D	84
Tileum	540
Title Page	3
Torch and Shield	199
Track	249
Treble Clef	107
Trumpeters	93

U

Ukulele Club	171
University, The	15
University, The (Review)	34
Upper Division Bonnheim Contest	111
U. N. X.	192

V

Varsity Smoker Rally	71

W

Wheeler Hall	33
Winged Helmet	175
Women's Athletics	295
Fencing	298
Hockey	297
Rowing	298
Swimming	300
Tennis	299
Women's "C" Society (Members)	333
Women's College Year	56
Women's Mandolin and Guitar Club	169
Women's Parliamentary Society	151

X

Xi Psi Phi	464

Y

Y. M. C. A	146
Y. W. C. A	147

Z

Zeta Psi	390
Zeta Tau Alpha	518

www.ingramcontent.com/pod-product-compliance
Lightning Source LLC
Chambersburg PA
CBHW021222300426
44111CB00007B/402